Peace, Decolonization, and the Practice of Solidarity

Peace, Decolonization, and the Practice of Solidarity

Rob Skinner

BLOOMSBURY ACADEMIC
LONDON • NEW YORK • OXFORD • NEW DELHI • SYDNEY

BLOOMSBURY ACADEMIC

Bloomsbury Publishing Plc, 50 Bedford Square, London, WC1B 3DP, UK
Bloomsbury Publishing Inc, 1385 Broadway, New York, NY 10018, USA
Bloomsbury Publishing Ireland, 29 Earlsfort Terrace, Dublin 2, D02 AY28, Ireland

BLOOMSBURY, BLOOMSBURY ACADEMIC and the Diana logo are trademarks of
Bloomsbury Publishing Plc

First published in Great Britain 2024
This paperback edition published in 2025

Copyright © Rob Skinner, 2024

Rob Skinner has asserted his right under the Copyright, Designs and Patents Act, 1988,
to be identified as Author of this work.

Cover image: Ivashutin Sergey/Alamy Stock Photo

All rights reserved. No part of this publication may be: i) reproduced or transmitted in any form, electronic or mechanical, including photocopying, recording or by means of any information storage or retrieval system without prior permission in writing from the publishers; or ii) used or reproduced in any way for the training, development or operation of artificial intelligence (AI) technologies, including generative AI technologies. The rights holders expressly reserve this publication from the text and data mining exception as per Article 4(3) of the Digital Single Market Directive (EU) 2019/790.

Bloomsbury Publishing Plc does not have any control over, or responsibility for, any third-party websites referred to or in this book. All internet addresses given in this book were correct at the time of going to press. The author and publisher regret any inconvenience caused if addresses have changed or sites have ceased to exist, but can accept no responsibility for any such changes.

A catalogue record for this book is available from the British Library.

A catalog record for this book is available from the Library of Congress.

ISBN: HB: 978-1-3501-5976-1
PB: 978-1-3504-2719-8
ePDF: 978-1-3501-5977-8
eBook: 978-1-3501-5979-2

Typeset by Deanta Global Publishing Services, Chennai, India

For product safety related questions contact productsafety@bloomsbury.com.

To find out more about our authors and books visit www.bloomsbury.com and
sign up for our newsletters.

Contents

1	Introduction: Peace, decolonization and the practice of solidarity	1
2	Peace, the state and development	21
3	Practices of anti-colonial activism in the 1950s	53
4	Anti-colonialism and the bomb	83
5	From 'nuclear imperialism' to armed struggle	119
6	Africa Freedom Action and the march that never happened	151
7	Aftermaths: Peace and decolonization	189
Bibliography		217
Index		233

1

Introduction

Peace, decolonization and the practice of solidarity

In September 1964, the veteran American peace activist A. J. Muste circulated a short mimeographed essay to an array of sympathizers including the editor of *Sanity*, the journal of the Campaign for Nuclear Disarmament (CND), in the UK. The essay set out Muste's analysis of the prospects for non-violent protest, which was, on one level, far from optimistic. In fact, he declared that in popular imagination 'the concept of nonviolence has fallen upon hard times'.[1] This was a significant indictment of a movement that had been a part of his life as an activist for nearly half a century. In 1916, Muste had joined the Fellowship of Reconciliation (FOR), a Christian pacifist movement formed by the British pacifist Henry Hodgkin at the outbreak of the First World War. Often overlooked in histories of twentieth-century social movements and political protest, the FOR had influence far beyond its own small circle thanks to members, including Muste, who played leading roles in high-profile socialist, civil rights and disarmament organizations and campaigns, particularly in the United States. As Joseph Kosek has argued, the FOR brought together individuals engaged in 'an active process of interpreting religion in the modern world', who identified violence itself as the specific and central problem of the twentieth century.[2] Over the century following its foundation, the vision of Christian non-violence articulated by FOR faced numerous challenges amidst industrialized war, mass civilian death and the invention of atomic weapons that had the potential to obliterate human society. Militant resistance and revolution, moreover, offered seductive visions of progressive transformation, which had attracted Muste himself as a radical socialist leader in the interwar years.[3] Thus, when Muste wrote of the problems of the radical peace movement, just three years before his death, it was with the recognition that his hopes for establishing a movement against violence were in retreat.[4]

[1] A. J. Muste, 'Problems of the Radical Peace Movement', 10 September 1964 LSE CND, 2018/9 1964–65.
[2] Joseph Kip Kosek, *Acts of Conscience: Christian Nonviolence and Modern American Democracy* (New York: Columbia University Press, 2011), 1.
[3] Leilah Danielson, *American Gandhi: A.J. Muste and the History of Radicalism in the Twentieth Century* (Philadelphia: University of Pennsylvania Press, 2014), 154–201; see also Leilah Danielson, 'Christianity, Dissent, and the Cold War: A. J. Muste's Challenge to Realism and U.S. Empire', *Diplomatic History* 30, no. 4 (2006): 645–69.
[4] Jo Ann Robinson, 'A. J. Muste and Ways to Peace', *American Studies* 13, no. 1 (1972): 95–108.

In the 1950s and early 1960s, Muste had been a central figure in efforts to mobilize the 'creation of a non-violent third way' that incorporated non-violent tactics within civil rights and anti-racist movements in the US and Afro-Asian anti-colonialism.[5] Again, by 1964, Muste had to acknowledge that these efforts had little success. In his view, the declining power of non-violence was evident the world over, from the civil rights movement in the United States to India, where the founding figure of modern non-violent philosophy, Mahatma Gandhi, had become little more than a 'ritual name'. Muste observed similar developments in South Africa, where the influence of advocates of non-violence such as the leader of the African National Congress, Albert Lutuli, had diminished with the rise of a new generation of figures, including Nelson Mandela, Govan Mbeki and Walter Sisulu, who had just a few months earlier been sentenced to life imprisonment for their role in launching an armed struggle against the apartheid state.[6] Across Africa, he argued, non-violence was losing support:

> in as diverse countries as Ghana, Kenya, Tanganyika and North Rhodesia nonviolence was a concept which elected interest and some support among leaders and, in less measure, peoples. This is no longer the case, and . . . violence is generally accepted as alone realistic and that Communism, often of the Maoist kind, gains ground.[7]

But, despite these indications of its demise, Muste insisted that the international peace movement had not been defeated. Instead, he called on those who shared his radical pacifist vision to search for new forms of non-violent protest that might better inspire those who sought an end to colonialism and racial injustice and bring about a radical transformation of the world. 'Violence has become a threat to the whole social fabric of the race', he concluded, and it was 'time for us to raise and not lower the banner of nonviolence'.[8]

As Muste acknowledged, violence figured prominently in discussions of contemporary developments in Africa in the mid-1960s: the bitter war in Algeria had eventually led to independence in 1962, but elsewhere on the continent the transfer of political power had been followed by civil conflict and violence, perhaps most starkly in the Congo, where the assassination of the Prime Minister Patrice Lumumba by Belgian agents highlighted enduring neocolonial power. Observers of the situation in South Africa, where members of the African National Congress and Communist Party had launched a sabotage campaign against the apartheid state in late 1961, concluded that violence was inevitable unless the policies of apartheid were rapidly dismantled. The 'way to avoid national suicide', wrote the South African journalist Colin Legum in

---

[5] Ibid., 104.
[6] Raymond Suttner, 'The African National Congress (ANC) Underground: From the M-Plan to Rivonia', *South African Historical Journal* 49, no. 1 (2003): 123–46; Thula Simpson, *Umkhonto We Sizwe: The ANC's Armed Struggle* (Cape Town: Penguin Books, 2016); Thula Simpson, 'Nelson Mandela and the Genesis of the ANC's Armed Struggle: Notes on Method', *Journal of Southern African Studies* 44, no. 1 (2018): 133–48.
[7] Muste, 'Problems of the Radical Peace Movement'.
[8] Ibid.

late 1963, 'is to find alternatives to White Supremacy before it is destroyed by violence'.[9] Similarly, the *New Statesman* reported earlier in that same year on the inaugural meeting of the Organisation of African Unity, noting that debates were dominated by calls to support violent resistance to intractable white colonial regimes in southern Africa. 'The only insurance against this new hazard to world peace', the editorial declared, was 'to cut out the cancers before they become malignant'.[10] In this sense, evocations of incipient violence and impending crisis were a threat that could be employed as a spur to redouble efforts to oppose racial segregation, colonialism and apartheid. For Muste, though, and for the other activists that form the focus of this book, the menace of violence was the essence of political struggle. In his efforts to organize a movement for non-violence, built on practical action as much as spiritual guidance, Muste embodied the core precepts of the radical international peace movement that emerged in the first half of the twentieth century.[11]

Born in the Netherlands in 1885, Muste had migrated to the United States with his family in the early 1890s and spent his childhood in Michigan before travelling to New York as a theological student. Brought up within the Calvinist Church, he then became a minister in the Congregationalist Church, but it was the Christian pacifism of the FOR that had a formative influence on Muste, forcing a break with his church in 1917 and the start of a career of activism that embraced pacifism, conscientious objection, socialism and engagement in the labour movement.[12] During the interwar years, his primary focus turned to progressive trade unionism and left-wing politics, helping to form the American Workers' Party in the mid-1930s. He was drawn into the complicated and fraught politics of the radical left as a consequence of the Party's merger with the Trotskyist Communist League of America in 1934 to form the Workers' Party of the United States.[13] When the strains of navigating the tense factionalism of the radical left began to take their toll, Muste travelled with his wife to Europe in 1936. While in Paris, he experienced a form of religious epiphany during a visit to the Church of St Sulpice, which resulted in his resignation from the Workers' Party and return to Christian pacifism and the Fellowship of Reconciliation.[14]

Muste's assessment that the mid-1960s was a critical moment for the peace movement therefore came at the culmination of over two decades of dedication to the cause of peace and non-violence but was also inflected with a revolutionary vision that set him apart from both the liberal and Communist peace movements of the post-1945 era. This book tells the story of a group of radical pacifists who, like Muste, sought a third way for radical politics in the era of decolonization and Cold War. The key figures in this story shared a spiritual and ideological faith in non-violence, which they brought to bear in campaigns for civil rights, colonial freedom and nuclear disarmament. For

---

[9] Colin Legum, 'South Africa: The Doomed Republic', *Africa Today* 10, no. 9 (1963): 4–7.
[10] 'War Drums in Africa', *New Statesman*, 65, 4 January 1963, 817.
[11] Scott H. Bennett, *Radical Pacifism: The War Resisters League and Gandhian Nonviolence in America, 1915–1963* (Syracuse, NY: Syracuse University Press, 2003).
[12] Danielson, *American Gandhi*.
[13] Ibid., 189–94.
[14] Ibid., 200–1; see also Bryan D. Palmer, 'The French Turn in the United States: James P. Cannon and the Trotskyist Entry into the Socialist Party, 1934–1937', *Labor History* 59, no. 5 (3 September 2018): 610–38.

them, the animating principle was not freedom, or justice, democracy or human rights – although these too were central to their political vision – but non-violence. As the aphorism widely attributed to Muste put it, they believed that there was 'no way to peace: peace is the way'.[15] At the heart of the campaigns and networks examined in this book was a core concern with the practice of political activism; peace as a form of action that could construct solidarity between groups and individuals from diverse backgrounds with divergent interests and ideals.

The efforts to mobilize non-violent responses to colonialism explored in this book were, moreover, experiments in transnational activism, insofar as they took shape within networks that spanned and connected activists and organizations in Europe, North America, Africa and Asia. As such, efforts to draw together peace and anti-colonialism constituted projects that fostered 'global connectedness', whose work was enacted through 'networks based on information exchange, project collaboration, participation in meetings and forums', as well as shared participation in larger international coalitions.[16] More precisely, the concept of transnational activism emphasizes the ideological and ethical ambivalence within and across the group of activists explored in this book. This is not a story of the emergence of a universal narrative of peace and freedom but of the ways in which such ideas informed, and were informed by, engagement in the particularities of national political cultures and the local dynamics of political activism.

This is, perhaps, most clearly illuminated by the career of the book's central figure, the Anglican cleric, anti-colonial campaigner and advocate of Gandhian non-violence, Michael Scott. Born in 1907, Scott's childhood was shaped by the divergent influences of middle-class family life and the working-class district of Northam in the port city of Southampton in which Scott's father served as the parish priest.[17] According to his autobiography, *A Time to Speak*, this dichotomy contributed to the development of a life-long struggle with what Scott called the 'question'.[18] This, it seems, was a hazy expression of doubt and uncertainty that enveloped political, religious and psychological anxieties. This ambivalence became manifest in a political journey that led Scott from ordination in the Anglican Church to induction into the Communist Party while serving as a parish priest in the East End of London during the Depression. In the 1930s he travelled to India, combining covert work for the Communist Party with his duties as chaplain to the Bishop of Bombay.[19] He returned to Britain at the start of the Second World War, and amidst the trauma of the Blitz in London, his ideological, spiritual and psychological anxieties reached a new level of intensity. He initially continued to work for the Communist Party but felt increasingly drawn to enlist as a combatant in the Royal Air Force, despite the Party's opposition – and

---

[15] Robinson, 'A. J. Muste', 105; see also fn. 54, 108.
[16] Hagai Katz and Helmut K. Anheier, 'Global Connectedness: The Structure of Transnational NGO Networks', in *Global Civil Society 2005/6*, edited by Helmut K. Anheier, Mary Kaldor, and Marlies Glasius (London: SAGE Publications, Limited, 2005), 240–65, p. 240.
[17] Anne Yates and Lewis Chester, *The Troublemaker: Michael Scott and His Lonely Struggle against Injustice* (London: Aurum, 2006), 4–8.
[18] Michael Scott, *A Time to Speak* (Garden City, NY: Doubleday, 1958), 13.
[19] Yates and Chester, *The Troublemaker*, 21–30; Scott, *A Time to Speak*, 67–82.

that of his family, who were shocked that he would abandon his religious vocation.[20] This internal crisis came to a climax when Scott was hospitalized with an acute illness diagnosed as Crohn's disease, which would affect him for the remainder of his life.

In 1943, he thus travelled to South Africa to improve his health, taking up a post with an urban Christian mission in the rapidly expanding city of Johannesburg. He quickly became entangled in the wartime politics of South Africa, which was shaped by the antithetical forces of a progressive left-liberal tendency towards loosening of the strictures of racial segregation, and the rising power of Christian nationalism that sought to entrench white supremacy and extend policies of racial control. As Director of the Campaign for Right and Justice, Scott's work became focused on networks of activism rather than his duties as a priest. Tensions between the Communist and liberal elements of the Campaign led to his resignation as Director in 1945, but the movement's emphasis on social welfare and development would remain one of the central features of his political agenda.[21] It also led to a decisive – although never fully explained – break with Communism. Instead, his political and spiritual faith would come to be centred on Gandhian non-violence, which he first encountered when he joined the civil disobedience campaign launched by the South African Indian Congress in 1946, to protest the extension of segregationist laws to South Asians. His participation in passive resistance in Durban led to a short prison sentence, after which he became notorious as a 'turbulent priest' actively involved with squatter movements and working with the journalist Ruth First to expose the use of prison labour on Transvaal farms.[22] Such activities created increased tensions between Scott and the Anglican authorities but gave him a burgeoning reputation as a 'fighter for African rights' among a younger generation of African political activists including Nelson Mandela.[23] Scott's experiences in South Africa and India were formative, but his activism was underpinned by the doubts, uncertainties and conflicting values that had characterized his double lives as priest and Communist agent. His advocacy of non-violence drew him into activist networks that straddled the political cultures of Britain, the United States and Africa but also underlined the distinctions and contradictions within these networks.

As these brief introductions to the life stories of Muste and Scott suggest, the networks that form the focus of this study reflected the personal experiences through which transnational activism was enacted. Their individual actions illuminate, in broad terms, the themes with which this book is centrally concerned: the ideologies of peace and pacifist campaigns for disarmament and anti-militarism, the diffuse array of future possibilities that influenced processes of decolonization, and the focus on activism as an endeavour formed by practice and methodology rather than agenda and outcomes. My main contention is that this final point – the question of methods

---

[20] Yates and Chester, *The Troublemaker*, 33–5.
[21] Rob Skinner, 'Christian Reconstruction, Secular Politics: Michael Scott and the Campaign for Right and Justice, 1943–1945', in *South Africa's 1940s: Worlds of Possibilities*, edited by Saul Dubow and Alan Jeeves (Cape Town: Double Storey, 2005), 246–66.
[22] Scott, *A Time to Speak*, 168–90; see also Ruth First, 'Bethel Case Book', *Africa South*, June 1958.
[23] Nelson Mandela, *Long Walk to Freedom: The Autobiography of Nelson Mandela* (London: Abacus, 1995), 121; see also Yates and Chester, *The Troublemaker*, 57–73; Scott, *A Time to Speak*, 152–68.

and practice – needs closer consideration in histories of decolonization and that the interactions of peace activists and anti-colonialism in the late 1950s and early 1960s serve as a reminder that solidarity ought to be understood primarily as a practice.

Peace: The lost cause of decolonization?

Through the work of Scott, Muste and many others, transatlantic networks emerged during the late 1950s that sought to connect strands of anti-colonial, civil rights and peace activism. These networks coalesced around mutual concerns around freedom, democracy and racial justice but came to focus on the existential threat posed by the rapidly expanding nuclear arsenals of the Cold War superpowers. The conjuncture of nuclear disarmament, anti-colonial and anti-apartheid movements in the 'new politics' that emerged in Britain and elsewhere in Europe at the end of the 1950s has been widely acknowledged.[24] Similarly, the ways in which networks of intellectuals and campaigners bridged the boundaries of Cold War divisions in the early Cold War have been the subject of attention in recent scholarship.[25] The wider discourse of peace was itself moulded by Cold War politics, with the Soviet-led World Peace Council (WPC) establishing an international network of national affiliates that fostered international solidarity between former colonial territories in Asia and Africa, as well as providing a platform for engagement with Western disarmament movements and, later, global protests against the Vietnam War.[26] But the relationship between the WPC and what Lawrence Wittner has described as 'non-aligned' disarmament movements could be highly antagonistic.[27] The movements examined in this book fall into the latter camp, although advocates of non-violence often exhibited positions that were more anti-Communist than non-aligned.

---

[24] Håkan Thörn, 'The Meaning(s) of Solidarity: Narratives of Anti-Apartheid Activism', *Journal of Southern African Studies* 35, no. 2 (2009): 430; see also Rob Skinner, 'The Anti-Apartheid Movement: Pressure Group Politics, International Solidarity and Transnational Activism', in *NGOs in Contemporary Britain: Non-State Actors in Society and Politics since 1945*, edited by N. J. Crowson, Matthew. Hilton, and James McKay (Basingstoke: Palgrave Macmillan, 2009), 129–46; George McKay, 'Subcultural Innovations in the Campaign for Nuclear Disarmament', *Peace Review* 16, no. 4 (2004): 429–38; but the most detailed recent study is Jodi Burkett, *Constructing Post-Imperial Britain: Britishness, 'Race' and the Radical Left in the 1960s* (Basingstoke: Palgrave Macmillan, 2013).
[25] Holger Nehring, *Politics of Security: British and West German Protest Movements and the Early Cold War, 1945–1970* (Oxford: Oxford University Press, 2013); Nancy Jachec, *Europe's Intellectuals and the Cold War: The Society of European Culture, Postwar Politics, and International Relations* (London: Bloomsbury, 2020).
[26] Carolien Stolte, '"The People's Bandung": Local Anti-Imperialists on an Afro-Asian Stage', *Journal of World History* 30, no. 1/2 (2019): 125–56; Günter Wernicke, 'The Communist-Led World Peace Council and the Western Peace Movements: The Fetters of Bipolarity and Some Attempts to Break Them in the Fifties and Early Sixties', *Peace & Change* 23, no. 3 (1998): 265–311; Kim Christiaens, '"To Go Further Than Words Alone": The World Peace Council and the Global Orchestration of Vietnam War Campaigns During the 1960s', in *Protest in the Vietnam War Era*, edited by Alexander Sedlmaier. Palgrave Studies in the History of Social Movements (Basingstoke: Palgrave, 2022), 13–49.
[27] Lawrence S. Wittner, *Resisting the Bomb: A History of the World Nuclear Disarmament Movement 1954–1970* (Stanford, CA: Stanford University Press, 1997), 83–5.

The focus of this book centres on two key moments in the late 1950s and early 1960s when anti-colonialism and the growth of militant Third World liberation movements intersected with the intensification of the Cold War nuclear arms race. The first was an attempt to despatch an international team of disarmament campaigners from Ghana to infiltrate the French atomic weapons test site in southern Algeria in late 1959. The protest drew on the support of the Direct Action Committee in Britain and Committee for Non-Violent Action in the United States and received significant political and material support from the government of Ghana. In December 1959, the team travelled northwards from Accra and crossed into the French West African territory of Upper Volta (Burkina Faso), before being halted a few miles beyond the border. After several failed attempts to progress towards the test site, the Sahara team abandoned their plans and sought instead to lobby African governments and political movements to support disarmament campaigns and non-violence. The French duly tested their first atomic weapons in February 1960.

The relationship between activists and the state is a key reference point in the analysis of the Sahara protest, but as its participants persevered in their efforts to engage anti-colonialism and anti-apartheid in a broader struggle against violence, they found themselves in a contest with a burgeoning shift towards militant armed resistance, particularly within anti-colonial movements in southern and central Africa. The second key moment examined in this book came in 1962, when peace campaigners under the auspices of the newly formed World Peace Brigade (WPB) aligned with pan-African networks in central and eastern Africa to launch Africa Freedom Action, a planned mass march from Tanganyika (Tanzania) into neighbouring Northern Rhodesia (Zambia). The march aimed to bolster the campaign of the Zambian nationalist United National Independence Party (UNIP), led by Kenneth Kaunda, whose public adherence to Gandhian non-violence attracted the attention and admiration of the WPB. But the march was never more than a proposition, and the plans were put on hold when Kaunda announced that UNIP would participate in the Northern Rhodesian elections held in October 1962.

Should an event that never in fact took place be filed alongside lost causes and paths not travelled, of passing interest to the specialist, but not, in the end worthy of serious attention? The events that feature in this account have been of marginal interest to historians of national liberation in southern Africa, where the 'turn to armed struggle' figures strongly in popular memories and official narratives. Academic histories of the struggle for freedom and democracy in South Africa, Zimbabwe and Angola have revealed the complexity and significance of violence in shaping colonial and post-colonial politics and society. Accounts of the liberation war in Zimbabwe, for example, have examined the individual experiences of fighters in detail, as well as the formative influence of violence on social memory, ethnic and national identities.[28] Similarly, narratives of liberation war have been central to studies of decolonization – and post-

---

[28] Ngwabi Bhebe and Terence Ranger, eds, *Soldiers in Zimbabwe's Liberation War*, vols 1 and 2 (London: James Currey, 1995/96); Jocelyn Alexander and JoAnn McGregor, 'War Stories: Guerrilla Narratives of Zimbabwe's Liberation War', *History Workshop Journal* 57 (2004): 79–100.
Jocelyn Alexander, JoAnn McGregor, and T. O. Ranger, eds, *Violence & Memory: One Hundred Years in the 'dark Forests' of Matabeleland*. Social History of Africa (Oxford: James Currey, 2000).

colonial conflict – in Angola and Lusophone Africa. These have often emphasized the role played by Cold War dynamics, particularly during the 1970s and 1980s.[29] In histories of South Africa, furthermore, the formation of militant movements by anti-apartheid and Communist organizations in the early 1960s has placed the adoption of armed struggle and the supposed failure of non-violence at the centre of the historical narrative of liberation.[30] This book does not seek to offer a revision or critique of these debates or claim that non-violent passive resistance was predominant in southern African liberation movements. But the episodes explored here are a reminder that no single narrative, however compelling, can fully capture the complex and contradictory contingencies involved in the processes of social and political transformation.

The scheme to launch a protest march across the border into the heavily-policed Northern Province of Northern Rhodesia in May 1962 actually happened, even if no march took place and the centre of gravity of decolonization in Zambia was far from Makonde and the Great North Road. The existence of a group of Gandhian activists determined to offer their support to the cause of national independence in Africa cannot be denied, even if their plans were never implemented. Similarly, the Sahara protest had no impact on the process of nuclear proliferation. After its tests in Algeria in 1960, France established itself as a nuclear power and provided support for the development of a nuclear weapons programme by the Israeli government. Despite the Partial Test Ban Treaty, signed by the United States, UK and Soviet Union in 1963, France's atomic weapons tests were followed by China in 1964. Recent work examining the welcome given to China's tests by international anti-colonial campaigners such as Claudia Jones further suggests that the relationship between narratives of peace, decolonization and Third World solidarity was complicated.[31] Questions of peace and nuclear proliferation also underlined the fragility of state-level Afro-Asian solidarity, as in the case of the Indo-China border war of 1962, which prompted the World Peace Brigade's final sustained effort to intervene in conflict. The war raised fears about future conflict that were compounded when China tested its first atomic weapon, prompting

---

[29] Natalia Telepneva, *Cold War Liberation The Soviet Union and the Collapse of the Portuguese Empire in Africa, 1961–1975* (Chapel Hill: University of North Carolina Press, 2021); The role played by Cuba has been a particular interest:
   Piero Gleijeses, *Conflicting Missions: Havana, Washington, and Africa, 1959–1976* (Chapel Hill: University of North Carolina Press, 2002).
   Piero Gleijeses, *Visions of Freedom: Havana, Washington, Pretoria and the Struggle for Southern Africa, 1976–1991* (Chapel Hill: The University of North Carolina Press, 2013); Edward George, *The Cuban Intervention in Angola, 1965–1991: From Che Guevara to Cuito Cuanavale* (London: Routledge, 2005).

[30] Stephen Ellis, 'The Genesis of the ANC's Armed Struggle in South Africa 1948–1961', *Journal of Southern African Studies* 37, no. 4 (2011): 657–76; Stephen Ellis, *External Mission: The ANC in Exile, 1960–1990* (London: Hurst; McKinley, 2012); T. Dale, 'Umkhonto We Sizwe: A Critical Analysis of the Armed Struggle of the African National Congress', *South African Historical Journal* 70, no. 1 (2018): 27–41; Simpson, *Umkhonto We Sizwe*; Simpson, 'Nelson Mandela and the Genesis of the ANC's Armed Struggle: Notes on Method'. One of the most nuanced accounts of the changing tactics of the ANC is Simon Stevens, 'The Turn to Sabotage by The Congress Movement in South Africa', *Past & Present* 245, no. 1 (2019): 221–55, and see also Jonathan Hyslop, 'Mandela on War', in *The Cambridge Companion to Nelson Mandela*, edited by Rita Barnard (Cambridge: Cambridge University Press, 2014), 162–81.

[31] Zifeng Liu, 'Decolonization Is Not a Dinner Party: Claudia Jones, China's Nuclear Weapons, and Anti-Imperialist Solidarity', *Journal of Intersectionality* 3 (July 2019): 21–45.

the Indian government to develop a nuclear weapons programme, which culminated in its own atomic bomb test in 1974.[32] And the apartheid state in South Africa developed and built a small number of nuclear weapons during the 1980s, before the programme was halted shortly before the launch of formal negotiations between the government and the ANC.[33] But the Sahara team would not have been assembled without the emergence of a conjunction of anti-colonial and disarmament movements in global politics in the late 1950s.

This book offers an alternative perspective on the politics of peace and the global Cold War, that blurs distinctions between passive resistance and armed struggle. The changing character of decolonization in the early 1960s certainly represented a critical moment for international peace campaigners, as calls for violent revolution against colonialism simultaneously undermined confidence in their capacity to inspire popular non-violence and inspired a new generation of activists to interrogate imperialism and militarism at the level of the state.[34] Visions of peace and Third World revolution were co-constitutive of the New Left and other radical forms of political activism that took shape in the 1960s. Attempts by international teams of peace activists to intervene on behalf of African independence movements might therefore be regarded as more than merely tangential and marginal moments in the history of decolonization.

Decolonization

The process of decolonization defies easy categorization. As one recent general history suggests, accounts of the process by which the world of European empires became a world of independent nation states are ultimately shaped by scholars' chronological or geographical frameworks, their emphasis on imperial, local or international perspectives, or narratives that centre on imperial withdrawal, national liberation, neocolonialism or globalization.[35] At its narrowest, the history of decolonization focuses on a narrative of institutional transformation, notions of contractual negotiation and transitions of formal political power, 'not a process but a clutch of fitful activities and events', as one authoritative account has put it.[36] Others view decolonization as a distinctive historical process with a much broader significance, marking the disintegration of a 'global colonial order' and the subsequent formation of a world of sovereign nation states.[37] This book focuses narrowly on the historical

---

[32] Itty Abraham, *The Making of the Indian Atomic Bomb: Science, Secrecy and the Postcolonial State* (London: Zed Books, 1998), 125.
[33] Anna-Mart Van Wyk, 'Apartheid's Atomic Bomb: Cold War Perspectives', *South African Historical Journal* 62, no. 1 (1 March 2010): 100–20; J. W. de Villiers, Roger Jardine, and Mitchell Reiss, 'Why South Africa Gave up the Bomb', *Foreign Affairs* 72, no. 5 (1993/1992): 98–109.
[34] Petra Goedde, *The Politics of Peace: A Global Cold War History* (Oxford: Oxford University Press, 2019).
[35] Jan C. Jansen, Jurgen Osterhammel, and Jeremiah Riemer, *Decolonization: A Short History* (Princeton, NJ: Princeton University Press, 2019).
[36] Raymond F. Betts, *Decolonization* (London: Routledge, 2004), 1.
[37] John Darwin, 'Decolonization and the End of Empire', in *The Oxford History of the British Empire, Vol V: Historiography*, edited by Robin Winks (Oxford: Oxford University Press, 1999), 543; see also

moment in the late 1950s to mid-1960s that saw a transfer of political power across much of the continent of Africa, following a similar process of decolonization in Asia over the previous decade. But it also highlights the complexity and contradictions of the broader process of the emergence of the nation state as a norm of international politics. The relationship between the loose networks of individuals and organizations promoting peace and nuclear disarmament, and the emerging African political elite, whose popular authority increasingly depended on their legitimacy as nationalist leaders, was the basis for the alignment between anti-colonial and peace movements but also its main weakness. In terms of analytical approaches to political protest and social movements, this might be configured as a tension between transnational and national modes of political participation. The friction between national and transnational forms of political action reflects a conceptual tension in histories of decolonization.

This tension should not be understood as an interaction between a complex and sophisticated transnational politics of peace and a homogenous and straightforward politics of African nationalism. Studies of the latter have shown that nationalism in Africa was itself a contradictory and diffuse phenomenon. While early Africanist histories sought to narrate the nascent nation, recent works have examined countervailing tendencies, including the ways in which ethnic and nationalist political affiliations emerged in parallel, or post-colonial forms of national citizenship and subjecthood remain shaped by colonial legacies.[38] And, more recently, work has focused on the histories of nationalism as a distinct category of analysis, contending that scholarship ought to focus, not on the histories of nations but on the 'rigorous historicization of nationalism in Africa'.[39] Many nationalist movements were, moreover, forged in the context of political exile and the experience of armed struggles based outside the borders of the nation state, leading to what has been described as 'un-national' nationalism.[40] Similarly, the experience of exile and engagement with wider pan-African and Afro-Asian networks shaped regional as well as national identities.[41] The ambiguous relationships between nationalist leaders and transnational networks detailed in this book constituted connected but distinct political formations

John Darwin, *Britain and Decolonisation: The Retreat from Empire in the Postwar World* (London: Macmillan, 1988).

[38] Pioneering 'nationalist' histories might include Thomas Hodgkin, *Nationalism in Colonial Africa* (New York: New York University Press, 1957); Terence O. Ranger, *Revolt in Southern Rhodesia 1896-7* (London: Heineman, 1967); on the parallel emergence of ethnicity and nationalism, see Jean Marie Allman, *The Quills of the Porcupine: Asante Nationalism in an Emergent Ghana* (Madison: University of Wisconsin Press, 1993); on citizenship see Mahmood Mamdani, *Citizen and Subject: Contemporary Africa and the Legacy of Late Colonialism* (Princeton, NJ: Princeton University Press, 1996).

[39] Miles Larmer and Baz Lecocq, 'Historicising Nationalism in Africa', *Nations and Nationalism* 24, no. 4 (2018): 912. On the emergent interest in the histories of nationalist movements, see also the editor's introduction to Éric Morier-Genoud, ed., *Sure Road?: Nationalisms in Angola, Guinea-Bissau and Mozambique* (Leiden: Brill, 2012).

[40] Luise White and Miles Larmer, 'Introduction: Mobile Soldiers and the Un-National Liberation of Southern Africa', *Journal of Southern African Studies* 40, no. 6 (2014): 1271–4.

[41] Ismay Milford, 'Harnessing the Wind: East and Central African Activists and Anticolonial Cultures in a Decolonising World, 1952–64' (PhD Thesis, European University Institute, Florence, 2019); Ismay Milford, 'Federation, Partnership, and the Chronologies of Space in 1950s East and Central Africa', *The Historical Journal* 63, no. 5 (2020): 1325–48.

that emerged from the processes of decolonization. While the emerging structures of the nation state operated as a constraint on the ambitions and universal visions of peace campaigners, the two forms of activism are, perhaps, best understood as parallel, rather than rival, paths of activism. Rather than operating at cross-purposes, transnational and national movements might instead be regarded as distinct but related aspects of a global history of activism. In this sense, the connections between European, US and African movements were part of a transnational history of peace that was 'made in different places but . . . constructed in the movement between places, sites, and regions'.[42] As Martin Thomas and Andrew Thompson suggest, 'anti-colonial nationalism, insurgency, and popular protest were themselves globalising factors' in the 1950s and 1960s, which laid the foundations for the forms of global integration that came to prominence in the late-twentieth century.[43]

The practices and the processes of decolonization were, moreover, strongly affected by the geopolitical context of the Cold War. Decolonization, as one recent collection suggests, resulted in the formation of post-colonial states that were 'independent but not self-sufficient' and the process of establishing national sovereignty and identity was complicated by the ideological struggles of the Cold War.[44] Importantly, as recent debates in the history of the Cold War have illustrated, in the formerly colonized world, the era of superpower tension was far less peaceful and more 'hot' than the experience of those in Europe and North America would suggest. Westad has made great efforts to reconfigure the history of the Cold War and take account of the overlapping histories of political change in the Third World. In focusing on the ways in which the United States and Soviet Union responded to political transformation in Africa and Asia, Westad argues, analysis of Cold War 'shifted south'.[45] And yet his works say little of the ways in which the threat of atomic weapons and what was described at the Accra conference in 1960 as 'nuclear imperialism' (see Chapter 5) played out in Africa; rather than a site of debate around the moral and political dimensions of nuclear proliferation, Africa is presented as a site of resource extraction, in the form of uranium.[46] Similarly, while accounts of the emergence of disarmament movements are presented as world histories, there has been a tendency to structure these accounts around national or regional rather than transnational or global criteria.[47] Nevertheless, accounts such as Wittner's multi-volume world history of nuclear disarmament have shown how the late 1950s and 1960s saw a rapid growth in opposition to nuclear weapons in Africa

---

[42] C. A. Bayly, Sven Beckert, Matthew Connelly, Isabel Hofmeyr, Wendy Kozol, and Patricia Seed, 'AHR Conversation: On Transnational History', *The American Historical Review* 111, no. 5 (1 December 2006): 1444.
[43] Martin Thomas and Andrew Thompson, 'Empire and Globalisation: From "High Imperialism" to Decolonisation', *The International History Review* 36, no. 1 (2014): 142.
[44] Leslie James and Elisabeth Leake, 'Introduction', in *Decolonization and the Cold War: Negotiating Independence*, edited by Leslie James and Elisabeth Leake (London: Bloomsbury, 2015), 3–4.
[45] Odd Arne Westad, *The Global Cold War: Third World Interventions and the Making of Our Times* (Cambridge: Cambridge University Press, 2016), 1; see also Odd Arne Westad, *The Cold War: A World History* (New York: Basic Books, 2017).
[46] Westad, *Global Cold War*, 133, 137.
[47] For example, Lawrence Wittner's account of the 'world movement' nevertheless tends to divide international movements by nation or region. The Sahara protest is therefore an example of 'Third World' activism in Africa, not of US or European activism: Wittner, *Resisting the Bomb*, 266–7.

that paralleled the emergence of disarmament movements in the West.[48] Moreover, groups such as the Campaign for Nuclear Disarmament (CND) in Britain articulated a transformative vision of Britain's future role as a post-imperial power.[49] Disarmament campaigns in the early Cold War suggest, again, that decolonization was a global but heterogeneous phenomenon. For disarmament campaigners and post-colonial African states, nuclear weapons and neocolonialism were inseparable threats, although this did not necessarily mean that opposition to nuclear imperialism equated to support for non-violence.

Alongside its concern with fears of global nuclear annihilation, the Cold War frames this study in other ways that align with Leake and Leslie's assertion that the Cold War should primarily be understood as a 'global ideological struggle'.[50] The emphasis on Western-led development efforts and anti-Communist stance of the Africa Bureau under Michael Scott, for example, suggest that anti-colonialism was a movement framed by contemporaries as a struggle to keep nationalists within the orbit of the West. And yet, Communism was anathema to Scott, not on purely ideological grounds but because of his engagement with Communists in specific national contexts, in Britain, India and South Africa. Other accounts of Cold War history return to the tension between national and transnational frames of reference. As Westad argues, in the context of the Cold War, nationalism 'had its clear limitations as a global framework . . . it was always a challenge to those who thought the future belonged to universalist ideologies'.[51] Similarly, as Nehring suggests, Cold War disarmament movements were co-constructed simultaneously in national and transnational frames of political activism. In his comparative analysis of disarmament movements in Britain and the Federal Republic of Germany, Nehring demonstrates that anti-nuclear weapons campaigns both illuminate the impact of national political cultures and emphasize 'the complexities of transnational protest'.[52] These histories reveal, Nehring also argues, the ways in which social movements are formed by a transnational 'politics of communication' across borders.[53] Ultimately, it was in the interactions between Western and African understanding of the wider context of disarmament as well as efforts to centre peace in the struggle for national liberation that the development of a transnational movement against violence was impeded by its encounter with anti-colonial nationalism.

The story of the intersection of peace and anti-colonialism in the early Cold War suggests a definition of decolonization as a process of historical transformation shaped by a complex interplay between multiple conceptualizations of nationalism, democracy, freedom and sovereignty. Decolonization seems to have eventually led to

[48] Wittner, *Resisting the Bomb*, see especially 267–71.
[49] Nehring, *Politics of Security,* 188–9.
[50] Leake and Leslie, *Decolonization and the Cold War*, 4.
[51] Westad, *The Cold War*, 7.
[52] Nehring, *Politics of Security*, 14.
[53] H. Nehring, 'National Internationalists: British and West German Protests against Nuclear Weapons, the Politics of Transnational Communications and the Social History of the Cold War, 1957–1964', *Contemporary European History* 14 (November 2005): 559–82. See also H. Nehring, 'The British and West German Protests Against Nuclear Weapons and Anti-Colonialism, 1956–64', *Socialist History Journal* 31 (2007): 9–39.

the construction of a world of nation states built on the foundations of the Western model of states that emerged in the eighteenth and nineteenth centuries. And yet, the entangled networks of activism explored in this book suggest that decolonization should not be read as a process in which the world took on Western forms of political organization but something contested and moulded at a local level. As Emma Hunter has noted in the context of Tanzania, the public sphere in Africa helped shape 'what independence could and should mean, how political subjecthood should be reconstituted'.[54]

The history of attempted engagement between peace campaigners and African nationalist movements in the late 1950s and early 1960s highlights the tension between claims centred on supposedly universal notions of freedom, democracy and peace and the distinctive agendas and more localized contextual concerns of nationalist movements. The episodes chronicled in this book demonstrate that this tension was most starkly illuminated when peace campaigners sought to utilize the patronage of African political leaders to serve an ideal – non-violence – that was not necessarily a priority (or even a viable option) for post-colonial states. Furthermore, as Lydia Walker argues, the work of transnational activists such as Michael Scott became a conduit for marginalized groups whose political claims highlight the limits of decolonization centred on the nation state.[55]

The end point of the process – the formation of a world of nation states – was, however, far from inevitable. Extensive support for federalist – as opposed to nationalist – visions of independence in the 1940s and 1950s.[56] Many other recent accounts have similarly emphasized the complexity, contextuality and contingency of decolonization, not as an event but as a series of interconnected processes of political transformation.[57] As Lee suggests in his overview of the 'afterlives' of the Bandung conference of 1955, 'decolonization equally constitutes a complex dialectical intersection of competing views and claims over colonial pasts, transitional presents, and inchoate futures'.[58] And, in his own most recent contribution to this ongoing debate, Cooper has argued that presenting decolonization as a narrative of the emergence of independent nation

---

[54] Emma Hunter, *Political Thought and the Public Sphere in Tanzania: Freedom, Democracy and Citizenship in the Era of Decolonization* (Cambridge: Cambridge University Press, 2015), 234.
[55] Lydia Walker, 'Decolonization in the 1960s: On Legitimate and Illegitimate Nationalist Claims-Making', *Past & Present* 242, no. 1 (2019): 227–64. Lydia Walker, *States-in-Waiting: Global Decolonization and its Discontents* (Cambridge: Cambridge University Press, Forthcoming 2023).
[56] Frederick Cooper, *Citizenship between Empire and Nation: Remaking France and French Africa, 1945–1960* (Princeton, NJ: Princeton University Press, 2014). Frederick Cooper, 'Possibility and Constraint: African Independence in Historical Perspective', *The Journal of African History* 49, no. 2 (2008): 167–96; Michael Collins, 'Decolonisation and the "Federal Moment"', *Diplomacy & Statecraft* 24, no. 1 (2013): 21–40.
[57] This has been particularly evident in recent comparative studies of decolonization including Martin Thomas, Bob Moore, and L. J. Butler, *Crises of Empire: Decolonization and Europe's Imperial States, 1918–1975* (London: Bloomsbury, 2008); Prasenjit Duara, *Decolonization: Perspectives from Now and Then* (London: Routledge, 2004).
[58] Christopher J. Lee, 'Introduction Between a Moment and an Era: The Origins and Afterlives of Bandung', in *Making a World after Empire: The Bandung Moment and Its Political Afterlives*, edited by Christopher J. Lee (Athens: Ohio University Press, 2010), 8.

states, 'misses the extent to which political movements focused on issues of social and economic justice, not just sovereignty'.[59]

But this story, of the overlapping campaigns for peace and against colonialism, suggests that decolonization was also framed by another set of concerns, largely absent in recent accounts: the political and activist practices through which decolonization was enacted. An examination of peace and anti-colonialism suggests that models of decolonization ought to address *methods* as well as ends.

The practice of solidarity

My main argument in this book is that histories of decolonization ought to show greater regard for the practices of resistance, protest and solidarity through which claims to universal concepts such as peace, sovereignty and freedom were enacted in particular local contexts and circumstances. By the early 1960s, the dynamics of transnational engagement with anti-colonial and anti-apartheid movements in southern Africa centred not on concepts of political rights but the ways in which independence might be achieved. As Muste noted with regret in 1964, the defining feature of the relationship between peace activists and movements for Third World liberation was the tension between violent and non-violent tactics of protest. The activists whose lives are explored in this book were concerned with the ways in which definitions of independence and subjecthood were formed through the practice of politics. Ultimately, the dividing line that emerged between peace and anti-colonial movements was defined by the difference between ends and means. So, just as Cooper has reminded us of the need to account for the different forms of political institution that were under debate during the process of decolonization, we ought also to engage with the ways in which, contemporaries imagined, political and transformation would be brought into being.

On the eve of the founding conference of the World Peace Brigade in 1962, the US Quaker and peace activist Charles Coates Walker suggested that non-violence was a defining feature of modern activism. It was, he argued, not until the twentieth century that non-violence became a 'political theory of action'. In the past, it had been an expression of religious faith or an ad hoc response to circumstances, but it was only with 'the Gandhian experiments in South Africa and India that non-violence has a mode of political action commanded the attention'.[60] Walker noted a series of contemporary challenges to Gandhian non-violence. It was, some asserted, 'ideological', a 'counsel of the privileged', whose material interests were served by a focus on non-violence and opposition to those who called for the overthrow of exploitation by any means. Others, he continued, argued that non-violence was a 'utopian' form of political action that avoided problematic discussions around the nature of political power, but he maintained that non-violence should not be understood as the fanciful desire to

---

[59] Frederick Cooper, 'Decolonizations, Colonizations, and More Decolonizations: The End of Empire in Time and Space', *Journal of World History* 33, no. 3 (2022): 524.
[60] Lydia Walker, 'The Idea of Non-violence and its Role in a World Movement', 28 December 1961, Swathmore College Peace Collection (SPC), Muste 89/22 WPB Founding Convention.

eradicate conflict, but a challenge to the idea that violence was a legitimate solution to conflict. He concluded that advocates should not be satisfied with 'a few platitudes nobody can disagree with, or a syncretism that picks up principles as one might gather firewood' and that campaigners needed both 'a vision of reality' and a 'sense of direction', or 'nonviolence will degenerate into uncoordinated and sporadic protests'.[61] For Walker, then, Gandhian non-violence was a potent force as a programme of action, not a body of ideas.

Although many, perhaps all, of the activists and campaigners who feature in this study, would have regarded Gandhi as a principal guide for proponents of a politics of non-violence, Gandhi's presence in this book is ghostly. As such, it draws inspiration from Sean Scalmer's recent work, *Gandhi in the West*, which has examined many of the same networks of British and American activists that are the focus of this book.[62] Like Scalmer, I would argue that the late 1950s and early 1960s can be described as a 'summer of satyagraha', in which Western radical pacifists undertook experiments in Gandhian non-violence for the first time, before they were overtaken by new forms of political campaign that no longer placed Gandhian principles of non-violence at their centre.[63] But, I would also argue that our historical understanding of this moment of satyagraha must also take into account the attempts by Western advocates of non-violence to support and influence anti-colonial movements in Africa. Moreover, in contrast to Mukherjee's recent reassessment of the significance of Gandhi in modern Indian intellectual history, I would argue that the Gandhian ideas of freedom explored by peace activists in the late 1950s and early 1960s suggest that the universality of Western categories of political freedom have been, for some at least, insecure for some time.[64] Mukherjee centres her argument on the fundamental distinction between Western concepts of political freedom, centred on identity, and 'the Gandhian discourse of renunciative freedom', which underpinned the largest non-violent mass resistance campaigns of the twentieth century, the Indian interwar anti-colonial movement.[65] It is striking, though, that while Mukherjee's analysis focuses on concepts and discourses, her account of Gandhi's political activism often centres on practice; the Gandhian non-violent resistance movement adapted Indic traditions of freedom through renunciation and located them, not within withdrawal from political and social life, but as an ethic of engagement.

In key regards, it was in the practices of renunciative freedom that connected the Gandhian movement in India to its Western counterparts. The campaigners who sought to connect anti-colonialism and non-violence in the late 1950s and early 1960s employed practices, or repertoires, that had been central to Gandhian satyagraha campaigns in India: marches, boycotts, fasting and self-sacrifice to legal authority. The Gandhian discourse of protest was thus connected to post-war social movements

---

[61] Ibid.
[62] Sean Scalmer, *Gandhi in the West: The Mahatma and the Rise of Radical Protest* (Cambridge and New York: Cambridge University Press, 2011).
[63] Ibid., 7.
[64] M. Mukherjee, 'Transcending Identity: Gandhi, Nonviolence, and the Pursuit of a "Different" Freedom in Modern India', *American Historical Review* 115, no. 2 (2010): 453–73.
[65] Ibid., 472.

through a shared vision of political and social transformation through practices of collective action. In 1963, the US peace activist David Dillinger wrote in the pacifist magazine *Liberation* that 'the power of a nonviolent movement stems from the actions it undertakes, not from its political statements or the private beliefs and associations of its participants'.[66] Dellinger, who would later achieve public prominence as one of the Chicago Seven anti-Vietnam War protestors charged for inciting a riot at the 1968 Democratic Party Convention, saw Gandhian ideas of protest as legitimating the claim that alternative forms of mass action could be effective. In Marian Mollin's account of radical pacifism in the United States, the echoes of Western Christianity in Gandhian philosophies of action meant that his 'otherwise foreign ideas' were readily adopted in the West.[67]

Collective action has been central to studies of political protest and social movements, but often these tend to focus on the ways in which practice shapes the organization and structure of movements or in the instrumental value of particular forms of public practice. For Tilly, collective action such as marches and other forms of mass public demonstration constitute 'contentious performances' that embodied the distinctive message of protest events; in time, though, these actions became 'repositories of knowledge' relating to the routines and repertoires deemed legitimate and meaningful within specific political cultures.[68] But the practices of Gandhian non-violent protest employed by transnational peace campaigners might also be understood as Tarrow has described as 'modular' forms of protest.[69] In Tarrow's account, focused on eighteenth- and nineteenth-century collective action in Europe and North America, protest forms such as the strike by industrial workers became a generalizable mode of collective action that could be understood and repeated across a range of local settings. In his work, Tarrow addressed shifting paradigms of protest that reflected the broader social transformations associated with modernity: industrialization, urbanization and the entrenchment of Western capitalism. But, in the case of mid-twentieth-century peace campaigns, the adoption of Gandhian ideas required an engagement with a set of political practices that, as Mukherjee argues, built on conceptual foundations that were inherently and necessarily different from those of Western political philosophy.

In assessing the adoption and adaptation of Gandhian practices of non-violence as universal principles for collective action it is perhaps necessary to take account of broader processes of cross-cultural translation. As Liu contends, in the context of colonialism, translation constituted an exchange of 'meaning value' that paralleled the

---

[66] David Dellinger, 'Policing the Peace Movement', *Liberation* 7 (January 1963): quoted in Marian Mollin, *Radical Pacifism in Modern America: Egalitarianism and Protest. Politics and Culture in Modern America* (Philadelphia: University of Pennsylvania Press, 2006), 6 See also Andrew E. Hunt, *David Dellinger: The Life and Times of a Nonviolent Revolutionary* (New York: New York University Press, 2006).

[67] Mollin, *Radical Pacifism in Modern America*, 14.

[68] Charles Tilly, *Contentious Performances* (New York: Cambridge University Press, 2008), 73–4; Sidney G. Tarrow, *Power in Movement: Social Movements and Contentious Politics* (Cambridge: Cambridge University Press, 1998), 29.

[69] Sidney G. Tarrow, 'Modular Collective Action and the Rise of the Social Movement: Why the French Revolution Was Not Enough', *Politics & Society* 21, no. 1 (1993): 69–90.

unequal forms of economic exchange that marked colonial encounters.[70] But, unlike the struggles over the definition of terms examined by Liu, the radical pacifists sought to translate Gandhian practices into their Western equivalents. Resonances with Western Christianity, as Mollin argues, offered one way of communicating Gandhian ideas.[71] But, although Christian faith provided a shared point of reference for many of the activists examined in this book, Gandhian principles of non-violence could also be defined in a more general concept of discipline, self-control and submission. In 1962, for example, the African American civil rights and peace activist Bayard Rustin was asked to provide a set of characteristics that would define suitable volunteers for the non-violent protest in support of the Zambian nationalist movement. These included a directive to insist that volunteers consider the potential consequences of participation in non-violent protests, which included 'facing guns and being shot'; 'being killed' or 'being surrounded by police and cut off for a long time from water or food'.[72] Leaders of the protest, Rustin continued, should exhibit a 'profound dedication to a free united Africa', although not in a form that would 'express itself through emotional excitability'.[73] Maintaining discipline in practice could be addressed in terms that highlighted the modularity of non-violence, adaptable to pan-African ideals just as it had been employed in the service of a political movement rooted in Indic tradition.

In outlining these criteria, Rustin reflected his experience of American passive resisters in civil rights protests since the 1940s. When the Congress of Racial Equality (CORE) began to organize non-violent protests against segregation in the United States, it produced detailed guidelines for volunteers that encoded discipline and planning and a level of control over individual protestors that, Scalmer has remarked, seems in contrast to the 'libidinous chaos of later generations of loving and peaceful protest'.[74] The practice of passive resistance was both carefully planned – including the use of role-play and theatrical improvisation to simulate the challenges that protestors might face – and evaluated through a careful process of reflection and discussion. Through such forms of carefully managed discipline, Gandhian non-violence could be adapted to the political cultures of Europe and North America. When these same activists turned their attention to the struggle against colonialism, they again understood non-violence not merely as a set of principles but as an experimental political practice.

Practices can thus define a movement and legitimize its claims, but protest is also a form of individual practice, not a resource or repertoire but an end in itself.[75] As other studies of modern social movements suggest, however, individual activist practice also shapes the collective identity of movements; in the case of the anti-apartheid

---

[70] Lydia H. Liu, 'The Question of Meaning-Value in the Political Economy of the Sign', in *Tokens of Exchange: The Problem of Translation in Global Circulations*, edited by Lydia H. Liu (Durham, NC: Duke University Press, 2000), 13–41.
[71] Mollin, *Radical Pacifism in Modern America*, 14.
[72] Rustin to Africa Freedom Action Working Committee, 5 March 1962, SPC Muste 89/22 WPB Correspondence.
[73] Ibid.
[74] Scalmer, *Gandhi in the West*, 149.
[75] James M. Jasper, *The Art of Moral Protest: Culture, Biography, and Creativity in Social Movements* (Chicago and London: University of Chicago Press, 1997), 338–42.

movement for example, participation in demonstrations or boycotts was routinely defined as an act of 'solidarity' – the term which provided the 'central identity concept' of the movement.[76] The concept of 'solidarity' would thus come to define transnational action for, and advocacy of, the liberation movements. As Featherstone argues in his exploration of the term as a 'central practice of the political left', solidarity is not established through an external characteristic that connects otherwise distinct groups but emerges from a generative activity whose terms are not defined and whose relations are 'unfinished and in process'.[77] A history centred on the practice of solidarity thus involves an emphasis on multiplicity and plurality and on the production of ends that may not have been foreseen.

My approach to the overlapping histories of peace and anti-colonialism in the post-war period is not, therefore, motivated by a desire to uncover underlying social structures or organizational and institutional frameworks. I am interested instead in the ways in which individual protestors, through their practice as actors, narrated the accounts of a virtuous life and the social and political ideals that seemed possible within their own distinct historical moment. Three themes emerge from traces left by these activists in the archive: hope, in the context of the possibilities for a world transformed by the end of empire; fear, in the existential crisis of possible nuclear annihilation, but also in the broader sense of a crisis of modernity; and a determined belief that the resolution of that dilemma came, not through a singular vision or plan, but in action and 'the very fact of moving forward, step by step'.[78]

The following chapters can be roughly divided into two sections. Section one comprises two chapters, the first of which takes the work of Michael Scott as its initial focus, before widening to reflect the expansion of the transnational networks that addressed anti-colonialism. The narrative also shifts from colonial metropole of London and the international centre of New York towards Africa itself, as peace movements began to interact more closely with African nationalism. The chapter also examines the ways in which campaigners engaged with the wider ideological landscape that shaped attitudes towards colonialism in the early 1950s and in particular, the engagement of British activists with notions of colonial development. The following chapter examines ways in which activists' political and emotional lives became intertwined, before chronicling efforts to fuse transnational visions of Gandhian non-violence with expanding nationalist campaigns against colonial rule in Africa. The second section provides a detailed account of the ways in which peace and anti-colonial movements became interconnected in the late 1950s and early 1960s. Chapter 4 focuses on the Sahara protest against French atomic tests, and Chapter 5 examines the aftermath of that protest from the Accra conference on 'Positive Action' in 1960, through to the formation of the World Peace Brigade in 1962. Chapter 6 explores the story of Africa

---

[76] Thörn, 'The Meaning(s) of Solidarity', 207.
[77] David Featherstone, *Solidarity: Hidden Histories and Geographies of Internationalism* (London: Zed Books, 2012), 5; 246.
[78] Bill Sutherland and Matt Meyer, *Guns and Gandhi in Africa: Pan African Insights on Nonviolence, Armed Struggle and Liberation in Africa* (Trenton, NJ: Africa World Press, 2000), 145.

Freedom Action and the march that did not take place in Northern Rhodesia in 1962. The final chapter concludes the story of the World Peace Brigade via three sketches of international efforts to connect peace to the anti-colonial and post-colonial politics of the early 1960s and reflects on the ways in which we might locate these ambiguous stories in a broader historical context.

2

Peace, the state and development

While practices of non-violent protest are the principal concern of this book, attempts to generate a collective non-violent action movement in the 1950s were also framed by the dominant ideologies that shaped the ways in which activists imagined decolonization. In this chapter, I will use two examples of peace and anti-colonial activism to examine the more general ideals that would shape later attempts to build transnational non-violent action against colonialism. The chapter begins with the participation of British and American campaigners in the World Pacifist Conference held in India in late 1949 and explores the visions of faith and justice that circulated within the peace movement. In the second example, I assess the claims to political rights and the idea of the state that shaped Michael Scott's attempts to advocate for the Herero people of South-West Africa (Namibia) at the United Nations that began in the late 1940s and continued into the 1960s. Finally, the chapter examines the ideas of development that influenced Scott and the Africa Bureau, the campaign organization for which he acted as Director. An outline of the plans for colonial transformation promoted by Scott and the Africa Bureau was set out in the book, *Attitude to Africa*, co-authored by Scott and published as a Penguin Special in 1951. The chapter explores the broad visions of state-centred development that were set out in the book and the sense of a crisis of modernity that resonated within Scott's individual contribution.

Peace and international justice

In late December 1949, the itinerant Anglican priest Michael Scott attended the World Pacifist Conference, a meeting jointly held at Santiniketan in West Bengal and the Sevagram ashram founded by Mohandas Gandhi in Maharashtra, India. The conference brought together just over ninety advocates of non-violent political action from across the world. Rather than a convention of national peace movements, the organizers brought the delegates to India to engage in efforts to compose a global strategy for peace. The charismatic leadership of Gandhi at the head of satyagraha campaigns in support of the independence movement in India subsequently inspired anti-colonial movements around the world, but the 1949 meeting was intended to inspire the construction of a worldwide peace movement as a legacy of Gandhi's life work. But the presence of Scott demonstrated that the causes of peace and anti-colonialism remained intertwined. The Sevagram meeting was nevertheless a gathering of individual activists and idealists to explore the possibilities for peace at both a personal and social level. And for Scott, the World Peace Conference came at a critical juncture in his political activism. It took place just weeks after he had addressed the Fourth Committee of the United Nations on behalf of the Herero people of South-West Africa, the first time any non-governmental official had been granted permission to directly lobby national delegates. His efforts in New York elevated him to a kind of celebrity status and provoked public fury from the South African government whose plan to 'incorporate' South-West Africa Scott had implacably opposed. The visit to Sevagram seems to have allowed Scott a moment of withdrawal, respite and inspiration away from the public attention that had followed his presentation to the Fourth Committee. In Britain, the *Observer* newspaper described him as the heir of Livingstone and one of the few Europeans able to navigate the 'barrier of suspicion that separates black from white in South Africa'.[1] According to the profile, which was based on notes provided by the group of Quakers that assisted Scott in London, he was a 'controversial figure' characterized by 'diffidence and reserve', but also 'uncompromising where . . . principles of humanity and justice are involved'. Scott's biographers define this moment as the point at which he achieved genuine celebrity status, but note that rather than embark on a series of publicity meetings on his return from the United Nations, he flew immediately to Sevagram. For Scott, then, the Sevagram meeting was of key importance, as a sanctuary from the intensity of New York and the fraught diplomacy of the United Nations, and also an opportunity to enjoy the companionship of people who shared his global perspective on political issues.[2]

The World Pacifist Conference offered political and personal respite for Scott. Away from New York, and the attention of the British press, Scott was able to spend time alongside like-minded individuals seeking to define a philosophy of action in response to the major issues that confronted the post-war world. Moreover, the discussions were interwoven with syncretic forms of religious and spiritual practice that appealed to Scott's maverick form of Christianity and, he reckoned, 'reached beyond the confines of institutional religion in a way that expressed humanity's search for the divine'.[3] It was in this setting that Scott began to formulate ideas that would form the basis of his autobiography, *A Time to Speak*. But what is clear in this later text (and somewhat glossed in the more recent biography) is that seems to have been a moment of heightened emotion for Scott. The day after his address to the UN Trusteeship Committee, he received news of the death of his father, Perceval Scott. In later accounts, Scott positioned his father as a central pillar of his childhood, higher than God in his regard and understanding, but also seemingly the source of both spiritual stability and existential guilt. When Perceval suffered a heart attack while playing with his children, Michael supposed he was responsible; when he informed his parents of his decision to enlist in the Air Force in 1940, Perceval collapsed with a stroke.[4] And yet his onward journey from New York to India was diverted only for a brief visit to his bereaved mother. The meeting, he recalled, was fraught, but emotionally guarded; his mother

[1] 'Profile – Michael Scott', *The Observer*, 4 December 1949, 3.
[2] Yates and Chester, *The Troublemaker*, 113.
[3] Ibid.
[4] Ibid., 7, 34.

conceded that it was appropriate for him to continue with his trip to India, but he 'had gone with a righteous sense of duty only half aware of the burden I had left her alone to bear'.[5]

The thoughts that Scott recorded of his time in India betray something of the internal struggle that shaped his political being. He felt that this inner conflict could not be separated from, or resolved independently of 'the external struggle for justice for the oppressed people of the world'.[6] In *A Time to Speak*, the account of his time in India in early 1950 shifts rapidly from his personal and private conflict to visions of a global contest between good and evil; the plight of the Herero people became a moral quandary alongside the legacies of the Holocaust and Hiroshima. This was, Scott surmised, a 'struggle to affirm what is true' with neither beginning nor end. In this struggle, he believed, 'ordinary people became transfigured by a sort of glory'. It was in the efforts of his friends and associates, from the Herero leader Hosea Kutako to his companion and fellow activist Mary Benson, that Scott located the 'stuff of life' that powered the continuous resurrection of the 'spirit of resistance to evil'.[7] The moral poetry of Scott's account is evident. It offers a vision of a transfiguration seen on a mountainside, but in place of a single Christ, Scott presents a series of dedicated activists, and rather than a singular doctrine, Scott turned to a spiritual message that transcended institutional religion. Although he presented it as the wisdom of Buddha, Scott concludes his account of Sevagram with a quotation from Edwin Arnold: 'Enter the Path! There is no grief like hate, No pains like passions, no deceit like sense'.[8] This moment of reflection and revelation from 1949 is followed immediately in his autobiography by an account of the final months of his mother's life, beginning with the news of her illness, which Scott received while attending the independence ceremonies in Ghana in 1957.

What his biographers describe as an 'Indian detour' were woven by Scott into something profoundly central to his political and spiritual vocation and his vision of a continuous struggle between good and evil. Instead of the sublime personality of a Christ or a Buddha, however, this struggle was fought by ordinary people and their individual sacrifices. In his account of the later pacifist endeavours in Central Africa, Jake Hodder offers an instructive insight into the mentality that shaped the development of pacifist activism over the first half of the twentieth century.[9] Hodder cites the American pacifist William James' 1906 call for a national service that 'would preserve in the midst of a pacific civilization the manly virtues which the military party is so afraid of seeing disappear in peace'.[10] For James, bringing this vision into being would create a 'moral equivalent to war', maintaining but repurposing the socially admired elements of military service, including discipline, bravery and service. It has been suggested that James' emphasis on the need for a 'heroic' form of pacifism stemmed

[5] Scott, *A Time to Speak*, 295.
[6] Ibid., 296.
[7] Ibid., 297.
[8] Edwin Arnold, *The Light of Asia*, quoted in Scott, *A Time to Speak*, 297–8.
[9] Jake Hodder, 'Waging Peace: Militarising Pacifism in Central Africa and the Problem of Geography, 1962', *Transactions of the Institute of British Geographers* 42, no. 1 (2017): 29–43.
[10] William James, 'The Moral Equivalent of War', *Peace and Conflict: Journal of Peace Psychology* 1, no. 1 (1995): 17–26.

from his relationship with his father, who had persuaded James not to participate in the American Civil War, psychological interpretations that might equally be applied to Scott.[11] Like James, Scott had an ambivalent relationship with his father and, although, unlike James, Scott had volunteered for military services, beginning training as a gunner in the Royal Air Force in the early 1940s, Scott's discharge on medical grounds meant that he also felt a sense of failure.[12] But for Scott, these psychological elements were necessarily combined with a spiritual purpose. The heroism and service of peace activism was not only the 'moral equivalent of war', but it was also an embodiment of faith and Christian praxis.

In his study of the peace movement in Britain, Martin Ceadal defined pacifism as a 'faith not a policy', albeit split between two distinct modes of thought.[13] Until the 1930s, Caedal argued, the British peace movement was shaped by 'pacificism', which did not oppose all war, but defined it as an irrational policy that should be prevented. But from the mid-1930s, the movement became dominated by an absolutist 'pacifism', which opposed war under any circumstances. But, some have argued, the conceptualization of pacifism as a form of faith was focused too narrowly. Many pacifists were of course connected with churches and religious humanitarianism, but pacifism itself was a broad church, whose leaders conceptualized peace as [much more] than opposition to military conflict. Prominent figures such as Richard Roberts, a founder of the Christian Fellowship of Reconciliation (FOR), considered pacifism to be concerned with radical social visions that went far beyond a singular fixation on war.[14] In many ways, Scott fit Ceadal's model of a 'pacificist': his opposition to war was not absolute and, following his involvement with Indian passive resistance protests in South Africa in the mid-1940s, was invariably concerned with 'non-violence' as a means of political action, rather than pacifism as a principle. Nonetheless, many of his closest supporters in London during the late 1940s were pacifists, including Quakers Esther and Gordon Moorhead and John Fletcher.[15] As Ceadel has suggested, the peace movement in Britain had lost some of its idealism by 1945, but 'its sense of special mission remained undiminished'.[16] Scott, in combining the vocation of non-violence with a powerful advocacy of democracy and anti-colonialism, offered a vision that would resonate with his neo-missionary vocation.

In the United States, pacifist movements drew on Gandhi in similar ways. Pacifists connected with Christian anti-war organizations such as the Fellowship of Reconciliation and the American Friends Service Committee had begun to spread

---

[11] Morton Deutsch, 'William James: The First Peace Psychologist', *Peace and Conflict: Journal of Peace Psychology* 1, no. 1 (1995): 27–35. See also G. Cotkin, *William James, Public Philosopher* (Baltimore: Johns Hopkins University Press, 1990); H. M. Feinstein, *Becoming William James* (Ithaca, NY: Cornell University Press, 1984).

[12] Scott, *A Time to Speak*, Yates and Chester, *The Troublemaker*.

[13] Martin Ceadel, *Pacifism in Britain, 1914–1945: The Defining of a Faith* (Oxford: Clarendon Press, 1980), 194. See also Michael Pugh, 'Pacifism and Politics in Britain, 1931–1935', *The Historical Journal* 23, no. 3 (1980): 641–56.

[14] Bert den Boggende, 'Richard Roberts' Vision and the Founding of the Fellowship of Reconciliation', *Albion: A Quarterly Journal Concerned with British Studies* 36, no. 4 (1 December 2004): 608–35.

[15] Yates and Chester, *The Troublemaker*, 101.

[16] Martin Ceadel, *Semi-Detached Idealists: The British Peace Movement and International Relations, 1854–1945* (Oxford: Oxford University Press, 2000), 423.

the message of satyagraha during the interwar period, which by the 1940s had crystallized into a series of movements that incorporated both pacifist and anti-racist agendas. J. Holmes Smith, a Methodist missionary in India whose support for the independence movement had led the British authorities to enforce his removal from the country, founded an ashram in Harlem in 1940 and led supporters on an 'Interracial Pilgrimage' between New York and Washington, D.C. in 1942.[17] Perhaps the most extensive experiment in Gandhian methods came in the shape of the Congress of Racial Equality, launched in 1942 by pacifists including future civil rights leader James Farmer and an individual who would go on to play a central role in coordinating white liberal anti-colonial and anti-apartheid campaigns through the American Committee on Africa, George Houser.

Having become a pacifist as a student, Houser had been imprisoned for resisting conscription in late 1940. After his release, he became part of a group of more radical activists drawn to the Fellowship of Reconciliation under the patronage of Christian pacifist and former trade union activist, A. J. Muste. Under his guidance, Houser, Farmer and Rustin worked to extend the appeal of the peace movement beyond its privileged and moderate base, extending pacifist concerns into wider social issues including racial injustice. They sought direct confrontation with segregation rather than efforts at amelioration and asserted the claim that pacifism was concerned with social as well as moral relations between humans.[18] Their most prominent collective action, the 1947 'Journey of Reconciliation', provided a training ground in the tactics of non-cooperation with segregation on public transport employed by the later 'Freedom Riders'.[19] It was a conscious experiment in the effectiveness of Gandhian techniques of non-cooperation in the context of American civil rights. But they did not seek to simply replicate the form of Indian independence campaigners; the Congress of Racial Equality was 'united around a common discipline' that incorporated both a strict array of behaviours, but also called for particular emotional responses. As Sean Scalmer has suggested, this was a 'western' adaptation of Gandhian methods, with the removal of the unfamiliar practices of 'self-purification' in Indian versions of satyagraha and their translation into a series of activities that were primarily designed to arouse the public conscience.[20]

The form of pacifism that Scott espoused, with its focus on radical action and an agenda that drew connections between anti-militarism, political rights and racial equality, was perhaps more closely aligned with the 'radical pacifism' that emerged in the United States during the early 1940s.[21] There, conscientious objectors began to align their efforts with those of social campaigners around civil rights, which in the 1950s would further extend to support for anti-colonial nationalist movements, especially in Africa. As Marian Mollin suggests, these efforts would ultimately founder

[17] Kosek, *Acts of Conscience*, 185–6.
[18] John D'Emilio, *Lost Prophet: The Life and Times of Bayard Rustin* (New York and London: Free Press, 2003), 54.
[19] Derek Catsam, *Freedom's Main Line: The Journey of Reconciliation and the Freedom Rides* (Lexington: University Press of Kentucky, 2009), 35.
[20] Scalmer, *Gandhi in the West*, 147.
[21] Mollin, *Radical Pacifism in Modern America*.

as a consequence of contradictions and fault lines that marked this American prototype 'counterculture' as much as they did mainstream society.[22] But racial equality and civil and labour rights were all on the agenda of radical pacifists of the early 1940s. A. J. Muste, head of the US branch of FOR, had been a labour activist and founder of the American Workers' Party during the interwar years, while another FOR worker and Black activist, James Farmer, took a leading role in the formation of the Congress of Racial Equality (CORE) in 1942. The founders of CORE also included George Houser, a white peace activist who had been jailed as a conscientious objector, and the Black FOR member and later key organizer of the civil rights movement, Bayard Rustin, among its leading members. In 1946, Houser and Rustin led the Journey of Reconciliation, a prototype non-violent protest against segregation on buses in the southern United States.[23] As Mollin's account attests, the Journey also highlighted the contradictory form of egalitarianism taken by the radical pacifists, as would-be women participants were excluded. While safety may have been a genuine concern, the Journey of Reconciliation was a demonstration of the extent to which radical pacifists 'reified and perpetuated the relationship between masculinity and militancy'.[24]

Similarly, the vision of activism for peace and social transformation presented at Sevagram revealed other forms of social myopia, for the networks within which Scott operated were the embodiment of elite privilege. As Hodder suggests, it was 'a key moment in the internationalisation of the peace movement ... where prominent leaders developed personal relationships – like that between A. J. Muste, Rev. Michael Scott and Jayaprakash Narayan'.[25] In providing a space for a non-governmental peace summit, the Sevagram meeting thus represented the possibilities for an 'alternative vision of internationalism', one of a series of conferences in which mid-century conceptions of internationalism were brought into being through lived experience.[26] This was a gathering of a uniquely global community, in contrast to the discussions between national delegations that characterized meetings such as those held by the United Nations or the World Council of Churches. It was also, as the *Times of India* suggested, a fitting opportunity for international pacifists to reflect on the experiences of the twentieth century in a country with a rich tradition of humanism and pacifism. Delegates such as A. J. Muste, who spoke on the oppression of African Americans, 'must have had much to say by way of comparison with the Indian experiments in revolt and resistance to evil force and war'.[27]

Hodder argues that the Sevagram meeting can also be read as a deliberate 'sensual immersion in Gandhi's India.[28] Aside from Gandhi's ashram in Sevagram, groups of

---

[22] Ibid., 7.
[23] Ibid., 31–5; see also Marian Mollin, 'The Limits of Egalitarianism: Radical Pacifism, Civil Rights, and the Journey of Reconciliation', *Radical History Review* 88, no. 1 (2004): 112–38, Catsam, *Freedom's Main Line.*
[24] Mollin, *Radical Pacifism in Modern America*, 43.
[25] Jake Hodder, 'Conferencing the International at the World Pacifist Meeting, 1949', *Political Geography, Special Issue: Historical Geographies of Internationalism* 49 (1 November 2015): 48.
[26] Ibid., 2; see also Stephen Legg, Mike Heffernan, Jake Hodder, and Benjamin Thorpe, eds, *Placing Internationalism: International Conferences and the Making of the Modern World* (London: Bloomsbury Academic, 2022), 2–8.
[27] 'Posers of World Pacifist Conference', *Times of India*, 8 December 1949.
[28] Hodder, 'Conferencing the International', 45.

participants travelled across India to all points of the compass, including the most southerly tip of the subcontinent to a group (which included Scott) to within sight of the Nepalese Himalayas. These seem to have been conscious attempts to infuse global peace activism with Indian thought and practice as an alternative to Western models of education and represent a counter to the tendency to 'westernise' Gandhi.[29] These efforts to root the meeting deeply in Indian culture could be viewed as part of an effort to build a new form of universalism, which would transcend the Western liberal forms of internationalism that had hitherto framed world pacifist meetings. Moreover, they resonate with the efforts by Indian delegates at the United Nations to position their country as a leading force in international efforts to interrogate colonialism and racial injustice. In his own campaign on behalf of Herero opposition to the incorporation of South-West Africa, Scott had been supported by the Indian delegation to the UN, which had quickly become a forum for criticism of South African race policies, predating both Indian independence and the introduction of apartheid policies from 1948.[30] Alongside claims centred on the rights of citizens in independent nation states and the ideological politics of anti-colonial nationalism, the tenets of Gandhian non-violence were an important foundation of activist politics across the world.

But the conference received little public attention outside India. Moreover, the meeting is entirely absent from histories of the Gandhian influence on British and American pacifist movements. Scalmer's recent work, for example, moves directly from an analysis of the pacifist response to a war against Nazi Germany to the more confident launch of self-consciously Gandhian campaigns in the 1950s, beginning with 'Operation Gandhi', the brainchild of British activist Hugh Brock in 1951. Thus, the Sevagram meeting and its attempts to internationalize the peace movement were marginalized, despite the presence of figures, including the US pacifist Richard Gregg, who are prominent in his account of the translation of Gandhian ideals in the United States and Britain.[31] European and American peace movements of the 1950s would adapt Gandhian ideas and practices for Western contexts, rather than assimilate Asian spirituality and philosophy, and it was not, as we will see, until the early 1960s that global peace activism and anti-colonialism sought to integrate American, European and Indian activists in a worldwide peace movement. Internationalization in the context of post-war peace movements tended to mean transatlantic cooperation and communication rather than a form of globalization. Still, pacifist groups such as the International Fellowship of Reconciliation would exert subtle but significant international influence on anti-colonial nationalism in Africa, on the anti-apartheid and civil rights movements and on anti-nuclear weapons protests. In each case, non-violence was the intersection of principle and practice, method and ideal.

---

[29] Scalmer, *Gandhi in the West*.
[30] Newell Maynard Stultz, 'Evolution of the United Nations Anti-Apartheid Regime', *Human Rights Quarterly* 13, no. 1 (1 February 1991): 1–23; See also Gerard McCann, 'From Diaspora to Third Worldism and the United Nations: India and the Politics of Decolonizing Africa', *Past & Present* 218 (2013): 258–80; Mark Mazower, *No Enchanted Palace: The End of Empire and the Ideological Origins of the United Nations* (Woodstock: Princeton University Press, 2009).
[31] Scalmer, *Gandhi in the West*, 136–40.

One of the participants at the Sevagram meeting was the South African academic and political leader Davidson Jabavu. The son of one of the pioneers of African political organization, John Tengo Jabavu, D. D. T. Jabavu was the first Black lecturer at the South African Native College (later University of Fort Hare) and, in the 1930s, was President of the All-Africa Convention established to coordinate opposition to the raft of segregationist legislation (including the abolition of voting rights for Black South Africans in the Cape Province). Although viewed by many as a moderate figure who had withdrawn from political activities in the late 1940s, Jabavu remained influential in Black political circles in South Africa. In his trip to India in 1949, he accompanied his close friend, the son of Mohandas Gandhi, Manilal, who had remained in South Africa when his father returned to India to devote himself to the independence movement. But Jabavu's interest in the principles of mission education and Social Gospel also drew him to the holist pacifist agenda espoused by the organizers of the Sevagram meeting.[32] His journey to India in 1949 was an embodiment of the integration of post-war pacifist networks into a transnational space of resistance that drew together advocates of peace, opponents of war and anti-colonial nationalists. His account of the trip, published in isiXhosa in 1951 as *E-Indiya nase East Africa*, may not have reached a widespread audience, and the Sevagram meeting has not figured in the accounts of a transnational anti-colonial conferencing centred on the more well-known Bandung and Accra meetings of the mid-to-late 1950s. And yet it testifies to the efforts to internationalize the peace movement, and the impact pacifist ideas had on the emerging generation of anti-colonial activists in both Africa and the West. Pacifist networks played a role in shaping the tactics and principles of independence movements in Africa during the 1950s and, in many senses, underpinned the relationship between African nationalists, African American civil rights campaigners and solidarity movements in Europe and the United States. And Scott, of course, made these connections tangible in his journey from New York to Sevagram in 1949.

Anti-colonialism and the state

Scott's testimony on behalf of the Herero people at the United Nations session at Lake Success prior to the World Pacifist Conference was a landmark for non-governmental organizations seeking to represent anti-colonial nationalism and indigenous rights. His testimony, as noted above, made him a kind of political celebrity in London and New York and when he returned from India, he sought to exploit this attention to garner support for African political claims more widely. By 1952, helped by several powerful mentors, including the editor of the *Observer* newspaper David Astor, Scott had helped to launch a new British organization dedicated to African politics, the Africa Bureau. During the 1950s, the Bureau became the centre of Scott's anti-colonial activities. It built its operating principles around the body of ideas articulated in the 1951 book *Attitude to Africa* discussed at length in this chapter, but the manifesto

---

[32] Tina Steiner, 'Ports as Portals: D. D. T. Jabavu's Voyage to the World Pacifist Meeting in India', *English Studies in Africa* 62, no. 1 (2 January 2019): 8–20.

and aims of the Bureau were shaped by the political context revealed in international debates around the status of South-West Africa that brought Scott into the spotlight in late 1949.

South-West Africa had been established as a German 'protectorate' in 1884, but it was in the 1890s that it became the country's primary site of settler colonialism.[33] In the two decades following the formation of the protectorate, systems of racial segregation and the appropriation of land for white settlement were established that paralleled similar processes across southern African territories under British and Portuguese control. German colonialists sought to exploit tensions between Herero and Nama indigenous groups, but as tensions increased between colonial settlers and the African population, officials turned increasingly to violent means. In early 1904, Herero leader Samuel Maherero launched an armed uprising, which met initial success. In June, a new military commander, Lothar van Trotha, who had combat experience in both Africa and the Boxer Rebellion in China, defeated Herero military forces and pushed the civilian population deep into the Kalahari desert, many of whom fled en masse into the neighbouring British-controlled territory of Bechuanaland. At the end of the year, the German authorities began to establish concentration camps (taking inspiration from tactics employed by British forces during the South African War that had ended just two years earlier). One recent account of brutal suppression of the uprising and resistance has portrayed German policies as a complex and deadly combination of racism and fear, which fed the genocidal destruction of the Herero people.[34] Although contemporary reports of the German 'campaign of vengeance' were published in the British and US press, Scott's testimony in 1949, which included a lengthy description of the Herero genocide, was perhaps one of the first times the events were introduced to a wider international public.[35]

But South-West Africa became a subject of international concern in the aftermath of the First World War. The South African military defeated German forces and seized control of the country in 1915 and following the Versailles Peace Conference, the South African government was granted power over the former German colony under a League of Nations mandate. The terms of the Mandate empowered the South African government in Pretoria to administer South-West Africa 'as integral portions of its territory'.[36] In essence, South-West Africa became a province of South Africa. From the mid-1920s, relations between the South African government and the Permanent Mandates Commission cooled over the meaning of sovereignty in South-West Africa. Did the Covenant of the League merely denote the right to administer the territory or

---

[33] Sebastian Conrad and Sorcha O'Hagan, *German Colonialism: A Short History* (Cambridge: Cambridge University Press, 2012); Bradley Naranch and Geoff Eley, *German Colonialism in a Global Age*. Politics, History, and Culture (Durham, NC: Duke University Press, 2014).

[34] Matthias Häussler, *The Herero Genocide: War, Emotion, and Extreme Violence in Colonial Namibia* (New York: Berghahn Books, 2021). For post-colonial debates on the Herero genocide in Germany, see Reinhart Kossler, *Namibia and Germany: Negotiating the Past* (Windhoek: UNAM Press, 2015).

[35] *Guardian*, 30 August 1950, 10; *New York Times*, 27 August 1950; Scott's testimony was also incorporated into Freda Troup, *In Face of Fear. Michael Scott's Challenge to South Africa* (London: Faber & Faber, 1950).

[36] Article 22, The Covenant of the League of Nations, *The Avalon Project: Documents in Law, History and Diplomacy*, Yale Law School, https://avalon.law.yale.edu/20th_century/leagcov.asp#art22, Accessed 28 October 2022.

sovereignty in the customary sense of the term? While South Africa in 1930 acceded to the former definition, its leaders remained convinced that South-West Africa could be incorporated into the Union if its settler population expressed a wish to do so. As Pedersen notes, this was despite the fact that William Rappard, Director of the Mandates Division, had explicitly stated that any changes to mandates would be determined by the will of their indigenous population.[37] In her account, Pedersen acknowledges that the Mandates system had not transformed the governing ideologies of colonial powers but had brought into being a system of diplomatic surveillance that required powers to address questions of international oversight, albeit in limited ways. Although South Africa resisted, challenges from the League of Nations Mandates Commission meant that its officials were 'obliged to *say* they were governing . . . differently'.[38]

As in the interwar period, South African officials in the 1940s considered the desire of the white population of the territory sufficient to justify a transfer of sovereignty to South Africa. After 1948, not only were these arguments being made by more determined and confident settler nationalists than those who had debated with the League in the 1920s, but they were also engaged with a new organization whose competence in matters relating to the League's mandates could be plausibly contested – in legal, if not moral terms. The South African government had consistently refused to provide the UN with details of conditions in the territory, a former German colony, which had been administered by Pretoria under a League of Nations mandate since 1919. In 1946, the then prime minister of South Africa, Jan Smuts, had announced the country's intention to 'incorporate' South-West Africa as a Province of the Union of South Africa, effectively rejecting United Nations competency with regard to the League of Nations Trusteeship system.[39] By the time of Scott's appearance before the Trusteeship Committee, then, the status of the territory was a matter of intense debate, which reflected the incomplete and emergent nature of the scope and remit of the United Nations itself. In this sense, the issue represented a test case in attempts to forge a new system of international order, building on – but not simply an extension of – the systems of discipline and oversight that Pedersen has referred to in her work on the League of Nations. Scott's 1949 testimony did not internationalize the issue of South-West Africa specifically or colonialism more generally. The cracks in the system had been created in the interwar period, with the principle that colonial administration ought to be subject to International scrutiny, albeit in a small number of exemplary cases. What made Scott's efforts new, however, was that he spoke with the authority of a colonized people, not merely *for* the Herero but at their bequest.

More accurately, perhaps, Scott's quest was undertaken at the prompting of Tshekedi Khama, leader of the Ngwato people of the Bechuanaland Protectorate (now Botswana).[40] A large group of Herero, led by Frederick Maherero, who had fled the

---

[37] Susan Pedersen, *The Guardians: The League of Nations and the Crisis of Empire* (Oxford: Oxford University Press, 2015), 220.
[38] Ibid., 4.
[39] Michael Crowder, 'Tshekedi Khama, Smuts, and South West Africa', *The Journal of Modern African Studies* 25, no. 1 (1 March 1987): 25–42.
[40] Rob Skinner, *The Foundations of Anti-Apartheid: Liberal Humanitarianism and Transnational Activism in Britain and the United States, c. 1919–64* (Basingstoke: Palgrave Macmillan, 2010).

brutality of German colonial forces after 1904, had settled in the Ngwato territory. The Herero issue was thus of direct concern but also spoke to wider anxieties about the South African agenda to incorporate Bechuanaland into the Union. From his appointment as Regent in 1926, Tshekedi Khama had a combative relationship with colonial authorities, particularly in negotiations over mining concessions. His abrasive political style and tactical use of the courts strained relations with British authorities and tested the principle of indirect rule to its limits.[41] And it was Khama, with the support of Frederick Maherero and African political activists in South Africa, who initiated attempts to take the Herero case to the United Nations in 1946, in response to South African Prime Minister Jan Smuts' formal announcement of his intent to incorporate South-West Africa into the Union.[42] That same year, Scott met Khama and Mahereru for the first time, and at their behest travelled to South-West Africa to investigate claims that the referendum that had been presented to the UN as evidence of indigenous support for incorporation was an inaccurate representation of public opinion.[43] After hearing the reports that Scott had collected, Mahereru and his supporters drafted a petition that would be taken to the United Nations, calling for the reunification of the Herero people and the return of their territory, and for the country to be placed administered under a mandate under the auspices of the UN Trusteeship Council. Scott agreed to deliver the petition to the UN on the behalf of Herero leaders and travelled to New York and witnessed the debate on South-West Africa in November 1947. Alone in New York in the midst of a snowstorm, Scott set down his reflections on his encounter with the frenzy of international diplomacy:

> The organised power of the modern State, with its limitless capacity to pervert the truth and men's minds by every scientific means of communication, is driving men towards the madness of self-destruction. This hideous strength can only be met by the utmost detachment from the things of this world and the most selfless submissions to a power which is greater than the physical force that is available to the modern rulers of the darkness of the world.

As he contemplated the failure of his attempts to deliver the Herero petition, thwarted by the complex and soulless machinery of the United Nations, Scott railed against 'the impotence of this vast city'. Turning to Gandhi and Christ as guides to perseverance in the face of daunting obstacles, Scott began to configure the iniquities of colonialism as part of a universal struggle against modernity. Moreover, sophisticated diplomatic questions were, in his view, merely symptoms of a deeper moral struggle. His efforts in Britain in the first half of 1949 were thus aimed at making 'the British public, who were responsible for the welfare and destiny of so many millions of dark-skinned people, aware of the malady and their obligation to contribute to its cure'.[44]

---

[41] Michael Crowder, 'Tshekedi Khama and Opposition to the British Administration of the Bechuanaland Protectorate, 1926–1936', *The Journal of African History* 26, no. 2–3 (March 1985): 193–214.
[42] Crowder, 'Tshekedi Khama, Smuts, and South West Africa', 25–42.
[43] Troup, *In Face of Fear*, 142–7.
[44] Ibid., 197.

Supported by a coalition of allies in New York including the National Association for the Advancement of Colored People (NAACP) and the International League for the Rights of Man, Scott returned to Lake Success for the September 1949 UN session. In mid-November, the General Assembly adopted a resolution directing the Trusteeship Council to move quickly to examine petitions from Trust Territories. And Scott had travelled to New York carrying just such a petition, signed by a group of Herero leaders, setting out a long history of grievances, including mass incarceration and killing, alienation from land and segregationist policies. The South African delegation sought to bar Scott from speaking, but he was eventually granted the time to present the Herero case in late November. Scott's testimony was the first time a private individual had been allowed the right to address a UN meeting; it set significant precedents around the ability of NGOs to directly lobby United Nations bodies and created a space for colonial subjects to use the UN as a space to articulate claims around sovereign rights and independence.[45] And for Scott, it was an opportunity to set out the broader moral framework in which he set their claims:

> For the Africans the question of the destiny of South West Africa goes deep down to the fundamental principle of right and justice which involves the integrity of our relationship with the African people as this has developed over a kong period of colonial history. The great task confronting human civilisation in Africa will require for their fulfilment good faith between the white and coloured races and willing partnership in these tasks. [46]

The 'sacred trust of civilisation' should, Scott emphasized, be understood as a matter of 'good faith' that signalled obligations on the part of those tasked with upholding that trust. This moral argument drew on language that overlapped with the paternalist notions of trusteeship and development that continued to pervade the thinking of European officials. What made Scott's argument distinctive was its focus on the political claims of African leaders, although those with whom he was most closely associated – including Khama and Mahereru – held positions of political authority derived from recognition of their power as 'chiefs' by colonial authorities. This, in turn, aligned with the models of political reform espoused by moderate advocates of colonial reform such as Rita Hinden of the Fabian Colonial Bureau, Hinden held that a 'hybrid' system that incorporated both Western and African forms of political institution, might offer a solution to the tensions between 'modern' Western and 'tribal' African social and political forms.[47]

Scott would pick up these themes in publications and public meetings following his return to the UK after the Sevagram meeting, exploiting the public status he had

---

[45] Carol Anderson, 'International Conscience, the Cold War, and Apartheid: The NAACP's Alliance with the Reverend Michael Scott for South West Africa's Liberation, 1946–1951', *Journal of World History* 19, no. 3 (2008): 297–325.

[46] Troup, *In Face of Fear*, 202; See also 'Black Africa Speaks with a White Voice', *News Chronicle*, 29 November 1949.

[47] Hinden, 'African Tribes and Western Democracy', *Empire 1947*; See also Hunter, *Political Thought and the Public Sphere in Tanzania*, 75.

gained following his dramatic address to the United Nations. In March, Canon John Collins of St Paul's Cathedral arranged a meeting under the auspices of Christian Action on 'Christ and the Colour Problem', addressed by Scott alongside Margery Perham, the Oxford-based historian and expert in colonial administration, and publisher Victor Gollancz.[48] Two months later, he addressed an audience of students at Cambridge University and declared that the 'old tribal gods have fallen down and we are looking towards a new age' in Africa. If Christianity were to play a role in this future, he continued, 'it must find a means, of bringing a moral force to bear on these crises in the world'.[49] In June, he spoke at another London conference, sponsored by the National Peace Council, on the 'Human Crisis in Africa'.[50] The sense of living in a moment of transformative crisis, and the need to reconcile modernity and tradition via a revitalized moral force, encapsulated at these meetings, were threads that would bind together Scott's activities through to the early 1960s.

During 1950 and 1951, Scott's network of support in the UK began to transform. Following his speech to the UN Trusteeship Council in 1949 and his subsequent trip to India, Scott's base of operations centred on the Friends International House in Tavistock Square, London, and a 'Michael Scott Committee' was formed, including two Quakers – John Fletcher and Esther Muirhead – and a South African clergyman, George Norton. These built on the informal Quaker networks that sustained him during the late 1940s and further expanded when another South African, Mary Benson, joined the group as secretary. After serving in the military in North Africa and briefly working for the United Nations Relief and Rehabilitation Administration, Benson had been an assistant for the film producer David Lean in London when she read the *Observer* profile of Scott shortly before his breakthrough appearance before the Third Committee. She wrote to Scott offering her help as an administrative assistant. Despite initial suspicion, Benson quickly became a vital part of the support network around the itinerant activist, forming a 'perfect team' with Scott, who came to depend on Benson both professionally and personally.[51]

These contacts were, however, part of a wider constellation of support across groups in London that included the India League and the National Council for Civil Liberties. In the United States, Scott's New York support network included members of the Fellowship of Reconciliation and the International League for the Rights of Man. In mid-1950, Scott gave a sermon at St Paul's Cathedral and spoke at a conference on the Human Crisis in Africa, while his supporters attempted to establish an African Relations Council. But it was the Africa Bureau, whose formation will be discussed in the following chapter, that would provide Scott with an organizational base for his anti-colonial activities. Many of the principles and ideological foundations of this new organization were, however, sketched out in advance of its launch in the slim Penguin 'Special', *Attitude to Africa*, published in 1951.[52]

[48] *Times*, 31 March 1950.
[49] *Cambridge Daily News*, 17 May 1950.
[50] *The Observer*, 21 May 1950.
[51] Mary Benson, *A Far Cry: The Making of a South African* (Randburg: Ravan, 1996), 57–63.
[52] W. Arthur Lewis, Michael Scott, Martin Wight, and Colin Legum, *Attitude to Africa* (Harmondsworth, Middlesex: Penguin Books, 1951).

The book's publication coincided with the Penguin founder Allen Lane's first visit to Africa, which he considered to be an emerging market for paperback non-fiction. British government officials also took an interest in Allen's visit, resulting in a meeting with the publisher at the Colonial Office and the formation of the Penguin West African Library.[53] For British officials, the move was an opportunity to expand Cold War efforts at information management and cultural development; African readers would, it was hoped, take up special Penguin editions of worthy classics, in place of seductive works of Communist propaganda. But *Attitude to Africa* was no exercise in colonial propaganda; while it aligned with the broad aims of official development policy in many respects, the authors (led by Scott) offered a view of white minority governments in southern Africa that one reviewer described, regretfully, as 'one of despair and reproach'.[54] Although its authors promoted an engagement with African nationalism and feared the threat of Communist influence, *Attitude to Africa* did not entirely fit the official line on post-war development in Africa described by Buettner as an instrumental programme geared towards the 'cultivation of amenable working relationships with "moderate" (pro-Western) Africans'.[55]

The first half of the book, which comprised two chapters dealing with an overview of the contemporary circumstances in Africa and an outline of a policy for Britain, were authored by the *Observer* journalist Colin Legum and the academic and pioneer of the discipline of International Relations, Martin Wight. The third chapter, by the development economist W. Arthur Lewis, outlined a policy for agricultural development, while the final chapter, by Scott, offered an account of the particular issues concerning southern Africa. With the British electorate as their primary audience, the authors focused their attention on the policies they regarded as most relevant to questions of colonial governance. Its broad framework hinged on the relationship between, on the one hand, paternalist notions of responsibility and trusteeship, and on the other, universal conceptions of humanity. The task for Britain was, therefore, to establish policies that furthered 'the interests of dependent peoples', whose central desire was 'to be treated as fellow human beings'.[56] The reference to dependence is perhaps instructive and reflected a politics of anti-colonialism that sat at a point of articulation between reformist humanitarianism and a more radical vision of democratic anti-colonialism. *Attitude to Africa* built on a faith in the premise of trusteeship, just as that premise began to crumble under the normative pressure of national sovereignty and self-determination. Its prospectus for change in systems of colonial governance stood at the intersection between a system of world empires and one of nation states, between the constrained internationalism of the interwar period and the bipolar world of the Cold War.

Legum, a South African journalist, had relocated to Britain in 1949 and joined the staff of the *Observer* in 1951. His views on African political affairs closely matched those of Astor and were founded on the belief that colonial powers would be obliged to

---

[53] Jeremy Lewis, *Penguin Special: The Life and Times of Allen Lane* (London: Viking, 2005), 288.
[54] C. M. Harris, 'Racial Problems', *Times Literary Supplement,* 30 November 1951.
[55] Elizabeth Buettner, *Europe after Empire: Decolonization, Society, and Culture* (Cambridge: Cambridge University Press, 2016), 43.
[56] Lewis, et al., *Attitude to Africa*, 8.

address the claims and agendas of African nationalists. As the newspaper's diplomatic and Commonwealth correspondent, he would publicly champion sanctions against South Africa, both in the *Observer* and in publications such as *South Africa: Crisis for the West* (1964).[57] Martin Wight had also worked for the *Observer* as a special correspondent covering the United Nations in the late 1940s.[58] But he was better known as an academic and researcher, working at Chatham House in the late 1930s under the Directorship of Arnold Toynbee. During the 1940s, he registered as a conscientious objector and worked under Margery Perham on a project examining colonial constitutions.[59] His Christian faith was central to his work, particularly during the 1940s when he seems to have struggled to come to grips with the 'theology of crisis', both through engagement with contemporary thinkers including Bonhoeffer and Maritain and via direct engagement with scripture, eastern religion and mysticism.[60] Together, Legum and Wight brought to the book visions of the world that resonated with two central elements of Scott's thinking: that African nationalism needed to be central to the process of change and that the political crises of the 1950s were part of a universal spiritual struggle. Like Scott, they believed this struggle was manifest in the overlapping racial and ideological divisions that shaped their contemporary world. African issues would play out, they argued, within a global 'racial struggle' between Western powers, anti-colonial nationalism and Communism.[61]

For Legum and Wight, the fundamental dynamic of the crisis in Africa was racial division. Britain should not, they urged, follow the path taken by South Africa, to ignore African calls for political rights in favour of the protection of settler interests, nor should it fall into easy but fallacious claims that African nationalism was synonymous with Communism. In contrast, they suggested that African rural societies were politically conservative and less likely to nurture a radical peasant politics. But international Communism would, they felt, find not easier to present a model of autonomy – it was 'easy for the Communists to promise independence and freedom to colonial peoples' as they were not obliged to deliver on such promises. They noted, however, that appeals to the 'superiority of Western democracy over totalitarian government' were unlikely to succeed and hinted that Africans would not necessarily distinguish their experiences of 'Western democracy' from totalitarianism – or, at least, they would not be 'impressed by warnings that their democratic rights are at stake'.[62] Perhaps unsurprisingly, their analysis shared a number of features of Wight's former mentor Margery Perham's view of the prospects for democracy in Africa. Writing in the aftermath of the first elections under new constitutional arrangements in the Gold Coast in July 1951, which had resulted in a victory for Kwame Nkrumah's Convention Peoples Party, Perham suggested that it might appear that the second half of the twentieth century would be an 'age of liberation' in Africa.[63] But, unlike in Asia, where relationships with the

---

[57] Colin Legum and Margaret Legum, *South Africa: Crisis for the West* (London: Pall Mall Press, 1964).
[58] I. Hall, *The International Thought of Martin Wight* (New York: Palgrave Macmillan US, 2006), 5–8.
[59] Martin Wight, *British Colonial Constitutions, 1947* (Oxford: Clarendon Press, 1952).
[60] Hall, *The International Thought of Martin Wight*.
[61] Lewis, et al., *Attitude to Africa*, 15.
[62] Ibid., 29.
[63] Margery Perham, 'The British Problem in Africa', *Foreign Affairs* 29, no. 4 (1951): 637.

Western world were refracted through 'historic cultures', Africans had encountered colonialism within social frameworks shaped by 'the multi-cellular tissue of tribalism' and 'primitive poverty'. As such, she argued, Western policies in Africa needed to be 'assimilative in the broadest sense'.[64] Similarly, Legum and Wight concluded that British policy needed to show 'how democracy works'; and yet Scott argued that the survival of a Western form of democracy required 'its ever-widening application to peoples of other lands'. Although Perham and the authors of *Attitude to Africa* seemingly shared a view that democracy was a Western cultural artefact to be donated to 'non-European' peoples, Scott was typically uncertain about its prospects. He argued that crises in Asia and Africa represented a failure of democracy, which ought to address 'the economic needs and growing political aspirations of those peoples and the lands which history has placed under our rule'.[65]

Like Perham's analysis of the prospects for political transformation in Africa, Legum and Wight focused much of their attention on the development of a colonial policy that could address the special characteristics of 'plural societies' comprising largely separate and distinct social units within single territories. Drawing on the work of former colonial civil servant John Sydenham Furnivall, they suggested that east, central and southern Africa represented the plural society in its 'classic form', structured by divisions between indigenous, South Asian and European communities.[66] Furnivall's ideas would later be elaborated by South African sociologists seeking to elaborate the structural conditions for political change within a society determined by 'ethnic pluralism', but for the authors of *Attitude to Africa* they underlined the difficulties posed to policymakers by powerful communities of European settlers, especially in southern Africa.[67] The Gold Coast elections, which had been denounced by the South African Prime Minister D. F. Malan as 'the good principle of democracy wrongly applied', seemed to presage even greater difficulties for colonial policymakers.[68] As Perham noted, Malan and other leaders of white minorities seemed 'obliged to defend their domination by principles of racial superiority which are an absolute denial of those upon which Britain is acting in her tropical colonies'.[69] Africa as a whole, the authors of *Attitude to Africa* argued, had 'become a cockpit of inter-racial conflict', which meant that efforts to confront economic social and political problems had to grapple with the particular qualities of local tensions and conflicts.[70] But, in general, African and European nationalisms were 'locked together in a dialectic of interdependent fears and antagonisms'.[71]

---

[64] Ibid., 638.
[65] Lewis, et al., *Attitude to Africa*, 29, 105, 106.
[66] J. S. Furnivall, *Netherlands India: A Study of Plural Economy* (Cambridge: Cambridge University Press, 1939), see 446; see also Lewis, et al., *Attitude to Africa*, 45–7.
[67] On Furnivall in South African sociology see Saul Dubow, 'Ethnic Euphemisms and Racial Echoes', *Journal of Southern African Studies* 20, no. 3 (1 September 1994): 360; see also John Rex, 'The Plural Society in Sociological Theory', *The British Journal of Sociology* 10, no. 2 (1959): 115; Leo Kuper, *Race, Class and Power: Ideology and Revolutionary Change in Plural Societies* (London: Duckworth, 1974), 252.
[68] 'Commonwealth in Peril', *Guardian*, 24 February 1951.
[69] Perham, 'The British Problem in Africa', 642.
[70] Lewis, et al., *Attitude to Africa*, 22.
[71] Ibid., 43.

Legum and Wight proposed a progressive policy in Africa that would support economic and social development as well as extending the appeal of Western forms of democracy. Again, such a policy, they believed, could only succeed when working in alliance with African nationalist movements. Nationalism, the authors contended, had emerged as a consequence of the 'social disintegration which Western ascendancy has started in Africa'.[72] In their assessment, the movement was not led by 'traditional' leaders nor Marxists but the European trained middle classes; nationalist politics in Africa was in effect the same 'struggle for jobs in the bureaucracy' that contemporary historians viewed as formative of nineteenth-century European nationalism.[73] Furthermore, they regarded support for African nationalist ambitions, not as a matter of political expediency but as a confirmation that social and political progress needed to be driven from within, rather than imposed by outsiders. In this, their approach was aligned with the official thinking on nationalism that has been chronicled by Frank Heinlein. Government ministers aligned with Fabian thinking on colonial policy, such as Creech Jones, and Colonial Office officials including Andrew Cohen regarded nationalism as a potentially positive influence that required a policy oriented towards cooperation rather than opposition.[74] Nationalists, Legum and Wight argued, should be viewed as allies rather than rivals for power. But, for many parts of Africa, support for African nationalism had to be balanced against the competition for power that was emerging between African and settler nationalisms, with the latter's ambivalence towards democracy a function of a fear of being 'overpowered by the Africans'.[75] Like Perham, their overall assessment was presented as a kind of realist incrementalism. They recognized that the rights of settler communities (both European and Asian) ought to be respected, but not to the extent that they alienated the 'non-white' majority in both Africa and the 'new multi-racial Commonwealth'.[76] The view set out in *Attitude to Africa* was, therefore, a reflection of the established views of the British political class rather than a radical manifesto for change.

At the start of the 1950s, progressive thinkers on colonial policy shared a common ground shaped by a discourse of civilization. This framework allowed white advocates of social and political change to analyse African developments as part of a universal pattern of historical movement. The 'revolt of the non-Western peoples against Western ascendency', Legum and Wight declared, was 'a world-wide movement, in which all non-white peoples share'. Pluralism, moreover, was not merely a model for understanding the structures of colonial societies, but an acknowledgement of a new kind of post-war reality in which individuals in a Western country such as Britain had 'become a citizen of a world-wide plural society'.[77] Although the concept of 'western civilisation' played a central role in their thinking, the idea represented a post-war re-evaluation of the concept of civilization and reflected a broader process

[72] Ibid., 32.
[73] The authors quote AJP Taylor *Hapsburg Monarchy*, 30 in Lewis, et al., *Attitude to Africa*, 34.
[74] Frank Heinlein, *British Government Policy and Decolonisation, 1945–63: The Empire Commonwealth* (London: Routledge, 2013), 24.
[75] Lewis, et al., *Attitude to Africa*, 42; see also Colin Legum, 'Race War in Africa', *The Observer*, 28 January 1951.
[76] Lewis, et al., *Attitude to Africa*, 45.
[77] Ibid., 14, 17.

of intellectual renewal that has been perceived across Europe after the mid-1940s.[78] There was a danger that this mode of thinking might simply reproduce eurocentric paternalism, and the book made numerous comparisons between Western culture and its impact on African social formations; while colonial cultures had reshaped African political consciousness, the process had resulted in 'the subversion of existing tribal society'.[79] However, the authors of *Attitude to Africa* offered a far from confident view of Western civilization in Africa:

> the argument of the 'backwardness' and historical incapacity of Africans is one that is indecent for Europeans to use, unless it has first provoked them into reflexion on how Europe in the past four centuries has insulted and exploited that backwardness and has contributed to the continuance of the historical incapacity ... African nationalism, it is true, has not yet produced a Gandhi or a Nehru; but in Africa today, the ill as well as the good, is largely what Europe has helped to make it.[80]

'Civilization' had a dual meaning. In a descriptive sense, it was a marker of the complex of cultural characteristics that marked the different groups that constituted plural societies; but it also appeared as a measure of capacity, in the context of differential 'standards of civilisation'. For Perham, Africa had been 'locked away from the influences of civilisation', until the advent of European colonialism which brought both 'subjection and civilisation', and for Legum and Wight, Africa was a 'continent without indigenous civilisations'.[81]

But, for Scott, civilization had a universal meaning. 'Civilisation', he argued in 1952 in a pamphlet published by the pacifist Fellowship of Reconciliation, 'is not in fact the invention of any one race'. Moreover, it was not something that could be created, or protected, by the forms of segregated societies proposed by advocates of apartheid in southern Africa. Only 'a multi-racial civilisation can survive' in Africa, he declared. There could not be 'equal rights for all civilised men' – as Cecil Rhodes had put it – without 'equal opportunity for all human beings to become civilized'.[82] That, Scott suggested, was the ultimate meaning of the Universal Declaration of Human Rights. And yet, aside from a brief reference to 'fundamental human rights' in Scott's chapter of *Attitude to Africa*, there is little discussion of normative and universal entitlements. This suggests that Moyn was correct in his contention that 'human rights' in the post-war period were far from central in the claims of independence movements more concerned with civil and political rights and popular sovereignty.[83] In the early 1950s, those willing to consider the dissolution of colonial power focused debate on the need to reconcile African and white settler nationalism and development. But Scott, whose

---

[78] Paul Betts, *Ruin and Renewal: Civilizing Europe After World War II* (New York: Basic Books, 2020).
[79] Lewis, et al., *Attitude to Africa*, 20.
[80] Ibid., 37.
[81] Ibid., 35, see also Perham, 'The British Problem in Africa', 650.
[82] Michael Scott, *Civilization in Africa* (London: Fellowship of Reconciliation, 1952).
[83] Samuel Moyn, *The Last Utopia: Human Rights in History* (London: Belknap Press of Harvard University Press, 2010; see also Roland Burke, *Decolonization and the Evolution of International Human Rights* (Philadelphia: University of Pennsylvania Press, 2010).

contribution to political debates was shaped by 'independence of mind and capacity for personal witness', hinted at something different.[84]

In late 1949, Scott entered the debates around trusteeship at the United Nations as a new kind of political actor. Without any official connection to any state, his presentation set the precedent that non-governmental voices might be heard and accorded some degree of authority in international organizations. To a significant extent, that authority derived from the principle – established in those earlier debates at the League of Nations – that indigenous peoples, as the subjects of the sacred trust of civilization, would have the final say in matters of sovereignty. But this was not a debate framed solely in terms of formal, legal competence and legitimacy. Scott's reflections on his experiences at the United Nations in the late 1940s reveal a different form of authority at work – a kind of charismatic authority that combined claims to African tradition with a spiritual vocation for action. In Scott's judgement, secular political debate was subordinate to a moral authority that combined the transcendent power of the Christian God with Gandhian practices of non-violence. At times, this presented itself as a desperate critique of the modern state and modern society. But this did not mean that Scott was ambivalent towards ideas of progress and development.

In the context of the international politics of decolonization, Scott's lobbying efforts at the United Nations represented a transformation of sorts in the character of Western anti-colonial activism. In the 1920s and 1930s, international anti-colonialism had largely centred on radical groups aligned along ideological lines, such as the League Against Imperialism, or more liberal and humanitarian efforts to ameliorate the impacts of colonialism and modernity on colonized peoples. The latter, which overlapped with the internationalization of missionary religion, emphasized social reform over political and economic transformation, and spoke of needs rather than rights. In his words and actions, Scott assumed the equal legitimacy of African political and social claims. But his arguments against settler colonialism and segregation also rested on the foundational principles of the League of Nations Mandates system. This had resulted, as Pedersen has suggested, in the construction of an international forum for debate that 'created new risks for imperial powers', but it stopped short of questioning the ideological foundations of empire and colonialism.[85]

When this system was reconstructed by the United Nations after 1945, campaigners such as Scott drew on the earlier language of benevolent imperial trusteeship, while anti-colonial groups such as the Fabian Colonial Bureau and the Africa Bureau looked to rebuild the structures that had been established in the interwar period. They saw their own activities operating in an international sphere that was in essence a space for humanitarians and nationalists to stake their claims. But, despite the rhetorical continuities, post-war thinking on colonial policy in Britain wars not seeking to rebuild the order of nation states with 'varying capacity' that emerged in the mandates system. Even for more cautious moderates, there was 'no alternative' to a policy centred on gradual decolonization.[86] For Scott, though, notions of 'sacred trust', despite their

---

[84] Yates and Chester, *The Troublemaker*, 130.
[85] Pedersen, *The Guardians*, 13.
[86] Perham, 'The British Problem in Africa', 650.

resonance with older narratives of colonial paternalism, implied a telos of eventual independence and decolonization. Such views overlapped, but did not perfectly align, with what Buettner identifies as the 'rose-tinted' view of the Labour Commonwealth Secretary, Patrick Gordon Walker, who insisted (in retrospect) that post-war ideals of development and Commonwealth reflected the exceptionalism view that 'British imperial rule increasingly assumed such a nature that it could fulfil itself only by annulling itself'.[87] For Scott in 1951, trusteeship and empire did have an end point, which could only be brought about by an alliance of African and European action centred on a programme of social and economic development.

Partnerships for development

Alongside the outline of the struggle between nationalism, Communism and Western democracy presented by Legum and Wight, the chapters of *Attitude to Africa* contributed by Scott and William Arthur Lewis emphasized another issue: social and economic development. This had become a central focus of British colonial policies of the British government during the 1940s, embodied in the 1940 and 1945 Colonial Welfare and Development Acts. The concept and practice of development was a fundamental dynamic of the process of post-war decolonization. Assessments of the intellectual history of development have configured the idea in contrasting ways. Earlier accounts presented it as a discourse of power in the service of a project of modernization and a foundational practice of the modern state.[88] Another view identified the historical roots of development in nineteenth-century efforts to reconfigure the role of the state in order to address the challenges of industrialization.[89] Others, notably Frederick Cooper, have viewed the interwar period and the exigencies of the Depression as the main drivers of the emergence of colonial development policies. Cooper has highlighted a divergence between intentions and impacts in development policy, and the degree to which development, whatever the intentions of colonial officials, had the effect of giving colonized peoples and anti-colonial movements a stake in the game of social and economic progress. Development, as Cooper suggests, became a 'claim-making construct for post-war social and political movements' in Africa and Asia.[90]

By the 1940s, then, the idea development was becoming aligned with a notion of 'modernization' which, though modelled on and assuming Western standards and practices, provided a framework for nationalist leaders to contend that Africans ought

---

[87] Patrick Gordon Walker, *The Commonwealth* (London: Secker and Warburg, 1962), 15; quoted in Buettner, *Europe after Empire*, 59.
[88] Arturo Escobar, *Encountering Development: The Making and Unmaking of the Third World* (Princeton, NJ: Princeton University Press, 1995). James C. Scott, *Seeing Like a State: How Certain Schemes to Improve the Human Condition Have Failed* (New Haven, CT: Yale University Press, 1998).
[89] Michael Cowen and Robert W. Shenton, 'The Invention of Development', in *Power of Development*, edited by Jonathan Crush (London: Routledge, 1995), 27–43; Michael Cowen and Robert W. Shenton, *Doctrines of Development* (London: Routledge, 1996).
[90] Frederick Cooper, 'Writing the History of Development', *Journal of Modern European History* 8, no. 1 (2010): 11.

to enjoy the entitlements of citizenship. The same language of modernization could equally be employed to justify the ruthless and violent suppression of anti-colonial resistance, demonstrated perhaps most starkly in the mid-to-late 1950s in Algeria and Kenya.[91] Even in these more perverse latter examples, development was characteristic of what Cooper described as the 'double transformation' that seemed underway in the mid-twentieth century: an 'expansion of the entitlements of citizenship' embodied in the construction of the European 'welfare state', together with the confidence that colonized peoples might develop the 'qualities' of citizenship.[92] The view of development presented in *Attitude to Africa* largely aligns with this broader historical analysis. As Legum and Wight suggested, development was needed to demonstrate the benefits of Western democracy in the face of the challenge of Communism, but their outline of the prospects for colonial policy offered few little detailed proposals on social and economic development.

This was instead provided by the pioneering development economist W. Arthur Lewis. Born in St Lucia in 1915, Lewis had travelled to Britain in the mid-1930s to study at the London School of Economics. Despite his academic success, as an undergraduate, Lewis had been rejected by the range of institutions, from the Colonial Office to Fleet Street, that might have been expected to welcome the talents of a prize-winning graduate with First Class Honours. Instead, Lewis had been persuaded to enrol as a doctoral student at the LSE and, in 1938, became its first Black member of staff. He remained on the teaching staff after the outbreak of war and by the mid-1940s had developed pioneering courses in colonial economics.[93] A decade later, Lewis had left London for Manchester, where he had become the first Black Professor at a British university. And, three years after the publication of *Attitude to Africa*, Lewis would go on to make his primary (and ultimately Nobel Prize-winning) contribution to the field of development economics, in an essay on 'Economic Development with Unlimited Supplies of Labour'.[94] The article set out a model of a 'dual economy' in less-developed societies, in which growth and economic development was driven by the movement of workers from a subsistence economy into wage-labour in a second capitalist economy. But there are few hints of this model in Arthur's contribution to *Attitude to Africa* which, unlike the other chapters, had been previously published, in the *Three Banks Review* in 1949.[95] The focus of Lewis' chapter was not the dynamics of labour but the collaborative development of peasant agricultural production to stimulate higher

---

[91] Moritz Feichtinger and Stephan Malinowski, '"Eine Million Algerier Lernen Im 20. Jahrhundert Zu Leben" Umsiedlungslager Und Zwangsmodernisierung Im Algerienkrieg 1954–1962', *Journal of Modern European History* 8, no. 1 (2010): 107–35; See also Fabian Klose, *Human Rights in the Shadow of Colonial Violence: The Wars of Independence in Kenya and Algeria* (Philadelphia: University of Pennsylvania Press, 2013); B. Rebisz, 'Discourses of Development and Practices of Punishment: Britain's Gendered Counter-Insurgency Strategy in Colonial Kenya', in *The Oxford Handbook on Colonial Insurgencies and Counterinsurgencies*, edited by Thomas and Curless (Oxford: Oxford University Press, 2022).
[92] Cooper, 'Writing the History of Development', 14–15.
[93] Robert L. Tignor, *W. Arthur Lewis and the Birth of Development Economics* (Princeton, NJ: Princeton University Press, 2020).
[94] W. Arthur Lewis, 'Economic Development with Unlimited Supplies of Labour', *The Manchester School* 22, no. 2 (1954): 139–91. On Lewis's wider significance, see Tignor, *W. Arthur Lewis*, 265–6.
[95] W. Arthur Lewis, 'Developing Colonial Agriculture', *Three Banks Review* 2 (June 1949): 3–21.

levels of production.⁹⁶ He suggested that state interventions in the form of improved education, infrastructure and state assistance in marketing could encourage greater efficiency and output in peasant agriculture, and was sceptical of the value of market-led policies. Lewis proposed significant increases in financial investment and argued that development policy should operate within the framework of existing farming practices and that policymakers needed to move beyond 'the stages of thinking in terms of new highly mechanized plantations'.⁹⁷

While Michael Scott's chapter in *Attitude to Africa* focused on questions and concerns relating to southern Africa, he too placed a systematic policy of development at the heart of his account. These reflected a long-standing interest in social and economic policy that dated from his involvement with the Campaign for Right and Justice in Johannesburg in the early to mid-1940s.⁹⁸ As Chair of the Campaign, Scott had worked with trade union representatives and liberal activists to lobby the Smuts government on the need for government-led efforts at post-war reconstruction. This brought him into contact with academics, officials and ministers who had begun to formulate plans for regional development. These plans resonated with policy initiatives that have been assessed by Bill Freund in his work on the 'developmental state' in South Africa. For Freund, the period between the onset of war in Europe in 1939 and the election victory of the National party in South Africa in 1948 might be characterized by the formation of a 'near developmental' state. It was true that a number of development initiatives were introduced by the wartime government, including plans for industrial decentralization, the establishment of parastatal entities and discussions around health and welfare. But, for Freund, official thinking on development in South Africa in the 1940s regarded social welfare as an enterprise coupled with, and in the service of, economic growth fostered by industrialization.⁹⁹ Efforts to introduce improvements in areas such as housing, education and health provision were largely focused on Black workers in urban areas, but the fundamental principles of segregation were never really open to debate.

For Scott, though, development was a practice rooted in paternalist obligation. It was aligned with broader liberal and humanitarian concerns and in a number of ways represented a continuation of the nineteenth-century missionary ethos. In order to achieve a renaissance in Africa, Scott argued that Africa needed 'men of faith and integrity' who would dedicate themselves to this task, or efforts at planned development would be nothing more than 'hollow externalism lacking inner confidence'.¹⁰⁰ Like Lewis, Scott contended that development in Africa could only succeed with the participation and support of Africans themselves. But, he saw development not purely,

---

⁹⁶ Lewis, et al., *Attitude to Africa*, 79–81.
⁹⁷ Ibid., 104. See also Matteo Rizzo, 'What Was Left of the Groundnut Scheme? Development Disaster and Labour Market in Southern Tanganyika 1946–1952', *Journal of Agrarian Change* 6, no. 2 (2006): 205–38. Nicholas Westcott, *Imperialism and Development: The East African Groundnut Scheme and Its Legacy* (London: Boydell & Brewer, 2020).
⁹⁸ Skinner, 'Christian Reconstruction, Secular Politics', 246–66.
⁹⁹ Bill Freund, *Twentieth-Century South Africa: A Developmental History* (Cambridge: Cambridge University Press, 2019), 21–3.
¹⁰⁰ Lewis, et al., *Attitude to Africa*, 110.

or even primarily, in terms of economic models and practical realities, but as a process that necessitated policies centred on the protection of African

> human rights, their God-given talents and divinely sanctioned opportunity to exercise them, and to ensure their own gradual adaptation of their social organisation and culture to modern methods of agriculture and peaceful community life.[101]

For Scott, development could only be successful if it proceeded from a basis of willing cooperation and due deference for the 'creative purpose in man's life'. Nor did he envisage development as a task for government alone; state investment and planning, he argued, was 'not incompatible with individual enterprise and investment'.[102] The new civilization that Scott visualized would not be a consequence of any pure ideological approach but through partnership between state, private enterprise and African peoples. But the consequences of failure would be to intensify racial and cultural tensions that might easily result in confrontation, violence and destruction that would require much larger and more complex efforts of social reconstruction.

Set alongside the model of development policy sketched by Lewis, Scott's vision of development seems a little idiosyncratic. Moral and theological rather than rational, it both aligned with and cut across the ways in which development ideology was articulated by contemporaries (and has subsequently been interpreted by academic commentators). More recent historical analysis suggests that, from the 1940s, development emerged as a new language of late colonialism as well as the context in which debates around moral and political authority in colonial territories operated.[103] Smith and Jeppesen suggest that it replaced a series of interwar concepts, including indirect rule and trusteeship, but the language of development employed by Scott, in particular, was interwoven with these earlier ideas.[104] In his interpretation, trusteeship centred on its implied purpose in fostering the maturity of African civilization. In June 1950, before Scott has come into the orbit of Astor, he set out these same principles for development in a sermon preached at St Paul's Cathedral at the invitation of Canon John Collins. The task for Britons in Africa, he proclaimed, was to be found 'not in extensive exploration, but in intensive cultivation'.[105]

Scott's definition of development resonated with the dimension of British colonial development policy under the post-war Labour government that Charlotte Riley has characterized as 'ethical' imperialism. But, as Riley notes, the distinction between authentic and performative adherence to a policy centred on a partnership between

---

[101] Ibid., 109.
[102] Ibid.
[103] Cooper, 'Writing the History of Development'; M. Cowen and R. Shenton, 'The Origin and Course of Fabian Colonialism in Africa', *Journal of Historical Sociology* 4, no. 2 (1991): 143–74.
[104] Chris Jeppesen and Andrew W. M. Smith, 'Introduction: Development, Contingency and Entanglement: Decolonization in the Conditional', in *Britain, France and the Decolonization of Africa: Future Imperfect?*, edited by Chris Jeppesen and Andrew W. M. Smith (London: UCT Press, 2017), 1–14, pp. 6–7.
[105] Michael Scott, 'Africa Challenges Our Faith', sermon preached at St Paul's Cathedral, London, 13 June 1950.

British officials and Africans was not always clear. Moreover, British policies rooted in a Fabian desire to promote welfare were in tension with a different agenda that sought to serve Britain's material and trade interests.[106] For Scott, development drew together the moral and the material spheres, the sacred and the profane purposes of political activism. The moral conception of development created a space for imagining both new forms of colonialism and post-colonial futures. Moreover, development required that these ideological processes were materialized in various tangible schemes that involved techno-scientific interventions intended to foster social and economic improvement.

In his 1950 sermon, Scott offered a clue to the practical application of his vision. 'In the Kalahari Desert', he declared, 'we have an opportunity of achieving something with the enthusiasm of the African people'.[107] What he had in mind was a scheme to irrigate the Okavango delta region, harnessing the waters of the Okavango River, which rise in southern Angola and flow into a land-locked basin in the northwest of Botswana. The plan, which he had promoted throughout the late 1940s and early 1950s, had been proposed by John Wellington, head of the geography department at the University of the Witwatersrand in Johannesburg. Wellington had published various analyses of the viability of the irrigation scheme in the Okavango and claimed that there might have been 'no other place in Africa where so much agricultural development is possible at so little cost'.[108] Similar schemes were imagined in the first decade of the twentieth century, and Scott drew comparisons between the Bechuanaland plans and the Gezira scheme in the Sudan and outlines CRO pilot projects that had been announced for the Okavango region, which according to the Colonial Office official Frank Debenham, suggested that the Okavango delta had the capacity to 'become a second Sudan'.[109] In *Attitude to Africa*, Scott called for widespread consultations including a round table of various experts as well as local leaders. He condemned earlier examples of 'consultation' that had been inadequate and urged that Africans were involved in a manner that would enable an informed understanding of proposed development projects.

Attitude to Africa represented a vision for a form of collaborative development that was aligned with the Fabian principles that were such a strong influence on British government policy in the aftermath of the Second World War. Its projects and outcomes were imagined rather than evidenced, and it was to a great extent an expression of change viewed from a metropolitan perspective. But its authors, and the organization that they would go on to establish, had a genuine belief that the vision could connect European and African interests and agendas, albeit through interlocutors who were largely representative of elites, such as Tshekedi Khama. None of the proposals regarding development in *Attitude to Africa* came close to the blunt, ideological and state-centred vision of 'development' that found its most stark

---

[106] Charlotte Lydia Riley, '"The Winds of Change Are Blowing Economically": The Labour Party and British Overseas Development, 1940s–1960s', in *Britain, France and the Decolonization of Africa: Future Imperfect?*, edited by Andrew W. M. Smith and Chris Jeppesen (London: UCL Press, 2017), 43–61.

[107] Scott, 'Africa Challenges Our Faith'.

[108] John H. Wellington, 'Zambezi-Okovango Development Projects', *Geographical Review* 39, no. 4 (1949): 552–67. p. 567.

[109] Frank Debenham, *The Water Resources of the Bechuanaland Protectorate* (London: Colonial Office, 1948), 125.

embodiment in the 'separate development' of apartheid in South Africa, but nor did they represent an alternative to the expert-led, technocratic governmentaility of the 'anti-politics machine'.[110]

The crisis of modernity and world history

Underpinning Scott's prospectus for a new approach to southern Africa was a powerful sense of incipient crisis. The concept of 'Crisis in Africa' was one of the abiding narratives that shaped post-war Western views on the continent and was a formative influence upon the ideological and intellectual basis of liberal anti-colonialism in the 1950s. From the point at which he addressed the 'Human Crisis in Africa' at Kingsway Hall in London in June 1950, though to his final excursion to Africa as an activist in 1962, Scott presented Africa as almost continually on the edge of crisis. In many ways, the continent was marked by political and social uncertainty throughout this period (and indeed beyond), but a closer view of *Attitude to Africa* suggests a particular set of entwined concerns. One envisaged a crisis of colonialism and social breakdown along the lines of race. A second imagined a geopolitical crisis, in which African stability was threatened by superpower rivalries and Cold War tensions. Third, was a social and economic crisis, which would require external agencies managed by colonial powers or international organizations such as the United Nations to work in collaboration with Africans to promote economic development and social improvement. Finally, and most important in Scott's view, Africa was facing a moral crisis, which was itself but one dimension of a worldwide struggle to reintegrate the spiritual into secular world. But Scott was by no means alone in considering their task urgent – and nor was he the only one of the authors to consider Christianity to be central to political progress. Martin Wight – who regarded Christian theology as an essential dynamic in international relations – and Colin Legum expressed a sense of urgency similar to that of Scott. The task, they felt, was to encourage policymakers to shape plans for development 'that will anticipate events, rather team having to improvise one in the middle of a crisis'.[111] *Attitude to Africa* exuded a palpable sense of a critical moment in time, making multiple references to the frequency of contemporary change, in which events were moving so fast that careful planning and strategic thinking were increasingly difficult.

Scott's conceptions of crisis also owed much to the framework of world history that had emerged in the aftermath of the First World War in the works of the German historian Oswald Spengler and his British counterpart Arnold Toynbee. The influence of Toynbee was palpable, illustrated most obviously in his references to Toynbee's 1948 book, *Civilisation on Trial*, in the titles of both his 1952 FOR pamphlet and the

---

[110] James Ferguson, *The Anti-Politics Machine: 'Development,' Depoliticization, and Bureaucratic Power in Lesotho* (Cambridge: Cambridge University Press, 1990).
[111] Lewis, et al., *Attitude to Africa*, 21.

amateur documentary film he produced to illustrate his public lectures.[112] Toynbee provided activists grappling with the political future a model of the world that aimed to reconcile the material and moral dimensions of human activity and confront the tensions between the dynamic of every-greater global unity and the evidence of an increasing diversity of interests and agendas that was embodied in the clash between settler and African nationalisms. His intellectual development in the early years of the twentieth century had been shaped by concepts of evolutionary ideology and 'civilization', the latter being an idea that combined the material and moral dimensions of collective existence, but one that had become synonymous with the history of 'European civilization'. The breadth of the European empire, technical innovation and material wealth seemed persuasive evidence of the universalizing potential of 'Western civilization', although more sceptical views had begun to emerge. Perhaps most powerfully, Gandhi had portrayed 'civilisation' as a disease of that 'enslaved by temptation' even while it failed to secure material needs.[113] Gandhi had spoken to an audience of Indians in the cause of anti-colonialism, but Toynbee too came to question the supremacy of Western civilization, after witnessing atrocities against civilians by Greek and Turkish forces in the early 1920s.[114] The disintegrating effect of Western influence became a theme of Toynbee's vision of World History, which drew on a comparative account of the history of civilizations in the plural, with a view to understanding which would, in the long view, come to the forefront of a unified world. That is, of course, if humanity was able to avoid the 'supreme catastrophe' that might occur as a consequence of learning 'how to tap atomic energy before we have succeeded in abolishing the institution of war'.[115]

Post-war decolonization would usher in a 'postmodern' moment that Toynbee had to a degree predicted with his first use of the term in the 1930s as a description of the threats to Western global power.[116] Similarly, in drawing on Toynbee in his own struggle against forms of colonial power he deemed immoral, Scott revealed the uncertainty and insoluble contradictions that were embodied in his vocation. An advocate for African nationalist movements, Scott saw development as the path to the formation of a new African civilization; he nonetheless built that vision in part on assumptions inherited from the privileged and protected social world in which he lived. But, like Toynbee whose vision of universalism was fragmented in the aftermath of the First World War, Scott's experiences in the east end of London, India and South Africa in the 1930s and 1940s forced him to attempt to synthesize the facts of increasing global unity and expanding diversity of ideas. Scott took from Toynbee a world view shaped from 'complementary and contradictory' elements, that sought after a universal truth but

---

[112] Rob Gordon, 'Not Quite Cricket: "Civilization on Trial in South Africa": A Note on the First "Protest Film" Made in Southern Africa', *History in Africa* 32 (January 2005): 457–66.

[113] Mohandas Karamchand Gandhi, *Hind Swaraj: Or, Indian Home Rule* (Madras: G.A. Natesan, 1921), 21.

[114] Rebecca Gill, '"Now I Have Seen Evil, and I Cannot Be Silent about It": Arnold J. Toynbee and His Encounters with Atrocity, 1915–1923', in *Evil, Barbarism and Empire: Britain and Abroad, C. 1830–2000*, edited by T. Crook, R. Gill, and B. Taithe (London: Palgrave Macmillan UK, 2011), 172–200.

[115] Arnold Toynbee, *Civilization on Trial* (London: Geoffrey Cumberlege, Oxford University Press, 1948), 160.

[116] Michael Lang, 'Globalization and Global History in Toynbee', *Journal of World History* 22, no. 4 (2011): 781–2.

was constantly uncertain of its nature, and was forever torn between a politics centred on utopian vision and one centred on the purity of its practice.

The development schemes that Scott proposed alongside his denouncement of segregationist colonialism and its reliance on migrant labour exhibited a similarly uncertain and contradictory conception of civilization. Development – in the social and economic sense – was, he believed, part of a 'great drama' underway in Africa under the oversight of colonial powers that entailed an expansion of Western forms of democracy to the peoples of Asia and Africa. The looming crisis in Africa that Scott envisaged in the early 1950s resulted, he argued, from the frustration of the economic and political aspirations of colonized peoples. But he couched this problem in terminology that sought to reconcile its material and metaphysical dimensions: the failures of colonialism had been 'failures of faith', arising from 'over-confidence on the part of scientists and white administrators, lack of long-term values and of any vision of the ecological significance of what is being attempted'.[117] The use of the term 'ecology' is intriguing and is difficult to parse in a way unaffected by current usage in the context of environmentalist ideologies and the relationship of humanity with nature. The term was first employed by the zoologist Ernst Haeckel to express the relationship between organisms and their wider environment, but its Greek root, *oikos*, inflected the term with a sense of 'home' or, potentially, 'community'. Subsequent references offer few clues to Scott's conception of development as ecology. W. H. Auden used the term once in his 1940 *New Year Letter*, in the context of Dante's understanding of 'The Catholic ecology', which might be interpreted as a gentle critique of scientific rationalism or as a reflection on the 'evolution from catholic community to protestant personality'.[118] At the centre of the *New Year Letter* was a deep disquiet concerning the human journey from a world centred on community to one dominated by 'Empiric Economic Man' who 'had found the key/To Catholic economy', a brooding reflection on the machine age, mass society and the atomization of human society. In that regard, at least, Scott's account of colonialism and development accords with Auden's bitter account of the world of the mid-twentieth century.

But there is no evidence that Scott had been influenced by Auden when he wrote of the 'ecological significance' of development. Nor is it clear that his thinking had been shaped by another earlier use of the term in a social context, in H. G. Wells' interwar studies of economic and social life, *The Science of Life* and *The Work, Wealth and Happiness of Mankind*.[119] In these works, Wells presented economics as a 'branch of ecology' that in turn formed part of a wider framework for understanding human life in terms compatible with emerging integrative models of nature, perhaps most

---

[117] Lewis, et al., *Attitude to Africa*, 106.
[118] W. H. Auden, *New Year Letter* (London: Faber and Faber, 1941), 23. Rainer Emig, 'Auden and Ecology', in *The Cambridge Companion to W. H. Auden*, edited by Stan Smith (Cambridge: Cambridge University Press, 2005), 213, 218; W. H. Auden, 'Tradition and Value', *The New Republic*, 1940 quoted in David Mason, 'The "Civitas" of Sound: Auden's "Paul Bunyan" and "New Year Letter"', *Journal of Modern Literature* 19, no. 1 (1994): 115–28.
[119] H. G. Wells, Julian Huxley, and G. P. Wells, *The Science of Life* (London: Cassell, 1931); H. G. Wells, *The Work, Wealth and Happiness of Mankind*. New and rev. Ed. (London: William Heinemann, 1934).

fully elaborated in Jan Smuts' *Holism and Evolution*.[120] But the assessment of the prospects for a development policy in Africa in the 1950s in *Attitude to Africa* paid close attention to environmental factors alongside its social and political dimensions. Legum and Wight argued that it was not a history of class exploitation of land owners that had shaped social and economic relations in Africa, but 'the low productivity of the soil itself'.[121] And Scott suggested that the need to combine environmental, social and political concerns was understood by some officials and administrators, who had begun to demonstrate

> a greater appreciation of the need for this faith and these values and for an ecological perspective of Africa's problems. The conservation and balanced use of Africa's soil, minerals and other natural resources cannot be achieved by technique alone, nor by any mechanical means. Nor can it be achieved if initially there is a disregard of the human factor.[122]

Scott's conceptualization of development in organic and holistic terms thus reflected an emergent intellectual interest in the integration of human social and economic relations within their environmental context. He would also have recognized Auden's use of 'ecology' to mark the contrast between 'community' and modern mass society. But the 'ecological perspective' to which Scott referred owed most to the American social and cultural critic Lewis Mumford. In his works *Technics and Civilisation* (1934) and *The Culture of Cities* (1938), Mumford developed a model of human social organization and material culture that owed much to the British pioneer of urban planning Patrick Geddes, with whom Mumford shared an extensive correspondence in the interwar period. From Geddes, Mumford inherited a vision of human society inflected by biological thinking that avoided the 'false biological analogies' presented by Victorian Social Darwinists. The ecological perspective in Mumford's vision of the city – and Scott's vision of development – was a form of thinking that centred on the organic:

> With the organism uppermost we begin to think qualitatively in terms of growth, norms, shapes, interrelationships, implications, associations, and societies. We realize that the aim of the social process is not to make men more powerful, but to make them more completely developed, more human, more capable of carrying on the specifically human attributes of culture – neither snarling carnivores nor insensate robots.[123]

Scott quoted extensively from *The Culture of Cities* in setting out a programme for regional development in South Africa, drawing in particular on Mumford's assertion that planning could reintegrate urban and rural areas and create 'cooperative' societies 'united by a common feeling for their own landscape'.[124] For Scott, development policies

---

[120] Jan Christiaan Smuts, *Holism and Evolution* (London: Macmillan, 1927).
[121] Lewis, et al., *Attitude to Africa*, 28.
[122] Ibid., 108.
[123] Lewis Mumford, *The Culture of Cities* (London: Secker & Warburg, 1944), 303.
[124] Ibid. quoted in Scott, *A Time to Speak*, 126, 128.

structured around social integration and cooperation were the key to escaping the threat of interracial conflict that all feared. After meeting with groups of white South African and African students at the University of Cambridge in May 1950, Scott called explicitly for Mumford's vision of a 'more serviceable and cooperative civilisation' to be built in southern Africa.[125]

The crisis of modernity and the practice of peace

Scott viewed the crisis he believed was underway in Africa to be an expression of the wider predicament of modernity, embodied by atomic weapons, racial conflict, and a struggle between hope and fear. His conviction that the world was amidst a fundamental moral and political crisis would be a repeated theme of his speeches and public statements throughout his activist career in the 1950s and early 1960s, and in some regards his thoughts on decolonization and peace were secondary expressions of a more thorough-going sense of unease with the world. In May 1956, just five years after the publication of *Attitude to Africa*, he preached again at St Paul's, focusing on 'beauty, truth and goodness': the means employed boy Christ to thwart evil. These means, he argued, had been abandoned in the modern world. Instead of providing a universal religion, Christianity had been divided, weakening its power to defeat 'the dangers of an arrogant nationalism, and the doctrine of self-interest, hatred and violence, that are poisoning the spirit and the mind of man, making him prey to tyranny and totalitarianism'.[126]

One of the examples of the tyranny of modernity Scott cited in his sermon was the Lyons Electronic Office (known as Leo), a large computing device which had been constructed between 1949 and 1951 to manage stock and maintain the company payroll across the chain of Lyons Tea shops in London. The world's first business computer might have seemed an eccentric topic for a sermon, but it captured the public imagination in 1954 not only as a tool to remove the 'drudgery' of clerical work but also as a threat to workers. In the place of clerks and warehouse workers, large companies could harness 'slave electrons' to undertake basic clerical processes just as nineteenth-century machines had replaced the labourer's muscle power.[127] Scott's sermon in 1956 echoed these fears and suggested that vigorous social and political efforts would be needed to develop 'skills in the use of leisure in the great urban manhives that we call cities'. In order to confront the challenges of this new electronic age, Scott argued, planning would be critical. Moreover, careful effort would be required to overcome the widening gulf between the developed and 'undeveloped' world of colonial territories. Overcoming this inequality would, he insisted, require an immense increase in the consumer power of ordinary people in the Third World, alongside a rapid growth

---

[125] *Cambridge Daily News*, 17 May 1950.
[126] Michael Scott, 'Sermon at St Paul's', 27 May 1956 Bodleian Library (BOD), Astor Papers, MSS 15363/203 1955–58.
[127] 'Electronic Clerk Takes Over', *Guardian*, 27 September 1954; Ritchie Calder, 'Slave Electrons', in *New Statesman and Nation* (London: Statesman and Nation Publishing, 27 February 1954), 246–7.

in global production. These ideas would have sounded familiar to those who had been involved with Scott in South Africa during the 1940s, where the combination of an integrated economy and 'common society' had become a central pillar of the ideology within the left-liberal circles in which he became politically active.[128] But for Scott, social and economic development was also divinely sanctioned. Conscious planning, he suggested in his 1956 sermon, was part of God's plan for humanity, and an expression of 'the freedom He has given us to exert that will in harmony with His upon our environment'.[129] He concluded his sermon with a call to arms:

> We stand at the beginning of a new era in the life of men with endless possibilities opening up before us. Nationalism is not enough. Nationalism is too much. Totalitarianism has failed, and at what cost! We need you the pioneers of this new age, new creatures born out of the fire which comes down at the Pentecost to those who live themselves in penitence, and in utter submission to the will which is greater than their own will – none other than the creative spirit of the universe.[130]

For Scott, activism was nothing if not a spiritual endeavour, and Christian faith was the nucleus of his commitment to a transformation of the political world. But his activism was shaped by two other, equally potent, elements: a fierce sense of justice and a commitment to non-violent action. His opposition to colonialism and later advocacy of nuclear disarmament stemmed from this twin ideals.

In the late 1940s and early 1950s, Scott was perhaps the most prominent example of an activist driven by the overlapping principles of non-violence and anti-racism. A significant number of individuals and organizations on both sides of the Atlantic whose political agendas included parallel strands of peace and anti-colonialism. There were key differences between Scott, Rustin and Houser, perhaps most noteworthy being the contrast between American activists' history of conscientious objection and Scott's decision to volunteer to serve in the Royal Air Force during the Second World War. His emergence as an advocate of Gandhian civil disobedience came later, during his time in South Africa in the 1940s.[131] Scott also exposed contradictory positions within British peace and anti-nuclear weapons movements; he espoused a kind of paradoxical paternalism that deployed the language of trusteeship to espouse independence and decolonization as the teleological purpose of Britain's 'mission' in Africa. At times, he seemed to regard the methodology of passive resistance, which he had encountered via involvement in the civil disobedience campaigns launched by the Indian National Congress in South Africa in the 1940s, as being of equal importance to the aims of independence and democracy.[132] Other British peace campaigners demonstrated comparable commitment to the legacy of satyagraha. In 1951, Peace Pledge Union activist Hugh Brock proposed 'Operation Gandhi', a series of non-violent protests against nuclear weapons, US military bases in the UK and British membership of

---

[128] Skinner, 'Christian Reconstruction, Secular Politics'; see also Yates and Chester, *The Troublemaker*.
[129] Scott, 'Sermon at St Paul's'.
[130] Ibid.
[131] Scott, *A Time to Speak*, 133–9; Yates and Chester, *The Troublemaker*, 50.
[132] See, for example, Michael Scott, *Shadow over Africa* (London: Union of Democratic Control, 1950).

NATO.[133] But it was Scott who did most to interweave anti-nuclear and anti-colonial campaigns into the fabric of transnational peace campaigns during the late 1950s and early 1960s. As we will see, his activities formed an encounter between Western visions of national morality and Gandhian (and by extension broader Third World) tactics of resistance.

What British and American activists shared, therefore, was a conviction that the means of political engagement were central to its ends. Social and political transformation was not a matter of achieving a set of predetermined objectives through any advantageous means, but a process in which the actions taken would influence the eventual outcome. Their engagement with British and American political culture also demonstrated that these methodologies of protest were shaped by contingencies and employed radical acts of political resistance alongside practices of political lobbying, publicity-making and fundraising that had marked humanitarian, anti-racist and civil rights movements for over a century. In the United States, the social foundations of anti-colonial and pacifist activism were similar but not identical in form to those which pertained in Britain. But, as the discussion of the ideas of development and British 'responsibility' towards Africa in this chapter suggests, the ideological framework and political focus of activists in Britain reflected a direct relationship between African colonial issues and the British state. The focus of campaigners in Britain – in the early 1950s at least – was on the political system and the operation of power within state institutions rather than alternative forms of power and resistance. While there were hints at radical forms of social thought, such as those described by Scott as an 'ecological' vision of development, the political agenda, with its emphasis on cautious and accommodationist notions of partnership, seemed in line with the broad aims of the colonial policy of the Labour government in Britain. Despite having contacts with African political leaders and activists, nationalist movements were regarded by the authors of *Attitude to Africa* in somewhat abstract terms. As the following chapters will show, Western anti-colonial movements would quickly be obliged to take account of the values and agendas of Africans. In contrast, US pacifists had begun to engage with domestic campaigns for racial justice and civil rights in the 1940s, even though it was more radical figures such as W. E. B. du Bois that had campaigned to connect national and international struggles for justice and freedom during the late 1940s.

---

[133] Scalmer, *Gandhi in the West*.

3

Practices of anti-colonial activism in the 1950s

During the 1950s, peace and anti-colonial campaigns were shaped not only by the ideas and ideals assessed in the previous chapter but within affective networks through which solidarity was constructed and contested. These networks were, in many regards, mid-twentieth century analogues of the 'anti-imperial subculture' that Leela Gandhi has described emerging from the complex and chaotic world of possibilities encountered at the colonial periphery in the late-nineteenth century.[1] The political culture of anti-colonial movements was formed within an emotional landscape of activism, contingent upon social structures and the opportunities and limitations afforded by class status and racial identities. The first part of the chapter considers this emotional landscape as it follows American and British activists through their engagement with Africa, the politics of anti-colonialism and anti-racism in the early 1950s. Their attempts to build connections with African independence movements were often viewed through a prism of hope and despair, whether manifest in encounters with rigid colonial world views, or the challenges of reconciling their political and personal lives, their inner struggles and intimate relations with others. These efforts illustrate the extent to which activism and solidarity were products of a politics of network-making, and the alliances and antagonisms that, along with campaign strategies, political visions, and shared values, drew individuals together into a collective enterprise. The chapter then traces the emergence of a political culture of anti-colonialism by examining the ways in which activists built institutional centres such as the Africa Bureau and identified issues of concern, including the elaboration of the system of apartheid in South Africa and the formation of the Central African Federation.

In Britain, Scott's work navigated a path between radical anti-colonialism and incrementalist visions of development and constitutional reform, and the work of the Africa Bureau illuminates something of the social history of class and status hierarchies that shaped anti-colonial movements. But it also reveals that these histories cannot be understood purely in terms of tactics and organization and illustrates the interpersonal relations that created and maintained such collective endeavours. The politics of peace and anti-colonialism was shaped by the emotions of political work and the ways in

---

[1] Leela Gandhi, *Affective Communities: Anticolonial Thought, Fin-De-Siècle Radicalism, and the Politics of Friendship* (Durham, NC: Duke University Press, 2006), 8.

which social and gender relations were both contingent to and constitutive of the ideologies of movements.

When he returned to Britain after the World Peace Conference in India, it seems likely that Scott intended to return to South Africa, as he had after his previous journey to the United Nations in 1948. But this became an increasingly difficult prospect. While in New York in 1949, his formal licence from the Anglican Church was withdrawn, and then, shortly after the June 1950 National Peace Council conference, he was hospitalized following a recurrence of Crohn's disease. Although Scott resumed his activities in Britain and returned again to the United Nations, any plans he may have had for a quick return to South Africa were frustrated in January 1952, when the South African government formally declared him a 'prohibited immigrant'. Stripped of his right to enter and reside in South Africa, Scott thus embarked on a path of transnational activism, travelling in an arc that would take him between activist networks in Britain and annual pilgrimages to the United Nations to maintain his campaign on South-West Africa.

In the year that followed the publication of *Attitude to Africa*, the political context of Western anti-colonialism shifted in significant ways. In Britain, a change of government in late 1951 returned the Conservative Party to power, significantly changing the complexion of colonial policy. In Anglophone Africa, political leaders increased the volume of their opposition to colonialism and mobilized popular nationalist campaigns. Local political cultures and concerns meant that the trajectories of anti-colonial protest differed significantly, but few seemed to be following the constitutional path that had opened for the Convention Peoples Party in the Gold Coast. As the authors of *Attitude to Africa* warned, the severity of political tensions was greater in regions with larger communities of European settlers, and perhaps at its most acute in Kenya, where violent resistance to colonial rule licensed the imposition of a State of Emergency in October of 1952. It was events in central and southern Africa, however, that drew the attention of pacifist campaigners in Britain and the United States. The Africa Bureau launched in London amidst debate around the formation of a Central African Federation and quickly began to provide support for African delegations from Nyasaland and Northern and Southern Rhodesia. And, in the United States, activists were invigorated by the launch of the Defiance Campaign against apartheid in South Africa, drawing on Gandhian tactics of civil disobedience similar to those employed by CORE and FOR in the 1940s. But the development of anti-colonial activism was not simply reflexive or a response to external stimulus, it also indicated the broader social structures and political cultures that shaped activist networks in early 1950s Britain and America. Moreover, anti-colonialism was also a reflection of the subjective experiences, emotions and psychology of those individuals prepared to dedicate their time and energies to campaigns of solidarity with Africans.

Peace and anti-colonial networks in the United States

In the 1940s, US peace activists, including A. J. Muste and James Farmer, had revitalized US pacifism through their efforts within the Fellowship of Reconciliation and new movements such as the Congress of Racial Equality. These networks of multi-racial activists would have an important influence on the development of anti-colonialism in the United States in the 1950s and 1960s. This interest, which had been stimulated by the adaptation of Gandhian tactics by African nationalist movements, represented a new dimension in a long history of US engagement with African issues. This had included agents of imperialism in the form of engineers and entrepreneurs, who brought expertise and resources to bear on the burgeoning extractive industries, notably in South Africa.[2] African Americans had played a part in missionary and humanitarian engagements with Africa in the nineteenth century, in a spectrum that stretched from the repatriation project of the American Colonisation Society in Liberia to the radical influence of missionaries from the American Methodist Episcopal Church.[3] Black Colleges and Universities in the United States provided a formative education for many pioneers of African political organizations and nationalist movements. By the interwar period, the Africanist diasporic politics of charismatic leaders such as Marcus Garvey had established transatlantic ideological connections of equal significance to those emanating from Moscow and the Comintern.[4] In the 1940s, the Council of African Affairs articulated a leftist critique of colonialism that emphasized the connections between domestic racism and imperialism.[5]

Like radical critics of colonialism and segregation, US pacifists emphasized the connection between domestic racism and colonialism, but central to their engagement with these issues was their bearing on the subject of peace. This would manifest in questions of political practice and the promotion of non-violent tactics transformed the politics of civil rights in the United States. But it also reflected a global view of world politics that shaped campaigns against nuclear weapons and framed decolonization and the Cold War within a narrative of existential threat. In the 1960s, the diffuse cultural influence of the notion of 'peace' would play help shape counter-cultural

[2] Elaine Katz, 'The Role of American Mining Technology and American Mining Engineers in the Witwatersrand Gold Mining Industry 1890-1910', *South African Journal of Economic History* 20, no. 2 (2005): 48-82; M. Z. Nkosi, 'American Mining Engineers and the Labor Structure in the South African Gold Mines', *African Journal of Political Economy/Revue Africaine d'Economie Politique* 1, no. 2 (1987): 63-80; Stephen Tuffnell, 'Engineering Inter-Imperialism: American Miners and the Transformation of Global Mining, 1871-1910*', *Journal of Global History* 10, no. 1 (2015): 53-76.

[3] J. T. Campbell, *Songs of Zion: The African Methodist Episcopal Church in the United States and South Africa* (Chapel Hill: University of North Carolina Press, 1998); see also Lawrence S. Little, *Disciples of Liberty: The African Methodist Episcopal Church in the Age of Imperialism, 1884-1916* (Knoxville: Univ. of Tennessee Press, 2000).

[4] Minkah Makalani, *In the Cause of Freedom: Radical Black Internationalism from Harlem to London, 1917-1939* (Chapel Hill: University of North Carolina Press, 2011); Mark Solomon, *The Cry Was Unity: Communists and African Americans, 1917-1936* (Jackson: University Press of Mississippi, 1998); Robert Trent Vinson, *The Americans Are Coming!: Dreams of African American Liberation in Segregationist South Africa* (Athens: Ohio University Press, 2012); Robert A. Hill and Gregory A. Pirio, '"Africa for the Africans": The Garvey Movement in South Africa, 1920-1940', in *The Politics of Race, Class and Nationalism in Twentieth-Century South Africa*, edited by Shula Marks and Stanley Trapido (Harlow: Longman, 1987).

[5] David Henry Anthony, *Max Yergan: Race Man, Internationalist, Cold Warrior* (New York: New York University Press, 2006); Charles Denton Johnson, 'Re-Thinking the Emergence of the Struggle for South African Liberation in the United States: Max Yergan and the Council on African Affairs, 1922-1946', *Journal of Southern African Studies* 39, no. 1 (2013): 171-92. See also Francis Njubi Nesbitt, *Race for Sanctions: African Americans against Apartheid, 1946-1994* (Bloomington: Indiana University Press, 2004).

protest against the Vietnam War and apartheid. After the initial crystallization of anti-racist activism within networks of conscientious objectors in the 1940s, the new threat of atomic weapons maintained the momentum of US pacifism, via groups such as the Peacemakers, whose members included Bayard Rustin as well as Muste and Houser.[6] But in part as a consequence of these efforts, in the early 1950s, some American pacifists began to engage with the politics of anti-colonialism in Africa.

As Scott and his collaborators began to draft *Attitude to Africa*, a group of Peacemakers travelled to Europe with the intention of cycling from Paris to Moscow in a high-profile campaign for disarmament. The young and relatively inexperienced activists ultimately failed in their aim and travelled only as far as the Soviet military base in Vienna before being halted. One of these visionary cyclists was Bill Sutherland, an African American peace campaigner who took a diversion to Britain before returning to the United States, hoping to learn more of the burgeoning African nationalist movements from Black students. There, during a visit to Birmingham for a meeting at the Quaker Selly Oak Colleges, Sutherland met the South African educationalist, linguist and editor of the journal *Bantu World*, Jacob Nhlapo.[7] Nhlapo informed Sutherland of plans for a non-violent resistance campaign against 'unjust laws' in South Africa planned for the following year.[8] When Sutherland returned to the United States, he reported the plans enthusiastically to Houser and Rustin at CORE. Sutherland urged South African political activists to contact CORE requesting support, and nascent anti-apartheid organization was formed, Americans for South African Resistance.[9] One of the key organizers of the group was George Houser, the Methodist minister and CORE activist, who had led the Journey of Reconciliation alongside Bayard Rustin in the 1940s. From early 1952, Houser had begun to correspond with leaders of the African National Congress and South African Indian Congress as well independent figures such as Manilal Gandhi.[10]

Another liberal pacifist and civil rights activist that began to engage with African issues during 1952 was Homer Jack, a Unitarian Universalist clergyman from Illinois, who witnessed the early stages of the protest when he arrived in Johannesburg in early July, during a three-month tour of Africa. Jack had been a key figure in the Chicago Council Against Racial and Religious Discrimination in the 1940s and had edited *The Wit and Wisdom of Gandhi*, a collection of aphorisms and quotations published in

---

[6] Leilah Danielson, '"It Is a Day of Judgment": The Peacemakers, Religion, and Radicalism in Cold War America', *Religion and American Culture* 18, no. 2 (2008): 215–48; Mollin, *Radical Pacifism in Modern America*, 49–68.

[7] For a recent account of Nhlapo's contribution to debates around African identity and language harmonization, see Finex Ndhlovu, 'Pan-African Identities and Literacies: The Orthographic Harmonisation Debate Revisited', *South African Journal of African Languages* 42, no. 2 (2022): 207–15.

[8] Jervis Anderson, *Bayard Rustin: Troubles I've Seen: A Biography* (New York: Harper Collins Publishers, 1997), 141.

[9] Interview with Bill Sutherland, 19 July 2003, Prexy Nesbitt, Mimi Edmunds, (interviewers) in 'No Easy Victories' collection, 'Struggles for Freedom in Southern Africa, https://jstor.org/stable/al.sff.document.nev001suth, Accessed August 2022; see also Anderson, *Bayard Rustin*, 142.

[10] William Minter, Gail Hovey, and Charles E. Cobb, eds, *No Easy Victories: African Liberation and American Activists over a Half Century, 1950-2000* (Trenton, NJ: Africa World Press, 2008), 62–3; George M. Houser, *No One Can Stop the Rain: Glimpses of Africa's Liberation Struggle* (New York: Pilgrim Press, 1989).

1951.[11] In London, en route to South Africa, Jack encountered Michael Scott, whom he found 'fascinating ... but somewhat distracted and disorganised' while hosting African delegations from central Africa. After a protracted visit to the humanitarian missionary-theologian Albert Schweitzer in French Equatorial Africa (now Gabon), Jack arrived in South Africa, where he embarked on a non-stop series of meetings with Black South African leaders including Yusuf Dadoo and Alfred Xuma, as well as other active anti-apartheid campaigners including the trades union organizer E. S. Sachs and the Anglican urban missionary Trevor Huddleston. He also spent time with Manilal Gandhi, who – at that point – had distanced himself from the Defiance Campaign on the basis that it had been instigated by Communists.[12] In late July, Jack delivered a speech for the Gandhi-Tagore Lectureship Trust in Durban, which brought him into conflict with both Afrikaner groups and liberal white opinion. After beginning with the observation that 'democracy ... is weakening and fast disappearing' in South Africa, Jack predicted that Gandhian influences would bring non-racial elections within a decade.[13]

In his view, Jack felt that debates around apartheid underlined the need to resist the polarization of Cold War international politics, but within South Africa, his ideas were highly divisive. The *Cape Times*, which published a lengthy interview in which he repeated many of the claims from his earlier talk, condemned his 'snap judgement' of the country in its editorial.[14] *Die Burger* bracketed Jack alongside Scott as 'confused minds' whose 'moral superiority' was called into question when they declared their support for 'organised infringement of the Law' by Black South Africans.[15] As a consequence, the Archbishop of Cape Town, Geoffrey Clayton, abruptly cancelled a planned appointment with Jack, sending him a note proclaiming that, after reading his interview with the *Cape Times*, it would be a 'waste of time' meeting him.[16] Jack's reflections on his visit, published in *The Forum* in October 1952, suggested that such criticism of foreigners' lack of knowledge was unfounded and that he had spoken to figures from a much wider political and racial spectrum than most South Africans would encounter in their daily lives. Moreover, he felt that no one in South Africa had developed a 'clear blueprint' for the transformation of race relations and although the Defiance Campaign was 'the most important movement south of the equator', few in South Africa – aside from Communists – were sympathetic. Jack's conclusions sharply illustrated the contrast between the developing anti-apartheid attitudes of international observers and South African liberals, whose increasing struggle to reconcile an instinctive determination to work within the structures of the South African state with the democratic demands of Black opposition groups. By the end of the 1950s, liberals such as Edgar Brookes would feel themselves to be working on the

---

[11] Mahatma Gandhi, Mohandas Gandhi, and Homer A. Jack. *The Wit and Wisdom of Gandhi* (Boston: Beacon Press, 1951).
[12] Homer Jack, 'Africa Diary', 9 July 1952, Swarthmore Peace Collection (SPC) Homer Jack Papers, JACK VI/9 - Africa Diary.
[13] Jack, 'Legacy of Mahatma Gandhi in South Africa Today', *Indian Opinion*, 1 August 1952, 229.
[14] 'Control by Blacks Predicted', *Cape Times*, 7 August 1952; 'Snap Judgements', *Cape Times*, 8 August 1952.
[15] *Die Burger*, 9 August 1952.
[16] Clayton to Jack, 7 August 1952, SPC Homer Jack Papers JACK VI-9 Africa Trip 1952.

'borderland between hope and despair', whereas international critics of apartheid had long begun to re-calibrate the focus of their political optimism.[17] For Jack, Scott was the embodiment of hope for Africa: a white man who aligned himself with Africans 'unambiguously and without political motives'.[18]

The politics of hope also attracted Bayard Rustin, whose first visit to Africa began as Jack was returning from Cape Town aboard the *Stirling Castle*. With backing from the Fellowship of Reconciliation and the American Friends' Service Committee, Rustin travelled to west Africa seeking to forge links with nationalist leaders in the Gold Coast (soon to become independent Ghana) and Nigeria. Like Jack, Rustin's African journey included a diversion to Britain, where he attended the World Conference of Friends in Oxford. In an effort to enliven the proceedings, Rustin and fellow American delegates presented a statement of faith that elaborated what he had described as a 'revolutionary faith' from the conference floor. While their statement was not deemed suitable for inclusion in the formal proceedings, the concept of a revolutionary faith was recalled as inspirational by one British Quaker, Godric Bader, whose father Ernest would later help design the framework for pacifist training discussed at the founding conference of the World Peace Brigade (see Chapter 5).

Arriving in Accra in late August, Rustin spent a fortnight in the Gold Coast before touring Nigeria. He met Kwame Nkrumah, the prime minister of the newly established Gold Coast legislative assembly, and Nnamdi Azikiwe, head of the National Council of Nigeria and the Cameroons. While African nationalist movements in each country reflected local histories of colonialism and political cultures, Rustin perceived clear parallels in both leaders. Nkrumah was a kind of African Gandhi, insofar as he was surrounded by an aura of almost supernatural abilities, while Azikiwe was an African Nehru, 'willing to expend his all for the people' while remaining true to 'the ideals of Gandhi'.[19] He reported to his US sponsors that Nkrumah and Azikiwe, 'who fervently desire freedom for their people, are convinced that the only right way to it is by non-violent means'.[20] Privately, though, he expressed fears that, for Nkrumah at least, non-violence was a matter of 'expediency' rather than faith.[21] But his discussions with Azikiwe led to an invitation to train National Council activists in methods of non-violent protest. Although some in the Fellowship of Reconciliation were reluctant, Muste backed Rustin's plan to return to Nigeria for six months in 1953. On his return to the United States, he embarked on a speaking tour discussing the connections between peace and anti-colonial movements, raising funds for his Nigerian project.[22]

Aside from Michael Scott, American pacifists took the lead in forging connections between peace movements and anti-colonialism in Africa. But, whereas Scott had adopted Gandhian techniques in South Africa which would underpin his advocacy

---

[17] Brookes, quoted in Paul B. Rich, *Hope and Despair: English-Speaking Intellectuals and South African Politics, 1896–1976* (London: British Academic Press, 1993), 202.
[18] Jack, 'A Memo to Liberals', *The Forum*, October 1952, 43.
[19] Anderson, *Bayard Rustin*, 144–7.
[20] Rustin, 'Report on trip to Africa', 20 October 1952, SPC Fellowship of Reconciliation Papers FOR IID, Rustin, Trip to Africa 1952.
[21] Anderson, *Bayard Rustin*, 145.
[22] Jerald Podair, Jacqueline M. Moore, and Nina Mjagkij, *Bayard Rustin: American Dreamer* (Lanham, MD: Rowman & Littlefield Publishers, 2008), 33; Anderson, *Bayard Rustin*, 148.

for nationalist movements in Britain and the United Nations, Muste, Sutherland, Houser and Rustin represented a different blend of American socialism and Christian pacifism. These were peacemakers awakened to the ties that connected struggles against segregation at home with anti-colonialism in Africa. As we will see, American initiatives in Africa were framed very differently than those which developed in the Africa Bureau and the Movement for Colonial Freedom, where the politics of colonialism was a field that connected British and imperial political institutions. But, in both settings, the practice of activism was also shaped by the emotional lives of activists themselves. In the case of Rustin in 1953, this nearly resulted in the end of his work as a pacifist organizer.

'A revolutionary power, austere and enduring'?

In late January 1952, after giving a talk in Pasadena sponsored by the American Association of University Women, Rustin was arrested after being discovered having sex with two men in a car outside his hotel. The next day, after pleading guilty to public indecency, he was sentenced to two months in jail. A. J. Muste, his mentor and almost a father-like figure, who had long been aware of Rustin's sexual orientation, insisted that he had no option but resign from the Fellowship of Reconciliation or be dismissed.[23]

One valid reading of Rustin's experience would be to present it as exemplary of the risks faced by gay men involved in political activism in 1950s America. One recent biography suggests that Rustin's refusal to hide or suppress his sexuality was making 'as strong a statement as a gay man could at a time when even radical leftists like Muste could not fit homosexuality into their understanding of the world'.[24] But, the relationship between Rustin's sexuality and his politics was, arguably, more complex and more intriguing that such an analysis suggests. As another biographer, John D'Emilio, has noted, Rustin did not proclaim his sexuality, but throughout his political career it 'resisted . . . marginalisation and insinuated itself at every turn'. For D'Emilio, despite the archival silences that obstruct analysis of the role of his sexuality in his politics, his homosexuality was never totally submerged.[25] Accounts of Rustin's sexual awakening ranged from those that emphasized a lack of guilt and others, including the recollections of Bill Sutherland, that spoke of self-harm and attempts to sublimate his sexuality via sport while at college.[26] He was reportedly charismatic, attractive and sexually confident, but other activists in the 1940s hinted that his behaviour could be predatory.[27]

After his arrest and imprisonment in 1953, the relationship between Muste and Rustin had irrevocably changed. Although Muste supported Rustin's right to live his life as he chose he also believed that homosexuality was a form of decadence

---

[23] D'Emilio, *Lost Prophet* , 217; Anderson, *Bayard Rustin*, 153–4.
[24] Podair, et al., *Bayard Rustin*, 34.
[25] John D'Emilio, 'Reading the Silences in a Gay Life: The Case of Bayard Rustin', in *The Seductions of Biography*, edited by Mary Rhiel and David Bruce Suchoff (New York: Routledge, 1996), 60–2.
[26] Anderson, *Bayard Rustin*, 155–6.
[27] Ibid., 158–9.

contrasted with the 'natural' norm of intimate relations between men and women.[28] The arrest thus struck at a partnership and political vision that was at the heart of a FOR and Muste demanded Rustin's resignation from FOR. The incident – or perhaps the reactions of Muste and other FOR officials – appears to have prompted Rustin to reflect deeply on the relationship between his sexuality and his work as an activist. In a letter to Muste's assistant John Swomley, Rustin confessed that 'sex must be sublimated, if I am too live with myself and in this world longer', although in the same letter he also claimed that sex had 'never been my basic problem'. The previous year, he had also written that of the 'inner discipline' that was central to non-violence, but that this rational pledge could be tested to destruction at moments of 'emotional crisis'.[29] For Muste, Rustin's sexual behaviour was at odds with the self-control that was required of radical pacifism, and it seemed that the 'Action Discipline' that lay at the heart of the non-violent protest repertoires of CORE and other Gandhian movements could not be insulated from an individual's personal life.[30] Rustin's 'promiscuity denied the "depth" and "understanding" of love' but, as Danielson argues, this view was blind to the social pressures to repress homosexuality.[31]

Moreover, the episode revealed the complex relationship between moral and emotional life, between the rational discipline of the principles of passive resistance and its messy lived reality. In his own life, Gandhi had been no stranger to this paradox and challenge. He had pledged himself to celibacy in 1906, shortly before he began to formulate the practice of satyagraha that would be published three years later in *Hind Swaraj*. Although central to his political philosophy, Gandhi's engagement with the practice of *bhramacharya* – a form of asceticism that included total sexual abstinence – was not without controversy even within his own lifetime. Nehru held that Gandhi's version of sexual abstinence was a potentially unhealthy denial of human nature that had been taken to extremes, particularly in the 1940s when he shared his bed with young female followers in order to 'test' his celibacy.[32] But Gandhi's vision of chastity could, as Alter has suggested, be regarded as not only genuinely utopian but also an attempt to offer practical solutions to contemporary social challenges. National celibacy was, in Gandhi's view, a logical and transformative response to problems of overpopulation, endemic disease and starvation.[33] Perhaps most importantly, celibacy was at the centre of his commitment to nationalist politics: 'If a man gives his love to one woman, or a woman to one man, what is there left for the world besides?'[34] The anti-colonial peacemakers of the 1950s were not slavish in their adoption of Gandhian ideals and, as Rustin's case suggests, were in many respects sceptical of political

---

[28] Danielson, *American Gandhi*, 263–4.
[29] Anderson, *Bayard Rustin*, 162–3; 161.
[30] See Scalmer, *Gandhi in the West*, 148–9; Danielson, *American Gandhi*, 264–5.
[31] Ibid., 264.
[32] Vinay Lal, 'Nakedness, Nonviolence, and Brahmacharya: Gandhi's Experiments in Celibate Sexuality', *Journal of the History of Sexuality* 9, no. 1/2 (2000): 105–36.
[33] Joseph S. Alter, *Gandhi's Body: Sex, Diet, and the Politics of Nationalism* (Philadelphia: University of Pennsylvania Press, 2000), 11–14.
[34] Quoted in Richard Lannoy, *The Speaking Tree, a Study of Indian Culture and Society* (London: New York University Press, 1971), 386.

asceticism. However, adherence to the discipline of non-violence did not always sit easily with activists' personal relationships.

Love also became a complicating factor in the development of the Africa Bureau in London. Perhaps the most important member of the inner circle of Scott's supporters in the early 1950s was Mary Benson, a South African who had worked for the United Nations Relief and Rehabilitation Administration in Europe after the Second World War before becoming an assistant to British film director David Lean. One of the many who had been introduced to Scott via the *Observer* profile of 1949, she first met him in person in early 1950 and quickly volunteered to undertake secretarial duties. After initial suspicion – there were worries that the young woman was an agent of the South African government – Benson became a mainstay of the organization in its formative years. At the heart of this was the relationship that developed between Benson and Scott, who quickly seemed to become 'a perfect team'.[35] There was, however, no mutual agreement between the two on the nature and source of this perfection. Scott came to rely on Benson in ways that far exceeded administrative assistance, 'sharing ... intimate anxieties and ... profound thoughts', which overcame her rational understanding that a highly driven activist with a spiritual vocation such as Scott would not find emotional space for a more 'personal' relationship. The physical attraction Benson felt for Scott would not be returned.[36]

A brief analysis of the relationship between Scott and Benson reveals something of the complex interconnections between political activism as an emotional endeavour, an embodied practice and multiple variations of desire. Political relations are human relations, and the power to 'affect and to be affected' might be taken as a fundamental characteristic of the transformative encounters that might generally be defined as 'political'.[37] This was, moreover, intensified by the dynamic of Scott's faith; his political work was intrinsically connected to spiritual vocation that allowed no space for "personal" relationships. During the first two years that the Africa Bureau was in operation, Scott and Benson's relationship had the appearance of effective collaboration – Benson's practical and organizational skills proving a valuable foil to Scott's driven, but distracted, political energies. This professional relationship seemed to quickly shade into something akin to romance, at least in terms of a mutual desire for companionship and emotional attachment. But Scott was driven by a 'universal love' that, despite Benson's hopes, was incompatible with personal love. Benson sought to sublimate her desire for something other than the idealized and chaste form of relationship that Scott offered, but the result seemed to be further frustration and anxiety. She worried that others would consider it wrong for a clergyman such as Scott 'to have such a neurotic relationship with a woman. Or to have any close relationship with a woman, however pure it may be, other than a wife'. She concluded that there was only one solution: 'I am convinced it should be marriage or nothing'. But she acknowledged that marriage on Scott's terms had little hope of success; 'even if I were to behave as he would have me', she confided to Astor, 'it would still be neurotic'.[38]

[35] Benson, *A Far Cry*, 63.
[36] Ibid.
[37] Brian Massumi, *Politics of Affect* (Cambridge: Polity, 2015), ix.
[38] Benson to Astor, [n.d *c.* 1955] BOD Astor Papers, MSS 15363/114 Benson.

Compelling explanations for Scott's apparent fear of intimacy can be advanced. His biographers suggest that his 'sexual impediment' was a consequence of long-suppressed abuse as a child, but it is difficult to confidently map cause and effect, especially when, as was the case with Scott, an individual's subjectivity was shaped by visions of an ascetic calling. For Benson, the emotional limits that Scott maintained stemmed from a self-deceptive belief that he had 'found a new superior form of love'.[39] This should not, however, lead to the conclusion that their relationship fell foul of a form of Anglican *brahmacharya*. Rather, Benson's characterization of Scott's relations with women as 'a mixture of something very good and something very neurotic' seems apt.[40] Disentangling Scott's emotional, psychological and political lives seems particularly difficult. Political activism enacts an individual's vision of the world as it might be, which in turn emerges from a complex array of material, social and emotional relations.

Moreover, Scott's activism in the early 1950s was shaped by physical and physiological constraints. His political activities had been influenced by the circumstances of his physical health for some years: the diagnosis of Crohn's disease in the early 1940s had prompted his re-location to South Africa and thence into encounters with the politics of segregation, notions of development and the practice of Gandhian non-violent protest. A major relapse of the disease in 1950 and the subsequent period of convalescence at Astor's house provided the physical backdrop to the development of the networks that would foster *Attitude to Africa*, the formation of the Africa Bureau and the burgeoning relationship with Benson. But there was evidence of the messy, complicated correspondence between corporeal, emotional and political spheres of life in much of Scott's activities and relations with supporters. As Benson would later reflect that their relationship was strongest not only when they were emotionally content but also when he was not physically incapacitated. But his physical health also determined the extent to which Scott would encourage Benson to remain close: 'every time I made a move to go he drew me back – by illness or the work or his own pleas. And I willingly returned'.[41]

Scott clearly had the capacity to enthral supporters to the extent that they were willing to sacrifice their own comforts. In 1952, Benson travelled to New York to assist Scott at the United Nations, staying as a guest in the Brooklyn home of artist and civil rights campaigners Betsy Graves Reyneau. Benson described the lengths to which Reyneau had dedicated herself to helping Scott, to the extent that she was unable to cover her rent and had 'entirely given up . . . painting, selling toilet paper and writing in order to help'. Benson continued:

> Of course, they wouldn't tell him this, but had got to the point of desperation when I arrived. Also none of them can type nor knows the background of the case, and with his constant changes mind, and refusal to eat very often, they were pretty frantic.[42]

[39] Ibid.
[40] Yates and Chester, *The Troublemaker*, 159,160.
[41] Benson to Astor, [n.d *c.* 1955] BOD Astor Papers MSS 15363/114 Benson.
[42] Benson To Astor, 23 November 1952 BOD Astor Papers, MS 15363/202 1952–52.

The practicalities of life often seemed unimportant to Scott. He was in many ways an itinerant activist who continued to rely on the hospitality of friends and supporters or cheap accommodation, even though his political fame – and his social network of wealthy mentors such as Astor – meant that he could travel in a degree of comfort. In New York, Benson wrote with frustration that she had 'quite failed to persuade him to move into a hotel despite the fact that people subscribed $1000 for this'.[43] Benson's attempts to convince him that personal comfort would help his work led to an argument that illustrated the degree to which personal relationships and the practical organization of activism were intertwined:

> when I say he's changed, meaning that before he never worried about money and it just came in when he needed it, and that now he's got masses available yet wastes time wondering where his fare for Africa next February is coming from, he thinks I am accusing him of being mean.

She concluded, angrily, that Scott was 'being so damn masochistic at the moment that he has to punish himself for any personal pleasures'.[44] For Benson, political life and personal comfort were by no means incompatible, but the exchange suggests that their political and emotional lives were intertwined. Moreover, such conflicts not only affected activists as individuals but as members of an organization. Already in 1952, Benson seemed concerned about the impact of the friction with Scott on the working of the Africa Bureau itself. It was, as she later reflected, a context that added to her developing frustration. She wondered how the kind of chaste relationship that Scott imagined might operate within the environment of the Africa Bureau, and whether she could contemplate arriving 'in the morning after lonely nights every night, 365 days in the year from the age of 30-70'. Would, she imagined, they be 'miraculously unaffected by this state of affairs – sufficient to do a good job together murmuring words of love over the lunch table?'[45] Others in the Africa Bureau shared her concerns, including its Chair, the Conservative peer Lord Hemingford, who told her that the organization was 'affected by . . . our ups and downs'.

As with Rustin and the Fellowship of Reconciliation, although in somewhat different circumstances, the fraught emotional dynamic of Scott's political activism eventually achieved a degree of catharsis via a psychological crisis. Again, Scott's health was a factor. In mid-1955, Scott had been admitted to hospital in London with symptoms of depression and insomnia, which may have been related to a new regime of treatment for Crohn's disease, which had recurred earlier in the year. This was itself a significant development, but, in July, Astor received a telephone call from Scott informing him that he had been arrested for indecent exposure in Oxford, seemingly in the vicinity of a well-known (and usually discrete) site for nudist sunbathing on the banks of the River Cherwell. Thanks to the intervention of Astor, who removed Scott to a specialist clinic and recruited an Oxford solicitor who ensured the case was deftly handled

---

[43] Ibid.
[44] Ibid.
[45] Benson to Astor, [n.d c. 1955] BOD Astor Papers MSS 15363/114 Benson.

without publicity, the obvious jeopardy to Scott's political career – and the future of the Africa Bureau – was avoided.[46] In the months before his hospitalization, Benson had presented Scott with a final ultimatum and began to make arrangements to return to South Africa. But even before his 'crisis in Oxford', she put these plans on hold and play a key role in managing Scott's access to and engagement with the outside world. In June, American activists including Roger Baldwin of the International Rights of Man and A. J. Muste of FOR launched a fundraising appeal as 'Volunteers for Michael Scott'. Their effort sought to ensure that Scott would not again 'have to impair his never adequate health for lack of money to provide a minimum office set up'.[47]

The emotional, psychological and physiological dynamics of anti-colonial activism are sharply illuminated by the personal crises experienced by Scott and Rustin in 1952. These moments demonstrate the intersection between personal and political life, long before it became a focus of the social movements that emerged in the 1960s and 1970s. They also prefigured – and possibly informed – the often intense discussion of the psychological aspects of activism within pacifist groups in the late 1950s and early 1960s. In one of the more intriguing contributions to the debates in advance of the launch of the World Peace Brigade in 1962, the evolutionary biologist Julian Huxley wrote to Anthony Brooke of the need to account for fundamental emotional responses when developing high-minded and idealistic political campaigns. For Huxley, attempts to formulate persuasive sermons on peace were mere 'verbal activities' that could have little impact on the 'sub-verbal' instinctive drives that humanity had inherited from animal ancestors and which, he was certain, underpinned the tendency towards social and international conflict. An effective pacifist programme would, Huxley insisted, need to include practical activities constructed to quieten the 'instinctive or quasi-instictive drives which we have inherited from xenophobic, territory-claiming and status-seeking animal ancestors'.[48] Huxley's insistence on the need to consider the 'instinctual and emotional factors involved in individual and collective violence' may not have been entirely convincing in historical or psychological terms, but they fed into a desire among peace campaigners to nurture and develop effective political activism through careful programmes of training. In the early 1950s, non-governmental political activism tended to focus on charismatic individuals such as Rustin and Scott. In Scott's case, as Benson suggested, such individuals were driven by 'a revolutionary power, austere and enduring, yet deep down very emotional, fighting for truth and justice for the weak and the dispossessed'.[49] In terms of their sexuality, Rustin and Scott were obverse faces of the same dilemma – how could political activism, as a highly public practice, reconcile high moral ideals with the frailties and complexities of human emotion?

For Scott, this predicament resulted in an approach to politics that was non-conformist and at times uncertain. And while he retained the sympathies of key supporters such as Astor, more cautious and moderate colonial experts were less understanding. As the Oxford academic Margery Perham put it, in her review of Scott's

---

[46] Yates and Chester, *The Troublemaker*, 165–8.
[47] Ibid., 170.
[48] Huxley to Anthony Brooke, 29 October 1961, SPC Muste Papers 89/22 WPB Founding Convention.
[49] Benson, *A Far Cry*, 90.

book *In Face of Fear*, the missionary zeal which Scott brought to his campaigns was 'profoundly disturbing not only to those whose interests he attacks but to all sluggish souls . . . who watch him with a mingled fascination and repugnance'.[50]

The Africa Bureau and the politics of the establishment

Following the publication of *Attitude to Africa*, Scott, with continued support from David Astor, worked to create an organization that could form a platform for his African political campaigns. The subjective psychological and emotional dynamics of individual activists addressed in the previous section had a significant role in the development of anti-colonial and peace activism in the 1950s. But these were situated, and played out, in social contexts that structured these movements in equally powerful ways. The Africa Bureau, launched in 1952 with Scott as its Director, Benson as its Secretary, Lord Hemingford as Chair and financially backed largely by Astor, reflected the social relations that structured the political values and practices of its main organizers. Histories of British anti-colonial critics have nevertheless tended to emphasize its political agenda over its social foundations. This agenda has been defined as one of 'colonial political advance which was primary and self-justifying', that is, the Africa Bureau pursued political campaigns independent of the social and economic interests of its executive.[51] An assessment of the political agenda of the Africa Bureau is necessary, but the social context and class dynamics within which it operated must also be addressed.

In contrast to the burgeoning interest in Africa developing among American pacifists at the same time, Scott's efforts developed within a pre-existing network of organizations and individuals with interests in, and often direct connections to, missionary enterprise and systems of colonial administration. But, like his American counterparts, Scott's approach prioritized the 'rightful aspirations of the peoples of Africa'.[52] From his experience of lobbying on behalf of the Herero both at the United Nations and in London, Scott concluded that an organization was required that could mediate between African political representatives and British state, media and public. It was this intermediary role that Scott and his associates regarded as distinctive. But London in the early 1950s was by no means bereft of reformist and radical anti-colonial voices. The Union of Democratic Control, who had published Scott's 1949 statement to the Fourth Committee of the UN in pamphlet form, had turned its focus to African issues in the early 1950s, led by its secretary Basil Davidson and other radical thinkers including academic Thomas Hodgkin. The pair would during the 1950s begin to shape popular understanding of African affairs that offered a revelatory view of the 'rich and complex histories, cultures, and civilisations on which the nationalist

---

[50] Margery Perham, 'Black and White', *The Observer*, 14 May 1950.
[51] D. Goldsworthy, *Colonial Issues in British Politics 1945–1961* (Oxford: Clarendon Press, 1971), 6; see also 264–71.
[52] 'Draft Statement of Aims', [n.d. March 1952], BOD Astor Papers, MS 15363/202/Africa Bureau 1952–55.

movements sought to build' political movements and new states.⁵³ But although the UDC under Davidson shared Scott's aim to create links between African organizations and sympathizers in Britain, their close links with the more moderate Fabian Colonial Bureau would have tied Scott's organization too closely to the Labour Party. Moreover, the FCB was associated with the right of the Labour Party and maintained a cautious position on decolonization and African independence.

London was also host to an array of campaign groups and committees that had formed to address specific African issues. Chief among these in 1952 was the friction between the British government and the leaders of the Bamangwato chieftaincy in Bechuanaland (Botswana), Tshekedi Khama and his nephew Seretse. Both had been stripped of their formal roles and forced into exile by the British authorities following a dispute over the marriage between Seretse and an English woman, Ruth Williams in 1947, which drew the internal conflict between Tshekedi and Seretse into the wider politics of race in southern Africa as the latter's marriage fell foul of the apartheid ban on interracial marriage that had been imposed in 1949.⁵⁴ Two key groups had emerged to support Seretse Khama – the Communist-connected Seretse Khama Fighting Committee and the Council for the Defence of Seretse Khama and the Protectorates, chaired by Fenner Brockway of the Congress of Peoples Against Imperialism. Beyond its geopolitical ramifications, the dispute had created a deep division between Scott's long-standing ally Tshekedi and his nephew, and Scott had sought to broker a reconciliation between the two and viewed the work of the various committees a threat to the resolution of what was a 'family affair'.⁵⁵

But, in Scott's view, the broad array of groups concerned with African affairs that appeared to exist in post-war London concealed a much smaller body of highly motivated individuals spread thinly across a range of causes, which he later likened to the 'stage army of the good' described by Henry Nevinson in his description of the small Quaker groups that organized humanitarian organizations after the First World War, 'who contrived by their ubiquitous energy to conceal the paucity of their numbers'.⁵⁶ But Scott used the phrase as a warning, of the danger that the causes adopted by these small and increasingly hard-pressed groups would also attract the 'mad, the bad and the sad who, when mixed together, are apt to make a motley and undisciplined army'.⁵⁷ Others, however, held a more optimistic and generous view of the public support for Scott, particularly when it came to the issue of apartheid in South Africa. In June 1950, in the first wave of Scott's celebrity in the British press, the *New Statesman* reported on the receptive audiences that had attended the National Peace Council meeting on 'the Human Crisis in Africa'. Those in attendance, it argued:

---

⁵³ Stephen Howe, *Anticolonialism in British Politics: The Left and the End of Empire, 1918–1964* (Oxford: Oxford University Press, 1993), 195.
⁵⁴ Ronald Hyam, 'The Political Consequences of Seretse Khama: Britain, the Bangwato and South Africa, 1948–1952', *The Historical Journal* 29, no. 4 (1986): 921–47.
⁵⁵ Skinner, *The Foundations of Anti-Apartheid*, 95; see also Howe, *Anticolonialism*, 196.
⁵⁶ Henry Nevinson, *Fire of Life* (London: Harcourt & Brace, 1935), 358.
⁵⁷ Scott, *A Time to Speak*, 268.

Represented something more than what H.W. Nevinson used to call 'the stage army of the good'. Potentially this movement has millions of supporters behind it; it already spreads far beyond those worthy should who collect good causes in their middle age as they did postage stamps earlier in their careers. The British conscience, puzzled and frustrated by the East-West complex, need not be troubled by issues of peace or communism when it protests against *Apartheid* . . . the denial of human rights to Africans who are, in effect slaves[58]

Opposition to 'South African Nazism', the article concluded, was a cause around which there might be a united front. Anti-apartheid thus stood apart from the broader array of worthy issues that began to attract attention in the early 1950s. But nonetheless, the article suggested that there was a tangible popular interest in, and sympathy for, African political ambitions.

Scott was, however, concerned that groups such as those sponsored by Brockway and others on the left of the Labour Party would exploit African political leaders and activists in the interest of their own political and ideological agendas. A new organization was required, Scott argued, as a way of building 'a more effectual means of exchange of opinion between Africa and Britain and Britain and Africa . . . to restore confidence and keep pace with the rate of present developments'.[59] The inaugural meeting of this new organization was held in late March 1952, at which its structures were formally constituted and its formal statement of aims agreed. A range of names were considered, including the 'African Vigilance Association' and the 'Committee for Justice in Africa', but ultimately the shorter and less specific 'Africa Bureau' was adopted.[60] A small executive committee was appointed, which, according to Goldsworthy reflected an intention to forge 'wide connections with various elements in public life', but also reaffirmed the ways in which the organization was embedded in left-liberal establishment circles.[61] Alongside Scott, Benson and Astor, these included the *Attitude to Africa* co-author Colin Legum; aside from the Conservative peer, Lord Hemingford, the committee drew largely from Liberal and Labour Party supporters, including John MacCallum Scott, a member of Liberal International, the former Colonial Secretary in Attlee's Labour government, Arthur Creech Jones, John Hatch, who would be the Commonwealth Secretary of the Labour Party from 1954 until the early 1960s and Elizabeth Longford, Lady Packenham.

Despite its left-liberal leanings, Scott was determined that the Bureau would be independent from party politics, although he was highly sensitive to party political influences. In particular, he retained a residual distrust for Communist activists, derived from his interactions with party members in South Africa during the 1940s, which would remain a thread within the Bureau into the 1960s.[62] In an early draft of

---

[58] 'London Diary', *New Statesman and Nation*, 17 June 1950, 678.
[59] Scott, 'Memo on need for African Representative organisation in London and at United Nations', [n.d. 1952] BOD Astor Papers, MS 15363/202/Africa Bureau 1952–55.
[60] Ibid.
[61] Goldsworthy, *Colonial Issues*, 265.
[62] Richard Cockett, *David Astor and the Observer* (London: Deutsch, 1991), 188; Goldsworthy, *Colonial Issues*, 266.

his plans for a new representative organization, Scott was blunt in his analysis that anti-colonial groups in Britain included one 'that may fairly be described as "Trotsykist"'; while 'another is almost certainly a Stalinist fellow-traveller organisation'.[63] Although couched in somewhat more measured terms, Astor repeated these concerns when he arranged a private meeting at the Waldorf Hotel in June 1952 for the executive committee of the Bureau to meet prospective sponsors and supporters. His invitation made clear the decidedly anti-Communist ideological orientation of the new organization:

> A considerable effort is being made by Communist and other extremist organisations to become the sponsors of agitation on behalf of those in Africa with genuine grievances. One of the merits of this Bureau is that it may be able to steer aggrieved Africans and others away from such organisations . . . unless liberal-minded people in this country back such efforts, the leaders amongst these people will naturally tend to gravitate towards the Communists and their fellow-travellers who offer them willing aid.[64]

Such fears might suggest that the work of the Africa Bureau – and Western anti-colonialism more generally – ought to be viewed primarily through a lens of Cold War ideological struggle. There is evidence that the Bureau was directly – although unwittingly – influenced by the covert mechanisms of superpower rivalry, with one of its most important sources of funding from the late 1950s coming from the Fairfield Foundation, a New York-based organization which channelled money from the Central Intelligence Agency. Part of a large-scale propaganda exercise centred on the Congress for Cultural Freedom under Nicolas Nabokov, by 1960 the Foundation provided a third of the total income of the Africa Bureau.[65] But, despite this, the anti-Communism of Scott and the Africa Bureau cannot simply be understood as a reflection of the Cold War power struggle; anti-Communism, as one recent study attests, was a broad term that provided a unifying thread for a diffuse array of groups and positions, not a worldwide campaign coordinated from the United States.[66]

The founders of the Africa Bureau viewed Communism as a very real threat to Western interests in Africa and a justification for closer alignment with African nationalist politics. Furthermore, such fears were not restricted to Western observers but were shared by African political activists concerned that Communism signified ongoing white political domination. In South Africa, Africanist figures, such as the former ANC Youth League activist Godfrey Pitje, condemned the Defiance Campaign as Communist-inspired, reflecting a 'racialised wariness' that inflected the country's

---

[63] Scott, 'Memo on need for African Representative Organisation in London and at United Nations', [n.d. c. 1952] BOD Astor Papers, MS 15363/202 1950–52.
[64] Astor, invitation letter, [n.d. June 1952], BOD Astor Papers, MS 15363/202/Africa Bureau 1952–55.
[65] Frances Stonor Saunders, *Who Paid the Piper?: The CIA and the Cultural Cold War* (London: Granta, 1999), 116; Yates and Chester, *The Troublemaker*, 215.
[66] Luc van Dongen, Stéphanie Roulin, and Giles Scott-Smith, *Transnational Anti-Communism and the Cold War: Agents, Activities, and Networks* (London: Palgrave Macmillan, 2014), 2.

emerging resistance to apartheid.[67] In this sense, the Africa Bureau's opposition to Communist influence stemmed from a perceived threat to the independent expression of African political agendas and the achievement of an undiluted democratic freedom. The analysis is further complicated by Scott's refusal in 1952 to sign the affidavit attesting that he had no previous connections with 'totalitarian organisations' that was required for US visa applications; after initially being denied entry to the United States in order to attend the UN sessions, he was eventually allowed to travel on the condition that he remained within the vicinity of the UN headquarters in Manhattan.[68] But Scott appears to have forced the hands of the US authorities rather than being the victim of an intensification of Cold War paranoia. Two years earlier, British officials signalled their willingness for the United States to grant him a visa to attend the UN sessions on South-West Africa, despite being aware of his contacts with the Communist Party and opposing the proposal that he be allowed to address the Trusteeship Committee.[69]

It was not ideological commitments, but style of approach, that seem to have distinguished the Africa Bureau from other anti-colonial movements of the 1950s. In one of the earliest assessments of the historical significance of the Africa Bureau, David Goldsworthy contrasted its emphasis on public campaigns, often coordinated across a range of groups and individuals, with the focus of the Fabian Colonial Bureau on more private efforts to secure influence via individuals in government and the Labour Party.[70] But both ultimately relied on a narrow fraction of British society for their support. The metropolitan elite networks that characterized British anti-colonialism in the early 1950s were sketched in brief but revealing detail by Homer Jack during his stay in London with his wife Esther in April and May 1952. As well as his brief meetings with Michael Scott, he also encountered the Africa Bureau Director while viewing a session of the House of Commons, which included questions relating to the government handling of the political controversy surrounding the marriage of Seretse Khama and Ruth Williams.[71] Jack's six days in London included meetings with delegations from both Nyasaland and Northern Rhodesia [CF Scott, Africa Digest], long-time acquaintances of Gandhi and Albert Schweitzer, visits to the offices of Fabian Society, public meetings at the London Ethical Society and the Seretse Khama [Fighting Committee] – 'a typical British meeting, with slower pace and some evidence of communist infiltration'.[72] The day after the latter meeting, he met the exiled Khama in his Surrey home, before returning to London for an Africa Bureau meeting on the Central African Federation. On their last day in London, after Jack gave a sermon at a small church in Brixton, he and Esther engaged in some pacifist tourism, visiting Kingsley Hall, Gandhi's base during the 1931 Round Table Conference on India. After

---

[67] Deborah Posel, 'The ANC Youth League and the Politicization of Race', *Thesis Eleven* 115, no. 1 (2013): 61; Stephen Plaatjie, 'Conflict of Ideologies: The ANC Youth League and Communism, 1949–1955', (M.A., South Africa: University of Johannesburg (South Africa), 1994), 76–7.
[68] *Chicago Daily Tribune*, 1 October 1952; Homer Jack, 'The Saga of Michael Scott' [n.d. 1953], JACK VI-7 Michael Scott.
[69] FO to UK UN Delegation, 27 September 1950, UK National Archives UKNA) KV/2/2052.
[70] Goldsworthy, *Colonial Issues*, 269–70.
[71] Jack, 'Africa Diary', SPC Jack Papers JACK VI-9 Africa Diary 1952, 'Bechuanaland (Bamangwato Chieftanship)', *Hansard*, HC Deb 29 April 1952 vol 499 cc1228-32.
[72] Jack, 'Africa Diary'.

a personal tour from the warden, the Jacks travelled through the East End, noting that the 'appalling' bomb damage 'should remind Londoners of the dangers of a Third World War', before boarding a ferry to the Netherlands that evening. In addition to the array of meetings listed previously, Jack had, since setting aboard ship in New York, also met the publisher Victor Gollancz and the editor Kingsley Martin. This was a close-knit network, whose sinews bound together left and liberal political circles, African nationalists, clergy of various denominations and veteran humanitarians.

The Africa Bureau and its supporters represented the political ethos of a particular echelon of the British ruling class, but its campaigns captured a popular mood of disillusionment with the inertia of empire – of the obstacles that stood in the way of the promise of development. But most importantly, it represented a new mood in public attitudes towards colonial governance and democracy – or more specifically, a new intolerance towards policies that could be tarred with the brush of 'fascism'. In principle, this might include all forms of colonialism, but the primary target was the policies emerging from territories in the southern and central part of Africa whose administration was controlled by the interests of minority settler populations.

The Central African Federation: experiments with non-violence

The Africa Bureau was situated within a particular stratum of British society, but its primary intended relationship was with African political leaders, which meant that it became a key mediator between British public life and African nationalism. Although the executive committee discussed a range of priority issues at their inaugural meeting, they did not ultimately control the agenda of issues that would become the primary focus of the organization. Where the Africa Bureau did establish a particular interest, it was related to Scott's own experiences, concerns and contacts within southern Africa, including the question of the British Protectorates (the High Commission Territories of Swaziland, Bechaunaland and Basutoland), the situation of South Asian communities in Africa and the question of South-West Africa. But the initial focus of the Bureau's activities, as Homer Jack chronicled in mid-1952, was an area that had not previously figured in Scott's campaigns: the proposed creation of a federation of the British central African territories of Nyasaland and Northern and Southern Rhodesia.

The Federation plan had its origins in the interwar period after Southern Rhodesia gained self-governing status in 1923, and the economy of Northern Rhodesia began to be transformed by the rapid industrialization of the Copperbelt. The political amalgamation of Nyasaland and Northern Rhodesia with the southern territory was seen by settler communities as a way of consolidating power, but by the mid-1940s this had been effectively ruled out in the face of African opposition and on the basis of significant differences in 'native policy' between the three territories. However, the notion of 'closer association' between the three territories remained an abstract aim and began to carry greater weight with the foundation of large-scale cross-territorial development projects such as the Kariba dam. By the early 1950s, the electoral success of the National Party in South Africa provided a political rationale for federation as a safeguard against the influence of the apartheid state.[73] White opinion and mining interests began to align themselves to the idea of federation, and Labour government in Westminster offered guarded support. White political leaders in central Africa, led by Roy Welensky sought to define federation in terms of a 'partnership' between Black and white, an idea that seemed to 'beguile' metropolitan humanitarian opinion, although the Southern Rhodesian prime minister Godfrey Huggins revealed more of the reality of the situation when he defined the partnership between Europeans and Africans as that of the 'horse and its rider'.[74] Thus, as Collins has suggested, while the post-war Labour government promoted a policy of 'developmental imperialism', centred on managerialism and socio-economic improvement rather than notions of racial hierarchy, debates around race remained salient.[75] While partnership could have various connotations, federation was anathema to progressive circles in London as it became clear that African opinion was unanimous in its opposition.

Perhaps most significantly, the Fabian Colonial Bureau, with its close ties to the parliamentary Labour Party, also aligned itself against federation, but was not able or willing to lead a public campaign. The newly formed Africa Bureau thus seemed perfectly suited to lead a public campaign against the Central Africa Federation, but a Central Africa Committee led by Fenner Brockway together with other members of the Congress of Peoples' Against Imperialism was formed in mid-1952, setting up a rivalry that exacerbated the confusing multiplication of anti-colonial groups. As Howe notes in his analysis of anti-colonialism in Britain, the fractured network of groups taking an interest in colonial issues was somewhat absurd but reflected the fragmentation and factionalism of the left in Britain. Even where groups sought to be non-partisan in their ideological alignment, as was the case with the Africa Bureau, colonial issues captured the interest of an array of groups who advocated a variety of strategic approaches.[76] African political figures, moreover, had themselves been influenced by pan-Africanist networks in London even before plans for federation took shape in the early 1950s. Harry Nkumbula, president of the Northern Rhodesian African National Congress, had studied at the London School of Economics in the late 1940s where he came into contact with African activists connected with the West African Students Union and the pan-Africanist movement, including the future president of Ghana, Kwame Nkrumah.[77] These London networks were integral to the growth of organized African opposition to federation, as Nkumbula becomes one of a group of students who convened at the home of the doctor and future Malawian leader,

[73] Robert I. Rotberg, *The Rise of Nationalism in Central Africa: The Making of Malawi and Zambia, 1873–1964* (Cambridge, MA: Harvard University Press, 1965), 214–19.
[74] Ibid., 228; Rob Power, 'The African Dimension to the Anti-Federation Struggle, ca. 1950–53: "It Has United Us Far More Closely than Any Other Question Would Have Accomplished"', *Itinerario* 45, no. 2 (2021): 304–24.
[75] Collins, 'Decolonisation and the "Federal Moment"', 33.
[76] Howe, *Anticolonialism*, 199–200.
[77] Giacomo Macola, *Liberal Nationalism in Central Africa: A Biography of Harry Mwaanga Nkumbula* (London: Palgrave, 2010), 22.
   Giacomo Macola, 'Harry Mwaanga Nkumbula, UNIP and the Roots of Authoritarianism in Nationalist Zambia', in *One Zambia, Many Histories: Towards a History of Post-Colonial Zambia*, edited by Giacomo Macola, Jan-Bart Gewald, and Marja Hinfelaar (Leiden: Brill, 2008), 20.

Hastings Banda, to formulate a strategy of opposition to the plans for federation that had been announced by Welensky in 1949. The group drafted a memorandum deriding the confederation proposals as merely a disguised version of the long-standing plans for amalgamation that would subject all Africans in the region to the discriminatory policies of Southern Rhodesia.[78] Although its founders sought to provide clarity and direction in the organization of anti-colonialism in London, the Africa Bureau was thus an addition to an already-existing array of groups fractured along many lines of difference, perhaps the two most important being, first, the ideological split between the radical left and more moderate or non-partisan groups, and, second, the racial boundaries that divided pan-African networks from the (largely) white network of British anti-colonial groups.

What set the Africa Bureau apart was the determination of its Director to forge his own path through the complexities of metropolitan and African anti-colonial movements. At the heart of this was a focused advocacy for African political ambitions, coupled with a set of principles that prioritized means of action over specific ideological ends. Scott's engagement with opposition to the Central African Federation was a blend of the radical and the traditional – both in its everyday and theological sense as unwritten moral principle. It came in the form of a pledge of support for the deputation of chiefs from Nyasaland who visited Britain during the January 1953 conference at Carlton House in London, at which the British government confirmed its support for the Federation scheme. The Africa Bureau helped to organize meetings in London and a tour of provincial Britain for the delegates, including a tour of Westminster Abbey. Stopping at the memorial to David Livingstone, Scott recorded the moment in his autobiography as an extraordinary reminder of the nineteenth-century missionary's 'endurance and faith and passionate campaigning', which had brought the people of what would become Nyasaland 'to the Christian religion and the protection of the English Queen'.[79] This he contrasted with the apparent acquiescence, save for muted private expressions of concern, of British churches over the Central African Federation. For Scott, the issue hinged on the obligation to honour historical guarantees between traditional leaders, between the chiefs and the British Crown. Like his interactions with Herero leaders, Scott seems to have regarded chiefly authority in Nyasaland as a political reality rather than a creation of colonialism. Such views would appear at odds with the historiographical consensus that formed by the 1980s around the notion of a colonial 'invention of tradition' in which social customs and political lineage were created by colonial officials in the service of the doctrines of indirect rule.[80] More recent accounts have begun to suggest that traditions, customs and ethnic identities were not 'invented' as such, but a consequence of the constant reinterpretation and adaptation of historical social practices and political subjectivities by both African and European agents.[81]

---

[78] Rotberg, *The Rise of Nationalism*, 224. See also Miles Larmer, *Rethinking African Politics: A History of Opposition in Zambia* (London: Routledge, 2016).

[79] Scott, *A Time to Speak*, 276.

[80] Terence Ranger, 'The Invention of Tradition in Colonial Africa', in *The Invention of Tradition*, edited by E. Hobsbawm and Terence Ranger, 211–62 (Cambridge: Cambridge University Press, 1983); Leroy Vail, ed., *The Creation of Tribalism in Southern Africa* (London: James Currey, 1989).

[81] Thomas Spear, 'Neo-Traditionalism and the Limits of Invention in British Colonial Africa', *The Journal of African History* 44, no. 1 (2003): 3–27.

Viewed in this light, the chiefs' petition to Queen Elizabeth and Scott's reflections on the legacies of Livingstone were not atavistic reminders of a waning politics of imperial loyalism, but attempts to deploy notions of traditional political authority as a form of resistance. Such tactics had their limits nonetheless; on the advice of government ministers, the new monarch refused to meet the deputation.[82]

The discourse of moral duty was also important to the delegates from the Nyasaland African Congress. In the aftermath of the Carlton House conference, they argued that Federation would amount to domination by the settler nationalist policies of Southern Rhodesia, which they deemed little different from apartheid, and emphasized the 'moral obligation' that the British people had towards their country, which had willingly sought its protection. Underlying such carefully worded displays of apparent loyalism, however, were implicit threats. Without a significant settler population, and with widespread African opposition, Central African Federation would, they argued, need to be imposed on Nyasaland in ways that would leave little option other than organized resistance.[83] With anti-colonial violence in Kenya as a reference point, British commentators began to warn of the dangers if Britain forced African people 'in a situation which offers them no peaceful and constitutional way of expressing their grievances'.[84] These warnings, together with reports that African leaders had 'predicted bloodshed' in the wake of the Carlton House conference, suggested that a political crisis in central Africa might overshadow attempts to present a united and stable Commonwealth at the coronation of a new monarch in June 1953.[85]

With Nyasaland facing civil unrest, Scott saw an opportunity to demonstrate the power of non-violence in Africa. Without informing other members of the Africa Bureau executive, in April 1953 he flew to the capital of Nyasaland, Blantyre, fulfilling his pledge to support the delegation of chiefs who had visited Britain in January.[86] By the time of his arrival during Easter, both the Nyasaland Congress and the Council of Chiefs had begun to mobilize protest across the country; as he landed at Blantyre airport a combined meeting of the Council and Congress was underway and had agreed to establish a joint committee to organize a civil disobedience campaign along the lines of the Defiance Campaign in South Africa, including a tax boycott and withdrawal from government bodies. At a public meeting, Scott announced that he would advise the protest leaders on ways of internationalizing their campaign in Britain and at the United Nations.[87] While Power has credited Scott's presence with giving the local struggle an international dynamic, the arrival of the English priest in Blantyre might equally be defined as emblematic of the multiple geopolitical scales at with the politics of opposition played out. True to the aims of the Africa Bureau, Scott presented his actions in terms of mediation between events in Nyasaland and London. Writing an account of his journey to central Africa within weeks of the formal

[82] Scott, *A Time to Speak*, 275.
[83] 'Resolve to Resist in Nyasaland', *Times*, 17 February 1953, 'Nyasaland Chiefs Warn Lyttleton', *Observer*, 8 February 1953.
[84] 'Second Thoughts on Africa', *The Observer*, 15 March 1953.
[85] Rotberg, *The Rise of Nationalism*, 248.
[86] Ibid., 250.
[87] Joey Power, *Political Culture and Nationalism in Malawi: Building Kwacha* (Rochester, NY: University of Rochester Press, 2010), 65.

launch of the non-cooperation campaign in early May, he stated that the trip had been arranged in haste when news arrived in London of the meeting between the African Congress and the Council of Chiefs. Scott's visit was therefore promoted by a desire to talk directly to African leaders before taking action in the UK as legislation passed through Parliament.[88]

For Scott, the launch of the protest campaign was a further indication that African politics was undergoing a transformation, and the old practices 'of petition and deputation may not avail to secure justice'.[89] He viewed the non-cooperation movement as a sign of a new form of action that aligned with his own faith in Gandhian tactics of civil disobedience, although saw this as complementary to his proposals for petitions to the British Parliament and United Nations. He asserted publicly that he had made it explicit that his advice to the Congress and Council of Chiefs should not be taken as an alternative to their own plans for action in Nyasaland. In part this stemmed from a desire to repudiate claims that he had instigated the resistance campaign, but his advice also reflected his fear that the 'power and authority of the Chiefs' was under threat in a territory that had been regarded by many an epitome of the principles of 'trusteeship':

> For the first time in the history of Nyasaland a substantial number of Africans including some of the leading chiefs and the more educated people such as teachers and civil servants have come to regard the white population including even many of the missionaries as an alien and hostile people who came to their country with profession of peace in order to deceive them and prepare the way for treacherously handing their country over to people of their own kind in Rhodesia.[90]

Scott reported that he was confident that there were serious efforts to launch non-violent protest against colonial authorities, but this would only be maintained if there were signs of political reform, 'some recognition of the opinion and worth of the too often despised intelligentsia' and the formulation of political processes that would satisfy popular demands for change. Despite the deep feelings of discontent, he noted that leaders 'went out of their way to repudiate violence' at public meetings, which, he added, tended to be held on Sundays and planned a greater emphasis on religion than had been the case with the meetings attended by delegates in Britain earlier in the year.[91]

For Scott, faith in civil disobedience was entirely compatible with Christian belief.[92] But for church leaders in Nyasaland, his advocacy of non-violent protest and the campaign against the Central African Federation was highly dangerous. The paternalist and conservative Bishop of Nyasaland, Frank Thorne, challenged Scott and demanded to know whether he would share responsibility if the protests resulted in violence.[93] In

---

[88] Michael Scott, 'Visit to Central Africa', 31 May, 1953, BOD Astor Papers, MS 15363/202 1952–52.
[89] Ibid.
[90] Ibid.
[91] Ibid.
[92] Scott, *A Time to Speak*, 278–9.
[93] On Thorne, see Andrew Porter, 'Missions and Empire: An Overview, 1700–1914', in *Missions and Empire*, edited by Norman Etherington (Oxford: Oxford University Press, 2005), 101.

response, Scott argued that non-violent action could 'awake the social conscience' and – unlike other forms of militant action – was compatible both with the Christian doctrine of forgiveness and able to promote the 'dignity and worth of the human person'.[94] Non-violent civil disobedience, it seemed, was in accord with both the traditional teachings of Western religion and the universal principles of the Declaration of Human rights. Scott also argued that one form of resistance to the state would necessarily lead to another: 'to prefer to accept the penalty of an unjust law rather than acquiesce in the injustice of its enforcement', he declared, was 'not an invitation to violence'.[95] In his response to Thorne, Scott implied that it was possible to compartmentalize different means of protest, even if they served the same outcome. But Scott accepted that he would be responsible for any violence insofar as he had failed in his attempts to alter British policy and thus prevent the primary injustice of federation. In somewhat dramatic terms, he concluded that Thorne's call to obey the decision of Parliament to create a federation was an 'authoritarian doctrine surely not far removed from the one which almost destroyed Europe'.[96]

Following the launch of the non-cooperation movement at the start of May, many chiefs undertook public actions in support of the campaign, including the paramount of the Chewa people, Chief Mwase, who declared that he had spurned an invitation to attend the coronation of Queen Elizabeth in June 1953.[97] The protests by chiefs constituted a breakdown of the system of indirect rule that had formed the defining doctrine of British colonial administration in Nyasaland and across Africa. A number of chiefs submitted their resignation, while others alleged to be in favour of Central African Federation lost popular support. But perhaps the most dramatic episode involved the Ngoni paramount Philip Gomani, who was deposed after refusing to rescind his order to support the Council's protest campaign.[98] Scott was staying at Gomani's residence when the chief was ordered to leave the district, and witnessed the attempt by police to enforce his removal:

> Tear gas was thrown amongst the crowd, who did not know what it was, and believed it to be poisonous. They scattered and the chief was hustled into the car and driven away. I followed on foot and found that it had been stopped some way down the road, and that about ten Africans were pushing it in the opposite direction ... then someone opened the car doors, and the chief was carried away on their shoulders.[99]

Gomani, along with his two sons and Scott, attempted to escape across the border to Mozambique but were quickly placed under arrest by the Portuguese authorities and returned to Nyasaland. Gomani's sons were subsequently tried for assault and Phillip

---

[94] 'Copy of Note by Rev. Michael Scott' [n.d 1953] BOD Astor Papers, MS 15363/202 1952–52.
[95] Ibid.
[96] Ibid.
[97] Power, *Political Culture and Nationalism*, 66.
[98] Ibid., 67–8.
[99] Scott, *A Time to Speak*, 281.

Gomani was banished from Ncheu and died a year later in the town of Cholo (Thyolo). Scott was declared a 'prohibited immigrant' and deported at the end of May.[100]

The events in Nyasaland in 1953 provide a significant example of the ways in which African politics was inflected with Gandhian practices of resistance, shaping emergent African nationalist movements and presenting a challenge to metropolitan sympathizers. Although he represented a minority voice, in both British and settler opinion, Scott blended militant pacifism with an older humanitarian ethos and, through his individual effort, became an influential point of reference for nascent solidarity movements. His efforts bridged different strands of political action in a transnational campaign that connected British and African political movements in novel ways. The protests over Federation that began in Nyasaland in 1953 would reshape colonial politics in the territory; three years later a younger group of Congress leaders would obtain a potent public platform following election to a new legislative council. The African protests – and the reaction of colonial authorities – upset the notion that 'partnership' was a genuine vision of multi-racialism, let alone democracy, within the plan for Federation. It was not only Africans that could see that partnership was a 'hollow creed'.[101] Scott's actions in 1953 linked British movements with African counterparts and contributed to the reshaping of debate around British sympathy, solidarity and support for African nationalist movements in the mid-1950s. During this period, through the efforts of high-profile campaigners, including Scott, those in Britain with interests in Africa – and eventually many who had not previously paid close attention to the continent – began to move from attitudes shaped by 'development imperialism' to those defined by solidarity.

The most prominent British campaigner on African issues was the Labour MP Fenner Brockway, one of those whom Scott regarded with suspicion as he sought to establish a new, non-partisan organization after 1950. Brockway came from a missionary family, had a background in radical nonconformism and, like Scott's transatlantic supporters in the Fellowship of Reconciliation, had been imprisoned as a conscientious objector, albeit during the First rather than the Second World War. He became an Independent Labour Party MP in the late 1920s before joining the Labour Party in the late 1940s. Highly sympathetic to nationalist leaders in Asia and Africa, his opposition driven to colonialism was driven by moral distaste rather than strong ideological conviction, despite his socialist views.[102] In the early 1950s, Brockway began to play close attention to the developing crisis in Kenya, developing contacts with the Kenya African Union leader Jomo Kenyatta and its representatives in Britain, Mbiyu Koinange and Joseph Murumbi. Through COPAI, Brockway began to organize support for the nationalist movement, drawing a distinction between organized groups such as the KAU and the violent resistance associated with the so-called 'Mau Mau'.[103] Both Brockway and Scott began to highlight claims that Kenyans were subject to arbitrary arrest and brutal

---

[100] Ibid., 280–2, see also Power, *Political Culture and Nationalism*, 67–8.
[101] Rotberg, *The Rise of Nationalism*, 253, 270.
[102] Howe, *Anticolonialism*, 170–3.
[103] Caroline Elkins, *Britain's Gulag: The Brutal End of Empire in Kenya* (London: Jonathan Cape, 2005), 98–100.

treatment at the hands of the colonial authorities following the imposition of a State of Emergency in October 1952.[104]

In 1954, Brockway took a leading role in the formation of another new organization, the Movement for Colonial Freedom, which began to coordinate the anti-colonial activities of the Labour left in Parliament, as well as in constituency groups and trades unions; it represented a left counterpart to the nominally non-political but effectively left-liberal Africa Bureau.[105] Elkins suggests that Scott and Brockway's efforts represented a redirection of the efforts British non-governmental organizations, away from seeking influence within government to public efforts to 'expose the injustice of colonialism' and campaign for independence.[106] Similarly, recent work on the responses of international relief organizations such as the Red Cross to the violence in Kenya highlights the fundamental challenges posed by the violence in Kenya to the values and beliefs of humanitarian agents.[107] Moreover, as Milford has shown, activists in Britain were part of a wider transnational network that integrated, as much as mediated between, movements in Europe, Africa and Asia. The career of Kenyan activist Joseph Murumbi in Europe in Asia during the 1950s and the regional identities fostered by the work of the Nairobi-based Anti-Federation League suggest that these campaigns cannot be fully understood as interactions between African nationalists and increasingly strident Western sympathizers, but as part of a wider history of decolonization and internationalism.[108] These recent historiographical interventions suggest the significance of anti-colonial networks is found in a global history of decolonization, rather than an account of interactions between national movements, although for contemporaries, the emphasis placed by Scott and Brockway on the legitimacy of nationalist calls for independence represented a significant shift of principles. While experiments in federalism remain worthy of closer attention, Scott's actions in Nyasaland in 1953 were undeniably in the service of national self-determination.[109]

Scott's efforts did therefore internationalize local opposition to federation, just as Brockway and others had begun to demonstrate that colonialism in Kenya was at odds with an emerging universal standard of human rights.[110] But it also represented a personal step, his first attempt to take the initiative in developing international solidarity for an African campaign of non-violent civil disobedience. Yates and Chester describe Scott's foray into the politics of Federation as a 'means of expression' for his activist urges, which might otherwise have been tethered to the bureaucratic and

---

[104] Howe, *Anticolonialism*, 206.
[105] Goldsworthy, *Colonial Issues*, 276–8; Howe, *Anticolonialism*, 231–7.
[106] Elkins, *Britain's Gulag*, 99.
[107] Yolana Pringle, 'Humanitarianism, Race and Denial: The International Committee of the Red Cross and Kenya's Mau Mau Rebellion, 1952–60', *History Workshop Journal* 84 (October 2017): 89–107.
[108] Ismay Milford, 'Federation, Partnership, and the Chronologies of Space in 1950s East and Central Africa', *The Historical Journal* 63, no. 5 (2020): 1325–48; Ismay Milford and Gerard McCann, 'African Internationalisms and the Erstwhile Trajectories of Kenyan Community Development: Joseph Murumbi's 1950s', *Journal of Contemporary History* 57, no. 1 (2021): 3–23.
[109] On federalism see Michael Collins, 'Decolonisation and the "Federal Moment"', *Diplomacy & Statecraft* 24, no. 1 (2013): 21–40.
[110] See Klose, *Human Rights in the Shadow of Colonial Violence*.

organizational tasks of the Africa Bureau.[111] This is a fair assessment, but his actions were arguably much more than an assertion of an individual impulse. The story of Scott's expulsion from central Africa emphasizes his personal determination to work for the agendas of African leaders at the expense of the establishment circles within which the Bureau executive was drawn. Scott and the Africa Bureau were rooted in the generational and social cultures against which younger activists would soon rebel, but in his willingness to follow a vocation directed by the principles of non-violence and an emotional engagement with political injustice, Scott's efforts had created cracks in the facade of moderate metropolitan opinion.

Anti-colonialism, civil rights and African nationalism

After Rustin's resignation from the Fellowship of Reconciliation in early 1953, he suggested that Bill Sutherland take his place working for the *West African Pilot* in Nigeria. He travelled to London and was introduced to the influential pan-Africanist organizer George Padmore by Hugh Brock, editor of *Peace News*. When Azikiwe arrived in Britain for the conference to plan a new constitution for Nigeria in August 1953, Sutherland was confirmed as Rustin's replacement on the *West African Pilot*.[112] Sutherland recalled that his vision of African social and political progress diverged from that of Padmore, whose approach to colonialism was shaped by Marxist analysis, but more particularly to 'uncomplicate British imperialism', emphasize its exploitative and racialized dynamics and render it into something that could be resisted.[113] Sutherland, in contrast, viewed African struggles for freedom from an idealized vision of African spirituality and science that 'would contribute a new dimension of human warmth'.[114] Nevertheless, Padmore introduced Sutherland into pan-African circles in London as he awaited permission to travel to west Africa. This never came, but drawing on Padmore's support as well, Sutherland instead moved to the Gold Coast, where he would stay until the end of the decade. In early 1954, supported by a subsistence grant from the American Committee on Africa, Sutherland became involved with education projects in the eastern region of the country and married Efua Morgue, with whom Sutherland founded a school in Tsito that combined academic studies with practical work experience in local government agencies.[115] When they met, Morgue was working as a teacher in Achimota, while beginning to develop a career as a writer; following Ghanaian independence in 1957 she would go on to become a leading writer and dramatist and a pioneering advocate for the arts in Ghana.[116] By that time, their

---

[111] Yates and Chester, *The Troublemaker*, 130.
[112] Sutherland and Meyer, *Guns and Gandhi*, 6–7.
[113] L. James, *George Padmore and Decolonization from Below: Pan-Africanism, the Cold War, and the End of Empire* (London: Palgrave, 2014), 196.
[114] Ibid.
[115] Ibid., 22–3.
[116] James Gibbs, *Nkyin-Kyin: Essays on the Ghanaian Theatre* (Amsterdam: Brill, 2009), 89–125; Anne V. Adams and Esi Sutherland-Addy, *The Legacy of Efua Sutherland: Pan-African Cultural Activism* (Banbury: Ayebia Clarke, 2007).

marriage had ended, and Bill had left Tsito to work as a private secretary to Komla Gbedemah, one of the three most powerful figures in the Gold Coast Convention Peoples' Party who became Finance Minister following independence.[117]

Despite the interconnections between British and US anti-colonial activists evident in Sutherland's journey from New York to Accra, the transnational dynamics of anti-colonialism were also shaped by transatlantic differences in the organization and focus of movements whose concerns included issues of race and empire. There were clear contrasts between British and US anti-colonialism, not least the direct political engagement with Africa that came with Britain's status as a colonial power. Scott conceived of development as 'Britain's task in Africa', threatened by policies of racial domination, and believed that support for nationalist claims was a responsibility. American activists, meanwhile, viewed the politics of colonialism in the context of worldwide racial tensions that linked to their own national concerns around segregation and racial justice. When it was formed in 1952, Americans for South African Resistance (AFSAR) drew together an alliance of religious, pacifist and socialist groups that reflected the 'natural community' not only of Houser but of many others within the nascent anti-colonial and pacifist network including Sutherland, Rustin and Muste.[118] But perhaps the most significant dimension of US support for the Defiance Campaign – and one that reflected a key difference between US and British networks – was its role in connecting between anti-colonial and civil rights movements. The launch of AFSAR took place in the Abyssinian Baptist Church in Harlem, followed by a motorcade from Harlem to the South African Consulate. But the solidarity between African American activists and multi-racial civil rights groups represented by the public support for the Defiance Campaign masked real fractures that had emerged among familiar ideological lines. On the same day that AFSAR held its opening meeting, the Council for African Affairs (CAA), led by more radical figures on the left including Paul Robeson and W. E. B. Du Bois, held a rally in Harlem and a picket of the South African consulate; in subsequent weeks, the CAA launched a petition and held a conference of African American church and trade union leaders, civil rights and peace activists.[119]

In 1953, as Sutherland travelled to Africa and Scott threw himself into the opposition to Federation, key organizers of Americans for South African Resistance formed a new organization, the American Committee on Africa. (ACOA)[120] This new venture would become the centre of Houser's activist career and a key node in US anti-apartheid networks. Drawing together the threads of pacifist activism leading from the Congress of Racial Equality, missionaries and other 'liberal Africanists', the American Committee might be regarded as an expression of the conscience of America as the country's economic ties and political engagement with Africa expanded from the late 1950s.[121] An alternative narrative would, however, suggest that the formation of the ACOA represented the point at which the radical anti-colonial and civil rights ideals

---

[117] Gibbs, *Nkin-Kyin*, 98.
[118] Minter, et al., *No Easy Victories*, 64.
[119] Njubi Nesbitt, *Race for Sanctions*, 19–20.
[120] Minter, et al., *No Easy Victories*, 60.
[121] Donald R. Culverson, *Contesting Apartheid: U.S. Activism, 1960–1987* (Boulder, CO: Westview, 1999), 30.

of the 1940s, espoused by prominent individuals connected with the CAA including Robeson, W. E. B. du Bois and Alphaeus Hunton, was superseded by a politics of race shaped by Cold War ideological struggles. Whereas in the 1940s, civil rights campaigners articulated a strong critique of US foreign policy and cast civil rights as part of a wider movement of racial solidarity, the 1950s saw the emergence of anti-Communist forms of anti-colonialism that divided US civil rights from worldwide movements against colonialism.[122] The CAA faced intense legal and financial pressures from US government agencies, targeting Hunton and Robeson for their Communist links until the Committee shut itself down in mid-1955. Bracketed with the equally radical Civil Rights Congress, the decline of the CAA was emblematic of the degree to which Cold War anxieties redefined liberalism in ways that were antagonistic with forms of radical socialism with which it seemed comfortable in the 1940s.[123] Similar pressures ushered long-standing movements for racial equality such as the National Association for the Advancement of Colored People, to retreat from its efforts to cast African American claims within a broader framework of human rights and refocus on narrower definitions of civil rights.[124] It remains possible to state that the US 'civil rights movement and what might be called the international civil rights movement of anti-colonialism ran on parallel tracks', but these tracks might be characterized as narrow gauge routes to different destinations.[125]

In Britain, activist organizations tended to regard colonialism in Africa and racism in Britain as separate campaigning issues, even though their connections were acknowledged. John Collins, the Canon of St Paul's whose offices became a hub for anti-apartheid and anti-nuclear activities in the late 1950s, noted in his autobiography that the political controversy around Seretse Khama's marriage to a white woman reflected British prejudices as well as the iniquities of colonial politics.[126] But the deeper social frictions and prejudice that were revealed in the treatment of Khama by the British establishment did not become a focus for organizations such as the Africa Bureau, which was able to maintain a specialist interest in racial issues overseas even while Britain's expanding Black communities began to face de facto segregation and colour bars.[127] Howe has suggested that anti-colonial activists in Britain promoted the idea that 'domestic race relations were ... presented as a colonial question', just as colonial issues such as the Central African Federation were becoming, as Schwarz has argued,

[122] Penny M. Von Eschen, *Race against Empire: Black Americans and Anticolonialism, 1937–1957* (Ithaca, NY: Cornell University Press, 1997), 2–3; see also Njubi Nesbitt, *Race for Sanctions*.
[123] Brenda Gayle Plummer, *Rising Wind: Black Americans and U.S. Foreign Affairs, 1935–1960* (Chapel Hill: University of North Carolina Press, 1996), 202–3; 213.
[124] Carol Anderson, *Eyes off the Prize: The United Nations and the African American Struggle for Human Rights, 1944–1955* (Cambridge and New York: Cambridge University Press, 2003).
[125] Thomas Borstelmann, *The Cold War and the Color Line: American Race Relations in the Global Arena* (Cambridge, MA: Harvard University Press, 2001), 46.
[126] Lewis John Collins, *Faith under Fire* (London: Frewin, 1966), 185–6.
[127] Susan Williams, *Colour Bar: The Triumph of Seretse Khama and His Nation* (London: Penguin, 2007); See also Chris Waters, '"Dark Strangers" in Our Midst: Discourses of Race and Nation in Britain, 1947–1963', *Journal of British Studies* 36, no. 2 (1997): 207–38; Peter Fryer, *Staying Power: The History of Black People in Britain* (London: Pluto Press, 1984).

a point of reference for 'the ideological recasting of the political right'.[128] British anti-colonial and anti-apartheid groups largely maintained a political distance between their concerns and domestic racial tensions and injustices, while decolonization provided a stimulus to new strands of Conservative thinking to emerge, centred on anti-immigration and racial whiteness.

In contrast to their aim to mediate between African nationalists and the British public, anti-colonial groups struggled to build any form of multi-racial diversity within their own organizations. By the early 1960s, the lack of African representation in the MCF was cited as a genuine failing on the part of the organization. In his report on the 1961 conference, for example, Hilary Fenton, of the MCF group in Merseyside, noted regretfully that 'it was surprising and rather discouraging to find so few coloured people at the conference'. It seemed, he felt, at odds with the assumption that 'the role of the MCF is to fight with Africans against colonialism, but this would hardly have been apparent to an outside observer'. Fenton doubted that he would have known anything of the movement's efforts to assist the escape of the Pan-Africanist Congress leader Philip Kgosana from South Africa in 1960 if he had not attended the conference in person. This was, Fenton suggested, 'exactly the sort of activity which will convince people, especially Africans in provincial centres, that MCF is actively helping their countrymen, not just passing resolutions'.[129] And yet, from the mid-1960s, the MCF (in contrast to the newly formed Anti-Apartheid Movement) readily participated in campaigns linking the issues of colonialism with domestic racial injustice. This, perhaps, reflected the extent to which the MCF mirrored the political agenda of its figurehead, Fenner Brockway, who persevered for years with the promotion of a Parliamentary Bill that would make racial discrimination an offence. Fenton's attitude in Merseyside thus appeared to chime with the agenda of the national body, and, in November 1961, John Eber wrote asking whether the Area Council would take an active role in the campaign against the Commonwealth Immigration Bill. Eber suggested that Fenton might work on plans that drew on the precedent of the Willesden Area Council, which had successfully lobbied for the formation of an International Friendship Council that would bring together local political parties, religious leaders and immigrant communities.[130]

Anti-colonial campaigners in the mid-1950s did not predict that decolonization would re-frame the politics of race in Britain in little more than a decade, but the disconnect between the struggle to achieve African freedom and racial justice in a multi-cultural Britain was in a real sense an unintended consequence of efforts to raise public sympathy for nationalist movements in the 1950s. Perhaps the clearest example of this can be seen in organized anti-apartheid campaigns that began to develop in the latter half of the 1950s, before coalescing into a formal Anti-Apartheid Movement in the following decade. The AAM, with close ties to South African political

---

[128] Howe, *Anticolonialism*, 325; Bill Schwarz, *The White Man's World* (Oxford: Oxford University Press, 2011), 342.

[129] Hilary Fenton, 'Notes on Annual Conference, 1961', Special Collections, School of Oriental and African Studies, London (SOAS) Papers of the Movement for Colonial Freedom MCF Box 28, AC 53, Merseyside Area Council, 1959–63.

[130] Eber to Fenton, 29 November 1961, SOAS MCF Box 28 AC 53 Merseyside Area Council 1959–63.

organizations, especially the African National Congress, openly avoided engagement with the domestic politics of race, even though apartheid was a fundamental issue of concern for Black community organizers and groups.[131] In both Britain and the United States, then, anti-colonialism and domestic anti-racism became overlapping, but in many respects disconnected ways of talking about rights and justice in the 1950s.

Racial identities, and the (often unspoken) conceptualization of whiteness that accompanied imperialism and colonialism, have begun to be understood as affective responses to encounters with African and Asian others. As Lake and Richards put it in their account of the 'Global Colour Line', notions of whiteness were built on 'the transnational circulation of emotions and ideas, people and publications, racial knowledge and technologies that animated white men's countries and their strategies of exclusion, deportation and segregation'.[132] At the same time, pan-African racial solidarity was an emotional, as much as an ideological, intellectual and cultural response to the forms of racial exclusion that structured the global experience of empire and colonialism.

Anti-colonial activism reflected these affective affinities, but in tangled ways which generally tended to be related to political and ideological divisions between liberalism, nationalism and Communism. These came together in the wave of enthusiasm that met the independence of Ghana in March 1957. By the end of the year, the pan-Africanist George Padmore settled in Accra to set up, at Nkrumah's invitation, the Bureau of African Affairs, which provided support for leaders of independence movements and collaborated with overseas organizations including the Africa Bureau.[133] Under Padmore's leadership, the Bureau of African Affairs sought to refocus efforts to forge pan-African unity and to internationalize national struggles for independence. Padmore envisioned the Ghanaian state, with Nkrumah at its centre, as a platform to build a new form of African socialism, although economic and trade policies would initially look towards the West.[134] The celebrations to mark Ghanaian independence in 1957 thus drew together a cross section of groups and individuals engaged with the process of decolonization process; it could be cast as a victory for constitutionalism, nationalism, passive resistance, pan-Africanism and left and liberal anti-colonial groups. Pacifists too saw Nkrumah and Ghana as a beacon. The philosophy of Positive Action, which had provided a symbolic and practical foundation for the anti-colonial protests of the Congress People's Party in the early 1950s, attracted activists such as Sutherland and inspired pacifist leaders such as Muste to encourage peace movements to pay greater attention to nationalist struggles in Africa. For pacifists in the United States, the cause of African liberation aligned principles of civil and democratic freedoms with the potential to create a new 'redemptive force' in a world increasingly divided by Cold War ideologies.[135] But nationalism would prove to be an ambiguous partner.

---

[131] Elizabeth Williams, *The Politics of Race in Britain and South Africa: Black British Solidarity and the Anti-Apartheid Struggle* (London: I.B. Tauris, 2012).
[132] Marilyn Lake and Henry Reynolds, *Drawing the Global Colour Line: White Men's Countries and the International Challenge of Racial Equality* (Cambridge: Cambridge University Press, 2011), 4.
[133] James, *George Padmore and Decolonization from Below*, 169-70.
[134] Manning Marable, *W. E. B. Du Bois: Black Radical Democrat* (London: Taylor & Francis Group, 1987), 208.
[135] Danielson, *American Gandhi*, 262.

4

Anti-colonialism and the bomb

This chapter outlines the alignment between peace and anti-colonial activism around the issue of nuclear disarmament. If the history of peace activism in the 1950s and 1960s was underpinned by a single emotion, it would be fear. In her cultural history of that emotion, Joanna Bourke describes the ways in which the threat of nuclear apocalypse added layers of dread and uncertainty to long-standing fears surrounding warfare. The development of atomic weapons created a new landscape of psychological anxiety as humans wrestled with the fact that their existence as a species had become contingent on politics. Moreover, military power had become 'ultimately more conclusive that those of God'.[1] From the early 1950s, moreover, Cold War and anti-colonial rhetoric converged within a language of 'peace' and condemnation of Western militarism, embodied by nuclear weapons.[2] The critical moment came, perhaps, with the explosion of a hydrogen bomb by the United States, which accelerated the pace of nuclear weapons development but more importantly shifted the power of atomic weapons from devastating force to one that had apocalyptic potential. In one prominent incident in 1954, the crew of the Japanese fishing boat, the *Lucky Dragon*, were exposed to radioactive material from US hydrogen bomb tests in the Pacific and returned to Japan suffering from radiation sickness, causing in the death of one crew member some months later.[3] The incident sparked widespread public debate and the rapid growth of anti-nuclear protests in Japan, intensified global fears of radioactive fallout and prompted cultural fascination with disaster, illustrated by the Japanese film *Gojira* (*Godzilla*) released in the same year.[4] The advent of the nuclear arms race and the first tests of the hydrogen bomb was the critical catalyst for the transformation of social and cultural responses to nuclear weapons and the launch of vigorous anti-nuclear weapons movements around the world.[5]

---

[1] Joanna Bourke, *Fear: A Cultural History* (London: Virago, 2006), 285.
[2] On Afro-Asian debates around western militarism in the early 1950s, see R. Leow, 'A Missing Peace: The Asia-Pacific Peace Conference in Beijing, 1952 and the Emotional Making of Third World Internationalism', *Journal of World History* 30, no. 1–2 (2019): 21–53.
[3] Wittner, *Resisting the Bomb*, 2, 8.
[4] Ibid., 8–11; Kerry Brougher, 'Art and Nuclear Culture', *Bulletin of the Atomic Scientists*, November 2013.
[5] M. Grant, *After the Bomb: Civil Defence and Nuclear War in Britain, 1945–68* (London: Palgrave Macmillan UK, 2009). Jonathan Hogg, *British Nuclear Culture: Official and Unofficial Narratives in the Long 20th Century* (London: Bloomsbury Publishing, 2016); Jonathan Hogg and Kate Brown, 'Introduction: Social and Cultural Histories of British Nuclear Mobilisation since 1945',

Very often, the new anti-nuclear weapons organizations were formed by individuals with a set of political and moral values that overlapped with those of anti-colonial movements. The principles of moral protest, concerns for the nascent idea of human rights, racial equality and the universal norm of democratic representation meant that movements, reflected a similar social profile. These also united 'old movements', such as those concerned with labour and class interests, as well as older forms of moral politics, drawing as we have seen in previous chapters, on the legacies of humanitarianism. As discussed in the first two chapters, campaigns in the United States against racial injustice had drawn on pacifist forms of direct action since the 1940s, and by the mid-1950s many of the key figures from these earlier campaigns had begun to engage directly in the politics of anti-colonialism. In Britain, anti-colonial movements had similar connections to a broader peace movement, through prominent individuals such as Fenner Brockway and, of course, Michael Scott. In the latter part of the decade, the emergence of direct-action-oriented movements for nuclear disarmament began to claim the attention of activists on both sides of the Atlantic, multiplying the connections between peace and anti-colonial movements.

The chapter centres on the development of protest against the French nuclear weapons programme, following the announcement of plans to test an atomic bomb in the Sahara. The case study is significant insofar as it represented the first time that the movements against nuclear weapons and colonialism intersected and was the first attempt to mobilize direct action around disarmament on the continent of Africa. The Sahara protest represents a tangible connection between the disarmament movement and the politics of decolonization but, as will be further discussed in the next chapter, also illustrated the frictions between advocates of peace and movements for African liberation. On one level, both disarmament campaigners and African nationalists had begun to recognize ways in which both the nuclear threat and imperialism involved the entanglement of state defence agencies and corporate business that Eisenhower would distil into the concept of the 'military-industrial complex' in 1961.[6] But the two also diverged in significant ways, some of which began to be revealed in the attempt to forge a connection between transnational disarmament movements and pan-Africanist networks in the late 1950s.

Peace, anti-colonialism and the emerging disarmament movement in Britain

In early 1959, colonial issues were prominent in the pages of *Peace News*, the pre-eminent journal of the British peace movement. Under the editorial leadership of

---

Contemporary British History 33, no. 2 (2019): 161–9; Jonathan Hogg and Christoph Laucht, 'Introduction: British Nuclear Culture', *The British Journal for the History of Science* 45, no. 4 (2012): 479–93.

[6] Dwight D. Eisenhower, 'Military-Industrial Complex Speech', *Yale Law School*, Avalon Project, 1961, https://avalon.law.yale.edu/20th_century/eisenhower001.asp, Accessed 27 February 2023. See also Petra Goedde, *The Politics of Peace: A Global Cold War History* (New York: Oxford University Press, 2019), 59.

Hugh Brock from 1955, *Peace News* had expanded its coverage of African and Asian affairs, which included a regular column by Fenner Brockway expressing radical support for nationalist movements as well as condemnation of authoritarian actions on the part of British and colonial forces, particularly in Kenya. Its readers were provided with reports on Kwame Nkrumah's speech to the All-African People's Congress, as well as a more critical perspective on the meeting from the American Quaker Arlo Tatum, highlighting the differences between Ghanaian and Nigerian positions on African unity.[7] Some reports suggest a political naivety such as an enthusiastic profile of Fidel Castro as 'Cuba's Robin Hood', who Brockway defined as 'an ascetic, [and] devout Roman Catholic' with 'no political ambitions'.[8] The activities of Michael Scott were a regular feature, including a profile from 'Phyz' in early February:

> A visit to New York to plead the African cause at the United Nations, promptly followed by the All-Africa People's Conference in Ghana. Less than 48 hours after returning to England he's in jail for obstructing the building of a missile base. Nine days in prison over Christmas before a hectic series of public meetings, articles and letters for the Press, TV interviews and debates, committee meetings, discussion and answering a stack of personal correspondence. Then another 14 days in jail to prepare for the next round of lectures, university debates, interviews and TV. Somehow, despite all this, he's full-time Director of the Africa Bureau! And, of course, the 'phone never stops ringing. A parson's work depends on the size of his parish.'[9]

The report described the publicity that had surrounded the sit-in led by the Direct Action Committee Against Nuclear War (DAC) protesting the construction of a base for US Thor intermediate-range ballistic missiles at Swaffham in Norfolk that had taken place in December 1958. Scott had joined the protest immediately after his return from Accra and, along with DAC organizers Michael Randle, Pat Arrowsmith and April Carter, the second prison spell resulted from his refusal to agree not to disturb the peace in future. The Swaffham protest represented both a new phase in Scott's activism and an intensification of public attention on a burgeoning movement against nuclear weapons that had been gathering pace in Britain since 1957. Reports of Swaffham protestors embarking on hunger strike in Norwich jail and Scott's arrest for refusing to 'keep the peace' featured in national newspapers throughout January 1959.[10] In a lengthy opinion column in *The Observer*, Scott evoked English traditions of freedom, declaring that the protestors 'would rather forgoe our liberty by deliberate choice than be party to a course which we believe to be fundamentally wrong'. He went on to describe the good-humoured interactions between the police and protestors,

---

[7] 'Each Territory Must Choose', *Peace News*, 9 January 1959, 3; 'Another Look at the All-Africa Peoples Conference', *Peace News*, 16 January, 1959, 1. Both Homer Jack and George Houser responded in letters published in *Peace News*, 13 February 1959, 5.
[8] 'Towards Democracy with Cuba's Robin Hood', *Peace News*, 9 January 1959, 7.
[9] 'At the House', *Peace News*, 6 February 1959, 3.
[10] 'Rocket Men on Hunger Strike', *Daily Mail*, 7 January 1959, 'Atom Protest Parson Arrested in His Office', *Daily Mail*, 9 January 1959, 'First Swaffham Arrests – The Rev. M. Scott', *Guardian*, 9 January 1959.

who represented a cross section of ordinary citizens ('even if some of them were vegetarians'). In all, a very polite British protest.[11]

Scott's account perhaps underplayed the tensions that were emerging with the advent of anti-nuclear weapons protest. On a personal level, Scott's involvement with passive resistance in Britain seemed a natural extension of his advocacy of similar protests in Africa, but they also conflicted with the views of others involved with the Africa Bureau, including both Astor and Hemingford who opposed to anti-nuclear weapons campaign. From 1958 through to 1962, Scott would nevertheless balance anti-colonial and anti-nuclear activism, insisting that his association in the latter was purely in a personal capacity.[12] The involvement of Scott in the protests nevertheless reflected the degree of interconnection between the new anti-nuclear weapons movement, older peace campaigns and anti-colonial protest. The tensions within the Africa Bureau were also replicated in the wider movement in Britain and in similar developments in the United States.

Following the first US hydrogen bomb test in the Pacific in 1954, leading public figures began to articulate concerns around the acceleration of nuclear weapons programmes, although public opinion (outside Japan) tended to oppose any form of disarmament. In the aftermath of the Bikini Atoll test in March 1954, Lewis Mumford wrote to the *New York Times* expressing his deep fear of the implications of 'the perfection of scientific weapons of total destruction and extermination'.[13] Instead of the secretive development of such weapons, Mumford – in terms that resonated with Scott's activist credo – called for pause, reflection and open dialogue between peoples, 'in the faith that love begets love'.[14] Significantly, as Wittner notes, Mumford's intervention recommended a halt to the further development of nuclear weapons.[15] Even before the Bikini test, radical pacifists in Britain had begun to call for a halt to the development of nuclear weapons; a statement on disarmament was included in the 'Operation Gandhi' campaign announced by *Peace News* editor Hugh Brock in 1951.[16] In the aftermath of the H-Bomb tests of 1954, though, calls for disarmament became more widespread, articulated by Labour MPs including Fenner Brockway who launched a Hydrogen Bomb National Campaign, supported by high-profile Christian activists including the Reverend Donald Soper and Canon John Collins. The following year, the philosopher Bertrand Russell published a joint statement with the physicist Albert Einstein warning of the danger that nuclear war would lead to human extinction. Their intervention was the catalyst for the Pugwash Conferences, bringing together scientists across Cold War divides, a form of international conferencing that paralleled but did not overlap, similar efforts within networks of Afro-Asian anti-colonial solidarity and pacifist internationalism.[17] In January 1957, Albert Schweitzer

[11] Scott, 'Our Aims at Swaffham', *The Observer*, 11 January 1959.
[12] Yates and Chester, *The Troublemaker*, 200–1.
[13] *New York Times*, 28 March 1954, 10.
[14] Ibid.
[15] Wittner, *Resisting the Bomb*, 10.
[16] The campaign had much broader and ambitious objectives, including Britain's withdrawal from NATO and the demobilization of the armed services, see Scalmer, *Gandhi and the West*, 138–44.
[17] A. Kraft and C. Sachse (eds.), *Science, (Anti-)Communism and Diplomacy: The Pugwash Conferences on Science and World Affairs in the Early Cold War* (Leiden: Brill, 2020).

broadcast a 'Declaration of Conscience' calling for an end to nuclear tests.[18] The latter seemed particularly significant, gaining public attention across the globe, its emphasis on nuclear tests and the power of public opinion struck a chord in many countries, with the exception of the United States.[19] But even there, with its echoes of Margaret Chase Smith's evocation of basic rights in the face of McCarthyite anti-Communism, the influence of Schweitzer's message might be seen in the 'Declaration of Conscience' on South Africa organized by the American Committee on Africa in December 1957.

In Britain, the hydrogen bomb test planned for May 1957 had intensified public condemnation of atomic weapons. In many accounts, the most powerful came from the novelist and playwright J.B. Priestley in an essay in the New Statesman in November 1957, which implored the British people to reject nuclear weapons and break the enchantment that had set 'industrial civilisation . . . hell-bent on murdering itself'.[20] Priestley's call invigorated public debate in Britain and inspired discussions that led to the formation of the Campaign for Nuclear Disarmament (CND) in the following year.[21] By the end of the decade, CND had become the largest anti-nuclear weapons movement in Western Europe. The connections between disarmament and anti-colonial movements were apparent from the outset, with Canon John Collins becoming the Chair of CND while his offices in Amen Court became a hub for meetings that regularly rotated between colonial and nuclear issues, often with many of the same personnel in the room.[22] It was not CND, though, that founded the most prominent British anti-nuclear protest event, but the DAC, formed in late 1957 by supporters of the Quaker pacifist Harold Steele, who had attempted to sail into the British atomic test zone near Kiribati in the Pacific.[23] In early 1958, the DAC announced plans for a march from London to the British atomic weapons research establishment at Aldermaston.[24] The march, also backed by CND, attracted thousands of participants and became an annual centrepiece of the British anti-nuclear weapons movement. A key figure at this first Aldermaston march, Scott also led delegations to the British prime minister calling for an end to the nuclear weapons programme. Through these activities, he met younger and radical activists associated with the DAC, including Randle and Carter, and the experience of working alongside them appeared to reinvigorate his activist energies. He would continue to undertake his annual pilgrimages to the UN in New York and maintain his involvement with the more formal activism of the Africa Bureau, but over the next five years, campaigns and protests campaigning alongside Randle and others connected with the DAC would be central to his political activism.[25]

Another prominent figure at the first Aldermaston march was Bayard Rustin. After his imprisonment and resignation from the FOR, Bayard Rustin had begun to

---

[18] Wittner, *Resisting the Bomb*, 5–7; 29–33.
[19] Ibid., 32.
[20] J.B. Priestley, 'Britain and the Nuclear Bombs', *New Statesman* 54, no. 1390 (2 November 1957): 554.
[21] Lawrence Wittner, *Confronting the Bomb: A Short History of the World Nuclear Disarmament Movement* (Stanford, CA: Stanford University Press, 2009), 59.
[22] Collins, *Faith under Fire*.
[23] Nic MacLellan, *Grappling with the Bomb: Britain's Pacific H-Bomb Tests* (Acton, ACT: ANU Press, 2017).
[24] Wittner, *Resisting the Bomb*, 48–9.
[25] Yates and Chester, *The Troublemaker*, Chapter 20.

rebuild his career as an activist. Based in New York, he began to work for War Resisters International (WRI) and, in 1956, with the support of Muste and A. Phillip Randolph, was despatched to Montgomery Alabama to offer advice on Gandhian tactics to Dr Martin Luther King. Rustin became a trusted adviser to King as he led the successful bus boycott in Montgomery and was elected to lead the newly formed Southern Christian Leadership Conference.[26] Throughout this period, Rustin remained convinced of the need to connect American peace and civil rights movements with African nationalism, arguing that there existed a 'very direct link between the campaign against nuclear weapons and the struggle of the African peoples for freedom'.[27] He therefore made strong efforts to extend his links with international peace movements, and, in April 1958, he was the only American speaker at the rally that began the first Aldermaston peace march. For Brenda Gayle Plummer, Rustin's participation at the rally in Trafalgar Square in London that launched the march placed him in a long tradition of African American campaigners involved with international activist movements, beginning with the campaign for the abolition of slavery in the nineteenth century.[28] He was, of course, also a leading participant in the American pacifist movement, which had developed its own 'ban the bomb' campaign in parallel with those that had formed in Britain and elsewhere. The National Committee for a Sane Nuclear Policy (known as SANE) had formed in November 1957, with a particular focus on banning atomic tests. Earlier that year, on the anniversary of the bombing of Hiroshima, a group of advocates of Gandhian civil disobedience, with Muste playing a central role, staged a protest at the US test site in Nevada.[29] One of the participants, Albert Bigelow, followed Steele in seeking to sail a yacht, the *Golden Rule* into the US Pacific nuclear test zone in early 1958, although his efforts were halted in the vicinity of Hawaii.[30] Following a series of loosely connected protests, the Committee for Non-Violent Action (CNVA) was launched in September 1958, as a kind of counterpart to the DAC in Britain.

The movements that emerged in Britain and the United States in 1957 and 1958 represented, Wittner argues, a shift of emphasis in anti-nuclear movements from attempts to curtail nuclear tests to disarmament, from test bans to calls to 'ban the bomb'.[31] The new wave of activism in 1958 also revealed significant differences in tactics and approach, between those movements, such as CND, that focused its efforts on raising public consciousness and parliamentary lobbying, and the DAC, which favoured passive resistance. The publicity that followed the Swaffham protest in late 1958 implied that this argument had some merit. CND focused, in particular, on the Labour Party in Britain, eventually persuading its conference to support a policy of unilateral disarmament in 1960 which, although swiftly overthrown by the party leader Hugh Gaitskell, set out a line of division between the moderate and radical

---

[26] Anderson, *Bayard Rustin*, 186–212.
[27] D'Emilio, *Lost Prophet*, 218.
[28] Brenda Gayle Plummer, *Window on Freedom: Race, Civil Rights and Foreign Affairs, 1945–1988* (Chapel Hill, NC: University of North Carolina Press, 2003), 1.
[29] Danielson, *American Gandhi*, 279–80.
[30] Wittner, *Resisting the Bomb*, 55–6.
[31] Ibid., 44.

wings of the party that, arguably, remains significant today.[32] For some, however, the historical significance of the anti-nuclear weapons movements that emerged in the late 1950s lies beyond their organizational history and impact on party politics. As Holger Nehring suggests, in his comparative analysis of the emergence of anti-nuclear weapons movements in Britain and the Federal Republic of Germany, groups such as CND both challenged and epitomized British post-war society.[33] By presenting these movements as one dimension of a broader 'politics of security', Nehring demonstrates that anti-nuclear weapons protests highlight the significant impact of the Cold War in shaping political cultures in Europe. These were, he suggests, transnational protest movements that reflected the global character of the Cold War.[34] The interaction of transnational peace protest, African nationalism and the politics of non-alignment examined in this chapter signals that the politics of security at these local, transnational and global scales also overlapped with the processes of decolonization.

The French nuclear weapons programme

The French atomic programme might easily be regarded as the epitome of the resurgence of Charles de Gaulle, who returned to power after the collapse of the Fourth Republic in 1958. The development of atomic weapons seemed perfectly aligned with the 'grandeur' of de Gaulle's robust foreign policy, but the programme had roots almost as deep as its British counterpart. The decision to embark on a military programme of atomic research was taken by Pierre Mendès-France in late 1954, in the context of the combined strategic challenges of anti-colonial resistance (in both Southeast Asia and North Africa) and the defence policy implications of debates around European integration. Mendès-France, like de Gaulle, saw an atomic programme as the key to increasing French influence with their strategic partners. Central to the decision was thus a desire to maintain French 'national independence' and build a European Defence Community that would be more than a 'supplementary militia . . . to protect Anglo-Saxon atomic bases'.[35] The formal decision to build a nuclear weapon was signed by Gaillard in April 1958 and confirmed by de Gaulle following his reappointment as prime minister in the midst of the May crisis following the rebellion by settlers and French military commanders in Algeria. Despite the political turmoil, there was thus continuity in French atomic weapons policy; although de Gaulle was sceptical of the depth of US defence guarantees to Europe, the nuclear programme did not represent a singularly Gaullist ambition but was part of a longer-term process of adaptation to,

---

[32] Stuart Croft, 'The Labour Party and the Nuclear Issue', in *The Changing Labour Party*, edited by Martin J. Smith and Joanna Spear (London: Routledge, 1992); Len Scott, 'Labour and the Bomb: The First 80 Years', *International Affairs* 82, no. 4 (2006): 685–700.
[33] Nehring, *Politics of Security*, 4.
[34] Ibid., 14.
[35] Jean-Marc Boegner, quoted in Béatrice Failles, 'Pierre Mendès France et la construction de l'arme atomique. Une responsabilité collective, un défi personnel', *Matériaux pour l'histoire de notre temps* 63, no. 1 (2001): 139–40.

and realignment of strategic thinking within, the new circumstances of the world after 1945.[36]

In March 1958, international observers remained uncertain of the French plans. It was reported in March that French nuclear scientists continued to focus their efforts on non-military programmes, working closely with the Atomic Energy Commission.[37] But by the middle of the year, the political message was clear. During the visit by US Secretary of State, John Foster Dulles, to Paris in July, de Gaulle confirmed that France had the capacity to build an independent nuclear deterrent, and suggested that 'much time and money could now be saved if America would admit France to the "Atom Club"'.[38] The following month, a high-profile visit by de Gaulle to the nuclear facility at Marcoulle fuelled speculation that France would be able to announce tests in 1959.[39] The formal announcement of the French plan to build and test a nuclear weapon came eventually in October 1958, cutting across the temporary moratorium on atomic tests agreed by United States, Britain and the Soviet Union which came into force at the end of that month.[40] The international politics of the French tests were fraught. Their conjunction with the rising wave of anti-nuclear weapons protests across Europe meant that some form of campaign against the tests would be inevitable, despite the lack of any extensive opposition within France itself, partially explained by French peace activists' focus on the war in Algeria.[41] Resistance to the French tests therefore originated within the international disarmament movement.

The British DAC raised the possibility of organized protests against the French nuclear test plans in January 1959, via their delegation to the European Congress for Nuclear Disarmament in London. Prior to the conference, DAC organizer Pat Arrowsmith wrote to European colleagues sketching initial plans for an international team to highlight the 'universal danger of nuclear weapons' by travelling to the French test site in the Sahara via either Morocco or Ghana.[42] At the meeting, the DAC announced that it hoped to establish an international coordinating committee for direct action and to oversee protests at both the British tactical nuclear missile base in Dortmund as well as the French tests in the Sahara. Although two key figures – Scott and Hugh Brock – were in jail during the Congress following the Swaffham protest, the DAC sought to persuade delegates to offer practical support for a 'journey by "a group of well-known persons" to the Sahara testing grounds'.[43] The Congress seemed sympathetic to direct action, but observers noted that the DAC plans were not supported by the conference as a whole.[44] The DAC held that the protests would have

---

[36] David Holloway, 'Nuclear Weapons and the Escalation of the Cold War, 1945–1962', in *The Cambridge History of the Cold War: Volume 1: Origins*, edited by Melvyn P. Leffler and Odd Arne Westad (Cambridge: Cambridge University Press, 2010), 390.
[37] *The Observer*, 30 March 1958, 13.
[38] *Guardian*, 7 July 1958, 1.
[39] *New York Times*, 3 August 1958, 11.
[40] 'France to Test Bombs Soon', *Guardian*, 24 October 1958, 9.
[41] Wittner, *Resisting the Bomb*, 74.
[42] Arrowsmith to Lore Frobenius, 12 January 1959, Bradford Peace Collection (BPC) Papers of the Direct Action Committee DAC 5/7/1.
[43] *Guardian*, 18 January 1959.
[44] 'Campaign for Nuclear Disarmament – note by the UK Delegation', NATO Committee on Information and Cultural Relations, AC/52-D(59)1/1.

a greater impact than any within France and would 'symbolise our common concern about the threat of nuclear weapons', but scepticism from the French delegation meant that plans for a large-scale campaign were put to one side.⁴⁵ The congress nonetheless recognized that the intense debate around disarmament – with its tensions between opponents of nuclear weapons and pacifists, between international agendas and national politics – ought to build towards a global campaign. During a visit to Germany in the immediate aftermath of the London conference, plans were set out for a world congress that would include representatives from African and Asian movements.⁴⁶

But the DAC revived their protest plans after the French authorities confirmed the construction of a test base at Reggane in southern Algeria.⁴⁷ Their first instinct was, again, to work with European anti-nuclear campaigners, including prominent French pacifists and anti-nuclear weapons campaigners. These included André Trocmé, head of the European section of the International Fellowship of Reconciliation and renowned pacifist who had protected Jewish refugees from the Vichy regime during the Second World War and in the 1950s had established a centre in Morocco to support French pacifist objectors to the war in Algeria. Trocmé had been an active organizer of international protest against nuclear weapons but, by 1959, had begun to question the extent to which global movements were fracturing along ideological lines. He attended the Fourth World Conference Against Atomic and Hydrogen Bombs in Tokyo in August 1958 but argued that the conflation, by African and Asian nationalist delegations, of Western colonialism and nuclear militarism undermined opportunities for a genuine meeting of like minds. 'It was upsetting', he argued, 'to see how skilled manoeuvres, under the cover of a struggle against nuclear weapons, would easily sow fear and hatred against the West alone'.⁴⁸ Trocmé's unease that critiques of colonialism were being deployed tactically to serve ideological purposes – which had been manifest since the formation of the World Peace Council in 1950 – reflected a dynamic that made French atomic tests in Africa a challenge as much as an opportunity for anti-nuclear weapons protestors. Cold War rivalries exacerbated anti-colonial sentiment, and French colonial policies, while differing sharply from those of other European powers, could easily be cast as an epitome of Western imperialism.

French activists had, in fact, begun to mobilize opposition to the planned tests following the London Congress in January 1959. Trocmé and the physicist Alfred Kastler became co-presidents of the French Federation Against Atomic Armament when it was formed in April 1959, and took a leading role, along with the editor of *France-Observateur*, Claude Bourdet, in coordinating a public campaign against the tests in France. By mid-1959, a petition had been circulated among academics and church officials, but these efforts had limited impact and did little to generate mass

---

⁴⁵ P. Arrowsmith to L. Frobenius, January 12, 1959, BPC DAC 5/7/1; 'Untitled Memo for European Congress', n.d. [January 1959], BPC DAC 5/7/1.
⁴⁶ *Guardian*, 20 January 1959.
⁴⁷ *Guardian*, 5 May 1959.
⁴⁸ A. Trocmé, 'Fourth International Conference Against A- and H-bombs', *Fellowship* 24, no. 21 (1958): 29–30.

appeal beyond an intellectual elite.[49] Moreover, there were few links between the DAC and their French counterparts. In developing the British plans for the Sahara protest in June and July 1959, April Carter wrote to European contacts seeking advice. French responses displayed a reluctance to commit to the DAC plan, and Trocmé himself argued needed to be 'genuinely French, organised by the French, with the approval of French popular good sense'.[50] Recent explanations for the failure to develop a consensus among European activists have focused on their distrust of the Gandhian methods of the DAC, the repression of French protests by the Gaullist regime (in contrast to the greater level of freedom for activists in Britain), but also the DAC's own unwillingness to work with more militant protest in France, which was led by Communist-aligned groups.[51] National feeling has also been cited as a reason for the relatively muted popular protest against the tests in France: many people shared the feeling that national prestige could be reclaimed through a nuclear weapons programme.[52] French attitudes to the British campaign against the tests hardened when pickets were organized outside the French Embassy in London, allowing critics to cast the protests as anti-French. In September, less than a month before team members began to arrive in Accra, April Carter herself admitted that she had no knowledge of how 'the French anti-atomic armament organisation argues its case'.[53]

The British campaigners connected with the DAC, and some of their French counterparts, such as Pierre Martin, regarded anti-nuclear weapons protests and anti-colonialism as two connected parts of a broader pacifist struggle. Many peace campaigners in France, however, sought to avoid making direct connections between the two issues. It seems likely that this was at least in part a consequence of the timing of the tests in Algeria at a delicate conjuncture in the independence war in the country. Given that the tests took place soon after de Gaulle publicly acknowledged the inevitability of self-determination for Algeria, it nevertheless seems significant that the location of the French test site did not appear to have resonated with the public.[54] Like their British counterparts, French peace activists were wary of being tainted as 'Communist or anti-colonialist inspired' in their opposition to the tests.[55] In general, pacifist campaigners sought to avoid any direct connection with or support for the National Liberation Front in Algeria, even though some leading political figures offered private support for the Sahara protests.[56] British campaigners nevertheless understood

---

[49] Wittner, *Resisting the Bomb*, 230–1.
[50] Trocmé, quoted in Carter, 'The Sahara Protest Team', in *Liberation Without Violence: A Third-Party Approach*, edited by A Paul Hare and Herbert H. Blumberg, 126–56 (London: Collings, April 1977), 152.
[51] Christopher R. Hill, 'The Activist as Geographer: Nonviolent Direct Action in Cold War Germany and Postcolonial Ghana, 1959-1960', *Journal of Historical Geography* 64 (April 2019): 36–46.
[52] Wittner, *Resisting the Bomb*, 230–1.
[53] A. Carter to A. Hamers and V. Hamers-Camatta, September 2, 1959, BPC DAC 5/7/1.
[54] Martin Evans, *Algeria: France's Undeclared War* (Oxford: Oxford University Press, 2011), 261–82.
[55] A. Carter to V. Hamers-Camatta, 17 June 1959, BPC DAC 5/7/1.
[56] According to A. J. Muste, the former Prime Minister, Pierre Mendès-France, expressed 'admiration' for the protest team during a lecture tour in the United States in early 1960. A. J. Muste to E. Peter, 28 January 28, 1960 SPC, Muste Papers, Reel 89/16/Sahara Protest Team. On the 'non-Communist Left' and Algeria, see, for example, Todd Shepard, *The Invention of Decolonization: The Algerian War and the Remaking of France* (Ithaca, NY: Cornell University Press, 2006), 64–5.

that the protest had to be insulated from any commentary on the war in Algeria to avoid alienating French opinion. In the context of a protest against French militarism, a 'complete pacifist demand' – that is, a campaign that embraced a call for an end to all violence in Algeria – was rejected as unworkable.[57]

For anti-nuclear weapons protestors in Britain more generally, however, peace and anti-colonialism were increasingly presented as intertwined issues, with the DAC as the 'chief interlocutor of anti-colonial practices in Britain'.[58] This status was in many respects a function of the group's Gandhian strategies of protest, and other leading pacifists were key to making the connection between nuclear weapons and colonialism. Hugh Brock, as editor of *Peace News*, ensured that colonial issues were a major editorial focus, and the veteran pacifist and anti-colonial campaigner Fenner Brockway wrote a regular column for the newspaper. By the middle of 1959, discussion of the French tests illustrated a strengthening connection between anti-colonialism and peace in the public pronouncements of campaigners. In mid-June, *Peace News* reported on the ongoing developments, noting that the planned tests had become a key concern for groups coordinating the 'struggle against colonialism in the Mediterranean and the Middle East'.[59]

Moreover, the DAC had other European contacts who were acutely aware of the impact of the French tests on colonial politics. These included the Swiss pacifists Ralph and Idy Hegnauer. Both had worked to provide humanitarian assistance for refugees in Palestine, India and Pakistan after the Second World War under the auspices of Service Civil International (SCI), who also employed the French pacifist and later participant in the Sahara protest team, Pierre Martin. They replied that an advance group should travel to Morocco and liaise with government authorities as well as Algerian representatives, but suggested that travelling from Ghana or Nigeria might be easier, given the strength of official opposition to the French tests in both countries.[60] As the Hegenauers suggested, the protests were not purely a question of non-governmental organizations and social movement activities but had taken a prominent position in colonial and post-colonial politics in west Africa.

Building a campaign

Efforts to organize a protest campaign began to develop in Europe during the summer of 1959. But, the earliest official declarations of opposition to the tests were moved by African political leaders in Ghana and Nigeria. From mid-1959, statements from both countries were vehement in their opposition, but those from Ghana were in many regards more radical. In July 1959, Krobo Edusei and George Padmore led a group of protestors to the French Embassy in Accra and attempted to deliver a formal diplomatic note opposing the tests in uncertain terms. The groundwork for the official

---

[57] A. Carter to Arno and Vera Hamers-Camatta, 2 September 1959, BPC DAC 5/7/1.
[58] Hill, 'The Activist as Geographer', 38.
[59] *Peace News*, 12 June 1959.
[60] Idy and Ralph Hengauer to April Carter, 13 July 1959, BPC Randle Papers Cw1 DAC5/7/1.

protest had been laid even earlier by academics and trades union organizers as well as editorial pieces in the Nkrumah-supporting *Ghana Times* and *Evening News*. The subject of nuclear tests had also been a topic of discussion at the first conference of Independent African states, held in Accra in April 1958, which called for a nuclear test ban 'not only in the interest of world peace, but also as a symbol of their avowed devotion to the rights of man'.[61] French Embassy Officials refused to accept the protest letter, taking particular offence at Ghana's claims to speak on behalf of African territories as a whole in its condemnation of the tests. The diplomatic dynamics of west African protests against the tests would play out alongside the organization of the Sahara protest over the coming months, but the stance taken by officials in Ghana encouraged closer alignment between pan-Africanist anti-colonial groups and peace activists in Britain.

In August, the DAC began to collaborate with the London-based Committee of African Organisations (CAO), organizing a demonstration in Trafalgar Square to protest against 'nuclear imperialism'. Formed in the previous year, the summer of 1959 was a moment of peak activity for the CAO, which included campaigns focused on Kenya, the Central African Federation and the unrest in Nyasaland. It worked closely with the MCF and took a leading role in the launch of the boycott of South African goods that laid the foundation for the Anti-Apartheid Movement in Britain.[62] The Trafalgar Square rally, held in the midst of a heat wave at the very end of August that had forced 'all but a few disconsolate tourists' from the streets, nevertheless attracted over a thousand protestors chanting 'Down with de Gaulle', while a smaller group formed a picket outside the French Embassy.[63] Pamphlets produced by the organizers leant strongly on the language of anti-colonial and pan-Africanism:

> For many years our lot has been humiliation and degradation, and now that our people are looking at the shining example of the nine independent African States, waiting, fighting and struggling for their chance to govern themselves, with the forces of imperialism on the run, the most atrocious of all enemies is creeping into our continent THE H-BOMB. . . . The centuries of slavery and imperial exploration are to be followed by the destruction of the lives of our people through the pollution of our air with radioactive fall-out from the impending French nuclear explosions. It is outrageous that the French greed for power and glory can only be satisfied by the destruction of our people. The entire African Continent has said NO to this nuclear madness.[64]

Behind the references to African unity, the CAO represented a particular body of African opinion. Mostly drawn from the ranks of African students in the UK, the

[61] Ghana protest letter (copy), 6 July 1959 UKNA DO 35/9340.
[62] Hakim Adi, 'African Political Thinkers, Pan-Africanism and the Politics of Exile, c.1850–1970', *Immigrants & Minorities* 30, no. 2–3 (2012): 263–91; Christabel Gurney, '"A Great Cause": The Origins of the Anti-Apartheid Movement, June 1959–March 1960', *Journal of Southern African Studies* 26, no. 1 (2000): 123–44.
[63] 'London Letter', *The Guardian*, 31 August 1959; *Times*, 31 August 1959; 'Africa Says No to French Tests', August 1959, DAC/5/7/7; *Daily Express*, 31 August 1959.
[64] 'Africa Says No to French Tests', pamphlet [n.d. August 1959], BPC DAC 5/7/7.

Committee's vision of African unity tended to have an Anglophone focus. Moreover, while recent research has emphasized the key role played by activists from east and central Africa, including the Tanzanian student and activist Dennis Phombeah, the Committee relied strongly on west African support, including financial backing from Nkrumah.[65] Connections between peace and anti-colonial protest in London in 1959 thus built on networks of pan-African influence, as official protest against the French tests in west Africa was led by individuals who had been important figures in the radicalization of African student politics in Britain in the 1940s.[66] These links would both facilitate and constrain the endeavours of the Sahara protest team when they arrived in Ghana.

Under close examination, the relationship between anti-nuclear weapons organizations and anti-colonial movements is revealed to be far more complex than a superficial account of an alignment between movements would suggest. Despite apparently shared ethical and political agendas, the life histories of key individuals within these networks tell a more nuanced story. The primary contact between the DAC and the Committee of African Organisations was its Secretary, Dennis Phombeah, a leading organizer for the Tanganyikan African National Union who had arrived in Britain in 1956 after studying in Zagreb. He continued his studies in the UK, but his academic work quickly took second place to political organization, especially after the formation of the CAO in March 1958. But, as James Brennan has argued, Phombeah's work as a political organizer was supplemented by covert activities as an informant for the British security services, alongside membership of the Communist Party of Great Britain.[67] In Brennan's account of his covert career suggest that it is better to view Phombeah as an informant rather than a 'spy' in the usual sense. His analysis of the political capacities of African leaders was trusted by British officials and bolstered the regard for Julius Nyerere during the process of constitutional negotiations leading to Tanganyikan independence.[68] Phombeah's role as an informant thus appears to have complemented, rather than contradicted, his work as a coordinator of anti-colonial activism in Britain at such a critical juncture in decolonization.

What was, however, problematic for the relationship between the DAC and the CAO as the plans for the Sahara protest took shape were the contacts and ideological affinities with Communist and Communist-aligned movements that both Phombeah and other CAO activists maintained. In the aftermath of the Trafalgar Square rally, Michael Randle and April Carter wrote to Phombeah and his co-organizer, Ali Bashoran, expressing misgivings around the presence of representatives of the British Peace Committee (BPC) on the platform. While the emergence of CND had both diminished the influence of the Peace Committee and encouraged an alignment of interests between Communist and anti-Communist peace campaigners, the DAC, with its close connections to the historical rivals of the BPC, the Peace Pledge Union,

---

[65] Milford, 'Harnessing the Wind', 113–19.
[66] Adi, 'African Political Thinkers, Pan-Africanism'.
[67] James R. Brennan, 'The Secret Lives of Dennis Phombeah: Decolonization, the Cold War, and African Political Intelligence, 1953–1974', *The International History Review* 43, no. 1 (2021): 153–69.
[68] Ibid.

remained wary of 'official association' with a movement so closely associated with the Communist left.[69] Randle and Carter recommended the formation of a joint-organizing committee for the Sahara protest, with equal representation from the CAO and pacifist organizations, operating on agreed principles, which for the DAC would include a commitment to non-violence and opposition to all nuclear tests including those undertaken by the Soviet Union. A meeting was arranged for mid-September, but when representatives of the CAO failed to attend, the DAC determined to press ahead anyway. Randle headed to France in the hope of persuading the leaders of the main anti-nuclear weapons movements to support the Sahara protest team. Meanwhile, the two main organizers of the DAC had entered into concurrent correspondence with George Willoughby of the Committee for Non-violent Action (CNVA) in the United States.[70] This would eventually become the mainstay of support for the Sahara protest team, but the key connection between the British, American and African dimensions of the project would be the African American pacifist campaigner Bill Sutherland.

April Carter had written to Bill Sutherland in Ghana in mid-June 1959, with the same general request for advice and outline of the protest plans that the DAC had sent to its European supporters.[71] Thanks to postal delays, Sutherland did not respond until a month later, after Ghana's official protest letter had been rejected by French diplomats in Accra. In contrast to the Hegenauers and others, Sutherland's comments on the plans for the protest focused on practical issues, drawing on the experiences of friends who had crossed the Sahara the previous year. In traversing the desert, international travellers relied on French authorities to monitor their progress and, when they went astray, to despatch search teams to locate groups and guide them back to established routes. A protest team, Sutherland suggested, would more likely be met by a military force than a search party.[72] He also urged that the team itself should include African participants as the Sahara tests were an 'opportunity to substantially broaden the base of the movement'.[73] As an adviser to Nkrumah's long-time ally and finance minister, Komla Gbedmah, Sutherland became an important interlocutor between the Ghanaian government and international peace networks. In July, he discussed the DAC proposals with Padmore and in August he had taken a principal role in establishing the Ghana Council for Nuclear Disarmament[74].

Like Sutherland, Gbedmah had links with movements that sought to draw together threads of anti-colonial, peace and internationalist movements in the late 1950s. Gbedemah opened the congress of the World Movement for World Federal Government in the Netherlands, in August 1959, where he was re-elected as its president. The

---

[69] Randle and Carter to Bashoran and Phombeah, 31 August 1959, Bradford, BPC DAC 5/7/3. See also Nicholas Barnett and Evan Smith, '"Peace with a Capital P": The Spectre of Communism and Competing Notions of "Peace" in Britain, 1949–1960', *Labour History Review* (Liverpool University Press) 82, no. 1 (2017): 51–90; Nehring, 'National Internationalists', 559–82.

[70] Randle to George Willoughby, 20 August 1959; Carter to George Willoughby, 14 September 1959, SPC Papers of the Committee for Nonviolent Activism CNVA VI Sahara Protest Correspondence.

[71] Carter to Sutherland, 17 June 1959, BPC Randle Cw1/DAC5-7-4, A. Carter to V. Hamers-Camatta, June 17, 1959, BPC DAC 5/7/1.

[72] Sutherland to Carter, 15 July 1959, BPC Randle papers Cw1/DAC5-7-4.

[73] Ibid.

[74] Wittner, *Resisting the Bomb*, 266.

conference passed several resolutions calling for an end to nuclear weapons testing and increased international intervention in debates around arms control.[75] The involvement of Gbedemah – who had been involved in the world federalist movement since the early 1950s – further signalled the increasing alignment between movements that took a generally globalized view of political organization with questions of colonial freedom and peace. Already in 1957, The World Movement for World Federal Government expressed support for Afro-Asian solidarity and called for the end of colonialism in Africa. In its October 1959 edition, the federalist publication *Towards World Democracy* included a version of an essay by the ethnographer Odette de Puigaudeau refuting the French government's claim that the region around the Sahara test site was 'empty desert'; in the same edition, it noted that the 'atomic menace' could only be overcome when 'world institutions are created to control disarmament'.[76] Moreover, while international campaigners focused their creative efforts towards protest against the French tests, there were signs that disquiet on the part of west African officials was becoming a concern for the British government.

Although Ghanaian officials had raised the strongest formal complaint against France, other African territories had also expressed concerns about the prospects of a nuclear explosion in the Sahara. A special meeting on Algeria attended by foreign ministers of nine independent states – mostly from North Africa, but also including Ghana, Liberia and Ethiopia – denounced all plans to test nuclear weapons in the continent.[77] Other territories still formerly under the control of colonial powers issued similar complaints, and in some cases these prompted serious diplomatic responses from British officials. In Nigeria, for example, the French test plans had been debated by the National Assembly in February 1959, and by August British civil servants began to worry that opinion in the country had begun to shift from criticism of France to anger that Britain had failed to support Nigerian protests. Frederick Hoyle-Millar noted that, if Britain ignored the 'genuine expressions of disquiet about the effects of the coming French tests, Nigerians may very well concede that we rate the emergence of France as a nuclear power as of greater importance than the welfare of a future Member country of the Commonwealth'.[78] In the following month, a high-ranking Nigerian delegation to the UK, including the prime minister designate Abubaker Balewa, visited the Harwell Atomic Energy Research Establishment, where they were briefed on the potential impact of the French tests. Before leaving the UK, Balewa issued a public statement expressing his satisfaction that there was 'no question of British indifference' towards the Nigerians' concerns about the tests and that delegates' concerns had been somewhat assuaged by their meeting with scientists at Harwell.[79] Balewa's comments elicited an immediate and angry response from the Ghanaian press. The *Ghana Times*

---

[75] Jean-Francis Billion, 'The World Federalist Movements from 1955 to 1968 and European Integration', *The Federalist – Political Review* 2 (1996): 96–118. See also Wittner, *Resisting the Bomb*, 266.
[76] *Towards World Democracy*, No. 20 October 1959, SPC CNVA papers VI Sahara project correspondence.
[77] 'Special Conferences', *International Organization* 16, no. 2 (1962): 444–6.
[78] Hoyle-Millar, memorandum, 21 August 1959 UKNA DO 35/9340.
[79] Overseas Press Telegram Service, 16th, 19th September 1959 UKNA DO 35/9340.

expressed surprise that the Nigerian delegation had 'succumbed so easily to lollipops' from British officials, who were accused of amplifying French claims.[80]

In public statements, Nkrumah alleged that Britain supported the French test plans, and, in private, British officials were clearly caught in a dilemma. The Moroccan delegation had secured an opportunity to bring protests against the tests to the floor of the United Nations in New York, forcing British diplomats to make preparations for what was likely to be a highly problematic confrontation. Under Macmillan, British policy was being steered in the direction of closer relations with Europe and decolonization, and a debate in the General Assembly was likely to alienate either, if not both, French and African leaders. Discussion between French and British diplomatic officials revealed the case that the French sought to make at the United Nations centred on the safety precautions that had been put in place and the relative isolation of the French test site. French officials planned to draw a contrast between their plans and early US atomic research, which had taken place much closer to centres of population; moreover, as British officials noted, the French site was closer to Gibraltar than Nigeria or Ghana.[81] It seemed impossible that Britain could not acknowledge the French right to undertake tests within its own territory (notwithstanding the anti-colonial struggle underway in Algeria), but at the same time diplomats recognized the genuine concerns of Africans. Ultimately, Britain's central concern was to maintain progress at the Geneva test-ban treaty negotiations, although that was unlikely to placate African concerns.

After the Nigerian delegation visited the UK, a technician from the UK Nuclear Weapons Research Establishment at Aldermaston visited Nigeria to demonstrate instruments designed to measure the levels of atmospheric radiation. The British authorities had shipped equipment to Nigeria that could be used by an 'officer used to handling meteorological instruments and recording data', with sites (predominantly in the north of the country) identified as suitable locations for monitoring stations.[82] Diplomatic channels were also used to make the Ghanaian authorities aware that such equipment would also be made available to them if it were requested, but Ghanaian officials instead reached out to the Canadian government who, with British encouragement, had offered nuclear assistance to the West African state.[83] These combined efforts were designed to provide concrete reassurances to African leaders, but anxiety in west African territories was by no means restricted to those with political interests at stake. Academics and government scientists were equally concerned. When Aldermaston scientist Noah Pearce travelled through Accra during his visit to west Africa, he met with H. O. Walker, Director of the Ghana Meteorological Service. A former colonial official who had remained in post following independence, Walker, informed Pearce that 'he would not care to have his wife in Ghana at the time of the explosions' and was not to be persuaded that his fears were unfounded.[84] The Deputy High Commissioner, Leonard Wakeley, subsequently remarked that, as a government

[80] Press clipping [n.d. September 1959], *Ghana Times* UKNA DO 35/9340.
[81] H. T. Morgan to A. Emanuel, 1 October 1959 UKNA DO 35/9340.
[82] Message to Acting HC Accra 4 September, UKNA DO 35/9340.
[83] 19 October Telegram CRO to Ottawa, 28 October Flack to Dorman UKNA DO 35/9340.
[84] 27 October R. J. Vile to Allen UKNA DO 35/9340.

official, Walker's interests might not have been best served by disagreeing with Nkrumah's position on the tests, and that similar claims had been made by the head of the Physics Department at UC Ghana.[85]

Reactions to the French atomic tests in west Africa illuminate the ways in which nuclear diplomacy reflected – and influenced – the changing geopolitical contexts for African and European relations in the late 1950s. W. Arthur Clark, working for the Commonwealth Relations Office, explained the rationale for Britain's vote against the condemnation of the French tests at the UN as a consequence of the need to balance the expected reaction of African members of the Commonwealth with the desire to 'restore our relations with France and Europe'.[86] Prior to this, equivocation by British Ministers had antagonized both political leaders in west African states and French opinion in equal measure.[87] African states, however, viewed the diplomatic situation through the lens of the Commonwealth. Anger at the French plans reflected widespread fears and suspicion regarding the effects (both physical and political) of the detonation of an atomic weapon in Africa by a colonial power. When African leaders expressed their 'indignation' when plans for the Sahara tests were officially announced in August 1959, the French government claimed that 'for several hundred miles around the testing ground there is no population centre and indeed hardly a single human being'.[88] In response, Odette du Puigaudeau wrote describing the test site at Reggane as part of a chain of oases that stretched towards the Moroccan border.[89]

Despite efforts on the part of the DAC to publicize du Puigaudeau's account, little attention was given to the potential impact to communities in the vicinity of the test site. In west Africa, however, official protests were accompanied by public demonstrations, heightened by the publication of images of survivors of Hiroshima. Public anxieties in Nigeria were particularly extensive, with the Christian Council of Nigeria voicing concerns that 'atomic particles' would be carried by the prevailing wind into the country, while the Federation of Nigerian Women's Organisations were reported to have sent a telegram to Queen Elizabeth II, asking her to 'protect the lives of Nigerian sons and daughters by appealing to the French government'.[90] Meanwhile, the University of Ibadan issued a statement expressing concern over contamination of the cereal crops upon which both human populations and their livestock were dependent.[91] African responses might also be viewed as an embodiment of a struggle around knowledge. In one sense, the British (and French) authorities acted in ways comparable with imperialist pioneers of the nineteenth century; at the same time, Nkrumah could secure access to scientific resources through Canada, without, as Hill

---

[85] 7 November LJD Wakely to M Allen UKNA DO 35/9340.
[86] WAW Clark to HC Accra 9 December 1959 UKNA DO 35/9340.
[87] Christopher Robert Hill, 'Britain, West Africa and "The New Nuclear Imperialism": Decolonisation and Development during French Tests', *Contemporary British History* 33, no. 2 (2019): 278.
[88] *Daily Telegraph*, London, 11 August 1959.
[89] O. du Puigaudeau, 'The Atomic Age Reaches the Oases', *Towards World Democracy*, October 1959, BPC DAC 5/7/10.
[90] *Observer*, London, 10 August 1959.
[91] *Times*, London, 15 July 1959.

notes, 'having to collaborate with its former colonial master or one of the so-called "bomb club"'.[92]

Meanwhile, the DAC in London had continued in their efforts to coordinate a high-profile international protest in Africa. By the time of the Trafalgar Square rally, two separate plans were under investigation: one focused on a team travelling to El Hammoudia from Accra in Ghana, another on a route heading south from Morocco. Both were discussed in a report sent to anti-nuclear weapons organizations in the United States, France and Belgium, as well as Bill Sutherland in Ghana. Discussions about the routes would continue through to November, and the possibility of a protest group from Morocco would be revived in January 1960, but the DAC outlined some key concerns that were to ultimately lead to the group setting out for Accra. A major objection to a route from Morocco was that the team would inevitably meet, and potentially rely on, the Algerian FLN and that the southward journey would traverse a militarized zone. The route from Ghana, while significantly further from the test site, was viewed as potentially less dangerous, while the authorities in Accra would be able to provide practical support and be less susceptible to pressure from France.[93] The report also recognized the complexities involved in coordinating a coherent international protest, whose participants would be likely to hold differing views alongside their opposition to the nuclear tests. In particular, the DAC report noted that while participants would 'undoubtedly be opposed to colonialism', Western peace campaigners and African activists would inevitably differ in their emphasis on the role of colonialism. Ultimately, the organizers felt that a 'joint protest by those who will suffer from the tests and those whose countries are responsible' was a key dimension of the enterprise.[94] The focus on suffering is noteworthy, perhaps, in comparison with French and British efforts to present the tests as unlikely to have a detrimental effect on the lives of those who considered themselves in danger.

In the immediate aftermath of the Trafalgar Square rally, before the CAO broke contact with the DAC organizers, correspondence between Carter and Sutherland spoke optimistically of an independent joint protest committee and of two groups of protestors leaving simultaneously from Morocco and Ghana. Encouraged by rumours that Malian political leaders in French Sudan (Mali) had opposed the French nuclear tests, Sutherland sought further advice on the practicalities of traversing the desert and Carter began to estimate the costs of the expedition.[95] Sutherland then accompanied Gbedemah when he attended the Commonwealth Finance Ministers' Conference in London on 22 and 23 September, the week after Balewa had led the Nigerian delegation to London. By this point, the DAC began to encounter significant hurdles as they sought to finalize arrangements for initial members of the protest team to head to Ghana in early October. As Sutherland travelled from Accra to London, Randle met with leading figures from French anti-nuclear weapons organizations in Paris,

---

[92] Hill, 'Britain, West Africa', 282. As Hill notes, within a year Nkrumah had turned instead to the Soviet Union for support in developing nuclear power, rather than Canada.
[93] 'Memorandum on Sahara Protest Entry' [n.d. 1959] SPC CNVA papers VI Sahara Project DAC.
[94] Ibid.
[95] Carter to Sutherland, 2 September 1959, Sutherland to Carter, 4 September 1959, Carter to Sutherland, 9 September 1959, Sutherland to Carter 12 September 1959, BPC DAC 5/7/4.

but despite support from André Trocmé, his attempts to establish a joint protest were unsuccessful. And then, on 17 September, the CNVA agreed to offer only 'moral support and encouragement' to the DAC protest project. The resources of the Committee, they felt, were already stretched by commitments to protest campaigns in the United States, and they moreover felt that general political support for anti-nuclear weapons protest was further advanced in the UK, citing the increasing support within the Labour Party for disarmament.[96] Furthermore, Willoughby noted reservations around the degree to which the Sahara protest could be defined as genuinely 'international' without significant numbers of French and African participants, including in leadership roles. It was at this juncture that Sutherland's efforts came to the fore. His work with Gbedmah took him to London and then on to New York, enabling him to liaise directly between the DAC and the CNVA, which resulted in a transnational alliance between African anti-colonialism, British and American peace movements and the US civil rights movement.[97]

Sutherland was a significant influence on the decision of the CNVA to reverse its earlier decision on the Sahara protest at a meeting held on 6 October. At the end of September, following his arrival in New York, Sutherland met with George Willoughby, A. J. Muste and Bayard Rustin, who concluded that they should reconsider the level of support offered by the CNVA. They were persuaded by the probable inclusion of several African participants in the protest and the support given to the project by Michael Scott. They agreed to arrange a special meeting of the CNVA once Scott had arrived in New York for his annual pilgrimage to the UN Trusteeship Committee.[98] Scott was one of a number of guests in attendance, including Sutherland himself and Igal Roodenko, a veteran of the Journeys of Reconciliation in the 1940s.[99] For Sutherland, the Sahara project was of particular significance for 'the future of nonviolent direct action', and after a lengthy discussion, the CNVA agreed to provide financial support and publicity for the campaign. They also tasked Committee member Bayard Rustin to travel to Ghana to coordinate plans with DAC activists and investigate the possible relationship between the protest and African anti-nuclear weapons movements. Meanwhile, Michael Randle and the artist Francis Hoyland travelled to Accra in early October, initially hosted by the development economist Walter Birmingham, who was teaching at the University College of Ghana.[100] Equipped with a list of contacts, including David Rees of the Ghana Broadcasting System, Randle and Hoyland were tasked with setting up practical arrangements for the team, including the procurement of radios in order to maintain communication.

The DAC prepared a full plan of logistical requirements prior to Randle and Hoyland's departure. A clear route had been identified, leaving Ghana at Bawku, travelling across French Sudan to Tessalit before heading north across the desert to

[96] Willoughby to April Carter, 18 September 1959, SPC CNVA VI Sahara Project Correspondence.
[97] Sutherland and Meyer, *Guns and Gandhi*, 36.
[98] Willoughby to April Carter, 26 September 1959, SPC CNVA VI Sahara Project Correspondence.
[99] 'Minutes of CNVA Committee Meeting', 6 October 1959. SPC Muste Papers, Reel 89/16/Sahara Protest Team.
[100] Carter to Birmingham, 22 September 1959, Birmingham to Carter 2 October 1959, BPC DAC 5/7/4.

El Hammoudia – a journey of just over 2,000 miles. The team planned to travel in three Land Rover vehicles, each carrying half a tonne of essential supplies. The costs, which Carter had initially estimated to be £1,000, had inflated to over £3,000. By mid-October, with logistical and political support from the Ghanaian authorities, and morally and financially underwritten by American supporters, the team might well have felt increasingly confident of success. Although the CNVA had been reluctant to commit fully to the protest before Sutherland had been able to make his case in New York in late September, the two organizations were in many respects a natural fit for a collaborative project. April Carter would characterize the CNVA as a 'sister organisation' to the DAC, which depended on many of the same transnational connections that served its British counterpart. These included a combination of informal Quaker networks, links with the Christian International Fellowship and War Resisters International.[101] It was thus through transatlantic and pan-African networks with well-established mutual connections, in contrast to more diffuse European anti-nuclear organizations, that allowed the formation of an international protest against the French tests.

The Sahara protest team in Ghana

The advance team of Randle and Hoyland, arrived in Ghana on the morning of 9 October 1959. The same day, George Willoughby wrote to April Carter setting out plans for Bayard Rustin to travel to Ghana via London in mid-October. The intention was for Rustin to assist the protest team until December 1959, but that he would not take part in the protest himself.[102] Rustin's first impressions of developments in London were not positive, however. Rustin felt that the project budget was 'extremely unrealistic' and that at least double the £3,000 they had estimated would be required. In fact, the DAC had raised no more than £200, and Randle and Hoyland's flights to Accra had been paid by Carter herself. Rustin had also investigated the withdrawal of the CAO from the project, drawing on the services of the Kenyan activist Joseph Murumbi, a behind-the-scenes 'internationalist' organizer who was working at the Moroccan Embassy and played a major role in the arrangements for the second All-African Peoples' Conference in Tunis in January 1960. Murumbi revealed that the Sahara project had fallen foul of the sharpening rivalry between Michael Scott and Canon John Collins, with the latter advising African activists in London to avoid working with the 'irresponsible and crackpot' DAC.[103] Although they had collaborated on anti-colonial campaigns in the early 1950s, Collins had become increasingly influential both as Chair of CND and a leading conduit for funds between Britain

---

[101] Wittner, *Resisting the Bomb*, 266.
[102] Willoughby to April Carter, 9 October 1959, SPC CNVA VI Sahara project Correspondence.
[103] Rustin to George Willoughby, 18 October 1959, SPC CNVA VI Sahara Project Correspondence. On Murumbi see also Milford and McCann, 'African Internationalisms and the Erstwhile Trajectories of Kenyan Community Development', 111–35.

and South African liberation movements.[104] In a sense, the rivalry between Scott and Collins embodied the divergent agendas, principles and methodologies of CND and the DAC, which would crystallize in the resignation of Bertrand Russell as president of CND and launch the direct action-oriented Committee of 100, along with Scott and Randle, in late 1960.

The Sahara project was thus hampered by underlying tensions between different strands of the British anti-colonial movement, but a wider array of sometimes contradictory political agendas complicated the DAC's efforts. With Murumbi's support, the CAO were persuaded to draft a statement in support of the Sahara protest which, Rustin believed, would be of particular use in Africa. The following day, Murumbi visited Rustin to deliver proposals from Moroccan officials to revive plans for a team – possibly in parallel with the Ghana-based group – to travel to the test site from the north. With promises of full (although indirect) financial backing from the Moroccan government, Rustin agreed to consider the proposals but was troubled by the same concerns that the DAC had earlier raised, including the difficulty of maintaining an independent and international protest if it had state support, and the likely entanglement with Algerian FLN agents. Despite the manifest problems with the DAC project – a lack of clarity about the route to the test site, no firm commitment of funds and little sense of the full costs of equipment, and no specific information about African participation – Rustin determined to continue on to Ghana and seek solutions.[105] In his response, Willoughby expressed caution about the Moroccan proposals and the likelihood of becoming entangled in 'international intrigue' in North Africa and suggested that, without significant African involvement, CNVA ought to withdraw its active support. But he reserved judgement until receiving further reports from Accra.[106] April Carter outlined the DAC position, which took the Moroccan proposals seriously, acknowledging the value of a second team in amplifying the public impact of the protest. Ultimately, though, the British committee were wary of accepting funds, even indirectly, from a state that had stakes in both the regional and geopolitical dynamics of the French tests.[107]

Carter's report to Willoughby in the final week of October presented a positive summary of developments with the team itself. Esther Peter, who had resigned from her work as a translator for the Council of Europe, had become the first French volunteer. Although not a representative of the official French anti-nuclear movements, she had been involved with the World Citizens' Movement established by former USAF bomber pilot Garry Davis in Paris in the 1940s and had attracted support from pacifist organizations including the War Resisters League.[108] Her presence thus allowed

---

[104] Denis Herbstein, *White Lies: Canon John Collins and the Secret War Against Apartheid* (Oxford: James Currey, 2004), 55–8.
[105] Rustin to Willoughby, 18 October 1959, SPC CNVA VI Sahara Project Correspondence.
[106] Willoughby to Bayard Rustin, 25 October 1959, SPC CNVA VI Sahara Project Correspondence.
[107] Carter to George Willoughby, 26 October 1959, SPC CNVA VI Sahara Project Correspondence.
[108] 'Progress Report on Sahara Protest', 12 November 1959, SPC CNVA VI Sahara Protest DAC. On Davis and 'World Citizens', see Scott H. Bennett, *Radical Pacifism: The War Resisters League and Gandhian Nonviolence in America, 1915–1963* (Syracuse, NY: Syracuse University Press, 2003), 182–3.

the DAC to describe the team as 'international' in its releases to the press.[109] Carter nonetheless admitted that no French journalists attended the press conference that the DAC arranged when Peters was in London en route to Accra. By mid-November, she reported that support from France would ultimately rely on the position taken by André Trocmé.[110] In her account, Randle and Hoyland had been embraced by the Ghanaian authorities on their arrival, which had been met with a champagne reception, a chauffeur and publicity officer. They had given radio broadcasts and had arranged screenings of two short anti-nuclear documentaries: the 1954 examination of the 'Lucky Dragon' incident, *The Japanese Fisherman* and *March to Aldermaston*, the 1959 film produced by the Film and Television Committee for Nuclear Disarmament depicting the previous year's march from London to the Atomic Weapons Research Establishment.[111] Willoughby would, however, have been able to contrast Carter's rosy picture with Rustin's earlier report of Michael Randle's complaint that their publicity officer was 'high handed and determined', suggesting that tensions between the peace campaigners and the Ghanaian authorities around the project agenda had already begun to emerge.[112]

During November, the make-up of the protest team began to coalesce, as more international participants began to arrive in Accra, and Ghanaian activists – many of whom were closely connected with Nkrumah and his government – increased their influence on the project. When Esther Peter's participation in the protest team was announced in October, an Indian participant, Hemlatha Devi, had been listed alongside Peter. Although Devi's involvement in the team was supported by the DAC, it appears that she encountered difficulties in securing a visa for Ghana. At one stage, Randle appeared confident that the main organizer of the Ghana Committee for Nuclear Disarmament, E. C. Quaye, would vouch for Devi, but she does not seem to have joined the other team members in Accra.[113] The CNVA and DAC discussed the possibility of replacing Sutherland with a white US participant, for 'representational' reasons, but no suitable candidates were found, and Sutherland was determined to continue his active role. The discussions about representation reveal something of the sensitivity of US campaigners to the racial dynamics of the protest, which would surface at several points throughout the time that peace campaigners worked in Ghana in 1959–60. One of those considered as a replacement for Sutherland was CNVA member Jim Peck who (like Willoughby) had been one of Albert Bigelow's crew members in the *Golden Thread* the previous year. Peck was dissuaded from travelling to Ghana on health grounds but clearly understood the value of the Sahara protest in bringing together two of the main strands of global activism in the 1950s. The project was, he insisted, 'a demonstration of brotherhood . . . and it is a demonstration against colonialism'.[114] In the American context, the interweaving of peace and anti-colonial movements obviously paralleled

---

[109] *The Guardian*, 1 October, 1959, 20; *The Times*, 1 October 1959, 8.
[110] Carter to Michael Randle, 19 November 1959, SPC CNVA VI Sahara Project Correspondence.
[111] Carter to Willoughby, 26 October SPC CNVA VI; see also Christopher R. Hill, *Peace and Power in Cold War Britain: Media, Movements and Democracy, C. 1945–68* (London: Bloomsbury Publishing, 2018), 116–17.
[112] Rustin to George Willoughby, 18 October 1959, SPC CNVA VI.
[113] Randle to Hemlata Devi, 13 November 1959, SPC CNVA VI Sahara Project Correspondence.
[114] Peck to Bayard Rustin, 16 November 1959, SPC CNVA VI Sahara Project Correspondence.

the history of interconnections between pacifist and civil rights activism. In 1959, these connections seemed to be literally embodied in the person of Bayard Rustin. Peck was one of those in attendance at meeting with A. Phillip Randolph to discuss Rustin's journey to Africa in the context of his commitments to the civil rights movement. Peck argued that Rustin's participation in the protest would enhance, rather than detract from, his work as a civil rights organizer. Moreover, he noted with concern that Rustin was apparently regarded as indispensable to all US non-violent protest campaigns – 'it is a sad situation when non-violent action ... depends on a single individual in order to take place', he concluded.[115]

On his arrival in Accra on 19 November, Scott demonstrated that he still seemed able to act as a bridge between peace and anti-colonial movements – and more significantly, between Western activists and Africans. His welcome was dramatic: a large crowd had gathered at the airport and carried Scott on their shoulders from the aircraft to an awaiting car. Such well-organized demonstrations of support concealed, however, the tensions that had begun to emerge between the protest team and their Ghanaian hosts. Underpinning much of the friction was the question of funding. The DAC organizers in Britain had continued to struggle to raise funds from their supporters – by mid-November their appeal had yielded only £500 in donations – but the resources of the CNVA were not limitless. By the end of October, Rustin had already spent $400 on travel expenses, which was $100 more than the donations that Muste had secured by that point.[116] When in early November, the CNVA nevertheless agreed to commit to the project, they aimed to raise $3,000 by the middle of the month. The committee also agreed that Rustin should remain in Accra and become an official participant in the protest.[117] But these efforts were shown into shade by the response within Ghana. The night before Scott landed in Accra, the Komla Gbedemah spoke in a radio broadcast of the refusal of Africans 'to permit our god-given land to be used for the destruction of humanity' and launched an appeal for £9,000 to support the team.[118] When A. J. Muste arrived in Accra at the end of the month, he discovered that nearly £10,000 had been raised in Ghana with significant amounts donated at mass meetings attended by the protest team. He concluded, somewhat drily that such 'local funds will take care African phase of project'.[119] In terms of material resources, Western campaigners relied on African support.

This had a direct effect on the dynamics of the network of supporters around the protest team. Initially, Nkrumah's Ministers had offered to fund the protest directly, but the protest team declined. Instead, a Working Committee was formed, under the joint sponsorship of the DAC and CNVA as well as the Ghana Council for Nuclear Disarmament and the Bureau of African Affairs.[120] The Working Committee itself

[115] Ibid.; Carter, 'Memorandum to Team in Accra', 12 November 1959, SPC CNVA VI Sahara Project Correspondence.
[116] Muste to Margaret Lamont, 19 October 1959; Rustin to A. J. Muste, 19 October 1959, SPC Muste Papers Sahara Protest Team, Reel 89/16.
[117] Willoughby to Bayard Rustin, 5 November 1959, SPC CNVA VI Sahara Protest Correspondence.
[118] Gbedemah, Radio Address, 18 November 1959, SPC CNVA VI Sahara Project Memos. Drafts etc.
[119] Muste to George Willoughby, 26 November 1959, SPC CNVA VI Sahara Project Correspondence.
[120] Jean Allman, 'Nuclear Imperialism and the Pan-African Struggle for Peace and Freedom: Ghana, 1959–1962', *Souls* 10, no. 2 (2008): 83–102.

comprised a number of African officials with close links to government, along with Sutherland, Rustin and Scott. Its African members included Quaye and Gbedemah, and its meetings were held in the offices of the Finance Ministry. The committee included another Ghanaian minister, Nathanial Welbeck, the former General Secretary of the Convention People's Party who would find himself briefly in the international spotlight the following year when, as Ghana's representative to the Congo, he was surrounded by Congolese troops loyal to President Kasu Vubu for aligning too closely with Patrice Lumumba.[121] The committee also included Abdoulaye Diallo, the Guinean former vice chair of the World Federation of Trades Unions, organizer of the Francophone transnational labour movement, the *Union générale des travailleurs d'Afrique noire* and, according to Rustin's notes in 1959, the representative of Guinea in Accra. Finally, the Committee included two members connected with the Bureau of African Affairs, E. J. Duplain and Ras Makonnen, who had taken over as the Director of the Bureau following the death of Padmore. Born in Guyana, Makonnen studied in North America before travelling to Europe in the mid-1930s and settling in London in 1937. He became a close associate of Padmore at the International African Service Bureau and became Secretary of the Pan-African Federation when it was revived in Manchester in 1944. A leading organizer of the pan-African movement in Britain, he founded the journal *Pan-Africa* in 1947. Makonnen moved to Ghana in 1957 and became active in the Bureau of African Affairs but would later criticize the failure to build on its capacity to become a foundation for pan-African politics after Padmore's death.[122] In Rustin's assessment, Muste and others had the 'very difficult' task of restraining Makonnen on the Working Committee and claimed that he was 'much disliked by most of cabinet'. In his summary of the arrangements in Accra, Rustin described the committee to Ralph Bunche as 'a peculiar group and not simple to work with', but it had been agreed that the team itself would have the final say on strategy and that an emphasis on non-violence would be maintained.[123] Issues of race came to the surface when Randle was barred from sitting on the Working Committee as he was 'open to suspicion', and Rustin noted that 'even Michael Scott is not fully trusted' by some of the committee. Muste described the situation as 'awkward', and Scott remained the committee's only white member.[124]

The final team assembled in Accra on 5 December. That night, Scott spoke on Ghana Radio, declaring that the protestors were about to embark on a 'non-violent war against the inhumanity of nuclear war'.[125] Ten Ghanaian volunteers, including Kwame Frimpong Manu, joined the international activists, along with Ntsu Mokhehle, the president of the Basutoland Congress Party (who would later become prime minister of Lesotho in the mid-1990s), and Nigerian student Hilary Arinze. The European participants in the protest comprised the British contingent of Hoyland, Randle and Scott, alongside Esther Peter and another French supporter, Pierre Martin, a member of War Resisters International and the humanitarian organization Service Civil

---

[121] *New York Times*, 22 November 1960.
[122] Marika Sherwood and Hakim Adi, *Pan-African History: Political Figures From Africa and the Diaspora Since 1787* (London: Routledge, 2003), 118–21.
[123] Rustin to Ralph Bunche, 22 November 1959, SPC CNVA VI Sahara Project Correspondence.
[124] Muste to George Willoughby, 26 November 1959, SPC CNVA VI Sahara Project Correspondence.
[125] Quoted in Allman, 'Nuclear Imperialism', 90.

International, who had been working for UNESCO in Ghana. The final members of the team comprised the US contingent of Rustin and Sutherland. Muste remained in Accra and reported on the team's progress to supporters in the United States.

The team set out from Accra on 6 December, after being given a 'tremendous farewell' from its local supporters.[126] Prior to their departure, the team had released a statement setting out their plans to provide, first of all, a 'symbol and focal point through which the people of Africa . . . might express their resentment and protest against the Sahara test', but if they were able to reach the test site, to 'place their lives in the way of the nuclear instrument that may ultimately wipe out thousands of lives'.[127] The team had awoken before dawn to attend a rally held at Accra Arena. An estimated crowd of around a thousand people had arrived by 6 am to greet the protestors, who had become known in the city simply as 'Sahara'. With Quaye as Master of Ceremonies, Gbedemah gave the main address to the crowd, which included forceful criticism – 'when Frenchmen assume high office, they become mad'.[128] Gbedemah's direct attack on French colonialism – something about which the DAC had, of course, expressed deep misgivings during their short collaboration with the CAO – culminated in the claim that 'every bad Frenchman will be driven from Africa'.

The protest, moreover, was defined by Gbedemah in decidedly Africanist terms – although an international team, he declared that its members were 'now a part of Africa . . . forever enshrined in the hearts of Africa'. Once Gbedemah had concluded, the team boarded their vehicles and set out through the streets of Accra, which were lined with supporters and well-wishers. They then drove to Gbedemah's family home. As guests poured libations for the success of the team, Muste reflected on the consequences of the extensive support that had been given by the Ghanaian government. No government, he acknowledged, could be 'truly devoted to non-violence and its revolutionary implications', but nor could organizers of non-violent actions operate if state authorities opposed them – as their experience would show. But Muste insisted that no compromise on matters of principle had been required and, in fact, for many in the Convention Peoples Party, 'Sahara' had resuscitated 'the idealism and enthusiasm of the hard struggle for independence'.[129] Although Muste was by no means an impassive observer of the ongoing debates around the legitimacy of violence in the cause of African freedom, his reflections suggest that the contemporary 'moral and methodological dialogue over what an independent Africa should look like' was not purely about the future, but also spoke to the personal histories of Ghanaian activists.[130] Moreover, Muste argued that the team's experience showed that popular support for non-violence was widespread in Africa and that the protest had 'crystallized' but not invented African concerns about nuclear weapons.

---

[126] Muste to Willoughby, 7 December SPC CNVA VI Sahara Project Correspondence.
[127] *Guardian*, 7 December 1959, 9.
[128] Muste, Draft account of Sahara Protest for *Liberation*, 6 December 1959 (Muste Sahara Protest Team Reel 89/16).
[129] Muste, Draft account of Sahara Protest for *Liberation*, 6 December 1959, SPC Muste 89/16 Sahara Protest Team.
[130] Jeffrey S. Ahlman, 'The Algerian Question in Nkrumah's Ghana, 1958–1960: Debating "Violence" and "Nonviolence" in African Decolonization', *Africa Today* 57, no. 2 (2010): 66–84.

Muste's optimism for the potential development of a non-violent pacifist movement in Africa was supported by the applications to join the protest team that had been received as they travelled north across Ghana. The would-be volunteers seemed, however, motivated by a sense of national and African solidarity rather than a dedication to non-violence per se. In a joint letter written a few days before the convoy set out, three municipal workers from Kumasi pledged themselves to be willing to 'die in the flower of youth at the verge of winning a noble chance than live as long a bull in a stall'.[131] Another would-be volunteer, Prosper Tsegah, suggested that 'the people representing us to the Sahara testing sight [sic] are not enough to represent a very big nation'; if people 'far from the north of Africa' could express their sympathies with Africans, he argued, then Africans themselves ought to be ready to help.[132] Alexander Asiamah, from Osiem in the Eastern Region, wrote in similar terms of his desire to join the team and show his 'sincere love to this new nation "Ghana" in particular and Africa in general, and to show my sincere love to humanity'.[133] More than one volunteer expressed their readiness to face danger if it would help to highlight African opposition to the tests; J. A. Ossei, a trades union organizer, stated bluntly that he would be prepared 'to die at Sahara for the sake of my brother Africans if French intend of killing Africans'.[134]

Whatever the root cause of local support, the Sahara team's journey north was followed avidly by official news services and marked popular support throughout the country. After leaving Accra, they had driven to the city of Kumasi before heading on to Tamale on the second day. In each city, crowds gathered and cheered the progress of the convoy, prompting Muste to raise the possibility of training a 'permanent nonviolent and pacifist movement'.[135] On the third day, the team reached Navrongo, close to the border with Upper Volta. Here, the team reportedly met with William Frances Hare, Governor-General of Ghana and former Cabinet minister during Attlee's Labour government. Hare knew Michael Scott and, in Muste's account, was sufficiently interested in the Sahara project to suggest that some British officials had misgivings about the French tests.[136] The following day, the convoy of vehicles left Navrongo and headed north into Upper Volta. Muste left the team at this juncture and waited at the nearby town of Baku to report on their progress. The main group managed to cross into French-controlled territory without incident, displaying anti-nuclear flags and singing as they journeyed through 'a near-desert no-man's land' until they reached the customs post in the town of Bittou.[137] Here, they were halted by police. Discussions ensued after the officers informed the group that they had been instructed to refuse them entry to

---

[131] Boyake, Arthur, Bobson and Halman to Michael Scott, 2 December 1959, SPC Muste 89/16/Sahara Protest Team.
[132] Prosper Desmond Tsegah to Sahara Protest Team, 9 December 1959, SPC Muste, 89/16/Sahara Protest Team.
[133] Alexander Asiamah to Sahara Protest Team, 1 December 1959, SPC Muste, 89/16/Sahara Protest Team.
[134] J. A. Ossei to Michael Scott, 2 December 1959, SPC Muste, 89/16/Sahara Protest Team.
[135] Muste draft account of Sahara Protest for *Liberation*, 12 December 1959, SPC Muste 89/16 Sahara Protest Team Reel.
[136] Ibid.
[137] Ibid.; *Guardian*, 11 December 1959, 1.

the territory. But, as they had not been told to arrest the protestors if they refused to return to Ghana, the local police had to travel to the capital Ouagadougou, for further instructions. In the meantime, local onlookers gathered, evidently aware of what had brought the strange visitors into their midst, and equally clear in their ambivalence towards the French bomb test. 'If it's harmless', one observer suggested, 'why not hold it in the country outside Paris, so that all the French people can see the wonder!'[138]

The situation quickly developed into a stalemate. When police officers returned at midday on Thursday (10 December) they had been given no clear directives, but nevertheless insisted the team hand over the keys to all their vehicles.[139] The team refused, whereupon police were deployed to surround the convoy. Rustin led some of the protestors back to Ghana, to report on developments, and after four days the remainder of the group retreated back across the border.[140] A week later, a smaller second group returned to Upper Volta, comprising Scott, Randle, Sutherland and four Ghanaians, including a teacher and musician Kwame Frimpong Manso, who Randle remembered entertaining the team with a protest song against nuclear weapons he had composed on the journey.[141] In an apparent test of local officials, this group travelled to the town of Pô around 20 kilometres beyond the border but some distance west of Bittou but, again, police officers halted their progress. They camped near the customs barrier, obstructing the main road and each day would make several attempts to cross before sitting in the road to maintain their public vigil, which included prayers and talks led by Scott.[142] On 21 December, Pierre Martin set up camp outside the French Embassy in Accra and, on Christmas Day, began a fast in protest at his country's refusal to grant the team permission to enter Upper Volta.[143] On 30 December, he was visited by a delegation of Ghanaian officials including Quaye, as well as Clarkson Nylaander, the Minister of Defence, and Tawiah Adamafio, General Secretary of the CPP. In response to questions from Martin, Nylander declared that Ghana would continue to prioritize spending on 'improving the social and economic welfare of the country' rather than the development of nuclear weapons.[144] Martin maintained his fast outside the Embassy until 8 January, culminating in a public meeting addressed by Gbedemah before Martin was then carried shoulder-high by Ghanaian supporters.[145] The protest team remained encamped in Pô, while local authorities reportedly sought to construct a new route around their vehicles. The protest was eventually broken up on 3 January, when the team set off on foot past the border post before being surrounded by police. The keys of their vehicles were confiscated, the vehicles themselves impounded and the

---

[138] Muste, A. J. 'Memo for Liberation', December 12, 1959. SPC Muste, 89/16/Sahara Protest Team.
[139] Telegram from Muste 11 December SPC CNVA VI Sahara Project Correspondence.
[140] *Guardian*, 11 December 1959, 1.
[141] Michael Levy, *Ban the Bomb!* (Stuttgart: Ibidem Press, 2021), 94.
[142] Muste to Bishop Horace Donegan, 23 December 1959, Muste to Gerald Petch, 29 December 1959, SPC Muste, 89/16/ Sahara Protest Team.
[143] DAC Press Release, 'Sahara Protest Against French Nuclear Tests', 22 December 1959, SPC CNVA VI Sahara Project DAC.
[144] Press Release, 'French Atom Bomb Explosion in the Sahara', 30 December 1959, UKNA DO 35/9340.
[145] Randle, Cable to CNVA, 8 January 1960, SPC CNVA VI Sahara Project Correspondence.

team were driven to the town of Léo, around 80 kilometres further west, before they were taken to Tumu in Ghana.[146]

An ill wind

The New Year brought an end to any realistic hope that the team would reach Reggane, but the core members of the Sahara team remained in northern Ghana, determined to find some way of maintaining their protest. At this juncture, however, another group of European visitors had arrived in Ghana as the final preparations for the French tests were underway. The British prime minister Harold Macmillan flew into Accra on 6 January, on the first stage of an extensive tour of Africa that would culminate in his famed 'Winds of Change' speech to the South African Parliament in late February. Although efforts were made to maintain cordial relations during Macmillan's stay in Accra, it was clear that the prevailing currents were not entirely hospitable. According to reports in the British press, the emphasis was on the 'friendly' encounter between Macmillan and Nkrumah, despite a recognition of the underlying tensions that marked the meeting between the leader of the former colonial power and one of the most prominent and outspoken critics of colonialism and neocolonialism. On his arrival at the airport, Macmillan announced his intention to 'come to see, to hear, and to learn' before being driven with Nkrumah through 'waving crowds' in Accra.[147] The *New York Times* offered a somewhat different assessment of the temperature of the meeting, noting that Nkrumah had been 'expected to pose as the militant champion of immediate freedom'; it also observed that the public reception was a little more muted than that suggested by the *Guardian*, as the convoy from the airport had skirted the centre of Accra, ensuring that 'few Ghanaians saw the British visitor'.[148] Over the course of the week in Ghana, Macmillan sought – with only limited success – to maintain control over the representations of the progress towards decolonization by British journalists, while local newspapers positioned their British counterparts as 'scapegoating outsiders' unable to portray the anti-colonialism expressed by Nkrumah and others in anything but a negative light.[149]

The veneer of friendliness may well be part of the standard performances of political summits, and both Macmillan and Nkrumah had compelling reasons to present their meeting in positive terms. Nkrumah, as the *Daily Mail* report on the initial meeting commented, was already showing signs of the paranoia that would increasingly mark his political style and the decision to arrange a press conference for Nkrumah, who had 'become almost a recluse as far as interviews go' was seen as a demonstration of the significance of Macmillan's visit.[150] The initial talks between the leaders focused on the Volta hydroelectric scheme, vital to Nkrumah's vision for economic development,

---

[146] Ibid.; *Guardian*, 4 January 1959, 7.
[147] *Guardian*, 7 January 1960, 1.
[148] *New York Times*, 7 January 1960, 8.
[149] Rosalind Coffey, *The British Press, Public Opinion and the End of Empire in Africa: The 'Wind of Change', 1957–60* (London: Palgrave Macmillan, 2022), 137–8.
[150] *Daily Mail*, 7 January 1960.

which Macmillan visited on 9 January. That same day, Macmillan met a delegation from the opposition United Party, signalling the British prime minister's 'concern for the standards of the Commonwealth'.[151] But Macmillan also had reasons to foster a positive impression of relations with Ghana. British journalists had challenged the Ghanaian Minister of Information, Kofi Baako, on the introduction of measures to allow 'preventative detention' of political opponents, to which the quick reply was that at least Ghanaian people – unlike those in Nyasaland – could exert their democratic will in elections; Macmillan was quick to cite this official response when he was challenged over the imprisonment of Jomo Kenyatta and continued imposition of emergency measures in Kenya, but the challenges posed by independence movements in central and eastern Africa could not entirely be brushed away.[152]

However, when the French atomic weapons programme was raised at Macmillan's final press conference in the country, it was difficult to maintain diplomatic balance. In response to questions from Ghanaian journalists, Macmillan stated his support for the French claims that the tests were 'too remote from inhabited areas to endanger health' and that Britain had no moral right to block French attempts to develop an atomic weapons programme when the country had a nuclear arsenal of its own.[153] In this reply, Macmillan stayed well within the boundaries of the briefing document on the tests that had been prepared in advance of the trip, and he concluded with the fundamental principle that had been held since the UN debates of the previous autumn, reasserting the focus of British policy on initiatives at the talks in Geneva that would lead to a ban on all nuclear tests, rather than efforts to single out individual countries such as France.[154] At another press conference, held on the day Macmillan left Ghana, Randle and Quaye claimed that Macmillan's statements had in fact encouraged France to press ahead with its test plans and, furthermore, they insisted that it was impossible to offer assurances that the tests would be harmless. Quotations from their statement accompanied Ghanaian press reports of the departure of Macmillan.[155] When Macmillan addressed the Nigerian Parliament on 13 January, he did not stray from the briefing lines on the French tests but did emphasize his desire 'for all nuclear tests to be brought to an end everywhere in the world, in Africa as much as in Asia, or Europe or America or in the Pacific'.[156] This was sufficient to prompt Quaye to send a telegram of congratulation to Macmillan, urging him to 'use his great influence to present France from carrying out tests on the soil of Africa'.[157]

By the time Macmillan left Ghana the Sahara team had regrouped in Bolgatanga. Although one replacement Land Rover had been secured, without a full complement of vehicles and with diminishing funds, they were forced to adjust their tactics. Another possible route, leaving from Nigeria, was rejected on the basis that the test was likely to

---

[151] *The Observer*, 10 January 1960, 1.
[152] *New York Times*, 11 January 1960, 13; *Guardian*, 7 January 1960, 1.
[153] *New York Times*, 11 January 1960, 13.
[154] '"French Atomic Tests" brief by the Commonwealth Relations Office', 31 December 1959, UKNA DO 35/9340.
[155] Randle Cable to CNVA, 14 January 1960, SPC CNVA VI Sahara Project Correspondence.
[156] *Times*, 14 January 1960.
[157] Randle Cable to CNVA, 14 January 1960, SPC CNVA VI Sahara Project Correspondence.

take place before resources and volunteers could be found.[158] They nevertheless began to formulate plans for one further attempt to cross into Upper Volta. Randle would later reflect that the project had been undermined by 'a too narrow interpretation of first principles', namely the idea of maintaining 'openness' with French authorities. It might, he suggested, not have been unethical to simply have informed the French of the group's general intentions. This was, in fact, the approach adopted when ten days after the breaking of the stalemate in Pô, the DAC announced that a third effort to cross the border would take place.[159] This time, the small group of volunteers were led across the border zone at night by locals and then hitched a lift northward aboard commercial vehicles. In this manner, they were able to travel 100 kilometres beyond the border before being recognized by the same French police officer they had encountered in Pô and forcibly returned again to Ghana.[160] Although they announced their determination to make another attempt to reach the test site, the team returned to Accra and Scott departed for the second All-African People's Conference in Tunis, which began on 24 January.[161]

Scott arrived in Tunis determined to maintain the momentum of the Sahara protest and to secure support for further attempts to infiltrate the test site. Although he acknowledged that the route north from Ghana was now impossible, he called for further volunteers to travel to Reggane by other means – one suggestion being that a team fly to Algeria and parachute into the testing zone and attempt to persuade workers on the site to strike.[162] The likelihood of such a plan succeeding seemed minimal, and French authorities had already announced plans for flight restrictions across most of southern Algeria in advance of the test itself. A mysterious central 'Zone 42', which obviously corresponded to Reggane itself, would be subject to the greatest restrictions and any attempt to fly into this area – even before the general restrictions had been announced – would have been difficult, to say the least.[163] The conference itself was something of a difficult encounter following the undoubted success (despite underlying tensions) of the Accra meeting in December 1958. Diallo, who had replaced Padmore as the key organizer of the conference, was met with criticism from Nigerian delegates for failing to report on the progress of the steering committee, Tom Mboya, chair of the Accra conference, had been demoted and the delegates from the Pan-African Movement of East and Central Africa were reportedly 'mutinous and on their guard'.[164] But the French tests provided a point of convergence within the pan-African movement. Following his opening address to the conference, the Tunisian president Habib Bourguiba addressed a crowd estimated at around 100,000, demanding the evacuation of the last remaining French military base at Bizerte and urged the protestors to march on the French Embassy.[165]

---

[158] Randle, Cable to CNVA, 12 January 1960, SPC CNVA VI Sahara Project Correspondence.
[159] Randle, untitled manuscript, 3, BPC Randle Cwl MR/1/3.
[160] *Guardian*, 18 January 1959, 2. See also Levy, *Ban the Bomb!* 95.
[161] *Guardian*, 23 January 1959, 6.
[162] *Guardian*, 30 January 1960, 7.
[163] *Times*, 9 January 1960.
[164] Catherine Hoskyns, 'Tunis Diary', *Africa South – In Exile* 4, no. 4 (July-September 1960): 105; *Guardian*, 30 January 1960.
[165] Ibid.; *New York Times*, 26 January 1960, 1.

The Sahara project helped to focus international public attention on the French tests, although in the early weeks of 1960 protests had begun to build their own momentum in Africa, Europe and North America. In some instances, team members and organizers worked in parallel with the Sahara team, and alongside Pierre Martin's vigil at the French Embassy in Accra, the Nigerian participant Hilary Arinze followed suit in early January at the French Consulate in Lagos.[166] In Britain, the DAC had turned its attention to new protest project aimed at the deployment of US 'Thor' Intermediate Range Ballistic Missiles. On 2 January, over eighty DAC activists were arrested at the Harrington air base in the Midlands after a protest march, while the following day leaders of CND delivered a protest to the US Embassy in London condemning the decision not to renew the voluntary test ban that had been agreed in 1958.[167] Over the following weeks, pickets were held at French government buildings in London, New York and Hamburg. In Accra, activists claimed to have links with the Convention Peoples' Party had gathered at the French Embassy at the end of January carrying placards calling on France to 'Test the Bomb on Your Own Soil'.[168] Police were deployed to protect the embassy, as Ghanaian authorities sought to balance continued official opposition to the French tests with attempts to dampen popular unrest. Calls for boycotts of French companies had been accompanied by rumoured threats of looting and loudspeaker vans toured Accra announcing that the police and army had been empowered to break up demonstrations with tear gas.[169] In North Africa, as well as Tunisia, large rallies were held in Libya and Morocco, and 500 African students were arrested in Paris at a demonstration on 11 February.[170]

The French military scientists detonated their bomb early in the morning of 13 February. The device, named *Gerboise Bleue*, was a plutonium bomb with a yield of 70 kilotons, much larger than any of the initial tests by the United States (1945), the Soviet Union (1949) and Britain (1952). In his public announcement later that day, President de Gaulle claimed that the test had been a 'national effort' that would 'reinforce her defensive potential, that of the community and that of the West'. In addition – and echoing the rational outlined by Pierre Mendès-France five years earlier – de Gaulle also claimed that the test would strengthen the ability of the French government to press for a disarmament agreement.[171] Muste put his feelings more bluntly: 'The French have exploded their damn bomb. The shadow of it has bean on all of as this weekend'.[172] Within hours of de Gaulle's official announcement, Nkrumah declared that the assets of French businesses in Ghana would be seized.[173] The Tunisian government threatened to take 'appropriate measures', while Morocco withdrew from the formal cooperation pact that had been signed with France at the country's independence in 1956, and the Japanese Embassy in Paris lodged a formal protest.[174]

[166] Carter, 'The Sahara Protest Team', 137.
[167] *Guardian*, 4 January 1960; *New York Times*, 4 January 1960.
[168] *New York Times*, 31 January 1960, 13.
[169] Telegram, Accra to CRO, 9 February 1960, UKNA DO 35/9340.
[170] Carter, 'The Sahara Protest Team', 137; 140.
[171] *New York Times*, 13 February 1960, 1.
[172] Muste to Bill Sutherland, 16 February 1960, SPC Muste 89/16.
[173] *Guardian*, 14 February 1960, 1.
[174] *New York Times*, 14 February 1960, 4, 16 February 1960, 1.

In India, with reports suggesting that winds were carrying radioactive material from the explosion across North Africa towards the Gulf and the South Asian subcontinent, government officials decried French action as 'injurious to the cause of world peace'.[175]

The Secretariat of the Afro-Asian Solidarity Conference had, meanwhile, issued an immediate call to its national bodies asking members to sever diplomatic relations with France.[176] Nor was the news welcomed in Washington. The French tests were an obvious insult to US authority and undermined the nuclear hegemony of Washington within the North Atlantic alliance. De Gaulle's determination to use the French atom bomb to strengthen the country's role in the Western alliance would come under further pressure following the victory of John F. Kennedy in the US Presidential election in November 1960. In the late 1950s, prior to launching his presidential campaign, Kennedy had been a supporter of Algerian independence and a critic of de Gaulle's atomic ambitions, and observed in 1959 that the 'French bomb is aimed at Washington rather than Moscow'.[177] The Sahara protest team had failed to halt the test, but as symbolic effort to link the politics of the Cold War and the processes of decolonization, it was a significant endeavour.

Disarmament and decolonization

A matter of weeks after the first test at Reggane, the British prime minister Harold Macmillan addressed the South African Parliament on the political trajectory of British colonialism in Africa. In his famous speech, Macmillan signalled the inevitability of decolonization and presented a challenge to the system of white minority rule in South Africa.[178] It has, rightly, become a landmark in the history of the British empire, but the events in southern Algeria meant that for contemporaries in west Africa, attention was focused on the anticipation of a very different set of air currents. While British and French scientists continued to claim that the impact of the test would be negligible, recent work suggests that the environmental consequences of the test were uncertain at the time, and much greater than those officially acknowledged to this day.[179] African responses to the tests were framed by fears of pollution that seem reasonable in the light of our expanded understanding of the impacts of radiation. In this context, the language of 'nuclear imperialism', employed by Nkrumah and other African leaders seems in retrospect, as Christopher Hill has put it, 'not so much as a propagandistic slogan as a compelling framework'.[180] Protests against the French tests had brought British and US anti-nuclear pacifists into alliance with African anti-

---

[175] *Times of India*, 17 February 1960, 1.
[176] *Times of India*, 15 February 1960, 7.
[177] Quoted in Constantine A. Pagedas, *Anglo-American Strategic Relations and the French Problem, 1960–1963: A Troubled Partnership* (London: Routledge, 2013), 129.
[178] Saul Dubow, 'Macmillan, Verwoerd, And The 1960 "Wind Of Change" Speech', *The Historical Journal* 54, no. 4 (2011): 1087–114.
[179] André Bendjebbar, *Histoire secrète de la bombe atomique française* (Paris: Le Cherche Midi Éditeur, 2000).
[180] Hill, 'Britain, West Africa', 274.

colonial campaigners who explicitly connected the history of 'centuries of slavery and imperial exploitation' with 'the pollution of our air with radioactive fallout'.[181]

It was not that the Sahara protest team were unaware of the underlying issues that shaped African opposition to the tests. In Michael Randle's view African anxieties were shaped predominantly by 'resentment of yet another colonialist outrage in Africa', rather than anti-nuclear pacifism. Ignoring this fact would, he felt, misunderstand the vital 'historical context' of the issue.[182] The principal lesson for peace campaigners was that genuine transnational connections would not be forged solely around nuclear disarmament, but its relevance to the politics of freedom and decolonization as it was understood in Africa. At the same time, pacifists were unwilling to compromise their own principles and thus sought to emphasize 'the importance of the non-violent tradition in the liberation struggle in Africa' and 'find responsible African leaders to play a leading part'.[183] The Sahara protest had suggested, however, that this would not be straightforward, although some peace campaigners argued that the problem was one of a lack of focus. The US Quaker and civil rights activist Ernest Bromley pronounced 'that the simple moral gesture of a small group determined to reach Reggane at all costs was side-tracked by extraneous political considerations'. Randle denied this was the case but acknowledged that the DAC had not originally expected that the protest would become entangled in Ghanaian politics. Ultimately, he admitted, the 'strong current of anti-colonial resentment' was an inevitable consequence of Ghanaian support. But at the same time, Randle saw this not as a failure of planning, but part of a learning process, in which peace campaigners were obliged to consider – and then 'state clearly and forcibly' – their position on the colonial context in which the French atomic tests were embedded.[184] As Sutherland noted, the campaign had made little effort to engage Francophone African support, and that, despite protests by Black students in Dakar and elsewhere in west Africa, the Sahara team could not 'overlook the fact either that we really haven't broken into the French African Community'.[185]

Thus, while the Sahara protest team had manifestly failed in its attempt to reach Reggane, it played a role in sustaining public interest in the tests despite French attempts to alleviate African concerns. But, the major failure of the project was, perhaps, that its attempts to construct an international and multi-racial protest that combined transatlantic disarmament movements with pan-African anti-colonialism, there seemed little sense of the need to address the underlying differences between them. The nuclear disarmament movement in Britain seemed at times to express a form of 'imperialist pacifism' and take the form of a 'romantic protest' characterized by a sense of nationalist exceptionalism.[186] A Britain free of nuclear weapons could,

---

[181] 'London Letter', *The Guardian*, 31 August 1959; *Times*, 31 August 1959; 'Africa Says No to French Tests', August 1959, DAC 5/7/7.
[182] M. Randle, '[untitled Memorandum]', n.d 1960, BPC Randle Cwl 1/3.
[183] M. Randle, 'Some Notes on the Positive Action Conference to Be Held in Accra', 20 March 1960, BPC DAC 5/7/20.
[184] Randle, untitled manuscript, BPC Randle Cwl MR/1/3.
[185] Sutherland to A. J. Muste, 17 March 1960, SPC Muste 89/16/Sahara Project.
[186] On 'imperialist pacifism' James Hinton, *Protests and Visions: Peace Politics in Twentieth-Century Britain* (London: Hutchinson Radius, 1989). On 'romantic protest', see Meredith Veldman, *Fantasy, the Bomb and the Greening of Britain: Romantic Protest, 1945–1980* (Cambridge: Cambridge

some campaigners argued, restore its international prestige by playing a mediating role between Cold War superpowers and non-aligned states.[187] Randle presented the Sahara protest in similar terms, suggesting that it offered an alternative vision of British internationalism, and claiming that, when he denounced Macmillan for his failure to condemn the French tests in early 1960, he had acted as 'an ambassador for radical Britain'.[188]

The academic and future Labour MP David Marquand offered another view of British disarmament campaigners, however, suggesting that the Aldermaston marchers were 'the lineal descendants of pious, upstanding Victorian pastors' whose 'language of internationalism' concealed an underlying nationalist pride.[189] More recent historical analysis has intimated that Aldermaston marchers seemed engaged in a form of 'civilising mission' and that the nuclear disarmament movement expressed its identity in terms that aligned with discourses of nationhood.[190] In her later study of post-1945 peace movements, April Carter contrasted the French and British experiences of decolonization, contending that Britain had been able to avoid 'provoking acute internal crisis' and activists could thus combine anti-colonial and disarmament in ways that their French counterparts were unable to match until after the end of the Algerian war.[191] Other accounts of British social movements also suggest that the mass peace movement of the late 1950s signalled the arrival of a new generation of protest that combined a critique of nuclear militarism with anti-colonial sentiment. According to Lent in his account of post-war British social movements, this had first been glimpsed with street protests against the Anglo-French military intervention in Egypt in 1956, organized by the MCF.[192] For British activists, the Sahara protest thus reflected the complex and contested legacies of the empire that marked a generation coming of age amidst the processes of decolonization.

In terms of its broader significance in the global history of decolonization, Allman suggests that the Sahara protest underlined the ways in which 'national liberation and nation-building, pan-Africanism and the radical, transnational peace movement were constitutive political struggles'.[193] Transnational peace campaigns were both enabled and constrained by decolonization, and while the Sahara team struggled to engage with the politics of the post-colonial nation state, the campaign against the French nuclear test programme also suggests that post-colonial politics had yet to coalesce in the early 1960s.[194] Ultimately, then, the Sahara protest revealed, but could

---

University Press, 1994), 120. See also Jodi Burkett, 'Re-Defining British Morality: "Britishness" and the Campaign for Nuclear Disarmament 1958–68', *Twentieth Century British History* 21, no. 2 (2010): 184–205.

[187] Ibid.,138.
[188] Carter, 'The Sahara Protest Team', 148.
[189] D. Marquand, 'England, the Bomb, the Marchers', *Commentary*, May 1960, 382; 385.
[190] Veldman, *Fantasy, the Bomb*; Nehring, 'National Internationalists', 28.
[191] April Carter, *Peace Movements: International Protest and World Politics since 1945* (London: Longman, 1992), 45.
[192] Adam Lent, *British Social Movements since 1945: Sex, Colour, Peace and Power* (Basingstoke: Palgrave, 2001), 31–2.
[193] Allman, 'Nuclear Imperialism', 84; 98.
[194] John D. Kelly and Martha Kaplan, *Represented Communities: Fiji and World Decolonization* (Chicago: University of Chicago Press, 2001), 9. See also John D. Kelly and Martha Kaplan, 'Nation

not reconcile, the underlying divisions between movements focused on nuclear weapons and colonialism. In Europe, national disarmament campaigns focused on the continued militarization of the continent, were shaped by distinctive political cultures and reflected the emotions of societies living through the aftermath of war.[195] In Europe, nuclear weapons made post-war fear manifest; in Africa they encapsulated the iniquities of colonialism, and the beginning of the 1960s would see utopian visions decolonization threatened by multiple crises. For the architects of the Sahara protest, the principles of non-violence were more vital than ever.

and Decolonization: Toward a New Anthropology of Nationalism', *Anthropological Theory* 1, no. 4 (2001): 419–37.

[195] Frank Biess, 'Feelings in the Aftermath: Toward a History of Postwar Emotions', in *Histories of the Aftermath: The Legacies of the Second World War in Europe,* edited by Frank Biess and Robert G. Moeller, 30–48 (New York: Berghahn Books, 2010), Incorporated, 37.

5

From 'nuclear imperialism' to armed struggle

Directly after the Sahara team's final effort was thwarted, Michael Scott travelled to Tunis to attend the second All-African People's Conference. He delivered a message outlining the attempts to travel to the site, before making a plea for support. 'We believe', he argued, 'that our way of civil disobedience and non-violent direct action can still at this last hour help to save the soul of France and the soil of Africa from the destructive violence that is being committed'.[1] Like Scott, this chapter picks up the themes of the Sahara protest, examining the attempts by peace campaigners to maintain their influence with African political leaders and activists in the face of increasing conflict and violence. Despite Scott's appeal to the conference and its unanimous condemnation of the French tests, African delegates were divided over the tactics of protest, with growing support for armed anti-colonial resistance. Just two months after the Tunis conference, this issue again became a focus of debate at an emergency meeting in Accra on 'nuclear imperialism'. But the Ghanaian government continued to provide support to former members of the Sahara team as they turned their efforts to planning the establishment of a training centre for non-violence based in Ghana.

However, political crisis in Africa, from the ongoing war in Algeria to the shooting of Black protestors at Sharpeville in South Africa, and, critically, the rapid collapse of post-independence Congo, gripped the attention of government officials. The chapter then turns to debates around the tactics of protest, as advocates of Gandhian non-violence began to lose ground to the claims of those such as Frantz Fanon who argued that colonial states had left nationalists no option other than violent revolution. This fed an emerging discourse of national liberation achieved through militant struggle against colonialism, in contrast to Gandian non-violence. The final section of the chapter explores the revival of an idea, first proposed in the interwar period, for the formation of a peace army that would stage interventions in zones of civil conflict and war. Discussions around the viability of a new peace army originated in India and the United States, but following a conference held in Beirut in January 1962, international campaigners announced the formation of the World Peace Brigade. As such, this chapter focuses on a kind of undeclared 'war of position' between peace campaigners, militant revolutionaries and militarized colonial states in the early 1960s.

---

[1] Scott, 'A Statement on the Sahara Protest Team to All-African Peoples' Conference at Tunis on behalf of the Ghana Council for Nuclear Disarmament', Papers from the Second All-African People's Conference, Tunisia [1960] British Library, EAP121/1/4/7, https://eap.bl.uk/archive-file/EAP121-1-4-7.

Against 'nuclear imperialism': Accra 1960

Even when viewed in isolation, the French atomic weapon test in mid-February 1960 represented a threat and opportunity for peace campaigners and revealed both the convergences and very real differences between the anti-nuclear and anti-colonial dynamics of the protest. In the wider context of events in Africa in the first months of 1960, the test embodied an almost bewildering set of contradictory developments. Just as the Sahara team returned to Africa after their third failed attempt to cross into Upper Volta, the French General Jaques Massu – the 'victor of the "Battle of Algiers"' revealed his deep unease with de Gaulle's aim of self-determination in Algeria and was recalled to Paris. On 23 January, settlers began to erect barricades in Algiers, and clashes between protestors and police led to twenty deaths. The stand-off lasted a week before de Gaulle asserted control.[2] Marking the moment at which France began to disentangle itself from Algeria, the near-coincidence of the week of the barricades and the explosion of *Gerboise Bleue* reflected the strength and weakness of French power; like Macmillan's tour of Africa (although with conflicting aims), de Gaulle's actions in Algeria in early 1960 reflected the entangled, yet divergent, agendas of European decolonization and Cold War strategic defence policy. For leaders of independent African states, however, the crisis in Algeria and the atomic test were presented as a straightforward manifestation of neocolonialism.

In the aftermath of their failed attempts to infiltrate the test site in early 1960, the Sahara team began to seek alternative ways of maintaining the protest against French tests. Although diminished in size, the team did not immediately disband following the detonation at Reggane, and the main figures remained in Africa. Sutherland had returned to work in Gbedemah's office, but Randle remained in Accra in an attempt to maintain the work of the team. After the conference in Tunis, Scott had travelled to Morocco to investigate the possibility of reviving the plan to send a team to Algeria from there – British officials noted reports from Rabat that Scott had told local reporters of plans to fly into the test zone using a chartered aircraft.[3] These schemes – which Rustin, at least, seemed to regard with some bemusement – came to little, and Scott returned to Ghana in mid-February. Having reconvened in Accra, the team began efforts to persuade the Ghanaians to keep up international pressure against the French test programme.

Scott was particularly enthusiastic to make plans for an international conference of African states to discuss actions in response to the French tests. Randle was pessimistic and felt that Gbedemah – the Ghanaian leader most closely aligned with the protest – was 'lukewarm' on the idea.[4] However, Kwame Nkrumah used Independence Day celebrations on March 6 to announce an emergency meeting of African states that would examine the issue of the French tests alongside wider concerns surrounding a 'new form of colonialism and its attempt to Balkanize the continent and destroy

---

[2] Martin Evans, 'Towards an Emotional History of Settler Decolonisation: De Gaulle, Political Masculinity and the End of French Algeria 1958–1962', *Settler Colonial Studies* 8, no. 2 (2018): 213–43.
[3] Telegram – Rabat to FO, 4 February 1960, UKNA DO 35/9340.
[4] Randle to A. J. Muste, 22 February 1960, SPC Muste 89/16 Sahara Protest Team.

African unity'.[5] While Nkrumah had already planned to convene a meeting to address the challenges of 'neocolonialism', Scott had reportedly persuaded him to include this within discussions of the specific issue of the French tests and 'continuing non-violent action against the French bomb tests'.[6] Scott then returned to Morocco before embarking on a tour of North African states but recommended that Michael Randle stay in Accra, where he was given a desk in Nkrumah's Bureau of African Affairs in order to assist in the arrangements for the conference.

Although Randle was anxious that the event would be an 'African initiative', rather than 'an attempt by "Westerners" to import and impose their own ideas', the conference was seen by peace campaigners as a moment of possibility.[7] As Sutherland noted in a message to A. J. Muste in New York, the mood at pan-African meetings suggested that African leaders were disillusioned by international organizations such as the UN and had begun to feel obliged to 'do something on their own'. The conference was thus a 'golden opportunity to write out own ticket' and shape the agenda of a conference that had originally been open to delegations from independent African states but would now include representatives from international anti-imperial and anti-nuclear groups that might influence 'change in Africa through non-violent techniques'.[8] A draft agenda produced on the day after the formal announcement of the conference split the discussion into three committees: one would focus on the future development of 'positive action' in Africa including the establishment of a permanent training centre in non-violence; the second committee would explore options for diplomatic and international interventions against France, alongside the Algerian war and apartheid in South Africa; the final committee was to examine the 'dangers of balkanisation', discussing issues including the French Community, economic imperialism and development.[9] This would eventually be amended to four committees, one examining the atomic tests, another the general question of liberation from colonial rule, and two looking specifically at Algeria and South Africa.[10]

Initially scheduled for mid-April, planning for the conference was accelerated when organizers realized that the Accra meeting would clash with the second Afro-Asian Peoples' Solidarity Conference due to take place in Conakry, and brought the conference forward to open at the end of the first week of April. The oversight exemplifies both the speed at which the Accra meeting was arranged, but also that transnational networks have the potential for dysfunction as much as interdependence. The Accra meeting was an opportunity for peace campaigners to engage with, and possibly shape, pan-African support for non-violence, but the diverse array of themes for discussion that might pull debate in other directions.

For campaigners such as Scott and Sutherland, non-violence was the moral force that underpinned their support for African anti-colonial nationalism and aligned it

---

[5] 'Cable Received from Accra', 6 March 1960, BPC DAC 5/7/20.
[6] Sutherland to A. J. Muste, 3 March 1960, SPC Muste 89/7/African Conference on Nonviolence.
[7] Randle, 'Some Notes on the Positive Action Conference', 20 March 1960, SPC Muste 89/7/African Conference on Nonviolence.
[8] Ibid.; Cable – Randle to DAC, 6 March 1960, BPC Randle Cw1 DAC 5/7/20.
[9] Randle, 'Conference on Positive Action for Peace and Security in Africa', 7 March 1960, SPC Muste 89/7/African Conference on Nonviolence.
[10] Randle, 'Article on Conference on Peace and Security in Africa', [n.d. 1960], BPC DAC 5/7/20.

with their own political philosophies.[11] The key concern, therefore, was not how to schedule the event within the wider context of African summits and Third World solidarity conferences, but how to ensure the opportunity to foreground principles of non-violence would not be sidetracked by the agendas of other delegates. Sutherland was anxious that the conference might be overshadowed by Cold War rivalries and 'the violence boys from Algeria and elsewhere'. But the greatest danger, in Sutherland's view, would be a failure to present viable and 'imaginative' proposals for non-violent action.[12] Randle, meanwhile, worried in particular that the conference debate would be shaped by the Algerian FLN, who had secured support for the establishment of a volunteer brigade of fighters during the All-African Peoples' Congress in Tunis in January.[13] Randle suggested that *Peace News* might enhance its growing coverage of African issues by publishing material aligned with the conference themes, in the hope that they might maximize the impact of anti-nuclear and pacifist ideologies on the discussions in Accra.[14] He proposed that *Peace News* publish a special edition to coincide with the conference, including contributions from United States, Asian and African advocates of non-violent resistance as well as clear proposals for further protests against France that would be 'challenging and concrete'.[15] Editions of *Peace News* in April 1960 duly focused on ways in which African states might build on the wave of international protest at the French tests, including a list of seventeen suggestions for an ongoing campaign set out by Fenner Brockway. The proposals set out action that might be taken by independent African states, including a joint appeal to the UN and possible economic sanctions, as well as actions that might be undertaken by African peoples themselves. Brockway noted that the greatest pressure on France would come from a popular protest from within the French Community, but his proposals were ultimately limited to forms of political action – petition and deputation – that in many respects marked a previous generation of activism. His final proposals were for a 'Sahara Bomb Day' that would be 'made the occasion of demonstrations in Africa and throughout the world demanding No More Tests'.[16]

Sutherland would later claim that the conference was the pinnacle of pacifist influence on African liberation.[17] But, despite the efforts of Sutherland, Randle and other anti-nuclear campaigners to create a moment of mobilization for an international peace movement, the Accra Positive Action conference was in essence a pan-African protest against 'nuclear imperialism' and neocolonialism. Opposition to nuclear weapons was, for most delegates, couched in anti-colonial rhetoric. Even its location, the Accra Community Centre, the site of the All-Africa Peoples' Congress of December 1958, underlined the strength of anti-colonial, rather than anti-nuclear, legacies. Nkrumah's opening speech included Scott's earlier proposal for a renewed protest efforts against

---

[11] See Scott, *A Time to Speak*, 295–312; Sutherland and Meyer, *Guns and Gandhi*.
[12] Sutherland to A. J. Muste, 17 March 1960, SPC Muste 89/16/Sahara Project.
[13] Randle, 'Some Notes on the Positive Action Conference', 20 March 1960, SPC Muste 89/7/African Conference on Nonviolence.
[14] Randle to Pat Arrowsmith and April Carter, 7 March 1960, BPC Randle Cw1 DAC 5/7/20.
[15] Randle to [Brock?], 8 March 1960, BPC Randle Cw1 DAC 5/7/20.
[16] Fenner Brockway, 'The Sahara Bomb Conference: Seventeen Suggestions for Action', *Peace News*, 1 April 1960, 7.
[17] Wittner, *Resisting the Bomb*, 268.

the French tests, based on mass protests from multiple destinations, making direct reference to Gandhi's Salt March. Amidst a series of references to the vital place of non-violent action, he condemned the French tests and declared that Africans 'renounce the foul weapons that threaten the very existence of life on this planet'.[18] But for much of his address, Nkrumah centred on the key themes of his political credo: unity and non-alignment. And while the question of nuclear disarmament was mentioned by many delegates, the conference speeches tended to focus as much attention on the contemporary crises in Algeria and South Africa as they did on the French tests.

The tension between non-violence and armed struggle was palpable. Fouad Galal, the head of the delegation from the United Arab Republic, declared that he supported all liberation movements, 'whether they use peaceful means or resort to arms. We believe that all means of liberation are justified by the very nature of colonialism which is nothing but aggressive'.[19] The French atomic weapons tests were thus, he argued, a further manifestation of French aggression. The struggle in Algeria, he claimed, represented the wider struggle for freedom across Africa, and Algerians had a fundamental right to ask for aid in their fight against France, just as France had sought the aid of others during German occupation. The Liberian delegate similarly singled out French colonialism in their condemnation of the test in Reggan, worrying that 'in desperation France who now possesses such a weapon may not use it either in Algeria or on the rest of us'.[20] But much of the Liberian statement was devoted to rights to self-determination and condemnation of colonial authoritarianism including the recent shootings by South African police of non-violent protestors in the township of Sharpeville.[21] Again, the conference was told that those calling for violent resistance to colonialism had a right to do so, although 'more effective methods' might also be found. But movements confronting colonialism were engaged in a moral cause, and 'every possible assistance should be rendered those beleaguered in such a struggle'.

The Algerian war was the key dividing line for advocates of armed struggle. In the speeches and comments of delegates at Accra, a clear distinction was drawn between French colonial violence, which was condemned on all sides, and the violence adopted by what Romesh Chandra, the representative of the World Peace Council, called the 'magnificent liberation army of Algeria'.[22] The French tests were, he argued, a manifestation of the 'monstrous crime that is colonialism', revealed in 'all its hideous colours before every man and woman in every land'.[23] The WPC championed the 'heroic struggle of the Algerian people', he asserted, and welcomed the decision taken at the Tunis conference to establish a volunteer brigade to fight alongside the FLN in Algeria. Galal, meanwhile, had used his speech to announce the opening of a bureau in

---

[18] Walter Birmingham, 'International Conference on Positive Action for Peace and Security in Africa', SPC Muste 89/16/Sahara Project.
[19] 'Speech Delivered by Mr M. F. Galal', BPC, DAC 5/7/21, Accra Conference April 1960.
[20] 'Statement of the Leader of the Liberian Delegation', BPC, DAC 5/7/21, Accra Conference April 1960.
[21] Tom Lodge, *Sharpeville: An Apartheid Massacre and Its Consequences* (Oxford: Oxford University Press, 2011).
[22] 'Speech by Mr Romesh Chandra', BPC, DAC 5/7/21, Accra Conference April 1960.
[23] Ibid.

Cairo to register volunteers for the brigade.[24] Chandra, however, concluded his address by stating that, 'as an Indian, as a citizen of the land of Mahatma Gandhi and Jawaharlal Nehru', his country stood in solidarity with the struggle for African independence.[25] Perhaps the most powerful advocate for armed struggle, however, was Frantz Fanon, who had recently moved to Accra to take up the post of representative of the Provisional Government of Algeria. Fanon had seized the attention of the delegates at the first All-African Peoples' Conference in 1958 with an intervention from the floor in support of the militant resistance of the FLN in Algeria, changing the tone of African anti-colonialism and laying out a challenge to the path of non-violence and positive action advocated by Nkrumah and the conference chair Tom Mboya.[26] When he returned to the Accra conference hall in April 1960, then, he spoke with authority on the question of violence and colonialism. Colonialism was, in Fanon's view, built on violence, 'in everyday behaviour, violence against the past that is emptied of all substance, violence against the future, for the colonial regime presents itself as necessarily eternal'.[27] If the conference was, as Sutherland suggested, the peak of pacifist intervention and Gandhian influence on African independence movements, Fanon's address articulated a new philosophy of anti-colonialism, at the centre of which was the belief that the means of resistance ought to meet the means of colonial authority head on.

Fanon would go on to define non-violence as 'a creation of the colonial situation' that signalled the mutual recognition of interests between colonial and indigenous elites. It was, he wrote somewhat dismissively, 'an attempt to settle the colonial problem around a green baize table'.[28] Although the Sahara protest appeared to attract widespread support among the Ghanaian people, the distinction drawn by Fanon between the popular masses and the bourgeois leaders of nationalist movements would become increasingly relevant as Western pacifists sought to extend their support for African liberation struggles in the early 1960s. But some African delegates to the Accra conference seemed more closely aligned with the aims of the Sahara protest that had provided the original impetus for the conference. Mainza Chona, the Zambian nationalist and key figure in the newly formed United National Independence Party (UNIP), also spoke at the Accra conference, condemning the French tests as 'both murder in cold blood as well as criminal trespass on our mother Africa'.[29] Chona's speech combined familiar references to French 'self-aggrandisement' with more intriguing – and prescient – comments on the debate surrounding the potential danger of radioactive fallout from the tests. The French authorities had claimed that the explosion would take place at a height sufficient to avoid significant volumes of radioactive material being swept up by high-altitude air currents, and British scientists working with Nigeria interpreted their measurements as demonstrating that the radiation fell below 'permissible thresholds'.[30]

[24] 'Speech Delivered by Mr M. F. Galal', BPC, DAC 5/7/21.
[25] 'Speech by Mr Romesh Chandra', BPC, DAC 5/7/21.
[26] Robert J. C. Young, 'Fanon and the Turn to Armed Struggle in Africa', *Wasafiri* 20, no. 44 (2005): 36.
[27] Frantz Fanon, *Alienation and Freedom,* edited by Jean Khalfa and Robert J. C. Young, translated by Steven Corcoran (London: Bloomsbury Publishing, 2018), 654.
[28] Frantz Fanon, *The Wretched of the Earth*, translated by Constance Farrington (New York: Grove Press, 1963), 48.
[29] M. Chona, 'Speech at "Positive Action" Conference', April 1960, BPC DAC 5/7/21.
[30] Hill, 'Britain, West Africa and "The New Nuclear Imperialism"', 283.

But, as Chona pointed out, there was no scientific consensus on the effects of radiation, and it would be 'nonsense to say that the increase of strontium 90 is "only" 1% because we do not know yet the effect of that 1%'.[31] Moreover, as Hill notes, recent evidence suggests that the February 1960 tests may have resulted in significant levels of radiation over 200 kilometres from the site of the explosion in Reggane.[32]

But Chona did not follow other delegates in calling for armed struggle, although he did express support for 'fellow freedom fighters', asking African states to provide them with financial backing and 'effective propaganda'. Further proposals included a 'total boycott' of central and southern African settler regimes, diplomatic pressure via the Commonwealth and the withdrawal of African states from the French Community. As a representative of a movement engaged in a regional independence struggle centred on the constitutional issue of the Central African Federation, it is noteworthy that Chona's address emphasized political and economic pressures rather than militant methods, and he concluded, with a hint of criticism, that African independence movements needed 'no more resolutions but positive action'.[33] Similar scepticism was expressed by the Tanganyikan Minister of State I. M. Bhoke Mananka, who spoke to the conference as the representative of the Pan-African Movement of East and Central Africa (PAFMECA). Mananka strongly criticized the tendency for pan-African conferences and meetings to pass numerous resolutions that had never been put into effect; these were, he argued 'merely an evasion or the best means of shirking responsibility. We are not interested in resolutions but POSITIVE ACTION'.[34] And, despite the emphatic support for armed struggle from some quarters, many of the debates at Accra focused on non-violent forms of protest. Over the course of the three-day conference, calls were made for a thousand African volunteers to form an enlarged Sahara protest, and it was suggested that African students could be deployed in Europe as potential interlocutors between pan-African and Western peace movements.[35] At the heart of Nkrumah's conference address was a pledge to fund a training centre where 'volunteers would learn the essential disciplines of concerted positive action'.[36] Sutherland's assessment of the conference may well have over-estimated the influence of pacifist movements, but it seems reasonable to suggest that the meeting represented both a genuine moment of opportunity for peace movements as well as underlining the limited degree to which Western activists might shape the direction of pan-Africanist debate and anti-colonial nationalism.

The conference resolutions included explicit references to issues of peace and disarmament. It called on governments to 'mobilise world public opinion and sympathy against further nuclear tests in general, and the existence of Atomic Missile Bases in Africa and for total disarmaments by collective and concerted actions through the United Nations', for economic sanctions and boycott of French goods and (in contrast

---

[31] M. Chona, 'Speech at "Positive Action" Conference', April 1960, BPC DAC 5/7/21.
[32] Hill, 'Britain, West Africa and "The New Nuclear Imperialism"', 284.
[33] M. Chona, 'Speech at "Positive Action" Conference', April 1960, BPC DAC 5/7/21.
[34] 'Speech by Mr I. M. Broke Munanka', April 1960. DAC 5/7/21.
[35] A. J. Muste, 'Reports from Abroad', *Africa Today* 7, no. 4 (1960): 4; A. J. Muste to A. Trocmé, 18 April 1960, SPC, Muste 89/7/African Nonviolent Movement.
[36] A. Carter, 'Draft Article on Conference on Peace and Security in Africa', n.d 1960, BPC DAC 5/7/20. BPC.

to the armed brigade envisioned at the Tunis conference), for 'Volunteer Training centres for future concerted action for non-violent demonstrations against further nuclear tests in the Sahara'.[37] But, in retrospect, peace campaigners had mixed feelings about the conference, which for April Carter, underlined the 'tremendous possibilities and tremendous problems' that accompanied the drive towards decolonization in Africa. Randle noted with disappointment that there were few representatives of Francophone territories.[38] Similar expressions of disappointment were expressed by delegates at the conference, who contracted Arab and Anglophone African opposition to the tests with an apparent lack of protest from French West Africa. In fact, there had been vocal opposition to the tests from Francophone African political leaders, although Randle recalled that only Mamadou Dia, prime minister of Senegal, had offered public opposition.[39] On non-violence more generally, Carter acknowledged the moral dilemmas raised by the war in Algeria, which had resulted 'in a situation in which it is both emotionally and politically almost impossible for African leaders to repudiate violent methods completely'. And most importantly, she suggested that 'ties of kinship' were stronger than support for principles of non-violence – the conference speeches and resolutions revealed feelings of identification *against* imperial and colonial power, rather than in support of a universal human solidarity.

Carter thus contrasted the resolution adopted on the tests, which included the calls for training in non-violent protest, with that concerned with Algeria, which supported the call for a volunteer brigade. She also recognized that this was not incompatible with Gandhi's view that fighting was preferable to 'cowardly submission'. But she raised concerns about the failure of speakers to differentiate between French leaders and the French people; this represented a failure to engage with progressive sections of French society, would she argued constitute an 'inverted nationalism'.[40] Furthermore, despite – or perhaps because of – Randle's desire to ensure that the Positive Action conference was an African initiative, the tensions that had arisen during the Sahara protest again rose to the surface. Many African delegates found the presence of Westerners advocating passive resistance far from welcome, while Western observers including the economist and Quaker Walter Birmingham, who taught at the University of Ghana, felt the conference speeches expressed rather too much visceral anti-French sentiment.[41] The conference committee on Algeria had, reportedly on the insistence of Frantz Fanon, refused to allow Pierre Martin to speak, while both Martin and Esther Peter were suspected of acting as French 'spies'.[42]

At the same time, there was scope for Western participants to articulate their views. Birmingham was able to intervene during the debates with a call for multi-racial unity that bridged divides:

---

[37] 'Resolution of the First Committee of the Positive Action Conference on French Atom Tests in the Sahara', April 1960, BPC DAC 5/7/21.
[38] Carter, 'Article on Conference on Peace and Security in Africa', [n.d.] 1960, BPC DAC 5/7/20.
[39] Ibid.; see also Wittner, *Resisting the Bomb*, 80.
[40] Carter, 'The Sahara Protest Team'.
[41] W. Birmingham, 'International Conference on Positive Action for Peace and Security in Africa', 9 May 1960, SPC Muste 89/16/Sahara Project; A. Carter, 'Article on Conference on Peace and Security in Accra', n.d 1960, BPC DAC 5/7/20.
[42] Ibid.

Victory in war vas not peace. At this conference hardly a word had been said as yet about peace. I wanted to say that there would and could be no peace in Africa until we had made of each enemy a friend. This embraced Frenchman and Afrikaners and all those we thought of as imperialists too . . . send out a manifesto of peace, friendship and goodwill to the common people of France and South Africa. We must speak to the many people in these nations with goodwill towards Africa, people like myself, whom, as some of you know, the product of an imperialist family.[43]

In response, Birmingham recalled, an African trade union delegate stood and called for the conference to endorse the 'application of Christian principle' in the struggle for freedom. Similarly, the sympathy and support that had been offered to the Sahara protest team by Ghanaian officials reflected shared principles that had been expressed in the 'Positive Action' than Nkrumah built as the foundation of his leadership of the independence movement in the 1950s. For Randle, this was a reflection of a shared faith in Gandhian non-violent action.[44] Despite the resolutions passed in support of armed struggle at the Tunis conference, Nkrumah's opening address to the Accra conference included the statement that non-violent positive action was 'the greatest single hope for peace, security and brotherhood among mankind'.[45] But the conference did little to alleviate the pacifists' anxieties about the growing influence of advocates of armed struggle. Western peace campaigners had come to Accra with the hope that international solidarity against nuclear weapons might provide a platform for a new era of peaceful cooperation; instead a new vision of liberation was emerging, centred on a sense of African solidarity rather than affinities with transnational pacifism. When it came to 'nuclear imperialism', the emphasis was most often placed on the second half of the expression.

Training camps for peace

For the Sahara team, one of the most significant developments of the Accra conference was the plan, announced by Nkrumah during his opening address, for a training centre 'where volunteers would learn the essential disciplines of concerted positive action. Such an establishment might also become the centre for much needed research into the philosophy and technique of positive action'. The centre would, he continued, become 'the greatest single hope for peace, security and brotherhood among mankind'.[46] For April Carter, this was the major success of the conference. If it was supported by all the participating countries – and those in Francophone territories especially – Carter suggested the centre would be 'a symbol of genuine African unity

---

[43] Walter Birmingham, 'International Conference on Positive Action for Peace and Security in Africa', SPC Muste 89/16/Sahara Project.
[44] Wittner, *Resisting the Bomb*, 266.
[45] A. Carter, 'Draft Article on Conference on Peace and Security in Africa', n.d 1960, BPC DAC 5/7/20.
[46] Walter Birmingham, 'International Conference on Positive Action for Peace and Security in Africa', SPC Muste 89/16/Sahara Project.

and an effective instrument of positive action'; but, she continued, if it was largely an effort by Ghanaian officials, it would be 'no more than a pawn in the African political power struggle'.[47] The initial signs were hopeful, and the day after the conclusion of the conference, Nkrumah met with leading pacifists including Muste and Scott and agreed to finance the establishment of a training centre and employ Sutherland and Randle to get the enterprise off the ground.[48] There were, however, significant difficulties for the establishment of a successful training centre, not least the perceived dangers of too close an affiliation with the government. As April Carter observed, 'at some stage the non-violent ideal will clash openly with power politics, and the government concerned will have to choose between the two'.[49]

From Gandhi onward, advocates of non-violent resistance had insisted on the vital need for training in both the principles and practical methods of pacifist protest. In the interwar period, Westerners attracted to the idea of *satyagraha* saw education as a fundamental requirement for would-be volunteers, some who wished to 'sit at the feet of the great man' in India, others who envisaged non-violent protest as more akin to an army than a monastic order.[50] In his pioneering handbook of Gandhian philosophy, *The Power of Nonviolence* (first published in 1934), the US pacifist Richard Gregg argued that training was essential for the formation of the habits and discipline necessary for non-violent protest.[51] The book provided a precise definition of Gandhi's method and set out a radical array of exercises in group meditation, exercise and folk songs as educational tools. These methods were described by contemporaries as akin to the marching drills of military training and were linked by Scalmer to the advocacy of 'selfless labour' by pacifists in the early 1940s.[52] Gregg's work shaped the thinking of the generation of peace activists that emerged in the 1940s and 1950s and inculcated a sense that non-violent protest was not merely a question of heightened moments of direct action, but a vocation built up through regular and disciplined effort.

But the fixation on training also revealed a lack of self-confidence that seemed in tension with peace campaigners' insistence on the urgency of their efforts. In the early 1950s, Bayard Rustin received a message from a pacifist group in Massachusetts who felt 'far from the self-disciplined, long-suffering, love-filled Satyagrahis who are probably necessary'; but, they argued, there were also dangers inherent in 'waiting to take action until we are "ready". Will that time ever come?'.[53] For leaders such as Muste, Rustin and Scott, training placed the emphasis on the moral character and world view of individuals; for them, activism was not a set of tools, but a way of life. These appeared at times to resonate with psychological practices of group therapy, such as the workshops organized by Muste, Rustin and A. Phillip Randolph on passive resistance for the Fellowship of Reconciliation in the early 1940s. Rustin's lectures would focus on a list of advice to activists to 'have no fear', 'admit their guilt', 'behave creatively'

---

[47] A. Carter, 'Draft Article on Conference on Peace and Security in Africa', n.d 1960, BPC DAC 5/7/20.
[48] Wittner, *Resisting the Bomb*, 268.
[49] A. Carter, 'Non-Violence and the African Future', *Peace News*, May 1960.
[50] Scalmer, *Gandhi in the West*, 116–17.
[51] Richard Bartlett Gregg, *The Power of Nonviolence* (Cambridge: Cambridge University Press, [2018 ed]), 166–73.
[52] Scalmer, *Gandhi and the West*, 120.
[53] Pat Perry to Rustin, 24 October 1951, quoted in Scalmer, *Gandhi in the West*, 122.

and 'raise the struggle from a physical to moral plane'.[54] In different – although not unrelated ways – education also provided a foundation for the ideas of development that were expounded by Scott and others in the 1940s. In *Attitude to Africa*, Scott highlighted the 'essential' need to train African technicians 'who would then enlist the understanding and enthusiasm of their own people'.[55] In Scott's experience, the principles of pacifist and developmental training might overlap, as in the case of St Faith's mission farm in Rusapi in Southern Rhodesia. The enterprise was organized by the pacifist Guy Clutton-Brook and his wife Molly, who had managed the Oxford House university settlement in Bethnal Green in London before migrating to Africa in the late 1940s. Scott described St. Faith's as a cooperative run 'on the basis of a true partnership between the races' built on the experience of 'practical living and working together'.[56]

Rustin continued to offer training sessions for peace activists through the 1950s, adding introductions to 'great practitioners of non-violence' from Jesus to Tolstoy, Thoreau and Gandhi and discussions of social issues from urbanization to racial integration, the economy and the international community.[57] But the primary purpose in 1960 was to create a training programme that would support the development of renewed protest against the French atomic tests. Michael Randle saw the centre as a base for new campaigns that would move on from the effective but symbolic work of the Sahara team to something that would directly challenge the French authorities. In sketching plans for a new phase of mass protest, Randle drew comparisons with British tactics in India where authorities had initially sought to ignore the resistance led by Gandhi. He envisaged groups of several hundred people converging on French West African territories. This would, however, necessitate the establishment of training centres, drawing again on the Gandhian model of the Ashram; Randle thus sent invitations to Asha Devi, a teacher at the Sevagram ashram, and Gandhi's protege Jayaprakash Narayan, asking for their support.[58]

It was critical, Randle believed, that the training institution maintained its independence from the state or other organizations. With the likelihood that such an enterprise would be based in Ghana itself or another emerging post-colonial nation, there would, he believed, be a duty to balance any obligations to government with its capacity to criticize; in essence, he believed that a pacifist organization could not 'remain a passive or silent spectator to the wrongs in the society in which it operates'.[59] Randle therefore warned against overambitious plans and recommended that the training centre focus on the short-term aim to continue (and expand) protests against the French tests. He welcomed Scott's proposal that multiple teams of African protestors should head towards Algeria from different starting points, but also noted that such

[54] Ibid., 129.
[55] Lewis, et al., *Attitude to Africa*, 130.
[56] Scott, *A Time to Speak*, 286, Scott, 'A Practical Hope for Africa', *The Observer*, 9 March 1952, 4.
[57] 'Training in Non-violence', *Peace News*, 5 June 1959, 3.
[58] Randle, 'Memorandum on Role of Direct Action in Campaign Against Sahara Tests', 13 March 1960, SPC Muste, 89/7 African Conference on Non-violence.
[59] Randle, 'Some Notes on the Positive Action Conference', 20 March 1960, SPC Muste 89/7/African Conference on Nonviolence.

a plan would create 'appalling problems of organisation and leadership'.[60] Instead, he suggested that around thirty Africans could be selected for an intensive training programme in leadership whose topics would include 'theoretical and practical issues and psychodrama' and engage in exploratory protests such as marches to the French Embassy before embarking on new attempts to reach Reggane. Ultimately, he argued, organizers would need to choose between non-violent and mass protest.

In late April 1960, Sutherland, Scott and Randle met with A. K. Barden, Nkrumah and Tawia Afamafio to discuss practical plans for the training centre, during which Nkrumah offered the use of a disused school at Winneba. Nkrumah was determined that the Accra conference should have a tangible result and that Ghana should take the lead, with other independent African states acting as co-sponsors. Adamafio was given overall responsibility for staffing and appointing a Board of Directors, but Randle and Sutherland were asked to draft staffing recommendations for Adamafio. Scott set out his own aspirations for the Centre, which ought to be 'place for thought, preparation, and planning for action by those who want to find the right means of struggle and liberation in the coming age of nuclear power and Neo-imperialism'.[61] The training programme would offer 'practical and academic training' that included histories of non-violent protest and African independence movements. But, Scott conceived of something much more ambitious: a hub for research focused on 'methods of liberation' undertaken within a community following the lines of a Gandhian *ashram*. At the same time, Scott's proposal avoided reference to specific philosophies of non-violence and stated explicitly that the curriculum would not follow a predetermined spiritual or ideological line. This was, the report suggested, because many African leaders saw non-violence as a tactic rather than a creed. In fact, Scott's plan envisaged that the centre might ultimately become a 'resistance headquarters' focused on militant methods. The report also predicted that the Directors would include individuals opposed to non-violent resistance.

In addition to these concerns, the report suggested that the degree to which the Centre would be oriented towards non-violent protest would be dictated by events in Algeria and South Africa. Randle had discussed the situation in South Africa with representatives of the Pan-Africanist Congress (PAC), the organization that had broken away from the ANC a year earlier and had organized the protest at Sharpeville in March that had been violently suppressed by police. In confirmation of his fears, the meeting suggested that the PAC had committed to armed struggle and to reject collaboration with progressive white supporters.[62] Randle's fear was that the non-violent training at the proposed centre would become preparation for 'psychological warfare' that would be pursued alongside militant resistance. The terms of reference of the training centre therefore required an explicit reference to support for non-violence. Randle had also begun to worry that the centre might struggle to navigate rivalries between sponsoring African states, as well as hostilities from factions within Ghana. He felt that the plans for the centre were falling foul of a fundamental tension between non-violence and

---

[60] Randle, 'Problems Arising from Positive Action Conference', BPC, DAC 5/7/20.
[61] [no author Randle?], 'Positive Action Centre', 10 June 1960, SPC DAC 5/7/20.
[62] Ibid.

the 'massive concentration of power' in the modern state. In particular, he raised concerns about the Preventative Detention Act that had been introduced in Ghana in 1958, allowing the prime minister to imprison individuals without due process. In his assessment, Randle felt that

> present trends in Africa seem to foreshadow strong central governments in the newly independent areas. It is the duty of those interested in non-violence to analyse and understand the economic, social and political factors that lead to arbitrary, or even dictatorial, rule, but they must never condone, or appear to condone, the violation of fundamental Human freedoms and rights.[63]

The plans for the centre should, Randle suggested, include an explicit and 'strong declaration about human rights everywhere'. Ultimately, he felt it would be necessary to state openly his (and Sutherland's) stance on rights and liberties and a belief in the need for the centre to be independent from government control and policy. But, to ensure that his proposals for the centre were constructive, he suggested three potential plans for protests. The first would be to launch a new campaign against the French tests from multiple points across west Africa. An alternative version would later be developed, centred on a 'Peace Flight' of high-profile international figures that would tour west Africa before travelling to France for a march on Paris itself.[64] The second plan comprised a march on South African jails led by an international team of protestors, and the third envisaged a protest march against slave labour in Angola. However, all three schemes were logistically-complicated, had not been endorsed by African movements, and in retrospect seem unlikely ways of reconciling pacifist and nationalist agendas.[65]

Moreover the plans for the Winneba centre were soon sidetracked by events elsewhere in Africa. Just weeks after achieving independence, the former Belgian colonial territory of the Congo descended into a political crisis and civil conflict. With the army in mutiny and Belgian forces deployed to occupy the mineral-rich Katanga province, the United Nations Security Council authorized the formation of an international peacekeeping force, which included a significant contingent from the Ghanaian army. Accra airport became a hub of activity:

> RAF Comets taking Ghana troops to the Congo sent off by Highlife from the army band; USAF Hercules planes bringing in Moroccan troops from Rabat, refuelling and taking off again; Globemasters bringing in refugees, many American missionaries, today Belgian refugees en route to God knows where. Often it's a Tragic-comic scene with Belgians full of bewilderment when they land at Accra and watch with an out-of-the frying pan look as they face hundreds of black troops going where they came from.[66]

---

[63] Ibid., 10.
[64] [nk], 'Action Against French Tests', 6 October 1960, BPC DAC 5/7/20.
[65] [no author Randle?], 'Positive Action Centre', 10 June 1960, BPC DAC 5/7/20.
[66] Sutherland to A. J. Muste, 18 July 1960, SPC Muste 89/16/Sahara Project.

Amidst the crisis, Sutherland secured a meeting with Nkrumah to discuss the centre, along with a proposal to send a 'non-violent positive action team' to the Congo. He left discouraged, with Nkrumah obviously having little concern for the training centre. This was, Sutherland believed, partly a consequence of the Congo crisis, but also because Nkrumah had been 'subjected to a barrage of Marxist interpretation' from W. E. B. Du Bois and C. L. R. James, who regarded non-violence as 'weak, fuzzy do-goodism which will lose Nkrumah the leadership of Africa'.[67] Nkrumah also revealed the plans to combine the centre with a CPP 'ideological school'. Although the news confirmed their fears, the African American sociologist John St Clair Drake advised them to agree to any plans for a six-month period.[68] Muste, however, was certain that American supporters would be unwilling to support the plans and that 'none of the organisations committed to nonviolence can participate, even in an informal way, in an institute responsible to the Central Committee of the CPP'.[69]

By the end of September 1960, it began to seem obvious that the non-violent 'positive action' centre would be subsumed within a college for trade union leaders and CPP party members. But Randle and Sutherland continued their efforts to present a viable and substantive programme of training to the Ghanaian authorities. Their planning was also reinvigorated by renewed French atomic tests in the Sahara, which added impetus to Randle and Sutherland's calls for the centre at Winneba to become a base for new protests across Africa. In a joint proposal written in early October, they argued that newly independent Francophone territories, whose silence had been the 'greatest weakness' of the Sahara protest, would be key to a new campaign. Bringing Francophone territories into protests would, they argued, have a beneficial impact on unity in west Africa, which had been hampered by 'France's undue influence'.[70] In a separate report, Randle argued that the French had created an official class closely aligned with France; that governments in the Francophone territories had also acted as 'stooges' for France, incarcerating nationalist leaders who demanded 'complete independence'.[71] Randle and Sutherland also set out highly detailed plans for the training programme itself, which comprised a daily schedule almost monastic in its rigour and focus. Volunteers would wake shortly after five o'clock and embark on 'work on land' before breakfast and private study. The remainder of the morning would be spent on lectures, discussion and further research, followed by an afternoon focused on practical work and physical exercise. After this, there would be a period of silence before the evening meal before volunteers would be free to enjoy 'creative recreation' including films or music.[72] The courses would include academic study of the theories and practices of non-violent action as well as African history and current affairs and discussions of pan-Africanism. Key reading would include Gregg's *Power of Non-violence* and *Defence in the Nuclear Age* by Sir Stephen King-Hall, a former

---

[67] Ibid.
[68] Randle to April Carter, 19 July 1960, BPC DAC 5/7/20.
[69] Muste to Bill Sutherland, 8 September 1960, SPC Muste 89/7/African Non-violent Movement.
[70] Sutherland and Randle, 'More Sahara Tests: The Need for Effective Protest', 1 October 1960, BPC DAC 5/7/20.
[71] Randle, 'Ghana Notebook', 1 October 1960, BPC Randle Cwl MR 1/3.
[72] 'Positive Action Training Centre', 1 October 1960, BPC, DAC 5/7/20.

naval officer who had become an advocate of unilateral disarmament, whose book advocated a system of national defence centred on reason and persuasion: a 'Battle of the Brains' rather than a 'Battle of the Bodies'.[73] Further readings included Nkrumah's account of Positive Action, as well as material on protest movements in Africa. The programme also included 'socio-drama' or role-playing of protest situations, which had been employed by the organizers of the Montgomery bus boycotts in the United States in 1956.

Despite the detail of their planning, Sutherland and Randle seemed unable to revive the interest of Ghanaian officials. Randle wrote to Nkrumah directly, declaring in somewhat over-optimistic terms that the Congo crisis had demonstrated the success of the Accra conference in 'keeping the Cold War out of Africa'. More revealing, perhaps, were his references to the ways in which Gandhian non-violent Shanti Sena groups in India had been critical of government policy, and that Nehru had even encouraged the leading Gandhian activist Vinoba Bhave to call him to account. Randle concluded by stating that he would 'feel honoured' to take on a role at the Centre, but would need to be clear that he could not support any developments at odds with his principles.[74] It is not clear how Nkrumah responded to Randle's letter, but Sutherland later recalled that after he contacted Nkrumah with his own concerns about the suppression of political dissent, an aide warned that such views would risk deportation.[75] The activists' original vision for the training centre no longer seemed viable, and before it could be established in its more limited form, Randle was recalled to the UK to support Scott and Bertrand Russell in the formation of the Committee of 100.[76] Sutherland would also leave Ghana the following year to work in Israel, which had developed close relations with Ghana through the influence of its ambassador to Accra, Ehud Avriel.[77] Sutherland had developed a friendship with Avriel and, following the collapse of his marriage, he left his role as an assistant to Gbedemah and accepted an offer to contribute to Israel's tilt to 'Afro-Asia' in the early 1960s.[78] Shortly after, the political tensions would reach Gbedemah, the 'outstanding peace leader in Ghana', who fled the country after Nkrumah had demanded his resignation.[79]

In the wider context of the developing multi-layer crisis in Africa in the early 1960s, it is perhaps unsurprising that the plans for close collaboration between international pacifists and the government of Ghana did not survive. The project to build a transnational peace movement in Africa was ultimately undermined by the strength of national and racial identities, which seemed to exert a more powerful influence than ideological affinities and moral principles. The Sahara protest has been more easily understood in terms of 'Black internationalism' and what Kevin Gaines has called

---

[73] Sir Stephen King-Hall, *Defence in the Nuclear Age* (London: Victor Gollancz, 1958), 31.
[74] Randle to Kwame Nkrumah, 1 October 1960, BPC Randle Cwl MR 1/3.
[75] Sutherland and Meyer, *Guns and Gandhi*, 45–6.
[76] M. Randle to Barden, 19 October 1960, BPC Randle MR 1/3.
[77] Zach Levey, 'Israel's Strategy in Africa, 1961–67', *International Journal of Middle East Studies* 36, no. 1 (2004): 74.
[78] Sutherland and Meyer, *Guns and Gandhi*, 46; see also Michael Brecher, 'Israel and "Afro-Asia"', *International Journal* 16, no. 2 (1961): 107–37.
[79] H. Jack to Buchbinder, 13 December 1961, SPC, Records of the Committee for a Sane Nuclear Policy (SANE) B5/Accra Assembly 1962. See also Sutherland and Meyer, *Guns and Gandhi*, 47.

a 'transnational culture of opposition' to Western colonialism; the failure to build a universal, multi-racial movement thus reflected the ways in which discourses of unity, such as pan-Africanism, drew peoples together in ways structured by political, social and cultural divisions determined by colonialism and Cold War.[80] The discontinuities between networks that were revealed in the Sahara protest were not simply a black and white issue but were a reflection of an increasingly sharp definition of the dividing line between colonial and anti-colonial visions of the future. Scott had envisaged the centre as a place for 'those who want to find the right means of struggle in the coming age of nuclear power and neo-imperialism', but the plans were transformed into an institution for training anti-colonial activists, a kind of non-violent variant of the military training camps that were being established to support liberation movements in Africa.[81] Perhaps the most significant aspect of the story of the Winneba Centre was, therefore, that it embodied in microcosm the shift from non-violence to armed struggle that was underway within African liberation movements.

The turn to armed struggle

Any assessment of the global history of the 'turn to armed struggle' requires an understanding of the overlapping vectors of political engagement with southern Africa, as transnational networks actuated by a sense of solidarity with African claims for civil rights, racial justice and political independence confronted the reality of political violence. Appeals for international solidarity built on shared tenets of Gandhian non-violent political action, and as a consequence leading figures in anti-colonial and anti-apartheid campaigns were also found at the heart of anti-nuclear weapons protests. As noted previously, Canon John Collins of St Paul's Cathedral in London combined anti-apartheid fundraising through the auspices of the Defence and Aid Fund with his role as Chair of the Campaign for Nuclear Disarmament.[82] Rank and file supporters of anti-nuclear weapons campaigns, likewise, viewed the threat of the hydrogen bomb and colonialism in the same moral frame. For many drawn to the rituals and routines of the annual Easter weekend Aldermaston March, Britain needed to renounce both its atomic weapons and its empire in order to secure its place as a world power – articulating a distinct form of 'British morality' in the process.[83] British nuclear disarmament might, therefore, be cast as a form of 'imperialist pacifism' and nationalist 'romantic protest', in which campaigners presented their movement as a pathway towards national redemption and the restoration of international power and prestige.[84]

[80] Allman, 'Nuclear Imperialism', 83–102; Kevin Kelly Gaines, *American Africans in Ghana: Black Expatriates and the Civil Rights Era* (Chapel Hill: University of North Carolina Press, 2006).
[81] 'Positive Action Centre', 10 June 1960, BPC DAC 5/7/20.
[82] Collins, *Faith Under Fire*; Herbsten, *White Lies*, see also Peggy Duff, *Left, Left, Left: A Personal Account of Six Protest Campaigns, 1945–65* (London: Allison and Busby, 1971).
[83] Burkett, 'Re-Defining British Morality'.
[84] On 'imperialist pacifism' Hinton, *Protests and Visions*. On 'romantic protest', see Veldman, *Fantasy, the Bomb*, 120.

Similarly, activists such as George Houser in the United States drew on radical pacifism as they sought to arouse the conscience of American citizens on the question of racial injustices in Africa from the mid-1950s. Inspired by the 'peaceful and orderly nature' of the Defiance Campaign, he had taken a leading role in the development of anti-apartheid protest in the United States and became Executive Director of the American Committee on Africa.[85] He served in this capacity for over twenty-five years, making a major contribution to US anti-apartheid activism.[86] During the 1950s he built connections with a number of Christian and pacifist African leaders, including fellow Methodist, Albert Lutuli, whom he met in South Africa in 1954. His engagement with African political affairs was by no means limited to South Africa, however, and he travelled to various parts of the continent through the 1950s. This included the Congo, which he visited in 1954 and again in 1957. He returned to the country in 1960 before its formal independence, and then again in November, amidst its political and constitutional crisis. His arrival coincided with gun battles between Tunisian UN forces protecting the representative of the Ghanaian government (and former member of the Sahara protest working committee), Nathaniel Welbeck and Congolese forces seeking to remove him from the country.[87] The fighting epitomized the changes that had taken place in the country since his first visit, and the forces challenging post-colonial Africa. For Houser, the issues at stake in Africa were no longer the struggle between colonialism and the democratic rights of Africans, as they were in South Africa eight years earlier. But perhaps most significantly, the crisis in the Congo seemed to reveal the limits of non-violence.

Houser maintained contacts with African advocates of Gandhian non-violence, including the Zambian nationalist leader Kenneth Kaunda, who he introduced to American pacifists when the ACOA hosted Kaunda in New York in mid-1960.[88] But Houser also maintained connections with individuals and movements that had inspired the supposed prophet of anti-colonial violence, Frantz Fanon. Anti-colonial movements in southern Africa were clearly evident in Fanon's vision of a wider anti-colonial struggle in the final months of his life. Of the various contacts he had made among the transnational community of nationalist exiles that orbited around pan-African conferences and centres of power such as Accra, Fanon had built up a relationship with a number of leading figures connected with the United Peoples of Angola (UPA) and had visited its bases in the Congo in 1960.[89] The revolt by rural workers in the coffee-growing regions of northern Angola in January 1961, referenced by Fanon in *Les Damnés de la terre*, and the subsequent uprisings in Luanda and UPA incursion into

---

[85] Americans for South African Resistance, 'Bulletin', n.d. [*c.* September 1952], Amistad Research Center, American Committee on Africa Collection.
[86] Culverson, *Contesting Apartheid*; David L. Hostetter, *Movement Matters: American Antiapartheid Activism and the Rise of Multicultural Politics* (London: Routledge, 2006); Njubi Nesbitt, *Race for Sanctions*.
[87] 'Houser', 28 November 1960, The Congo Revisited' SPC Fellowship of Reconciliation Papers, FOR IIC, General Corres 1960–62, Houser.
[88] 'Alfred Hassler to Houser', 18 May 1960, SPC FOR IIC, General Corres 1960–62, Houser.
[89] David Macey, *Frantz Fanon: A Life* (London: Granta, 2000); Joao Manuel Neves, 'Frantz Fanon and the Struggle for the Independence of Angola', *Interventions* 17, no. 3 (4 May 2015): 417–33.

the territory across the Congolese border were presented as a backdrop for the rapidly rising tensions in South Africa in mid-1961.[90] As well as a full-scale armed popular uprising against colonial rule in Angola, the South African government's mobilization of security forces in response to the ANC's call for a general strike in South Africa at the end of May 1961 strengthened the impression that remaining colonial states were entrenching themselves against the momentum of decolonization. The militarization of settler regimes took place amidst ongoing crisis in the fractured Congo, where the deployment of Belgian forces in the secessionist province of Katanga undermined international efforts to broker negotiations. The efforts to maintain colonial rule also took on a transnational dimension, as French security services advised their South African counterparts on the methods of interrogation and counter-insurgency that had brought stalemate in the war in Algeria.[91] This, then, was the burgeoning crisis that sharpened the thoughts of both Western and African anti-colonial activists in mid-1961.

In this context, arguments in favour of armed resistance seemed increasingly compelling. By the end of 1960, Nkrumah – who in many respects continued to embody the peaceful path to independence – had begun to take a more equivocal view of the merits of passive resistance. In parallel to the publicity surrounding the Sahara protest in early 1960, the Ghanaian press carried stories celebrating the popular response to the call for volunteers to fight in Algeria, and although the real numbers of recruits are unclear, the image of the African freedom fighter was coming to embody pan-African unity and liberation rather than the Gandhian passive resister.[92]

Between 1960 and 1962, anti-colonial and anti-apartheid politics in southern Africa had undertaken a decisive 'turn' towards armed resistance. In South Africa, the shooting of unarmed protestors by police in the South African township of Sharpeville marked an intensification of the state's authoritarian response to popular resistance, while conflict between security forces and the iKongo movement in the eastern Transkei signalled the possibility of rural insurrection.[93] Elsewhere in the region, beginning with the uprising against Portuguese colonialism in northern Angola in 1961, violent insurgency emerged as the central form of political protest.[94] Later in that same year, activists associated with the African National Congress and South African Communist Party (SACP) launched uMkhonto wi Sizwe (MK) and began a sabotage campaign that would last until its main leaders were arrested in July 1963.[95] Together,

[90] See, for example, *Fighting Talk*, 16, 4, May 1962.
[91] On Angola, see Malyn Newitt, 'Angola in Historical Context', in *Angola: The Weight of History*, edited by Patrick Chabal and Nuno Vidal (London: Hurst & Company, 2007), 19–92; David Birmingham, *Empire in Africa: Angola and Its Neighbors* (Athens: Ohio University Press, 2006).
[92] See Ahlman, 'The Algerian Question', 81–2.
[93] Thembela Kepe and Lungisile Ntsebeza, eds, *Rural Resistance in South Africa: The Mpondo Revolts after Fifty Years* (Cape Town: UCT Press, 2012).
[94] Patrick Chabal and Nuno Vidal, eds, *Angola: The Weight of History* (London: Hurst & Company, 2007); John A. Marcum, *The Angolan Revolution. Vol.1, The Anatomy of an Explosion, 1950–1962* (Cambridge, MA: MIT Press, 1969).
[95] Ellis, 'The Genesis of the ANC's Armed Struggle'; Paul S. Landau, 'The ANC, MK, and "The Turn to Violence" (1960–1962)', *South African Historical Journal* 64, no. 3 (27 February 2012): 538–63; Stevens, 'The Turn to Sabotage'.

these were significant moments in a tactical shift that would reshape the politics of liberation in southern Africa. Meanwhile, as the British federal experiment in central Africa became increasingly fragile, nationalist movements in Northern Rhodesia also appeared on the verge of provoking popular violence against the colonial authorities. By the middle of the decade, armed resistance had become a normative mode of Black politics across the region.

In histories of the movements against apartheid in South Africa, accounts of the beginnings of armed resistance have understandably focused attention on the decision to form MK.[96] Although there had been a long history of political violence in South Africa, and the emergence of an armed insurgency against the apartheid state was of course significant, there is a danger that these accounts become partial and partisan. More recently, the emotional intensity of this debate has increased as the argument has focused on the relationship between Nelson Mandela, the SACP and the role of Communist activists in the ANC's decision to allow a new armed body to be formed.[97] But, as Dubow has suggested, the development of an armed confrontation between resistance movements and a determinedly authoritarian state was by no means inevitable after Sharpeville. Similarly, Simon Stevens has shown that armed resistance was articulated alongside international sanctions as two faces of a global anti-apartheid movement.[98] There is, therefore, scope for a broader contextualization of the turn to armed struggle, taking a closer account of the relationship between violent and non-violent opposition to apartheid and colonialism in southern Africa.

In South Africa, key figures in the main anti-colonial movements, the ANC and PAC, who had been banned in the aftermath of the Sharpeville crisis in 1960, had begun to question the focus on passive resistance. By mid-1961, the leading advocate of radical tactics in the ANC, Nelson Mandela, proposed the formation of an armed movement and, despite opposition from Lutuli, the advocates of armed struggle were given the go-ahead to form a new organization, separate from the ANC, to carry out a sabotage campaign against the apartheid state. While many accounts of these debates have tended to focus on the narrow question of the degree to which these moves were manipulated by the South African Communist Party, recent work has begun to present a more rounded view of the rationale behind the change of tactics.[99] As Stevens notes, one of the key factors that shaped the thinking of ANC leaders in 1960–1 was the mounting evidence that violent protests were likely, and in the case of Mpondoland

---

[96] Simpson, *Umkhonto We Sizwe*.
[97] Ellis, 'The Genesis of the ANC's Armed Struggle'; Landau, 'The ANC, MK'; Stevens, 'The Turn to Sabotage'; Thula Simpson, 'Nelson Mandela and the Genesis of the ANC's Armed Struggle: Notes on Method', in *Southern Africa: History, Culture and Society Seminar Series* (University of London: Institute of Commonwealth Studies, 2017).
[98] Saul Dubow, 'Were There Political Alternatives in the Wake of the Sharpeville-Langa Violence in South Africa, 1960?', *The Journal of African History* 56, no. 1 (March 2015): 119–42; Simon Stevens, 'Strategies of Struggle: Boycotts, Sanctions, and the War Against Apartheid', (Ph.D., Columbia University, 2015).
[99] Stevens, 'The Turn to Sabotage'; Hyslop, 'Mandela on War'; Z. Pallo Jordan and Mac Maharaj, 'South Africa and the Turn to Armed Resistance', *South African Historical Journal* 70, no. 1 (2018): 11–26. For debates focused on the role of the SACP, see Ellis, 'The Genesis of the ANC's Armed Struggle'.

on the boundary of the Cape and Natal provinces, had already broken out.[100] Another critical point of reference was that of Cuba, where a small movement had acted decisively and ultimately triumphed in their revolutionary struggle. As Young suggests in his analysis of Fanon and the launch of armed resistance in Africa in the early 1960s, 'Cuba transformed everything, and gave armed struggle a prestige that almost instantly eclipsed that of Gandhi in India'.[101] Even *Peace News* covered Castro's revolution with interest.[102]

And yet, on the surface, the formation of MK in South Africa, the popular uprising in Angola and rising tensions in central Africa were the materialization of the worst fears of transnational peace activists, who had regularly predicted that nationalists would resort to violence if settler regimes did not address popular concerns. Even before the Sharpeville crisis, anti-apartheid activists had enthusiastically embraced the call for boycotts and sanctions as 'preferable to violence and bloodshed'.[103] But Houser's wider southern African connections suggest a more nuanced and fluid set of relations, beyond the obvious moral affinities that linked international solidarity movements to supposedly 'moderate' figures. In fact, there is little evidence of a coherent *theory of violence* developing in southern Africa in the early 1960s; for liberation movements, as for one of Fanon's sharpest critics, Hannah Arendt, violence was instrumental, not a creative force in itself, but a means towards a clear political objective. Defined thus, pacifist campaigners were able to resolve their dilemma by setting their sights on the ultimate aims of those political movements that had begun to take up arms against colonial regimes. For Houser and the American Committee on Africa, the critical issue of support for movements engaged in violent conflict had surfaced four years earlier, in relation to their support for the Algerian nationalist movement, whose representative, Mohammed Yazid, travelled to New York in 1956 to seek allies at the United Nations. For Houser, the question was 'could I be relevant to any struggle for freedom that was not clearly nonviolent?' Given a choice between aligning himself with groups following tactics of violence and abstention from action of any kind, Houser chose to rationalize his work as a conduit between nationalist groups and the US public, not as an advocate of their tactics but as an interpreter of a cause that was ultimately just.[104]

The violence in Angola in 1961 was regarded by many as a direct consequence of the actions of the colonial authorities. In a report in the South African liberal journal *Contact*, the Secretary General of the International Confederation of Free Trade Unions, Omer Becu described events in Angola as 'an explosion resulting from the oppressive policies of the Portuguese dictatorial regime'. The article asserted that Angolans had 'turned to armed revolt as their only escape from tyranny'.[105] Similarly,

---

[100] Stevens, 'The Turn to Sabotage', 237. On the Mpondoland rebellion, see Govan Mbeki, *South Africa: The Peasant's Revolt* (Harmondsworth: Penguin, 1964); Kepe and Ntsebeza, *Rural Resistance in South Africa*.
[101] Young, 'Fanon and the Turn to Armed Struggle in Africa', 37.
[102] 'Towards Democracy with Cuba's Robin Hood?', *Peace News*, 9 January 1959, 7; William Worthy, *Peace News*, 8 July 1960, 1.
[103] Bishop Reeves to Arthur Blaxall, 25 January 1960, Lambeth Palace Library, Collins Papers, MS 3294.
[104] Houser, *No One Can Stop the Rain*, 91–2.
[105] *Contact*, 18 May 1961.

a former missionary writing in the *New Statesman* suggested that the violence that accompanied the revolt in Angola might be explained by years of 'harshness and cruelty' under Portuguese colonialism:

> To kill with knife or panga produces more blood and more violent emotional reactions. The hand-to-hand struggle is more personal and primitive (and needs greater courage), but is it any more heinous than the impersonal and indiscriminate bombing of villages, the hunting of Africans 'like game' and the mass shooting of suspects?[106]

The comparison between the impersonal violence of the colonial state and the intimacy of killing in the name of anti-colonial revolution would be echoed by Fanon in *Wretched of the Earth*. Participating in violence was, in Fanon's account, an 'irrevocable action' that simultaneously severed the perpetuator from the colonial system and integrated them into the new nation; 'the colonised man finds his freedom in and through violence'.[107] The violence and counter-violence in southern Africa in 1960–1, from the napalm bombing of rural Angolan villages by the Portuguese air force to the deployment of military vehicles in South Africa, informed Fanon's provocative and formative analysis of decolonization but also heightened the sense of urgency felt by pacifists such as Houser.

In his first visit to Africa in 1954, Houser spent time in Angola, hosted by Western missionaries and also contacted the nascent Bakongo nationalist movement based in the Congo. The ACOA had provided support for the Angolan leader Holden Roberto in the United States in 1959 and had remained in touch when a major rural uprising began in early 1961. Houser, with his colleague John Marcum, visited rebel-held areas of Angola in January 1962, witnessing efforts to maintain what they described as 'ordinary village pursuits' alongside military preparations, as supplies of arms – reportedly from Algerian and Tunisian sources – had begun to arrive via the Congo.[108] On his return to the United States, Houser called for an expansion of humanitarian relief efforts, and for US officials to press their Portuguese allies in NATO to begin negotiations with the nationalist movements. Thus, by the early 1960s, the pacifist Houser, a veteran of Gandhian civil rights protests, had come to publicly support movements engaged in armed rebellion against colonial powers. If Houser, the experienced peace campaigner, could rationalize support for the armed struggle, then the efforts by pacifists to promote non-violence in Africa seemed unlikely to succeed. By late 1961, it seemed that African liberation movements had firmly rejected non-violence as their primary path to freedom.

Ten days before MK launched its first sabotage attacks in December 1961, and four days before the ANC president Albert Lutuli gave his acceptance speech for the Nobel Peace Prize in Oslo, Frantz Fanon died in Washington. The conjunction of these events was coincidental, and arguments for tangible connections between the

---

[106] 'The Agony of Angola', 6 January 1961, *New Statesman*, 61, 741.
[107] Fanon, *The Wretched of the Earth*, 67–8.
[108] George Houser, 'Report on a Journey Through Rebel Angola'; n.d. [c. March 1962], American Committee on Africa Collection, Amistad Research Center.

launch of armed struggle in South Africa and the publication of Fanon's *Les Damnés de la terre* in the same year are not fully convincing.[109] And yet, Fanon's assertion in 1960 that armed struggle was a last-ditch response to the 'violence of the everyday behaviour of the coloniser towards the colonised' resonates with the rationale of the leaders of MK, not least in Mandela's renowned testimony during the Rivionia Trial in 1964.[110] In Algeria, as in Angola and South Africa, Fanon argued, the violence of colonial racism was the precursor of armed struggle. Violent opposition to colonialism and apartheid was thus a realist response to circumstances in which Black political leaders found themselves in the early 1960s. During the 1940s and 1950s, there were clear ideological and methodological overlaps between peace movements and anti-colonial nationalism, and the language and tactics of Gandhian resistance provided a powerful reference point for transnational activists. The emphasis on violence and armed struggle that emerged in the 1960s was a palpable challenge to the efforts of peace campaigners such as Houser, Scott and Sutherland, but rather than providing a kind of counter-narrative that a retrospective Fanon-centred reading might suggest, contemporary peace activists saw it as a spur to reinvigorated efforts.

The formation of the World Peace Brigade

In January 1961 – the same week in which the uprising in Baixa de Cassanje saw the beginnings of the violent anti-colonial struggle in Angola – a meeting in New York City discussed a proposal for a World Conference on Non-violence, authored by the American Friends Service Committee member and Fellowship of Reconciliation activist Charles Coates Walker. The proposal suggested the practical agenda of an organizer rather than ideological innovation. The rationale for a new conference was straightforward: the global network of peace campaigners needed an opportunity to meet and share ideas. Between the lines, Walker's somewhat terse document was a testament to inertia within world pacifist movements rather than a manifesto for regeneration. A new conference would be a catalyst for the dissemination of research among peace campaigners which had hitherto been 'sporadic and uncoordinated'; previous attempts to maintain connections following world conferences had been promised but 'little apparently developed'.[111] Ultimately, what Walker was proposing was a permanent world peace body that had the power to coordinate intervention in crises across the globe; and these suggestions had in fact landed amidst a series of calls for renewed efforts at collaboration between pacifist movements. Specifically, Vinoba Bhave had founded the Gandhian Shanti Sena (Peace Army) in the late 1950s, and activists began to talk of ways of scaling such an enterprise up with the formation of an international pacifist corps. In 1960, Bhave's associate and former protege of Gandhi,

---

[109] Young, 'Fanon and the Turn to Armed Struggle in Africa'.
[110] Ibid.
[111] Charles Walker, 'A Proposal for a World Conference on Non-violence', December 1959, SPC – World Peace Brigade Collection, WPB – North American Council. Walker would go on to propose a 'World Peace Guard' in the early 1980s.

Jayaprakash Narayan, co-authored a letter on the subject to the UN Secretary General with Spanish diplomat Salvador de Madariaga. In their letter, they proposed that Hammarskjöld establish a 'Peace Guard' that could complement UN military forces. Their plan envisaged a parachute force of non-violent protestors who would block transport routes and airfields, equipped with technologies to allow media broadcasting directly from conflict zones. UN officials ignored the proposal, perhaps unsurprisingly, given that, as Margot Tudor's recent work on United Nations peacekeeping operations suggests, the ideals of the UN's humanitarian mission often resembled a 'reinvention of colonialism'.[112] The proposed peace force bore closer resemblance to the radical protest techniques pioneered decades later by environmental movements such as Greenpeace, rather than a viable framework for a pacifist companion to military and humanitarian efforts that were often coordinated by former colonial officials. The revival of the idea of a peace army was, it seemed, caught on the jagged edges of decolonization. But then, at the conference of War Resisters' International at Gandhigram held in December 1960, Narayan returned to the idea, using his keynote speech to restate his appeal for a peace army. In his intervention, as Lydia Walker's recent analysis shows, Narayan combined two pleas: first, that international peace campaigners transform their approach from one centred on pacifist disengagement with war to an active non-violent engagement with conflict; and second, that the violence involved in decolonization in Africa and Asia should be the primary focus of their efforts.[113] Much of the conference then focused on the formation of a 'world peace brigade' by pacifist movements.[114]

Charles Walker's January 1961 memorandum thus represented both an innovative proposal for international collaboration between peace movements, and a return to an idea that had long been debated by pacifist campaigners. Later in 1961, when the aims and scope of the new movement were under detailed discussion, the plans were announced in the *Guardian* newspaper in Britain as an attempt to create a body of 'unarmed volunteers, trained in the Gandhian techniques of non-violence, who would go to any area of tension in the world to practise what has been called moral "jiu-jitsu" on the warring inhabitants'.[115] Some contemporaries might have recognized this as a direct reference to Richard Gregg's 1934 book, *The Power of Non-violence*, which described the character of non-violent resisters, and how their 'human traits of love, faith, courage, honesty and humility', would undermine the 'moral balance' of an assailant.[116] And, as discussed in the opening chapter, the Sevagram meeting in 1950 had also considered the possibility of international 'satyagraha units'.[117] On one level, then, the World Peace Brigade was the final manifestation of a vision that had

---

[112] Margot Tudor, *Blue Helmet Bureaucrats: United Nations Peacekeeping and the Reinvention of Colonialism, 1945–1971*, Human Rights in History (Cambridge: Cambridge University Press, 2023).
[113] Lydia Walker, 'Jayaprakash Narayan and the Politics of Reconciliation for the Postcolonial State and Its Imperial Fragments', *The Indian Economic & Social History Review* 56, no. 2 (2019): 156.
[114] Thomas Weber, *Gandhi's Peace Army: The Shanti Sena and Unarmed Peacekeeping* (Syracuse, NY: Syracuse University Press, 1996), 16–18.
[115] *Guardian*, 10 August 1961.
[116] Richard Bartlett Gregg, *The Power of Non-Violence* (Philadelphia and London: J. B. Lippincott Co., 1934), Chapter 2.
[117] Weber, *Gandhi's Peace Army*, 53.

been sketched by peace campaigners since at least the interwar years, when the British activist Maude Royden proposed that an army of volunteers should be deployed to stand between Chinese and Japanese forces following the invasion of Manchuria in 1931. In February 1932, Royden, along with the Anglican priest and founder of the Peace Pledge Union Dick Sheppard, called on the League of Nations to form a 'peace army' that would place a 'human wall' between the combatants.[118]

India had retained its status as a lodestar of non-violent resistance throughout the 1950s, but since 1948 the focus and agenda of campaigns had diverged, with European and North American movements placing nuclear weapons at the centre of their efforts, while African movements deployed non-violence in the context of anti-colonial nationalism. And yet, although the formation of the Shanti Sena represented a continuation of a longer tradition of Gandhian non-violent action, it was essentially a parallel development to the Sahara team and World Peace Brigade. After the establishment of a formal Shanti Sena committee in 1958, Vinoba Bhave had spent much of the following year building up support and a national organizational structure. By the time the World Peace Brigade was launched, the Shanti Sena had deployed volunteers to various areas within India, including Belagavi on the disputed border between the states of Maharashtra and Karnataka. But, despite the legacy of a highly developed tradition of non-violent action in the frame provided by Gandhi, the development of the Shanti Sena should also be set within distinctive Indian debates around the relationship between pacifism and the institutions of the modern state.[119] Questions arose around the relationship between a non-violent movement and a state with a standing army and between non-violence and socialism. J. P. Narayan, making the inaugural address to the Gandhigram meeting, admitted that, while he believed war was a 'crime against humanity' he could also envisage circumstances in which he might offer moral support to those who had chosen to confront aggression with armed resistance.[120]

The Indian example seemed particularly important as an example of the challenges faced by non-violent movements in the context of the post-colonial state. While the anti-colonial struggle in India cannot be glossed as one shaped purely by non-violent action, the value of the moral leadership of Gandhi and the principles of satyagraha had granted the country a particular power in the imaginations of many – and not just pacifists – in relation to potential solutions to civil and international tension. But this reputation was tested with the Indian military intervention and annexation of the Portuguese enclave of Goa in December 1961. Narayan cited the decision to launch an armed assault on Goa as a reason to establish a Peace Brigade, to provide a pacifist alternative to military force. Narayan argued that to follow Gandhian teaching, activists ought to seek the creation of a 'non-violent society' through psychological,

---

[118] *Times of India*, 27 February 1932, 11; 29 February 1932, 9.
[119] On attempts by Bhave and the Bhoodan movement to apply Gandhian philosophies of practice to economic life for example, see Taylor C. Sherman, 'A Gandhian Answer to the Threat of Communism? Sarvodaya and Postcolonial Nationalism in India', *The Indian Economic & Social History Review* 53, no. 2 (2016): 249–70.
[120] Narayan, inaugural address, 1960, quoted in Devi Prasad, *War Is a Crime Against Humanity: The Story of War Resisters' International* (London: War Resisters' International, 2005), 322.

socio-economic and political transformation. But these were long-term aims, and pacifists needed to address ways in which situations of violence could be addressed in the meantime. Peacekeeping and defence had hitherto been considered within a framework of violence and the identification of institutions accorded the legitimate use of force. Instead, Narayan argued, pacifists needed to take steps to develop a positive alternative, which included the Shanti Sena. But, as he admitted, in the context of the Indian invasion of Goa, it had failed.[121] Similarly, writing in *Bhoodan*, the newspaper of Vinoba's movement, Suddharaj Dhadda noted that Nehru had hitherto accumulated 'moral prestige' on the basis of resisting the ejection of Portuguese officials from Goa by force of aims – a change of tactics, although apparently welcomed with feverish enthusiasm by sections of the Indian press, was likely to lose India a good deal of its moral credit. And – perhaps just as significantly – it meant that advocates of non-violence were 'found wanting' at a critical moment.[122] Western peace campaigners echoed such sentiments. Michael Randle, already considering a new pacifist project in central Africa, argued that 'Goa is both a symptom and a warning of a pattern that is likely to be repeated elsewhere'.[123]

The efforts to construct an international peace brigade between the Gandhigram conference – the first time a meeting of the War Resisters' International had taken place outside Europe – and the launch of the World Peace Brigade in early 1962 thus represented the first genuine attempt to bring the Indian, European and American strands of post-1945 non-violent action into alignment. The nuanced tensions around matters of principle embodied in Narayan's opening statement, moreover, presaged the difficulties in creating a viable organization that could meet the multifaceted aims and agendas of its participants and sponsors. By April 1961, the WRI plans for a World Peace Brigade had begun to coalesce around a committee, largely made up of English Quakers and pacifists including Michael Randle as well as Anthony Brooke, the 'Last White Raja' and former ruler of Sarawak and Ernest Bader, a Quaker industrialist who had converted his successful chemical company, Scott Bader, into a worker-owned enterprise in 1951. The committee was chaired by Scott and its secretary was Arlo Tatum, an American conscientious objector who had moved to Britain in 1955 when he became general secretary of WRI. As early as 1956, Tatum had been a strong advocate for the formation of a movement that could 're-create enthusiasm' for the pacifist movement.[124] In addition to prominent figures including Muste, Rustin and Martin Luther King, Tatum sought sponsorship from individuals based in the Communist bloc, in order to position the brigade outside Cold War alignment and to present it 'not as a method of protest but of constructive work'.[125] The plans for a World Peace Brigade would, Tatum asserted, need to move beyond 'the old idea of throwing ourselves between opposing armies'. For its planners, the new initiative would build on the foundations of interwar pacifism and non-violent resistance but would also need

---

[121] Narayan, 'Why a World Peace Brigade?', 23 December 1961, SPC Muste 89/22 WPB Founding Convention.
[122] Dhadda, 'The Challenge of Goa', *Bhoodan*, 23 December 1961.
[123] 'Memo on Project in Africa', 28 December 1961, BPC DAC Randle Cwl MR/1/4.
[124] Tatum, 1956, quoted in Prasad, *War Is a Crime against Humanity*, 320.
[125] Tatum to Alfred Hassler, 24 April 1961, SPC FOR IIC General Corres 1960–62, WRI.

to establish methods and principles geared towards the specific needs of the world in the second half of the twentieth century.

The challenges of the moment were summed up by the WRI organizer Tony Smythe:

> We are faced with major problems on a world-wide scale such as war, a variety of social tensions, the most extreme expressions of which takes a violent form, hunger poverty, loss of individuality and the concentration of power. Most of us would agree that all these are interrelated, that the causes are often the same and that any attempt at a solution cannot be rigidly confined to any particular evil.[126]

Hints of anarcho-pacifist principles appear in Smythe's account. The nation state, as a concentrated form of power, could not, he argued, provide the solutions to contemporary crisis nor usher peace into being, citing the experience of those connected with the attempt to establish the non-violent training centre in Ghana. His view was that a peace brigade should remain independent of government and instead launch 'parallel services' that could include microcosmic organization of local tax collection or alternative systems of international action such as monitoring of nuclear test bans. Others, such as Dhadda, invoked the existential threat of atomic war. He argued that there was no possibility of avoiding war as long as people rejected an 'attitude of genuine co-existence' and sought instead to exert dominance over each other. The advent of nuclear weapons had made such questions 'urgent and practical necessities' and non-violence had become a utilitarian matter of survival. Moreover, he argued that violence was rooted in 'the socio-economic order itself'. The 'non-violent' war that a peace brigade should wage, Dhadda asserted, would need to confront 'injustice, economic exploitation and political suppression and work for the establishment of a new order'.[127] Bill Sutherland, in contrast, suggested that the 'real question' was not the development of a 'constructive programme' but the formation of 'a dedicated, highly-efficient, mobile world non-violent force' that could 'act effectively in emergency situations . . . in areas of international tension or internal revolution'. For Sutherland, if notions of satyagraha were not sufficiently developed to achieve such a goal, 'we should bury this idea of a World Peace Brigade and concentrate on other methods of achieving our goals'.[128]

Some argued that the new organization should not launch emergency campaigns too quickly. The French activist and participant in the Sahara protest, Pierre Martin, suggested that extensive training was a vital first step that would require six months to a year before any effective campaign in Africa or elsewhere might be undertaken. He proposed that until April 1962 volunteers should focus on non-violent campaigns in their own countries, before travelling to Africa to undertake technical assistance work for six months. Discussions around a potential direct-action protest would therefore not take place until at least August 1962.[129] Others felt that the focus of the movement

---

[126] Tony Smythe, 'Study on the World Peace Brigade' [n.d. 1961], SPC - WPB - North American Council.
[127] Dhadda, 'The Task Before the Beirut Conference', 1 October 1961, BPC DAC Randle Cwl MR/1/4.
[128] Sutherland, 'Comments on World Peace Brigade', 1 October 1961, BPC DAC Randle Cwl MR/1/4.
[129] 'WPB - Comments by Pierre Martin', 28 December 1961, BPC, DAC Randle Cwl MR/1/4.

ought to be broadened. In November 1961, the London committee discussed a proposal that the peace brigade activities might extend to large-scale projects of social and economic development. In effect, this was one further opportunity for Scott to promote the plan that he had advocated since the 1940s, namely the Okavango delta irrigation scheme. Here, though, the proposal focused on a specific site – Chief's Island (now the site of a luxury tourist camp in the Moremi Game Reserve). Peace brigade volunteers might, together with local labour and overseen by expert engineers, construct a dike across the delta to the west of the island. The work would reclaim land potentially suitable for agriculture and provide a controllable supply of water for irrigation.[130] Later that month Scott took the same proposal to the UN Trusteeship Committee, but within the preparatory committee for the peace brigade, Pierre Martin expressed deep scepticism, suggesting that in his experience a project of the kind envisaged by Scott would be 'useless if it is not inserted into a development plan which foresees a collective system of ownership of the land'.[131] In its London conference on 24 November, the Okavango project was rejected by the World Peace Brigade preparatory committee. It was, conference delegates agreed, 'too vast an undertaking' and a 'small-scale project, preferably in a conflict situation' would be a better option.[132]

Perhaps the most ambitious proposition presented for consideration in the lead up to the Brummana conference came from the US pacifist Robert Swan. Imprisoned as a conscientious objector during the 1940s, Swan would later take a leading role in the community land trust movement in the United States. In December 1961, he set out a plan for an organization that could provide 'effective nonviolent action . . . and not merely a symbolic act'. As such the organization should establish a centre either in India or an African territory that would provide the main base for the activities of a 'nonviolent international Air Force' that would be on standby to deploy a non-violent paratroop force to set up vigils at the sites of atomic tests or sites of tension and potential conflict. The air force would also be able to distribute humanitarian aid, non-violent propaganda or combat forest fires. Alongside the air force, the centre would train and maintain a 'nonviolent corps of constructive workers'; although Swan does not provide specifics on the actual tasks such a corps would undertake, his plan suggested social and economic activities that might alleviate tensions that would require the services of the airborne 'interjection' force.[133]

Rather than grand projects, many of the preparatory discussions focused on the question of organization and training. Clear objectives and definition of the role of volunteers were needed, the US Quaker Arlo Tatum argued, in order to differentiate the peace brigade from notion of an international police force: the WPB would be independent from national govt and international organizations and an alternative to the idea of the Peace Corps being mooted by the new president of the United States,

---

[130] 'World Peace Brigade', 1 November 1961, SPC Muste 89/22 WPB Founding Convention.
[131] 22 November 1961 1220 Meeting of the UN Fourth Committee; 'WPB – Comments by Pierre Martin'.
[132] 'Minutes, WPB Second One-Day Conference', 24 November 1961, BPC DAC Randle Cwl MR/1/4.
[133] Robert Swan, 'Proposal for an International Non-violent Force', 7 December 1961, BPC DAC Randle Cwl MR/1/4.

John Kennedy.[134] At a preparatory conference of Indian activists held at Rajghat in October 1961, the training of volunteers was highlighted as a particular issue of concern. The delegates recommended that volunteers should be selected with careful regard to experience, age, health and capacity to communicate easily within an international context. As such, it was proposed that training should include courses in Esperanto, as well as a broad array of social and intellectual themes. The latter would include knowledge of satyagraha and ideologies of peace, set alongside training in social service and experience of 'community living'. With an additional focus on 'physical endurance' the general curriculum – like that sketched by Randle and Sutherland for the Winneba centre – evoked a degree of monasticism.[135] For others, training centres established by the peace brigade would be a vital intervention in the struggle to thwart the rise of armed resistance movements in Africa. Pierre Martin argued that the resolution agreed at the Positive Action conference in Accra had become even more significant and the World Peace Brigade, he suggested, would face the challenge of competition 'from rebels to whom certain African governments are giving military aid', as well as those who had travelled to China for 'military and terrorist training'.[136]

One of the more detailed proposals for a training programme was set out by the Gandhian activist Narayan Desai, who argued that training 'to cultivate attitudes' was a vital if neglected aspect of non-violent action. He proposed that an initial centre be set up, ideally in a neutral country whose government was generally supportive of the peace movement, where a national peace brigade was well established, and close to possible peace brigade projects. The training should, he suggested, centre on practical social service, including first aid, fire-fighting and construction. It would focus on developing the skills of 'community life' such as self-discipline, self-expression and leadership, as well as the history and philosophies of non-violence. Desai's proposal also suggested that the programme should employ the 'power of silence', the harmonious effect of music, and on the self-actualizing benefits of physical work and contemplation within nature. Again, the monastic qualities of the proposal are obvious. The final proposals put forward for discussion at Brummana, then, envisaged a training programme structured around 'local' efforts focused on social work and the formation of a 'civitia' (a non-violent militia) and 'zonal' training based on the programme of the Shanti Sena, established in the four continental regions of the brigade. Volunteers would, the plan suggested, normally undertake training in their nearest zone, following a curriculum which emphasized non-violence, social service, community responsibility and the formation of a collective identity. Practical elements of the training would include 'field work in non-violence' and efforts to instil physical and emotional endurance and discipline. The report highlighted a belief in the need to develop 'spiritual growth as essential to the development of integrated peace volunteers'.[137]

---

[134] Tatum, 'Thoughts on a World Peace Brigade', 1 October 1961, SPC FOR IIC General Corres 1960–62, WRI.
[135] 'Indian Preparatory Conference', 31 October 1961, SPC Muste 89/22 WPB Founding Convention.
[136] Pierre Martin, 'The Role of Pacifism in Africa', November 1961, BPC, DAC Randle Cwl MR/1/4.
[137] 'Note on the Training of Peace Volunteers for the World Peace Brigade', 1 December 1961, BPC DAC Randle Cwl MR/1/4.

African issues were prominent during both the preparatory discussions and the final conference at Brummana. Jean van Lierde, a Belgian pacifist, conscientious objector and adviser to Patrice Lumumba, called on pacifists to work to ensure that African states did not move into the orbit of either Cold War superpower, but instead promote 'positive neutralism', and focus on projects to promote agrarian reform and the development of 'communal socialisation'.[138] Pierre Martin added his own interpretation of African needs alongside van Lierde, noting that despite the vast social and cultural diversity within Africa, the peoples of the continent, in his experience, were united by strong anti-colonial sentiment and a genuine solidarity that prompted people to be 'concerned by an event, solely because it happens somewhere in Africa'.[139] Martin's account of an African personality was also suffused with a semi-colonial sense of collective psychology. 'All sorts of twists and turns are possible', he argued, where political cultures had evolved within an environment of slavery and colonialism and adapted to 'know how to use both cunning and violence'. But if Martin appeared to slip into the paternalist language of the expert who, through long experience, knows 'the African', he was at pains to counter examples of political violence in Africa – the most pressing being the contemporary conflict in the Congo – with those that testified to a heroic capacity for non-violence. The war in the Congo, he noted, did 'not involve even one twentieth of the black population of Africa'.

For Martin, the pious references to peace made by leaders of newly independent states in Africa were belied by the race to expand military strength, justified by national defence, international obligations and the fear of colonial powers. The military, moreover, had long functioned as a marker of prestige and a fundamental element of the public performance of state power. Like development policy, the military marching band represented a structural continuity between the colonial and post-colonial state. So, Martin called pacifists to 'concede a company for parades', but suggested alternatives to other functions of the military. National defence might, he argued, be secured through formal declarations of neutrality, but the international obligations of African states could not be de-militarized until states gained economic independence. For Martin, international aid would be a necessary part of the process of economic development, but he sounded a warning about the ease with which this blurred with military expansionism. He cited the example of the Peace Corps, who he imagined being deployed in advance of military missions in the guise of development assistance. The 'Kennedy Peace Boys', he concluded, would be 'imagined by the general population to be no more than American army officers in civilian clothes'.[140] But, in the face of the challenges he described, Martin's proposals for practical action were somewhat thin and unambitious. Given his background with SCI, his focus on civil service was understandable, but he offered little in the way of concrete proposals for an 'International Voluntary Service'. Instead, he emphasized the value of fostering friendship and personal contacts with African students, establishing civic partnerships with African cities, and collaborations between schools and trades unions.

---

[138] Jean van Lierde, 'Memo on Pacifism in Africa', July 1961, BPC DAC Randle Cwl MR/1/4.
[139] Pierre Martin, 'The Role of Pacifism in Africa', November 1961, BPC DAC Randle Cwl MR/1/4.
[140] Ibid.

Bill Sutherland also drew on his experiences in Accra in 1960. He noted that in his conversations with South African leaders passing through Ghana he found them open to ideas about non-violent approaches to combatting white domination. What they did not welcome, however, were 'lectures on Gandhi' as half a century of experience of this approach in South Africa 'entitled them to give the lectures'. Activists were looking to Egypt and the Soviet Union, Sutherland reflected, and he and Randle had nowhere to suggest as an alternative. He argued that peace organizations ought to involve themselves in conflicts in what Galling defined as a 'second party' – that is, by supporting a side with an obvious moral cause as Gandhi had done in his support for Congress in the interwar period. Pacifists like Scott, he added, were 'not promoting consensual goals', but revealing the fact that 'the status quo is a condition of static violence, not peace, and that creative conflict may be necessary to bring about true peace'. In essence, peace campaigners needed to be active and engaged in the wider politics of decolonization in order to demonstrate the effectiveness of non-violence. He proposed a 'hypothetical case' of a pacifist intervention in the Congo crisis. In Sutherland's imagined account, following the outbreak of civil violence, a group of leading pacifists would have been convened, while he and Randle flew to Tanganyika to set up a training centre. After a three-month training programme, volunteers would enter the Congo to liaise with and support UN technicians and local communities. The leaders of the main factions would be brought together in a 'neutral area' and engage in negotiations brokered by Nkrumah and Nyerere, supported by experts such as Muste and Narayan. This, Sutherland suggested, might sound 'way out' but represented the kind of 'second party' action that non-violent activists might provide.[141]

Michael Randle presented his proposal for an African protest project for discussion on the opening day of the conference. His plan was prefaced with a request for total secrecy, given the need for further consultations with African leaders. The outline was, however, very close to the project that would eventually be set in motion, although ultimately never carried out. Randle proposed a march from Tanganyika into Northern Rhodesia 'to assist in the struggle against minority rule' and to set up a training centre for non-violence (an initial centre would be established in Tanganyika prior to the march). If successful, a second stage of the protest envisaged a further march into South-West Africa 'to demand the return of lands of dispossessed Africans'. In a region whose politics were shaped by transnational links between settler and industrial interests, Randle argued that a 'victory for the freedom movement in any of these territories loosens the stranglehold of the ruling minority'.[142] The premise of the scheme ignored, of course, the extent of the economic and political hegemony of settler colonialism, centred on the apartheid regime in South Africa. It also suggested that activists had not fully grasped the challenges faced by, and transformations taking place within, the United Nations in the face of the entangled impacts of a nuclear Cold War and decolonization.

---

[141] Sutherland, 'World Peace Brigade – Further comments', 1 December 1961, BPC DAC Randle Cwl MR/1/4.
[142] Randle, 'Memo on Project in Africa', 28 December 1961, BPC DAC Randle Cwl MR/1/4.

After two conferences and the lengthy series of preparatory meetings in London, the World Peace Brigade was formally constituted at a conference held in Brummana, Lebanon, between December 1961 and January 1962. The venue for the conference was Brummana High School, founded by Quakers in the late-nineteenth century in a small resort town in the hills to the east of Beirut.[143] The conference opened on Thursday 28 December 1961 with an address from Michael Scott. The Anglican priest was undoubtedly a key figure throughout the conference, his appearance giving an air of dishevelled urgency, 'dressed in baggy tweeds' and carrying a portable radio constantly to keep in touch with world affairs'. He remained a charismatic figure, who seemed to win the support of younger activists just as he had excited Quaker pacifists and metropolitan liberals in the late 1940s.[144] Attended by fifty participants from across the world (save Latin America and the Soviet Bloc), the largest contingent of delegates came from the United States, followed by the UK, and then India and the Federal Republic of Germany. Nine other participants came from various European countries, five were based in Lebanon and two in Australia. Three Africans attended the conference, including E. C. Quaye from Ghana. Two notable absences were Jayaprakash Narayan, who sent a message of apology, and Vinoba Bhave. Each day, the conference discussed proposals from policy groups, focused on the aims of the brigade, its structure, the question of volunteers and training, and proposals for initial activities. On New Year's Day, the conference approved the naming of the organization as the World Peace Brigade for Non-Violent Action, and a Council was elected, whose members included Scott, Muste, Rustin, Randle and J. P. Narayan, as well as E. C. Quaye, together with Julius Nyerere and the Northern Rhodesian nationalist leaders Kenneth Kaunda. Three 'working committees' were established, for India, Europe and the United States. Later that evening, the meeting was closed with moments of silence followed by songs provided by Tatum, Rustin and Narayan Desai. All that remained was for the new organization to enact its founders' aspirations in the context of a real-world struggle:

> What is needed now is someone who possesses that strange power of moral and political imagination and perception which will lead him to see the action which history demands; and then a band of men and women who will act apart from fear of failure, ignominy, imprisonment or death. I do not know if the organizers of the Brigade will be able to escape the tolls of prudence, transcend purely political calculation, convince themselves that the purpose of life may be in giving their lives-so, that others may continue to see the blue sky, taste a potato, listen. to sweet music, or hold the hand of a friend.[145]

---

[143] The school – one of few co-educational institutions in the Middle East – was attended by a number of members of the Bin Laden family, including (briefly) Osama Bin Laden, in the late 1960s. Steve Coll, *The Bin Ladens: An Arabian Family in the American Century* (New York: Penguin Press, 2008), 134.

[144] Lyttle, 'Brummana Conference for a World Peace Brigade', 31 January 1962, SPC Muste 89/22 WPB Founding Convention.

[145] Lyttle, 'Brummana Conference for a World Peace Brigade', 31 January 1962.

The long-held aim of establishing a global peace army had come to pass, with anti-colonial struggles in Africa as its primary focus of concern. Its leading figures embodied, but also sought to galvanize, the interconnections between international peace campaigns and independence movements in Africa. 'The struggle of the anti-war movement', its founders argued, was 'essentially part of the struggle being waged by the African resistance movements for national liberation and independence'.[146]

---

[146] WPB Founding Statement, Brummana Conference, January 1962, SPC Muste 89/22 WPB Founding Convention.

6

Africa Freedom Action and the march that never happened

The World Peace Brigade embarked on its first project just months after its inaugural conference, with an ambitious plan to engage with the independence campaign in Northern Rhodesia led by Kenneth Kaunda. In what was a four-way scramble for power between the colonial state, the Central African Federation, the African National Congress led by Henry Nkumbula and Kaunda's United National Independence Party, the WPB aligned itself with Kaunda, whom they viewed as a kindred spirit and committed advocate of non-violence. This chapter follows the development of the relationship that developed between WPB activists and African political movements in east and central Africa in the months that followed the Brummana conference. As with the efforts of the Sahara protest team in Accra two years before, the WPB relied on the material support of independent African governments and pan-Africanist organizations. During the Addis Ababa meeting of the Pan-Africanist Movement of East and Central Africa (PAFMECA), WPB leaders reached an agreement to form 'Africa Freedom Action' in alliance with UNIP. The campaign, backed by the Tanganyika African National Union, the governing party since Tanganyikan independence in December 1961, involved a plan for a mass march across the border from Tanganyika into Northern Rhodesia in support of a national strike organized by UNIP.

No march took place, but the story of its planning and organization provides a window into the complex transnational and regional interchanges that were revealed in the history of the politics of decolonization in Zambia. In contrast to the Sahara protest, it was the first time that a peace movement had, albeit indirectly, become involved in the politics of national elections in Africa. The chapter thus examines the contradictions and difficulties highlighted by transnational peace campaigners seeking to advocate for African nationalist movements. Unlike the examples at the centre of Walker's recent works, however, the political claims made by UNIP aligned with dominant narratives of national liberation, although the WPB (and other international organizations such as the American Committee on Africa) took the conscious decision to support UNIP's claim to be the legitimate representatives of the majority.[1] Even when the focus of advocacy was a majority nationalism, it was involved in a rewiring of pre-existing systems of rule, a creative remaking of political culture.

---

[1] Walker, 'Decolonization in the 1960s'.

The WPB were in a sense instrumental to UNIP, but their value as transnational advocates was also bound up with a broader agenda of support for African political claims across southern Africa that set the nationalist struggle in Zambia within a wider perspective. The chapter examines these wider interests, noting the emphasis placed by WPB campaigners on the role of other sets of international interests, including corporate finance and mining groups, in a transnational politics of settler colonialism. It also addresses renewed attempts to establish training centres for non-violence in Africa, relying (as they had in Accra) on the patronage of African political organizations. Ultimately, the WPB campaigners that remained in Dar es Salaam struggled to identify a purpose, and there seemed little that peace campaigners could offer for post-colonial African states.

The challenge faced by the World Peace Brigade was significant. Prior to the early 1960s, transnational solidarity with southern African nationalist campaigns had been strongly attracted by its moral aspects, articulated by Christian and pacifist interlocutors in the West who emphasized its Gandhian and non-violent methodologies. But, as the process of decolonization across Africa gained momentum, international support for liberation movements began to be mapped out on African terms, and as a consequence violent resistance was taken as a rational and justified starting point. Accounts of the shift from passive resistance to 'guerrilla struggle' in South Africa attest to the global influences that informed activists, who closely followed the trajectories of anti-colonial revolutions, particularly in Algeria, Vietnam and Cuba. Many ANC leaders had read their Mao, while activists connected with the Communist Party felt a solidarity with global armed resistance led by Communist groups.[2] An analysis of the methodologies of 'struggle' should, then, be situated within the broader intellectual context of decolonization and the 'imperfect visions of the future' available to contemporaries.[3] The notion of a discrete 'turn' – away from civil disobedience, towards armed resistance – begins to seem an admirable motif for a national myth, but at best a partial vision of the complex, multifaceted and contradictory processes of decolonization. As explored in Gary Wilder's recent work on Francophone African visions of the end of empire, these processes were imagined as excursions into a potential future, as ways of enacting historical change.[4] Set alongside the various temporal possibilities that Wilder posits as integral to the process of decolonization, the 'turn to armed struggle' takes on a new dimension, in which an emotional politics of time emerges – a concept of crisis time or a moment of emergency. In essence, the chapter considers whether the singular notion of a definitive 'turn' can effectively capture the complex transnational history of this moment.

---

[2] Bernard Makhosezwe Magubane, et al., 'The Turn to Armed Struggle', in *The Road to Democracy in South Africa, Volume 1, 1960–1970*, edited by South African Democracy Education Trust (Cape Town: Zebra Press, 2004), 53–145.
[3] Smith and Jeppeson, *Britain, France and the Decolonization of Africa*.
[4] Gary Wilder, *Freedom Time: Negritude, Decolonization, and the Future of the World* (Durham, NC and London: Duke University Press, 2015).

Kaunda, UNIP and non-violence in Northern Rhodesia

In late January 1959, just after the Direct Action Committee had begun to advocate a protest campaign against the French atomic tests, Bill Sutherland wrote to Bayard Rustin on the subject of non-violence and African nationalist movements. Reflecting on his work at the All-African Peoples' Conference during the previous month, Sutherland reported that he had been particularly impressed with a delegate from the Zambian African National Congress, Kenneth Kaunda. Of all the delegates he had met, Sutherland singled out Kaunda as 'an individual who understands and is willing to go all-out on non-violent direct action'.[5] After the conference, Kaunda had remained in Accra and, with support from the sociologist St Clair Drake, studied the organization of positive action protests in Ghana. Sutherland wrote enthusiastically of the need to support Kaunda and endorsed requests for funds to purchase resources for a political campaign.[6] Muste noted the interest in Kaunda, initiated discussions with George Houser about ways in which American networks might offer support, and suggested that Kaunda might draft an article for publication in *Liberation*.[7] In the early 1960s, transatlantic pacifist networks thus championed Kaunda as a new hope for non-violence, fully embracing the idealized image of the leader of UNIP – and the organization itself – as the embodiment of a popular movement that shared their activist vision.

In Britain, African nationalist movements in Northern Rhodesia had been prominent in efforts to highlight opposition to plans for Federation in the early 1950s, but the roots of African political mobilization in the territory were deeper. Unlike the other states in the Federation, Northern Rhodesia had undergone a process of rapid industrialization in the first half of the twentieth century. Originally, the territory was an extension of Cecil Rhodes' grand conception of an African empire as a vast country estate, organized around colonial settlers in the frame of John Bull. But the landscape of colonialism in the territory became, quite quickly, shaped by industrialization and urbanization. Large-scale mining in the Copperbelt, stretching across the northern part of Northern Rhodesia and the Katanga province of the Belgian Congo, began to transform the region in ways comparable only to South Africa, where diamonds and gold had driven the rapid development of an industrial economy in the late-nineteenth century. From the late 1920s, rising global demand for copper resulted in the rapid development of a mineral industry across a region stretching from Elisabethville in the Congo across a series of new urban centres such as Ndola on the Northern Rhodesian side of the border. By the mid-1940s, African-initiated welfare associations began to rival official Advisory Councils as the authentic voice of African interests in the territory. In 1948, when representatives of settler communities began to agitate for new constitutional arrangements that would protect minority rule, representatives of

---

[5] Sutherland to Bayard Rustin, 20 January 1959, 4 February 1959, SPC Muste 89/16 Kaunda.
[6] Ibid.
[7] Muste to Sutherland, 13 March 1959, SPC Muste 89/16 Kaunda.

African welfare societies formed the Northern Rhodesian African Congress that, like its counterpart in Nyasaland, face a 'voice' to African political interests and aspirations.[8]

Kenneth Kaunda had become engaged with politics in the early 1950s when, alongside Simon Kapwepwe, he was a member of the Chinsali welfare association in the north-east of Northern Rhodesia, close to the main route to the border with Tanganyika.[9] When plans for Federation were announced in early 1952, Kaunda became a regional organizer for the Northern Rhodesian African Congress (NRAC); his public profile increased in October the following year when he made a public demand for equal political rights for Africans, who were braced for a struggle for their own country against the colonial 'enemy'. They were not, Kaunda argued, 'afraid of guns or atomic weapons'.[10] While compatriots in the NRAC including Harry Nkumbula engaged with socialist supporters in Britain, Kaunda was energized by the tactics of Gandhian civil disobedience and nationalist politics in India. He attributed his interest in the doctrine of *satyagraha* to an Indian shop owner in Lusaka, Rambhai Patel, whose translations of Gandhi's writing were integrated into Kaunda's public speeches as a young activist.[11] Over the course of the 1950s, Kaunda rose to prominence within the Congress, but clashed with the moderate leadership around Nkumbula after organizing a successful boycott of European-owned and Asian-owned stores.[12] His subsequent rise to national leader aligned with the standard narrative of African nationalist elites in the mid-twentieth century. After six months in Britain during 1957 under the patronage of the Labour Party, Kaunda returned to Africa and quit Congress the following year to become the leader of a new organization, the Zambian African National Congress (ZANC). As recent accounts of the history of Zambian nationalism have shown, the rupture between Nkumbula and Kaunda and formation of the ZANC was a contemporary personification of factional, regional and ideological fissures in the nationalist movement.[13]

The ZANC had particular regional and ethnic origins in the Copperbelt and Bemba-speaking peoples but did not constitute a homogeneous political movement.[14] It was, however, able to mobilize African opposition to white minority rule within the Federation and support for national independence. Kaunda took on the role as the figurehead for the movement, travelling to Accra for the All-African Peoples' Conference before returning to campaign for a boycott of elections to the legislative assembly in 1959. For his efforts, Kaunda was awarded a nine-month prison sentence, while the Governor of Northern Rhodesia accused the party of behaving like 'Chicago racketeers'.[15] Following his release, Kaunda joined the new organization, the United National Independence Party (UNIP), that had formed when the ZANC was banned during the election boycott. From 1959 – when the political tensions in Northern Rhodesia formed one part of a larger crisis for the Central African Federation which

[8] Ibid., 209–12, Larmer, *Rethinking African Politics*, 25–6.
[9] Rotberg, *Rise of Nationalism*, 239.
[10] Ibid., 242, 263.
[11] Kenneth Kaunda, *Kaunda on Violence* (London: Sphere, 1982), 15–16.
[12] Rotberg, *Rise of Nationalism*, 276–9.
[13] Larmer, *Rethinking African Politics*, 28.
[14] Ibid., 29–32.
[15] Rotberg, *Rise of Nationalism*, 301.

included widespread unrest, violence and the suppression of African political activity in Nyasaland – through to 1962, Kaunda and UNIP gradually strengthened their claim to represent the political aspirations of the majority in Northern Rhodesia, although Nkumbula and the ANC retained significant popular support.

During 1960, political unrest and tension increased still further, especially following the killing of a European woman, Lilian Burton, by UNIP activists on the Zambian Copperbelt in May. Burton's death took on significance for white conservatives as a 'viable symbol . . . for the purposes of political mobilisation', allowing them to present UNIP supporters as destructive and destabilizing, whose actions demonstrated the dangers of political reform.[16] It was also a direct challenge to the authority of Kaunda, who learned of Burton's death while on a tour of the United States organized by the ACOA. Setting his condemnation of all violence alongside evidence of the increasing authoritarianism of colonial government, Kaunda asserted that the 'dynamic' force of non-violence would be mobilized 'if we fail to get what we want from negotiations'. Independence was, he argued, a 'noble cause; let us employ noble ends'.[17] British officials began to recognize that Kaunda represented a leader untarnished in the eyes of Africans by any accommodation with federation but also sufficiently unthreatening to white opinion.[18] Kaunda would later define his political strategy as one which combined Christian faith and Gandhian hope. It was the latter, he argued, that would ensure that the Zambian nationalist movement could maintain civil disobedience without a descent into violence. For Kaunda, then, Gandhian tactics was 'a lifebelt thrust into the hands of a drowning man'.[19]

British government policy continued to search for a constitutional solution to the twin challenges of Federation and nationalism in central Africa. In October 1960, the Monckton Commission, appointed in the aftermath of the unrest in Nyasaland to reassess the political situation across the Federation, concluded that the federal arrangements required major changes, confirming, as the Africa Bureau had argued since 1952, that African opposition was 'widespread, sincere and of long standing'.[20] It recommended majority rule in Nyasaland and Northern Rhodesia. The report was rejected by Welensky who refused to countenance discussion of the possibility that territories would have the right to secede from the Federation. African leaders, meanwhile, opposed the proposals and called for immediate national independence. In early 1961, the British government convened meetings at Lancaster House in London to outline proposals for a new constitution for Northern Rhodesia. Kaunda convinced UNIP officials to maintain discussions with British authorities viaGovernor Evelyn Hone rather than boycott the process, but rejected the plans announced by the Colonial Secretary Ian McLeod for a complicated electoral system that seemed designed to block the ability of African nationalists to secure a majority.[21] In July,

---

[16] Walima T. Kalusa, 'The Killing of Lilian Margaret Burton and Black and White Nationalisms in Northern Rhodesia (Zambia) in the 1960s', *Journal of Southern African Studies* 37, no. 1 (1 March 2011): 63–77.
[17] 'Statement of Kenneth Kaunda', 13 May 1960, SPC, Muste Papers, Reel 89/16/Sahara Protest Team.
[18] Larmer, *Rethinking African Politics*, 35.
[19] Kaunda, *Kaunda on Violence*, 18.
[20] *Times*, 12 October 1960.
[21] Larmer, *Rethinking African Politics*, 38.

Kaunda sent out a plan for a campaign of non-violent protest; the subsequent 'Cha Cha Cha' protests including sabotage of infrastructure and government buildings seemed to suggest that Kaunda had limited control over local UNIP officials.[22] Press reports in Britain chronicled the widespread acts of sabotage and skirmishes between Africans and police across centres of UNIP support in the Northern Province and the Copperbelt. One account of the situation on the road to Chinsali on the border with Tanganyika described scenes likened to 'the wake of the German retreat in North-West Europe in 1945'.[23] Hundreds of UNIP supporters were arrested as it appeared Kaunda was in danger of losing control of the protest campaign.

There seems some evidence that Kaunda was not alone within UNIP in embracing Gandhian principles, such as the example of Nalumino Mundia who embarked on a fast during his internment in September 1961.[24] And UNIP assiduously compiled a compendium of arbitrary arrests, police beatings and political violence that was widely disseminated with overseas supporters in Britain and elsewhere.[25] Maintaining an international image of Kaunda as a principled advocate of non-violence was important, both within anti-colonial advocacy networks and government circles. As Larmer notes, Kaunda was identified by Western governments as a 'credible' figure who might fulfil the role of leader of a centralized authority in a post-colonial state, protecting relations with the former colonial power and Western interests, which, in the case of Northern Rhodesia, were largely represented by powerful multinational mining corporations. Both British and American officials recognized Kaunda's opposition to violence was genuine, and that he was a figure with 'outstanding moral qualities, sense of fairness and personal charm'.[26]

As with British officials, Kaunda became recognized by peace activists in Europe and the United States as a figure of hope. A profile in *Peace News* in July of that year said very little about the political manoeuvres within the Zambian nationalist movement, but instead presented Kaunda as one of a series of African leaders that remained keen advocates of non-violent direct action; his support, the article warned, was nonetheless dependent on the success of these tactics, as other nationalists willing to embrace violence were 'ready to usurp his leadership'.[27] Kaunda was thus viewed as a viable intermediary whose international influence was bolstered by backing from the American Committee on Africa as well as the Africa Bureau, Fabians, the Labour Party and Christian activists in Britain. Colonial officials, anti-colonial organizations and pacifist activists alike saw a potential ally in Kaunda. Were peace activists thus complicit in the construction of Kaunda as a unifying figure who would serve Western interests. The case for such an argument would be stronger, perhaps, if Kaunda relied solely on Africanist non-governmental organizations embedded in the political culture of New York and London, but the involvement of the World Peace Brigade suggests that

[22] Ibid., 40.
[23] *Guardian*, 13 August 1961, 1; see also *Times*, 9 August 1961, 10 August 1961.
[24] *Contact*, 21 September 1961.
[25] Kalulu and Chona to Macmillan, 7 April 1961, BOD Records of the Africa Bureau, MSS. Afr. s. 1681 Box 245 (Zambia) file 18.
[26] Quoted in Larrmer, *Rethinking African Politics*, 46.
[27] Keith Lye, 'Kenneth Kaunda', *Peace News*, 7 July 1961.

other dynamics were in play. In Scott, Rustin and Sutherland, Kaunda demonstrated an appeal to more radical movements in Britain and America that had begun to connect civil rights, anti-nuclear and anti-imperial values in novel ways. The rising tensions in Northern Rhodesia thus formed a background for the preparatory discussions around a World Peace Brigade. The efforts of Kaunda and other leaders of UNIP to present their movement as a supporter of non-violence struggling in the face of the kind of authoritarian provocation that had justified the recourse to armed resistance elsewhere in Africa made them an obvious candidate for support from the brigade following its official launch in January 1962.

The formation of Africa Freedom Action

Shortly after the Brummama conference, Scott, Randle and Rustin prepared a memorandum which outlined suggestions for 'Positive Action in Southern Africa'. The authors noted that the conference delegates had agreed that the anti-nuclear campaigns of Europe were 'essentially part of the struggle being waged by the African resistance movements for national liberation and independence'. They thus sought to capitalize on the shared ideological and moral principles, while recognizing the key distinctions between the movements, as well as the relations of power that shaped collaborations between Western and African activists. Pacifist principles were muted in the document, and the authors sought to reassure that they were not 'seeking to impose on the African leadership their view that positive non-violent action is the only realistic and effective method to obtain genuine peace and freedom'. Nevertheless, they called on African movements to persevere with 'militant but peaceful means of struggle' before 'resorting to policies of military violence'.[28] They nonetheless asserted their belief that armed struggle was not guaranteed to succeed, given the military resources available to colonial regimes, who would see armed revolt as a justification for reprisals, as had been the case in Angola, where Portuguese authorities had been given 'the excuse for a policy of genocide'. They also cited the dangers of armed resistance in undermining the capacity of the UN to broker a resolution to the crisis and heightening the likelihood that local conflicts would draw Africa into the Cold War. They claimed, in contrast, that non-violent positive action addressed the 'psychological' roots of inequality and baseless moral claims of the 'myth of racial superiority'. The economic impact of actions such as strikes would undermine the 'productive machine of an exploiting minority', while civil disobedience would target and weaken the 'whole administrative machine' sustained on the basis of 'unjust laws'. Advocates of armed struggle would no doubt have responded that such tactics had been tried and found wanting, but the significant point was not that pace activists were suggesting that liberation movements should simply persevere with the tactics of non-violence, but that they had a fundamental and tangible value. Non-violent action, they argued, had the capacity to be a catalyst for social transformation, along the lines of development in the southern United States

---

[28] 'Memorandum on Positive Action in Southern Africa', 28 December 1961, BPC DAC Randle Cwl MR/1/4.

as a consequence of civil rights protests. Its 'positive moral appeal', moreover, might fragment white solidarity and would offer no justification for 'terrorisation of the population'.[29]

Seeking willing partners, Rustin, Scott and Sutherland returned to Africa to attend the conference of the Pan-African Freedom Movement of East and Central Africa held in Addis Ababa in February 1962. At the conference, the peace brigade delegation entered into discussion with Tanganyikan and Zambian sympathizers and began to sketch more concrete plans for the project, which became known as 'Africa Freedom Action'. They approached the meeting at Addis Ababa with a knowledge of the ways in which debates around violent resistance to colonialism fed into widening divisions between African liberation movements and the consequences of this for the wider project of African Unity. They found some key African leaders supportive of their plans. Aside from Kaunda, Siddhartha Dhadda had been able to speak with the Tanganyikan leader Julius Nyerere before the conference, who had indicated his general approval of the plans set out in the memorandum presented to the Brummana meeting but was unwilling to act without approval from Kaunda.

When Bayard Rustin arrived in London en route to the Addis Ababa conference, he became aware of reports that the governments of Ghana and Egypt, although not members of PAFMECA, were advocating armed resistance to settler colonialism in southern Africa; Dhadda reported similar rumours in East Africa. Rustin wrote to Muste claiming that a 'School for Violence' had been established in Ghana, which intensified the need to present a viable alternative to the refugees beginning to congregate in centres such as Dar es Salaam in ever-increasing numbers.[30] Recent research confirms that, from late 1961, Ghana had indeed set up a guerrilla training camp, with Soviet instructors, in Mankrong, whose first intake in early 1962 included members of the South African Pan Africanist Congress.[31] These developments were significant both in terms of the light they shed on the longer-term history of the 'turn' to armed struggle in the early 1960s and, perhaps more significantly, in foregrounding the relationship between the politics of nationalism in South Africa and the politics of pan-Africanism. There had been attempts to calm tensions between the ANC and PAC in South Africa in the aftermath of the Sharpeville shootings, with the formation of a South African United Front, which operated an office in Accra from April 1960. But, despite official support from the government, many Ghanaians and the Bureau of African Affairs under A. K. Barden appeared to favour the PAC. Barden had been allegedly responsible for the expulsion of the leading ANC organizer Tennison Makiwane from Ghana in late 1961. As Grilli's account of relations between Nkrumah and South African liberation movements reveals, Barden had contributed to the collapse of attempts to foster unity between the PAC and ANC in March 1962 and undermined the capacity of the Ghanaian government to take a lead in coordinating pan-African support for South African liberation movements.[32]

---

[29] Ibid.
[30] Rustin to A. J. Muste, 22 February 1962, SPC Muste 89/16 Kaunda.
[31] Matteo Grilli, 'Nkrumah's Ghana and the Armed Struggle in Southern Africa (1961–1966)', *South African Historical Journal* 70, no. 1 (2018): 56–81.
[32] Ibid., 67.

For the South African ANC, the conference in Addis Ababa provided an opportunity for its leaders to present themselves as the legitimate voice of Black resistance to apartheid, and to gain ground on the PAC with regard to support across the African continent.[33] Before the conference, Oliver Tambo, who had left South Africa in 1960 in order to strengthen international support for the ANC, met Nelson Mandela, then working underground to coordinate ANC protest campaigns inside South Africa. Mandela had left the country secretly in February to begin a journey around Africa and Europe, and his appearance at the Addis Ababa conference was the first time he had addressed an African audience. In a speech that had been prepared in consultation with Tambo and another ANC leader, Robert Resha, Mandela described South Africa as a country 'ruled by the gun', whose regime faced an increasingly militant resistance movement. He warned that the sabotage campaign that had been launched in December would continue, but also asserted that non-violent protest had not been abandoned.[34] Correspondence from Bill Sutherland suggests that Mandela also met Rustin during the conference, although there does not appear to be a record of their discussion.[35] But Scott, Rustin and other peace campaigners judged Mandela's speech to be a warning that Africa faced a critical juncture between a non-violent path to decolonization or a descent into violent conflict that would, as the Congo crisis appeared to have shown, draw African states into a fatal Cold War confrontation.

The World Peace Brigade contingent gave their whole-hearted support to the UNIP delegation, which included both Kaunda and its treasurer, Simon Kapwepwe. The UNIP leaders had met with Mandela on the eve of the conference and had reportedly clashed over the relationship between the ANC and white Communists in the SACP.[36] During the conference, the WPB activists joined in lobbying for the election of Kaunda as president of the renamed Pan-African Movement of East, Central and Southern Africa (PAFMECSA). Under Kaunda's chairmanship, the conference blocked resolutions supporting violent action in South Africa and Angola but was unable to persuade delegates to commit to a policy of non-violence. But, the election of Kaunda, as a pacifist, as chair of the movement meant, Rustin argued that 'non-violence still remains the dominant tactic'.[37] Advocates of non-violence were successful, Rustin reasoned, because they offered a plan of action based on mass protest, rather than an 'elite' trained in militant tactics. In the hope of building on the success of the Gandhian activists at the Addis Ababa conference, the WPB members determined to establish a 'training centre for nonviolence' in Dar es Salaam, building on the support pledged by Tanganyikan prime minister Julius Nyerere.[38]

Directly after the PAFMECSA conference, Kaunda travelled to Egypt to convene with Zambian organizers before travelling to Tanganyika in late February. On the 20th, he held talks with Julius Nyerere, the three WPB organizers and TANU leaders

[33] Ellis, *External Mission*, 33.
[34] Anthony Sampson, *Mandela: The Authorised Biography* (London: HarperCollins, 1999), 163; Tom Lodge, *Mandela: A Critical Life* (Oxford: Oxford University Press, 2006), 97.
[35] Sutherland to Muste, 25 August 1962, SPC Muste 89/22 WPB Correspondence.
[36] Lodge, *Mandela*, 97.
[37] Rustin to Muste, 22 February 1962, SPC, Muste Papers, Reel 89/16/Kaunda.
[38] A. J. Muste, Jayaprakash Narayan, and Michael Scott, 'Report of the Chairmen, World Peace Brigade', 23 May 1962. BOD, Scott Papers (5770) 48/2.

including Rashidi Kawawa, who had taken over from Nyerere as the prime minister of Tanganyika in January 1962. During these meetings, the outline of the Africa Freedom Action project was determined. The plan was simple but hugely ambitious. Kaunda would return to Northern Rhodesia, assess the political situation and then announce a general strike. In Nyerere's view, Kaunda would be obliged to act quickly, or he would effectively gift 'the leadership over to the violent elements'.[39] Simultaneously with the launch of the strike, a mass of thousands of Tanganyikan African National Union (TANU) supporters would join international WPB protestors in a march across the border from Tanganyika into Northern Rhodesia. The international team – around thirty 'sound people' drawn from North America, Europe and India – would be, in Rustin's view, the fulcrum of the enterprise. 'We are the new factor that has struck the nerve', he asserted, 'We are the emotional drive in a very weary and difficult situation and we must not fail no matter what.'[40]

Rustin sketched a vision of a heroic 'ride' through Tanganyika from Dar es Salaam to Mbeya, just over seventy miles from the border with Northern Rhodesia. There, the marchers would join with Zambian guides and, once the general strike was launched in Northern Rhodesia, they would break into smaller groups before heading across the border for what was likely to be certain arrest. With the key details of the Africa Freedom Action plan in place, Rustin estimated that he, Scott and Sutherland would need to remain in Tanganyika for at least six weeks and had contacted all the participants at the Brummana conference. At the same time, he asked Muste to persuade specific individuals, including Arlo Tatum, Hugh Brock, J. P. Narayan, Dhadda and Desai, to join the team in Africa. On finances, Muste's area of specialist expertise, Rustin estimated somewhat vaguely that 'thousands of pounds' would be required despite the donation of transport and a large house in Dar es Salaam from TANU. Muste, as ever, coordinated forces in the background, cabling J. P. Narayan to request that he, together with Dhadda and Desai, join the others in Tanganyika, as well as launching public appeals in India to support Kaunda and UNIP.[41]

After the meeting between Kaunda and Nyerere on the 20 February, a joint press release was published welcoming the support of the World Peace Brigade, noting that they were 'convinced that such action applied now in Northern Rhodesia may yet prove to be the key to the liberation of Central and Southern Africa'. Africans needed the support of 'freedom loving people' around the world, they concluded, but the African struggle was in turn for all humanity, and a 'just and peaceful world'.[42] The press release prompted a series of messages between British officials in Dar es Salaam, Lusaka and London. Following an initial report on the TANU/UNIP press release, diplomats in Tanganyika sent an extract from the Swahili newspaper *MwAfrika*, which announced more details of a plan for a demonstration launched into the northern province of Northern Rhodesia, 'to awaken and stir the British government', led by

---

[39] Rustin to Muste, 22 February 1962, SPC, Muste Papers, Reel 89/16/Kaunda.
[40] Ibid.
[41] Muste Cable to J. P. Narayan, 2 February 1962, SPC Muste 89/22 Africa Freedom Project Tanganyika.
[42] 'Press Statement on East African Situation', 21 February1962, SPC Muste 89/22 WPB Correspondence.

Scott and Rustin.[43] By the evening of 22 February, British officials in Dar es Salaam confirmed American reports that the campaign was being organized by Michael Scott, along with two 'American negroes'. They went on to note that Kaunda was expected to hold a rally on 25 February to make further announcements. It was assumed that the main organizers would not have the required documentation to enter Northern Rhodesia, although Tanganyikans would not necessarily require formal visas to enter the neighbouring territory. It was nevertheless suggested that British officials urgently speak to Kawawa and warn of the 'embarrassing consequences' that would follow any Tanganyikan involvement in a protest.[44] Duncan Sandys guided officials in Tanganyika to warn Kawawa that 'active encouragement of lawlessness in a British Territory' would be regarded as an 'unfriendly act' and offer veiled threats of possible material consequences for the government in Dar es Salaam.[45] The following day, a telegram from Evelyn Hone outlined specific details of the legal jeopardy the marchers would face. First, immigration policy was within the remit of the Federal authorities, who Hone suggested would begin to apply immigration regulations on Tanganyikan citizens, which had hitherto not been enforced; he also noted that Scott was a 'prohibited immigrant' across the Federation territories following his activities in Nyasaland nearly a decade earlier and that it would be relatively easy to refuse to provide entry permits from American participants. Moreover, the march would be regarded as a 'procession' in Northern Rhodesia, requiring official sanction. Any Tanganyikan marchers would, therefore, be undertaking an activity that would break the laws of a neighbouring territory. In diplomatic terms, this was a clear warning to the Tanganyikan authorities.[46]

The British High Commissioner met with Kawawa on 23 February, followed by a letter outlining the 'grave concern' of the British government at the reports of the march.[47] The Tanganyikan prime minister flatly denied that he had offered support to the World Peace Brigade and any suggestions otherwise were mere 'speculation'. Despite strongly worded reminders that a 'friendly' government would not allow a major protest to be launched into a neighbouring territory, Kawawa refused to respond.[48] British officials recognized that the views of the Tanganyikan government on the Central African Federation were well known and that any implied or actual advocacy of the views of Welensky and Federal authorities would risk a serious breach in relations with Tanganyika. Both Kawawa and Nyerere had both declared in public that they would take the country out of the Commonwealth if it 'impeded their policies for African unity'.[49] Nyerere suggested to HC that the march aimed to rally support for the Zambian independence movement around the world, particularly in Britain, and when he challenged the High Commissioner to set out an alternative, he gave no reply.

---

[43] Dar to Lusaka, 22 February 1962, UKNA CO 1015/2524.
[44] Ibid.; Dar to Lusaka, 22 February 1962, UKNA CO 1015/2524.
[45] Sandys to Dar, 22 February 1962, UKNA CO 1015/2524.
[46] Hone to Secretary of State for the Colonies, 23 February 1962, UKNA CO 1015/2524.
[47] Dar es Salaam to Commonwealth Relations Office, 24 February 1962, UKNA CO 1015/2524.
[48] Dar es Salaam to Commonwealth Relations Office, 23 February 1962, UKNA, CO 1015/2524.
[49] Dar es Salaam to Commonwealth Relations Office, 24 February1962, UKNA, CO 1015/2524.

But, most importantly, for Nyerere the march was invaluable as a rallying point for African support, particularly for Kaunda himself.[50]

The diplomatic efforts underlined the importance of the timing of the Africa Freedom Action project, which paralleled increasingly fraught diplomatic efforts between London and central Africa to construct constitutional arrangements for Northern Rhodesia. The challenge was to deliver a solution that would secure agreement from both Zambians, who wanted independence and majority rule, and Welensky-supporting federalists, who wanted neither. Reginald Maudling, who had replaced McLeod as Colonial Secretary in October 1961, oversaw the drafting of revised proposals for elections, which aimed secure an outcome that would be supported by both African and settler communities without either gaining a significant political advantage. The aim, he claimed, was 'to avoid the degree and form of violence which would make a solution satisfactory to both races virtually impossible to obtain'.[51] The proposals were set out to Parliament at the end of February 1962 and were reported in the British press as a plan that 'very definitively tilts the balance in the direction of the African Nationalist parties'.[52] Welensky rejected the proposals and threatened to 'use force if necessary' to oppose them.[53] A week later, he announced new elections to the Federation Parliament under a racially restricted franchise and accused the British prime minister Macmillan of a 'surrender to violence'.[54] He claimed that the British government had shown a 'lack of faith' in the Federation, which faced a 'live physical threat'.[55] Africa Freedom Action was thus poised to make a potentially dramatic intervention in an increasingly fraught political situation.

Waiting at the border

On 27 February 1962, the day before the British Parliament was due to debate new plans for elections in Northern Rhodesia, the formation of Africa Freedom Action was announced in a joint.[56] A call was made for '20–30 international participants', including those with 'long association with the non-violence movement', those of 'outstanding international reputation', and more youthful volunteers 'prepared to carry out the arduous tasks' required before and during the march. There were also calls for pickets at British and Central African Federation offices, with the aim of attracting public attention to UNIP and its campaign.[57] Kaunda, meanwhile, announced that the marchers were on the border, 'Bible in hand'.[58] Three days before, British officials

---

[50] Rustin, 'Memorandum to Muste, Tatum, Dhadda, Brock', 5 March 1962, SPC Muste 89/22 WPB Correspondence.
[51] Reginald Maudling, *Memoirs* (London: Sidgwick and Jackson, 1978), 99.
[52] *Guardian*, 1 March 1962.
[53] Ibid.
[54] *Guardian*, 6 March 1962.
[55] *Times*, 9 March 1962.
[56] 'Africa Freedom Action Press Release', 27 February 1962. BOD, Scott Papers. (5770) 61.
[57] Rustin Scott, Sutherland, n.d. [1962], SPC, Muste, Reel 89-22, African Freedom Action Tanganyika.
[58] A. Paul Hare and Herbert H. Blumberg, eds, *A Search for Peace and Justice: Reflections of Michael Scott* (London: R. Collings, 1980), 147.

in Tanganyika reported that a UNIP organizer based in the country had travelled to Mbeya to test the levels of local support for the march. At the same time, American officials suggested that the protestors, despite being 'professional bleeding hearts', were 'responsible' and 'would only proceed with the demonstration if they were sincerely convinced that this was in [the] interest of Northern Rhodesian Africans'.[59] This was, in many respects, an accurate prediction of the subsequent developments, but British officials were less satisfied with reports that, despite Kawawa's insistence that the protest did not have official backing, two Tanganyikan government ministers had joined the Africa Freedom Action Committee. These were Saidi Maswanya, Minister without Portfolio, who had been a TANU organizer since the mid-1950s, and a parliamentary secretary to the prime minister, Isaac Bhoke Munanka, another TANU figure of long standing who had become party treasurer in the late 1950s.[60] At a second meeting, Kawawa did not appear persuaded by Maudling's new constitutional proposals and continued to insist that Tanganyikan participants in Africa Freedom Action were representatives of the party, and due to a shortage of experienced organizers, they 'could not avoid using individuals who happened also to be in Government'.[61]

At the start of March, representatives of the Northern Rhodesian and Federation administrations met in Lusaka to plan their response to Africa Freedom Action, whose volunteers had declared themselves 'determined to cross into Northern Rhodesia to identify themselves with the people struggling there for freedom'.[62] The Federal authorities were equally determined to keep them out, although they admitted that there was little that could be done to obstruct any Britons who had not been banned from entering the country. They split the protestors into various categories, the first being British subjects, including those who were already barred from entry such as Scott and Simon Zukas, a UNIP supporter who had arrived in Northern Rhodesia from Lithuania in the late 1930s and been deported to the UK in 1952. Other foreign nationals could, however, be held up if officials refused to grant residential permits. This would enable immigration officers to deal with 'American negroes' including Rustin and Sutherland. The final category of protestors were Tanganyikans, dismissed as 'hangers on to swell the numbers', who would, as the earlier communiques had suggested, be required to submit to existing control measures that had been held in abeyance.[63] If any marchers did manage to cross into Northern Rhodesia, they would fall foul of Public Security Regulations prohibiting any form of meeting in the Northern Province. While immigration officials may not have been able to halt a large group of marchers at the border, police were to be empowered to set up roadblocks on the Great North Road. The Federation armed forces would be sent to the area only to undertake

---

[59] Commonwealth Relations Office to Lusaka, 25 February 1962, UKNA CO 1015/2524.
[60] Dar es Salaam to Commonwealth Relations Office, 28 February 1962, UKNA, CO 1015/2524; see also Emma Hunter, '"The History and Affairs of TANU": Intellectual History, Nationalism, and the Postcolonial State in Tanzania', *The International Journal of African Historical Studies* 45, no. 3 (2012): 375; Henry Bienen, *Tanzania: Party Transformation and Economic Development* (Princeton, NJ: Princeton University Press, 1970).
[61] Dar es Salaam to Commonwealth Relations Office, 1 March 1962, UKNA, CO 1015/2524.
[62] Rustin to A. J. Muste, 22 February 1962. SPC, Muste 89-22, African Freedom Action Tanganyika.
[63] 'Report on a Meeting Held in the Administrative Secretary's Office', 1 March 1962, UKNA CO 1015/2524.

duties that would allow the local police to be redeployed to the march, and the police should ensure that 'only the minimum force' would be utilized against the marchers.[64] The colonial authorities seemingly believed that the planned march posed a significant political challenge. Although it was agreed that Air Force units that would be placed on standby should be equipped with tear gas, officials were reluctant to sanction its use merely to enforce immigration regulations.

As the US Charge d'Affaires in Dar es Salaam had acknowledged in his report to British diplomats, the leaders of Africa Freedom Action determined that the march would be 'non-violent, multi-racial and under their own (i.e. not U.N.I.P.) control'.[65] Although this was a matter of principle for Scott, Sutherland and the others, they also saw success as a practical necessity; they felt an urgent need to demonstrate the effectiveness of non-violence and counter the rising militant tendencies within national liberation movements. As Rustin argued in one of his regular reports to Muste, Africa Freedom Action was vital, because 'the leadership of Kaunda . . . and the fate of non-violence in southern Africa depends on the success of this project'.[66] Nyerere made a similar argument to Neil Pritchard when he was finally granted time with the TANU leader on 5 March. The 'essential consideration', Nyerere explained, was that 'Kaunda should retain control and leadership'; if Kaunda was able to accept the constitutional proposals, Nyerere would be content, but 'if he could not retain control except by rejecting new Constitution and calling for the protest march then Tanganyika must help him'.[67] Scott, meanwhile, argued that Africa Freedom Action might 'prove to be a last hope of securing . . . a more peaceful lasting solution than would be found by the methods of violence'. At the same time, he made it clear where the fault lay with the situation in Northern Rhodesia. It was with the 'crooked dealings' of European political leaders, who had sought to employ an 'arithmetical trick' to secure power in Northern Rhodesian elections, and whose 'cynicism . . . almost made a swear word of very term partnership on which the federation was founded'. The 'bullying and devious methods' of Welensky, Scott concluded, had 'brought the white man's prestige and the integrity of Britain and the West to a new low amongst Central Africans'.[68] The plan for the march was rooted in a deeply emotional opposition to settler colonialism in Africa, but it could only be successful if channelled into non-violent action.

There is no direct evidence of any discussion, either at Brummana or in Mbeya, around the decision to focus the action on a march. But it was by no means an arbitrary choice of tactic. Marches had emerged as a core element of popular protest during the nineteenth century, usually allied with mass public meetings in performances of public solidarity that articulated clear and sustained political claims. In theories of social protest and contentious politics, marches feature as 'modular' performances, known, mutually understood and repeatable acts in which public space was appropriated in the service of political claims that increasingly focused on national, rather than local, issues and grievances.[69] In the twentieth

[64] Ibid.
[65] Commonwealth Relations Office to Lusaka, 25 February 1962, UKNA CO 1015/2524.
[66] Rustin to Muste, [n.d. April 1962], SPC, Muste, 89-22/WPB-Africa-Bayard Rustin material.
[67] Pritchard to Maudling, 5 March 1962, UKNA CO 1015/2524.
[68] Scott, 'Africa Freedom Action', [n.d. March 1962], SPC Muste 89/22 WPB Founding Convention.
[69] Tarrow, *Power in Movement*, 50–1.

century, beginning with the *satyagraha* campaigns for Indian independence, marches became a central feature of non-violent anti-colonial resistance and, during the 1950s, were then reconfigured as forms of national and transnational protest by peace campaigners. As discussed earlier, from 1958 the annual march on the Aldermaston weapons research institute become a highly visible focus for anti-nuclear protests in Britain, while in the United States CNVA had turned to ambitious international marches, including a trek from San Francisco to Moscow in 1960–1 that provided an extraordinarily rare opportunity for Western activists to campaign openly within the Soviet Union.[70] The tactic had become a primary element of the protest repertoire of anti-nuclear weapons campaigners, although the logistics of organizing a mass protest through a remote region of central Africa created very different challenges to those faced in the Home Counties of Britain.

The pre-eminent issue was that this particular march did not directly serve the cause of its organizers, but would support another party, who, moreover, were themselves one of a number of groups engaged in a political conflict. The WPB activists acknowledged that this meant that Kaunda – 'the African who has his position by the support of his people' – would have the ultimate authority in the campaign. But they seemed less concerned that this also meant they had aligned themselves with one political movement amidst a contest for power and legitimacy. For some, the close affiliation between the WPB and UNIP was a significant problem. Lyle Tatum, the AFSC representative in Southern Rhodesia, suggested that there was a tendency to rely too heavily on the UNIP for an understanding of the situation in Northern Rhodesia. He felt, moreover, that the WPB had become seduced by the 'heady wine' of close relations with high-ranking leaders and that it had allowed nationalists to use the threat of the march as 'a secret weapon in a cold war'.[71] Zambian nationalism was a complex movement – 'a fluid coalition of people with diverse origins'[72] – but the apparent ideological affinities between Kaunda and the WPB activists meant that 'nationalism' was reduced, in the minds of the latter, to the agenda of the nationalist elite.[73] International support for Kaunda seemed to belie the ambiguous nationalist politics of UNIP. As a self-declared vehicle for popular nationalism, it cast its anti-colonialism in unequivocally absolutist terms. The rallying cry of the movement, *kwacha* ('dawn'), evoked a coming moment of salvation that, arguably, blurred the sovereignty of the Party with that of the People, cast the colonial state as 'satanic' and tied the nationalist mission to take possession of the colonial state to a more fundamental and spiritual claim to 'truth'.[74] But this kind of rhetoric was not merely conducive to the construction of a mass movement,

---

[70] Günter Wernicke and Lawrence S. Wittner, 'Lifting the Iron Curtain: The Peace March to Moscow of 1960–1961', *The International History Review* 21, no. 4 (1999): 900–17; Wernicke, 'The Communist-Led World Peace Council and the Western Peace Movements'.

[71] Lyle Tatum to Muste and Sutherland, 19 July 1962, SPC, Muste, 89/22 African Freedom Project Correspondence.

[72] Jan Kees van Donge, 'An Episode from the Independence Struggle in Zambia: A Case Study from Mwase Lundazi', *African Affairs* 84, no. 35 (1985): 268.

[73] The sense that the UNIP reflected a popular consensus has continued to mark scholarship, as Miles Larmer has recently argued, 'A Little Bit Like A Volcano – The United Progressive Party and Resistance to One-Party Rule in Zambia, 1964–1980', *International Journal of African Historical Studies* 39, no. 1 (2006): 49–83.

[74] David M. Gordon, *Invisible Agents: Spirits in a Central African History* (Athens: Ohio University Press, 2012), 129–30.

it could also facilitate the formation of relationships with international activists, like Scott and Muste, who built their campaigns against racial injustice and colonialism on their own Christian ethical framework. Kaunda's stance clearly impressed WPB leaders, who declared in May 1962 that he had 'become a leader of humanity' who was 'making a distinct contribution to the development of a peaceful and humane world society'.[75] Such sentiments were of enormous benefit to Kaunda, who engaged in a delicate balance between maintaining the respect of colonial officials and support within UNIP.[76] Moreover, with UNIP largely reliant on funds from outside the country, Kaunda's alliance with the World Peace Brigade represented an act of political realism as much as it was an expression of abstract moral principles.

Africa Freedom Action – involving as it did a global organization, and as a plan that was predicated on the literal crossing of national borders – represented an attempt to enact transnational protest within the confines of national politics. However, the international peace campaigners were by necessity dependent upon the will and nationalist agendas of Kaunda, UNIP and the Tanganyikan authorities. They were also subject to the whims of nature, as the border crossing at Mbala was closed on 7 March following torrential rainstorms. Conditions were so difficult that a lorry had reportedly taken four days to travel the hundred miles from Tunduma in Tanganyika.[77] That same day, the Northern Rhodesian authorities imposed their planned ban on political demonstrations and marches in the Abercorn and Isoka districts along the border; at the start of the month, reports from the region detailed thousands of Federal troops on patrol in the border region. Active efforts were underway to persuade local community leaders to support the security forces and to reassure 'unwilling people [of] the goodness and peacefulness of these Federal troops'.[78] One unintended consequence was that the increased police presence made it harder for political refugees to travel north into Tanganyika, including a group of South Africans who were arrested and returned to the country.[79]

But a small group of international supporters had begun to arrive in Dar es Salaam. One, John Papworth, would later spend the 1970s working as a personal assistant to Kaunda, but had already fallen foul of the Central African Federation authorities, who were in the process of declaring him a 'prohibited immigrant' across the three territories.[80] He came to Africa Freedom Action along a similar path to Scott, having been drawn to Communism but repelled by its authoritarian discipline, and had stood, unsuccessfully, as a Labour Party candidate in the 1955 general election in Britain. Imprisoned after joining direct action protest against nuclear weapons alongside Bertrand Russell, Papworth addressed a public meeting shortly after his arrival in Tanganyika, declaring that 'as sure as the sun will

---

[75] Statement to the Press, 21 May 1962, SPC, Muste, 89-22, African Freedom Action Tanganyika.
[76] Larmer, *Rethinking African Politics*, 33–43.
[77] Reuter telegram, 7 March 1962, UKNA CO 1015/2524.
[78] Masaiti to UNIP, 1 March 1962, SPC Muste 89/22 WPB Correspondence.
[79] Rustin to Muste, 1 March 1962, SPC Muste 89/22 WPB Correspondence.
[80] 'Report on a Meeting Held in the Administrative Secretary's Office', 1 March 1962, UKNA CO 1015/2524; on Papworth, see also Herbert Girardet, 'Obituary: John Papworth', *Resurgence*, October 2020, https://www.resurgence.org/magazine/article5616-obituary-john-papworth.html.

rise tomorrow, Zambia ... will be born and Kenneth Kaunda will be its leaders'.[81] At the same meeting, Scott added that Kaunda was 'not only a leader of African people, but of humanity', while Rustin asserted that the international volunteers had been attracted to Africa by a sense of justice and confident of victory. Other participants who had made their way to Tanganyika included Phillip Seed, a Quaker and Committee of 100 organizers from Yorkshire in the UK, and Niels Mathieson, an organizer of the Oslo branch of WR.[82]

In an effort to attract more volunteers, the PAFMECSA Secretary General, Mbiyu Koinange, wrote to members of the movement appealing for funds and high-profile figures willing to participate in the march.[83] Such individuals needed to be 'emotionally stable' and physically fit and would ideally be experienced political organizers, as 'persons suspected as mere adventurers might well be rejected'. In addition, Rustin had drafted a checklist of possible challenges that volunteers might face: they might be shot and killed; be deprived of water and food; be beaten, arrested, tried and imprisoned; or be held in detention without trial. Most importantly, volunteers were obliged to pledge their support for non-violence and be prepared to follow instructions from leaders, who would be selected on their 'profound dedication to a free, united Africa' as well as their ability to objectively assess the ways of applying non-violent resistance to specific issues.[84] Scott featured prominently in press coverage of the planned protest in East Africa, although the *Sunday Nation* asserted that 'Britain's "ban the bomb" preacher was completely over-shadowed by American Bayard Rustin, who answered most of the questions and generally took control of the assembly'.[85] But, when questioned about the purpose of the march, Scott 'became vehement' and asserted that the WPB supported Kaunda's opposition to the Central African Federation, a scheme, he argued, 'we have always believed ... to be crooked'.[86] The organizers thus articulated their determination to maintain their focus on the politics of federation and Zambian independence. The launch of the march, they insisted, would be determined by Kaunda. In a matter of days, the fate of the march would be sealed.

From resistance to electioneering

On 5 March, the UNIP national council announced conditional support for its participation in elections under Maudling's plan – a decision described by the *Guardian* newspaper in London as 'a considerable triumph for Mr Kenneth Kaunda and his powers of persuasion'.[87] The UNIP conditions included the release of political prisoners, a halt to arbitrary arrest of party organizers and members, and the lifting

---

[81] 'Zambia Will Be Born', *Daily Nation*, [Kenya] 5 March 1962.
[82] Sunday News (Tanganyika), 4 March 1962, SPC, Muste, 89-22, WPB Correspondence; *Peace News*, 2 March 1962.
[83] M. Koinange to PAFMECSA Members, 7 March 1962, SPC Muste 89/22 WPB Correspondence.
[84] Ibid.
[85] *Sunday Nation*, 4 March 1962; see also *Sunday News*, 4 March 1962.
[86] Ibid.
[87] *Guardian*, 6 March 1962.

of restrictions on their activities around the country. They called for an independent commission to assess the make-up of constituencies, for elections to be held before October, and that there would be no review of the Federal arrangements until after Northern Rhodesia had achieved majority rule.[88] For Larmer, this marked the moment at which the movement shifted its focus from 'popular resistance in favour of negotiations and electoral politics', necessitating a very different mode of organization and a transformed relationship with its grassroots supporters.[89] As a consequence of the changing tactical focus, Kaunda contacted the World Peace Brigade representatives in Dar es Salaam, asking them to cancel the launch of the march towards the border.[90] Speaking on the telephone to Rustin and the UNIP representative in Dar es Salaam that morning, Kaunda suggested that the Africa Freedom Action working committee should remain in Africa, but the other volunteers return to Europe to generate publicity for the campaign, raise funds for UNIP and seek further volunteers prepared to join a march if required. If the conditions demanded by UNIP were accepted by the British and Northern Rhodesian authorities, the general strike might be delayed by months, and thus Kaunda had concluded that the African Freedom Action volunteers, aside from the working committee, would be more effective away from East Africa. This was, Rustin recalled, only a day after Nyerere had called for additional volunteers to travel to Africa. Confusion was further compounded when the South African Press Association released a report declaring that the march had been called off completely.[91]

Even before Kaunda's decision, WPB organizers were aware that the decisions taken at the UNIP conference in Lusaka might place the march in a more uncertain position. Even if the constitutional proposals were unacceptable, it was acknowledged that UNIP could still agree to participate in elections. The march, like the general strike, was a political bargaining chip, but Nyerere was confident that Africa Freedom Action had already provided a 'great service to Zambia's independence'.[92] The reactions of British officials, and the deployment of troops and police to the Northern Province, indicated the depth of their concern over political developments in central Africa. The WPB organizers concluded that the march, alongside the Tanganyikan government's determination to support it, had already forced Britain to look seriously at the demands made by UNIP. Thus, even though the fate of the march effectively lay in the hands of UNIP, they would press ahead with preparations, including the planned launch of a fundraising appeal.[93]

Although they only had funds remaining to support themselves for no more than a few days, Rustin and the other main organizers determined to continue to gather resources to launch a march, but more ambitiously, to set up a permanent training centre in Dar es Salaam that would be financially independent of any African political

---

[88] Rustin to Tatum, Muste, Brock and Dhadda, 12 March 1962, SPC Muste 89/22 WPB Correspondence.
[89] Larmer, *Rethinking African Politics*, 48.
[90] Reuter Telegram, 8 March 1962, UKNA CO 1015/2524.
[91] Rustin to Muste Tatum, Brock and Dhadda, 12 March 1962; Africa Freedom Action Press Release, 9 March 1962, SPC Muste 89/22 WPB Correspondence.
[92] Rustin, 'Memorandum to Muste, Tatum, Dhadda, Brock', 5 March 1962, SPC Muste 89/22 WPB Correspondence.
[93] Ibid.

organization.⁹⁴ Although this would build on all the abortive plans and discussions since the Accra conference of April 1960, the new plan was also shaped by the political context of southern Africa; it would be a base for a series of further protests that were assumed would be needed 'before the rest of Southern Africa is free', and it would provide training for 'constructive work' that would be required to rebuild communities that had been displaced and disrupted by political violence.⁹⁵ Unlike their experience in Accra, Rustin was confident that they could trust the assurances given by Nyerere that the Tanganyikan government would allow the centre to operate entirely independently. Even before the march was finally called off, the organizers therefore turned their attention to another longer-term project, again centred on a centre for non-violent action in Africa.

In order to provide some clarity and what he acknowledged would appear to have been 'considerable indecision' in East Africa, Rustin provided a report on developments in mid-March. He began by explaining that communications between the protest group and Kaunda, a thousand miles away in Lusaka, were difficult, with telephone lines only open for two hours every morning. And, even when they were able to speak, the subjects they could discuss were limited by the knowledge that Federation authorities were monitoring the call. As such, the only safe lines of communication were via individual messengers who might take many days to make the trip. Second, Rustin noted that the Africa Freedom Action organizers had to liaise with three African organizations – UNIP, TANU and PAFMECSA – and although the groups usually concurred with the protest plans, it was still necessary to ensure that any decisions were agreed with Koinange and Nyerere as well as Kaunda. Furthermore, the political tensions in Northern Rhodesia were complicated by the decision to call Federal elections in late April. In Rustin's view, it was clear that African movements in all three territories would boycott these elections, but it was not obvious whether Kaunda's plans for a general strike in Northern Rhodesia would be extended across the Federation as a whole.⁹⁶ In conclusion, Rustin suggested that WPB groups around the world pause any plans to send volunteers to East Africa, but continue to identify potential recruits and focus efforts on raising awareness about the march and the UNIP campaign within their own countries. He also noted that, as further confusion had arisen over claims that 'thousands' of marchers were ready to cross the border, international supporters ought to prepare lists of signatures of those willing to be called to join a march.

Most of the international volunteers thus returned home, although John Papworth returned later in the year in an attempt to observe the Northern Rhodesian elections.⁹⁷ Scott and Sutherland remained, however, to coordinate Africa Freedom Action from Dar es Salaam The WPB North American Regional Council called Rustin back for consultations, but agreed in April that he should return to Dar es Salaam after a stopover in London to consult with Kaunda. Although the Council assumed that the march

---

⁹⁴ Ibid.
⁹⁵ Rustin, 'Memorandum to Muste, Tatum, Dhadda, Brock', 5 March 1962, SPC Muste 89/22 WPB Correspondence.
⁹⁶ Rustin to Muste Tatum, Brock and Dhadda, 12 March 1962, SPC Muste 89/22 WPB Correspondence.
⁹⁷ Rustin to Muste, 16 March 1962, SPC, Muste, 89-22, WPB Correspondence.

remained imminent, Rustin was charged with focusing his efforts on establishing the training centre in Dar es Salaam. They also agreed that his stay in East Africa would be reviewed at the end of May.[98]

The confusion surrounding the march did not only affect the would-be peace marchers. Throughout March 1962, British officials communicated details of the reported movements of Scott and others across, or close to the border. On March 15, it was rumoured that Scott had boarded a mail boat in Kigoma and planned to travel across Lake Tanganyika to Mpulungu in Northern Rhodesia. Plans for a 'reception party' in the Abercorn District were postponed however when diplomats in Dar es Salaam confirmed that Scott had not left the Tanganyikan capital.[99] Efforts to monitor the marchers continued through to May, when it was still believed that an 'incursion' into Northern Rhodesia, 'though unlikely [was] possible'.[100] The disquiet on the part of British officials was compounded by plans for the Home Secretary, R. A. Butler, who had, in a somewhat unusual step, taken responsibility for political discussions around the future of the Central African Federation, to visit Africa in May. Ahead of the trip, Parliament debated the situation in the region. Before the debates, Butler had held meetings with various parties, including Kaunda, in London. The World Peace Brigade, via Rustin, was provided with daily updates on their progress. Kaunda appeared confident that many of UNIP's conditions for elections would be met by the British and, although Rustin seemed less optimistic, he predicted that any 'large-scale action . . . will be put off until fall or early winter'.[101]

In London, parliamentary debates on federation rehearsed familiar themes. The dangers of violence figured prominently from both Conservative ministers and the Labour opposition, although the latter included thinly veiled criticism of supposed Conservative support for settler interests in their interventions. The Labour MP Denis Healey pointed to the example of Algeria, which had achieved independence in March 1962:

> In Algeria the Africans have won independence only by a long and ruthless war marked by fearful atrocities on both sides, and it is highly doubtful whether there will be any form of co-operation between the white minority there and the Africans who will dominate the new Algerian State as a result. We do not want that to happen in Central Africa. But can hon. and right hon. Members opposite imagine the attitude of the Africans who see their fellows in other countries becoming independent one after the other, through peaceful negotiations, while they see, on the other hand, that the only obstacle to independence in Central

---

[98] Minutes, WPB North American Regional Council, 24 April 1962, SPC – WPB – North American Council 1961–62.
[99] Hone to Secretary of State, 15 March 1962, UKNA CO 1015/2524; Dar es Salaam to Commonwealth Relations Office, 16 March 1962, UKNA CO 1015/2524.
[100] Dar es Salaam to Lusaka, 12 March 1962, UKNA CO 1015/2524.
[101] 'Summary of Report from Bayard Rustin', 7 May 1962, SPC Muste 89/22 Africa Freedom Project Tanganyika.

Africa, the same as the obstacle to independence in Algeria, is the existence of a large white minority?

He concluded by calling on Conservative MPs to pay heed to those African leaders who 'have been trying desperately hard for the last ten years to achieve change in these territories by peaceful methods'.[102] It seems reasonable to assume that Healey had Kaunda in mind. He referred to the UNIP leader directly in a discussion on Northern Rhodesia, asserting that Kaunda was 'risking his political life and, perhaps, his life as a human being by agreeing to take part in these elections' when the system of voting seemed intended to block an African majority.[103]

In the week following the debate in the British Parliament and just before Butler's planned visit to central Africa, PAFMECSA held an emergency meeting in Mbeya, the proposed assembly point for the volunteer marchers. The initial plan had been for Kaunda to attend the meeting, along with other political leaders, but in the event, the main participants were PAFMECSA officials, the African Freedom Action working committee and leading members of the World Peace Brigade, including J. P. Narayan and A. J. Muste. Without Kaunda, earlier suggestions that the meeting would conclude with a mass rally on the border with speeches from the UNIP leader as well as Scott, Nyerere and the Kenyan prime minister Jomo Kenyatta.[104] Prior to the talks in Mbeya, Scott, Narayan and Kaunda addressed a public meeting in Dar es Salaam, during which Kaunda declared again that the patience of his supporters was nearing its limit and that if he and other leaders of the movement were jailed, 'every follower of mine will become a general to himself'. The militant tone was sustained by both Scott, who described Welensky as the 'archbishop of moderation' and Narayan who claimed that Welensky could only redeem his 'stupidity and misbehaviour' by addressing African peoples' demands for freedom and rights.[105] At this point, British officials appeared to have lost patience and, unable to reflect on the toxicity of federation for the nationalist movement, leaned into outright condemnation: Kauda's public statements were 'deliberate hysteria' and inconsistent, they declared, while his international supporters were held in contempt. Narayan was dismissed as a 'meddlesome Indian intellectual' who, it was assumed, 'can no longer find social or constitutional problems of sufficient consequence in India to warrant his services'.[106] As the PAFMECSA conference was underway, immigration officials in Makonde, Northern Rhodesia, were 'discreetly reinforced', but while the choice of Mbeya as a venue for the conference may have been provocative, there seemed little likelihood of any march taking place. The delegates passed a series of resolutions calling for Britain to dissolve the Central African Federation, create the conditions to 'ensure that fair and free elections take place in Zambia' and initiate negotiations for a new constitution in Southern Rhodesia.[107]

[102] Healey, Debate on Central African Federation, *Hansard* HC Debates, 8 May 1962, Cols 254–5.
[103] Ibid., Cols 261–2.
[104] 'Summary of Report from Bayard Rustin', 7 May 1962, SPC Muste 89/22 Africa Freedom Project Tanganyika.
[105] 'Breaking Point Near in N. T. Says Kaunda', *Tanganyikan Standard*, 10 May 1962.
[106] O'Leary to Pugh, 12 May 1962, UKNA, CO 1015/2524.
[107] 'Resolutions Passed at an Emergency Conference of PAFMECSA', 13–14 May 1962, SPC, Muste, 89-39, Africa Freedom Action.

The latter point signalled that the politics of Federation were turning to focus on its southernmost territory, its most 'intractable problem'.[108]

A week after the Mbeya meeting, R. A. Butler, arrived in central Africa on a two-week long tour during which he conceded that Nyasaland would secede from the Federation, effectively bringing an end to Britain's federal experiment in Africa.[109] By the latter stages of Butler's tour of central Africa, the prospect of a protest march had dwindled further. On 22 May, the *Tanganyika Standard* provided a public account of what had been the position since March, namely that Africa Freedom Action marchers would 'remain in readiness' but would only cross the border if Kaunda felt that conditions for UNIP's participation in elections would not be met. World Peace Brigade organizers would, however, remain in Dar es Salaam to establish a Centre for Non-Violent Positive Action.[110] The official rationale for the decision was that, in contrast to the sense of crisis that had obtained during the Addis Ababa conference in February, changes in political conditions, and not least Butler's intervention, had persuaded Kaunda to 'make use of every constitutional means'.[111] In Kaunda's view, the international protest campaign had to be shelved in order that 'every possible concession of constitutional rights should be fully utilised'.[112] WPB leaders defined the decision by UNIP leaders to participate in planned elections as being 'in line with the Gandhian method' and acknowledged that this would halt any immediate plans for a march from Tanganyika.[113]

At the same time, the WPB leaders began to return to their home countries. Muste left Tanganyika on 21 May, and Rustin returned to the United States a week later. J. P. Narayan, meanwhile, embarked on a tour of East Africa with his wife Prabhavati Devi, during which they sought to enlist the support of Indian communities in Kaunda's independence movement and encourage interest in Gandhian ideas of *sarvodaya* – a combination of pacifism, economic socialism and liberty centred on village communities. Two other Indian supporters remained in Dar es Salaam with Scott and Sutherland – Suresh Ram, the veteran of the 'Quit India' and Bhoodan movements in India who had arrived in Tangyanika a few weeks previously as a representative of the Indian Regional Council of the WPB, and Rhandir Thaker, editor of the Swahili language *Ngrumo* newspaper.[114] The Narayans returned to India on 10 June after a final meeting with Sutherland, Ram and Thaker in Nairobi, where Narayan outlined the pledges of financial support he had secured from Asian communities, as well as his disappointment that African leaders had given little time to discuss the 'long-range problems' beyond the immediate aim of securing independence. After the Nairobi meeting, Sutherland and Ram travelled across

---

[108] L. J. Butler, 'Britain, the United States, and the Demise of the Central African Federation, 1959–63', *The Journal of Imperial and Commonwealth History* 28, no. 3 (2000): 140.
[109] *Guardian*, 18 May 1962, 1.
[110] 'Peace Marchers', *Tanganyika Standard*, 22 May 1962.
[111] Ibid.
[112] 'WPB submission to UN Special Commission on Colonialism', 5 June 1962, SPC, Muste, 89-39, Africa Freedom Action.
[113] Muste to Frank Loescher, 6 April 1962, SPC, Muste, 89-22, African Freedom Action Tanganyika.
[114] World Peace Brigade Positive Action Centre Newsletter, 30 July 1962, Muste 89/22 Africa Freedom Project Tanganyika.

Uganda and Kenya but found that the pledges of funds for UNIP that had been given to Narayan were much harder to collect.[115] As UNIP set about reorienting its activities towards an election campaign, Africa Freedom Action set aside plans for a march and embarked on a partial turn to fundraising. There had been, in the end, no demonstration of the power of transnational non-violent protest to counteract the wider trend to militant tactics in southern Africa. But this question would remain a key point of reference in the political discourse of decolonization in central and southern Africa.

Reflections and recriminations: The UN Special Committee on Decolonization

In the aftermath of the aborted march, the leading organizers of Africa Freedom Action began to search for a role that would allow them to maintain their efforts to build an alliance between international peace movements and anti-colonial movements in Africa. These continued to focus on their base in Dar es Salaam, relying on the political and material support of the pots-colonial government led by Julius Nyerere and the Tanganyikan African National Union. The city seemed the ideal location from which to spread the influence of the World Peace Brigade, located in close proximity to the centres of intransigent settler colonialism in central and southern Africa. This had resulted in the city becoming a focal point for regional resistance movements facing increasing political repression in their own territories. The South African ANC and PAC, as well as Namibian, Zimbabwean and Mozambican resistance movements, established offices in the city, in turn attracting diplomats and journalists from countries on either side of the global geopolitical divide. In 1962, Dar es Salaam was rapidly developing into a cosmopolitan 'Cold War city' that would, as George Roberts has shown, have an ambiguous influence on the TANU project to build an African socialist state.[116] In mid-1962, however, Scott, Sutherland and the other Africa Freedom Action organizers saw opportunities to pursue the plans that had proven unworkable two years earlier in Accra.

One of the most compelling, although ambiguous, achievements of the WPB organizers following the Mbeya conference was their interaction with the members of the UN Special Committee on Decolonization in June 1962.[117] The Special Committee had been established as a consequence of the General Assembly Resolution 1514 adopted in December 1960, which had declared colonialism (defined as the 'subjection of peoples to alien subjugation, domination and exploitation') was 'contrary to the Charter of the United Nations and is an impediment to the promotion of world

---

[115] Ibid.
[116] George Roberts, *Revolutionary State-Making in Dar Es Salaam: African Liberation and the Global Cold War, 1961–1974* (Cambridge: Cambridge University Press, 2021).
[117] WPB Positive Action Centre Newsletter, 30 June 1962, SPC, Muste, 89-22, African Freedom Action Tanganyika.

peace and co-operation'.[118] The following year, the UN General Assembly established a Special Committee on Decolonization to monitor the progress and effectiveness of the Declaration. Tanganyika was one of five African countries among the original seventeen members of the committee, which has continued to exist in enlarged form to this day.[119] In its initial investigations, the committee sought statements from a range of organizations including, in June 1962, a UNIP submission authored by its representative in Dar es Salaam, Robert Makasa. Largely focused on the reports of intimidation and violence against UNIP party agents, Makasa's report concluded by warning that 'a storm is brewing in Central Africa', accusing the Federation authorities of creating conditions that would allow the use of emergency powers.[120] The fundamental breakdown in trust implied in Makasa's statement seemed to underline the rationale behind the formation of Africa Freedom Action, as set out in the WPB submission. The project, they asserted, had been a direct response to the increasingly bitter divisions within the Central African Federation.[121] Moreover, these divisions were regarded as part of a much wider threat to decolonization in Africa and world peace in general.

In their assessment, the authors of the WPB submission emphasized the role played by transnational networks of commercial and industrial interests in shaping European economic and political hegemony from the Cape to the Copperbelt. Their analysis had been shaped by the work of US anthropologist Alvin Wolfe, who had begun to examine the impact of the mining industry after undertaking fieldwork in the Congo during the 1950s. After hearing Wolfe give a paper on the 'supranational' organization of corporate interests in the politics of central and southern Africa, Margaret Mead encouraged him to submit his paper to the journal *Human Organisation*, but publication was blocked, allegedly after a draft was shared with a mining executive.[122] Wolfe, who would later be denounced by US industrialist Clarence Randall as comprising, along with Scott, 'a highly articulate two-man team' damaging the reputation of the mineral industry in southern Africa, instead published the article in a series of non-academic journals including Muste's pacifist publication, *Liberation*.[123] By April 1962, Scott had integrated Wolfe's account into the political rationale for Africa Freedom Action, and Wolfe's vision of corporate interests had been woven into the fully formed account of the secretive connections between transnational capital and settler colonialism

---

[118] 'Declaration on the Granting of Independence to Colonial Countries and Peoples', United Nations General Assembly, GA 1514 (XV), 14 December 1960.
[119] Oliver Turner, '"Finishing the Job": The UN Special Committee on Decolonization and the Politics of Self-Governance', *Third World Quarterly* 34, no. 7 (2013): 1193–208.
[120] 'UNIP Submission to the UN Special Committee of Seventeen on Colonialism', 6 June 1962, SPC Muste 89/39 Africa Freedom Action.
[121] 'World Peace Brigade Submission to UN Committee on Colonialism', 5 June 1962. SPC Muste 89/39 Africa Freedom Action.
[122] Kevin Yelvington, 'Interview with Alvin W. Wolfe', *Practicing Anthropology* 25, no. 4 (2003): 42–6; see also Yelvington, Interview with Alvin Wolfe, 9 November 2009, Society for Applied Anthropology Oral History Project, https://www.appliedanthro.org/application/files/7915/6198/7259/Alvin_W._Wolfe_2.pdf, Accessed 15 May 2022.
[123] *New York Times*, 4 April 1963. Wolfe, Alvin W., "The Team Rules Mining in Southern Africa" (1962). Anthropology Faculty Publications. 2. https://digitalcommons.usf.edu/ant_facpub/2. Wolfe's academic paper was eventually published: Alvin Wolfe, 'The African Mineral Industry: Evolution of a Supranational Level of Integration', *Social Problems* 11, no. 2 (1963): 153–64.

presented in the WPB submission to the UN Special Committee.[124] In drawing on Wolfe's analysis the WPB submission represented arguably one of the first attempts to chart the relationship between settler colonialism and multinational corporations in southern Africa. Evidence of similar relationships between British and American corporate interests and the apartheid state in South Africa would later underpin anti-apartheid disinvestment and boycott campaigns.[125] The WPB submission also recommended that the UN supervise large-scale projects, centred on 'principles of regional planning', to promote organic and democratic industrial development in the region. Like the Okavango delta project, these suggestions closely match ideas that Scott had proposed as Director of the Campaign for Right and Justice in South Africa in the 1940s, influenced by the US intellectual Lewis Mumford.[126] The 1962 plan envisaged a programme of development that is founded upon the eradication of migrant labour and accumulation of capital within the region, whose ultimate aim, the *Tanganyika Standard* reported, was 'nothing less than the working out of an economic and social and political alternative to apartheid'.[127]

The WPB submission bore all the hallmarks of Scott's campaign agenda and personal political preoccupations. It likened the 'constitutional breakdown' in central Africa to the collapse of political institutions in Algeria and the Congo and predicted that further escalation of the crisis was likely. As peace activists, they shared a growing understanding that resistance to colonialism, 'to injustice and tyranny and unnecessary poverty and deprivation of rights are part of the struggle for peace'. Movements for 'national liberation', they argued, should be a key concern for the peace movement. In a context shaped by violent uprisings against colonialism, vicious attempts to suppress resistance by colonial regimes, and the fraught tensions between nuclear-armed Cold War superpowers, the WPB submission declared somewhat boldly that the 'world cannot be allowed to be destroyed because of constitutional failure in Central Africa'.[128] It is tempting to interpret the statement as mere bathos and an exaggerated understanding of the significance of Africa Freedom Action, but it is perhaps necessary to assess their concerns at face value and to consider how the statement communicated the peace campaigners' sense of living through a critical moment. The WPB had been launched in the shadow of the Berlin crisis of 1961, and those close to events in central Africa could be forgiven for conflating the politics of nationalism in Northern Rhodesia, the crisis that followed the secession of Katanga from the Congo, and the death of the UN Secretary General Dag Hammarskjöld at Ndola in September 1961 into a persuasive narrative of a world in peril. Their conclusion that the campaign for Zambian independence could easily become a frontline in the Cold War was by no means irrational. But, despite this wider context and despite giving the WPB members a hearing, the Special Committee appears to have given greater concern to the situation

---

[124] Scott, 'The Cape to Katanga Miners and Africa Freedom Action', 20/04/1962, SPC Muste 89/22 WPB Founding Convention.
[125] Ruth First, Jonathan Steele, and Christabel Gurney, *The South African Connection: Western Investment in Apartheid* (London: Temple Smith, 1972).
[126] Skinner, 'Christian Reconstruction, Secular Politics'.
[127] 'UN Team Warned', *Tanganyika Standard*, 6 June 1962.
[128] Michael Scott, 'World Peace Brigade Submission to UN Committee on Colonialism', 5 June 1962, BOD, Scott Papers, (5770) 48.

in Southern Rhodesia. A subcommittee on Southern Rhodesia chaired by Chandra Shekhar Jha of India met British Ministers in London in April, concluding that without constitutional changes acceptable to the African majority in Southern Rhodesia, 'a mood of desperation may set in which might lead to serious conflict and violence'. If there were no further developments, they recommended that the situation be debated at the next session of the General Assembly.[129] Thus, despite the apocalyptic warnings of the WPB – and the continued threat of unrest outlined by UNIP – the political process in Northern Rhodesia was not regarded as the primary threat to peace in central Africa.

Moreover, other pacifist activists in central Africa viewed the efforts of the World Peace Brigade in a less positive light. Arlo Tatum's brother Lyle, serving as the American Friends Service Committee representative in southern Africa, based in Harare, took a more critical view of Africa Freedom Action. Tatum's primary concern was that the WPB organizers had aligned themselves too closely with UNIP. Although he shared the others' admiration of Kaunda, he felt aggrieved that more sceptical views of UNIP claims, for example, around the degree of state repression in Northern Rhodesia had been treated with suspicion within pacifist circles. Furthermore, accusations that members of Nkumbula's ANC had been subject to attacks from UNIP and that the Governor, Evelyn Hone, favoured Kaunda's party over the National Congress had been ignored by the WPB. Tatum also had strong misgivings about the wisdom of submitting testimony to the UN Special Committee, suggesting that it included nothing 'which was anything like evidence under US law'. Information about corporate networks and the grievances of those who had been allegedly intimidated ought to have been presented by the representatives of UNIP rather than international supporters, he argued. It seemed, he continued, as if the WPB had been seduced by the 'heavy wine of high places' and the positive reception of their testimony by the committee 'says more about the political orientation and sophistication' of delegates.[130]

The WPB report, Tatum believed, betrayed an ideological bias towards Zambian nationalists and had shown implicit contempt towards Europeans in Northern Rhodesia. He objected in particular to the use of the term 'settler', which he felt was unnecessarily emotive and 'antagonises those with whom we seek reconciliation'. The word, he felt, should be seen as equivalent to 'native'. However, aspects of Tatum's argument seemed specious, at best. In questioning the claim that Welensky's mandate in Federal elections was based on fewer than 10,000 people, he argued that 'the problem was not the small vote . . . but the small size of the electorate'. It seems likely that WPB organizers – and indeed UNIP – may have regarded this as somewhat missing the point. Tatum was perhaps on more secure ground when he accused the WPB of overplaying their influence on events. Africa Freedom Action was not a critical element of the political manoeuvres in early 1962 as, he suggested, 'the wheels were in motion for change'. It was not, as the WPB had argued, likely that Federal authorities would block elections in Northern Rhodesia – Welensky needed

---

[129] 'Question of Southern Rhodesia', 21 May 1962, United Nations Registry (1946–1979), Trusteeship and Non-self Governing Territories, Reports of the Special Committee of Seventeen Members on the Implementation of the Declaration on the Granting of Independence to Colonial Countries & Peoples – TR 412.

[130] Lyle Tatum to Sutherland and Muste, 19 July 1962, SPC, Muste 89/22 WPB Correspondence.

the support of white communities and interventions in elections would not enhance that. It seemed obvious, he added, that after the constitutional amendments had been announced in February, there would be no march, but the WPB had allowed itself to be exploited by nationalist movements.[131] It had been clear from soon after the Brummana conference that the WPB had willingly aligned itself with the nationalist movement led by Kaunda, in order to bolster the popular support for an individual that international peace campaigners believed genuinely shared their political and ethical agendas. In their view, unlike Lutuli in South Africa, Kaunda had seemingly navigated a path between non-violent disobedience and implicit threats of violent resistance from followers in the movement he led. Although his adherence to Gandhian pacifism was complicated – and increasingly so as he came closer to executive power – Kaunda did seem to be the best candidate for an alliance between African nationalism and an international peace army.

Africa Freedom Action in Dar es Salaam: Searching for a purpose

In early June, just before the WPB submitted its report to the UN Special Committee of Seventeen, the Tanganyikan government agreed to grant a plot of land in Dar es Salaam on which the training centre could be built, although the WPB organizers had initially requested the use of buildings at the Salvation Army transit camp at Mgulani.[132] But neither of these plans transpired and the team members instead began to establish the centre in their accommodation on Garden Avenue, at the heart of the diplomatic quarter of the city. Along with Sutherland and Ram, four UNIP organizers had moved into the small bungalow and had begun a training programme centred around the discussion of non-violent action, the aims of the WPB, Central African politics and pan-Africanism, while Theresa Allain, an American UNIP volunteer, provided typing lessons.[133] The developments in Northern Rhodesia continued to be a focus of their attention, and reports from their UNIP contacts outlined an increased freedom of operation as they began to campaign for the upcoming elections. In his report to the WPB London Council at the end of July, however, Sutherland already outlined 'setbacks', including difficulties with transport and unspecified 'Communist anti-WPB activities'.[134] Scott was granted overall charge of the Dar es Salaam project but the WPB activists struggled to identify a focus of their activities. The group in Dar es Salaam nevertheless continued to maintain close contact with Kaunda and sought his advice as they developed plans for new actions aimed at tackling settler colonialism across the wider southern African region.

---

[131] Ibid.
[132] Kawawa to Bill Sutherland, 2 June 1962, SPC Muste 89/22 WPB Correspondence.
[133] World Peace Brigade Positive Action Centre Newsletter, 30 July 1962, SPC Muste 89/22 Africa Freedom Project Tanganyika.
[134] 'Minutes of Council Meeting, 30 July–2 August', 30 July 1962, SPC Muste 89/22 Council Meeting London 1962.

In August, Mbiyu Koinange relayed the desire of South African ANC activists that any action should focus on calls for the release of Mandela, who had been arrested by South African security forces soon after his return from his international tour. Kaunda, meanwhile, was focused on the somewhat different requirements of a national election campaign – funding and resources to maintain electoral campaigning across all of Northern Rhodesia, and propaganda efforts focused on alleged military activities that linked the NR ANC, Katanga mining interests and Welensky. An Africa Freedom Action meeting in late August agreed that the group should shift its efforts on the situation in Northern Rhodesia towards what was essentially UNIP progaganda – a 'constant exposé of Welensky, Nkumbula, Tshombe, and mining companies' in international press.[135] The group also discussed a plan mooted by Scott for a new protest focused on South-West Africa. The Tanganyikan minister, Saidi Maswanya, was sceptical, arguing that the country was 'too remote for Tanganyikans' and suggested that they should instead focus on neighbouring Mozambique. Sutherland countered that the president of the newly formed Mozambican Liberation Front (FRELIMO), Eduardo Mondlane, had suggested that their movement was not yet ready to work with international groups. Sutherland suggested instead that they should combine the South-West Africa protest with action aimed at 'smashing the Federation' *and* protest against jailing of Mandela.[136] Sutherland's somewhat over-optimistic proposals perhaps reflected the overall lack of enthusiasm he observed at the meeting and activists' pessimistic view of progress towards constitutional change in southern Africa.

Their base at the heart of Dar es Salaam nevertheless provided opportunities for Africa Freedom Action to meet an array of visitors from across the continent and beyond. These included European peace activists, such as Hagbard Jonassen of the Danish *Mellemfolkeligt Samwirke* (People-to-People Cooperation) movement, who focused on the kind of 'constructive' social work that had been put forward as a primary aim of the WPB.[137] Mbiyu Koinange had also introduced Sutherland to Waruhiu Itote, the former Mau Mau fighter 'General China', when he visited Dar es Salaam in August. Itote was, Sutherland reported, 'reticent to speak' but expressed optimism that the social divisions of the armed struggle would heal quickly after independence.[138] Sutherland reported extensive contacts with southern African campaigners, including Sam Nujoma of the South-West African Peoples' Organisation (SWAPO) and the South African Marius Schoon, an anti-apartheid activist who would be arrested and imprisoned in the following year for his part in a plot to bomb a Johannesburg police station.[139] Schoon and Sutherland debated the relative merits of non-violent protest and armed struggle, with the South African claiming that 'non-violence had been tried for 50 years' and that Africans had not been 'prepared temperamentally and religiously for non-violence'. Sutherland countered that Black South Africans were no less prepared than African Americans in the southern states, to which Schoon replied by noting that protestors in the United States had the 'weight of Federal law and the other parts of the

---

[135] Sutherland to Muste, 25 August, SPC Muste 89/22 WPB Correspondence.
[136] Ibid.
[137] see Wittner, *Resisting the Bomb*.
[138] Sutherland to Muste, 26 August 1962, SPC Muste 89/22 WPB Correspondence.
[139] *Rand Daily Mail*, 18 September 1963, 3.

country behind them'. Sutherland suggested that the 'the force of world opinion and the United Nations' in support of African struggles for independence and political rights placed South Africa in a similar relationship to that between southern states and the federal government in the United States.[140] In discussions with South Africans more generally, Sutherland believed that a consensus had emerged that nothing other than a military struggle similar to that fought in Algeria would overcome the apartheid state. South African activists appeared to acknowledge that the majority of the population were not deeply politically engaged and that movement could not expect a general strike to be successful.[141] Sutherland also noted the increasing divisions between the PAC and ANC. The former were viewed by their rivals as 'opportunists', while the latter were denounced as 'communist-controlled and too much influenced by whites' by the PAC. Sutherland reflected that 'those I talk with are willing to have reprisals upon the majority of non-whites for acts of sabotage', but continued to argued for 'one more all out effort at coordinating world action and internal nonviolent action'.[142]

In his reply to Sutherland, Muste argued that the central issue for Africans was that they did not have a focused programme for action and if one did exist, the question of violence would be less significant. The ANC, he suggested, had developed a clear strategic goal with the adoption of the Freedom Charter in the mid-1950s, and the problem with which national organizers had grappled with was tactical, compounded by the imposition of ever more strict measures of suppression against Black political opposition. But, Muste's central point was that 'non-violence has . . . not yet been fully tried', which seemed to offer little more than a rebuttal of the argument that ANC figures had made both in public and in private conversations with WPB activists. Muste suggested that 'action from within' was needed in South Africa and declared that it would be preferable if Lutuli was 'actually imprisoned by the SA government'.[143] Sutherland would later suggest that Muste's emphasis on Lutuli, while understandable given his staunch advocacy of non-violence, sat rather awkwardly alongside the ANC campaigns for the release of Mandela and might suggest that the WPB were 'out of touch'.[144] In his letter to Sutherland, Muste also noted that the success of non-violent action was not necessarily dependent on the plan being viable or rational: 'even if the kind of thing the World Peace Brigade proposes and tries to carry out seems foolish and actually is foolish in a sense, it is, nevertheless, of great importance, since it keeps attention focussed on the situation in Africa and lessons will be learned from experimenting, one experiment will lead to another which is more "practical" and effective'. Sutherland and the other WPB activists were engaged in a unique form of pacifist diplomacy in Dar es Salaam, he maintained, which made their efforts to train volunteers even more urgent and necessary.[145]

---

[140] Sutherland to Muste, 30 August 1962, SPC Muste 89/22 WPB Correspondence.
[141] This argument replicated the public justification for the formation of MK set out by Mandela; see Mandela, *Long Walk to Freedom*; Sampson, *Mandela*.
[142] Sutherland to Muste, 30 August 1962, SPC Muste 89/22 WPB Correspondence.
[143] Muste to Sutherland, 7 September 1962, SPC Muste 89/22 WPB Correspondence.
[144] Sutherland to A. J. Muste, 30 October 1962, Muste 89/22 WPB Correspondence.
[145] Muste to Sutherland, 7 September 1962, SPC Muste 89/22 WPB Correspondence.

At the beginning of September, Sutherland travelled to London for the annual meeting of the WPB Council. Much of the discussion centred on work in Africa, although details of the plans under discussion with southern African activists were coyly hidden from the newsletter circulated to supporters and sponsors. Instead, the newsletter presented an update on the preparations for elections in Northern Rhodesia that largely comprised reports on the activities of UNIP, which almost give the impression that the Zambian nationalist party was an official affiliate of the World Peace Brigade – 'only UNIP' the report declared, 'has published a detailed election manifesto' in its account of discussions at the UNIP party conference in August. Looking towards the elections in October, the WPB report defined the main challenges for UNIP. One was the danger of the 'Welensky-Tshombe-Nkumbula clique' manufacturing a political emergency that could justify cancellation of the elections, the other was the need for resources, and the WPB supporters were encouraged to send donations to the PAFMECSA Freedom Fund in Dar es Salaam. Sutherland also highlighted discussions between Suresh Ram and Simon Kapwepwe, during which he reiterated the support for non-violence from the UNIP leadership – 'a policy and creed not only for today but also for tomorrow and for the day after!' which had excited great praise when reported to Vinoba Bhave.[146] Sutherland's report also hinted at the development of a 'constructive programme' that would involve cooperation between the WPB and other international groups including the AFSC, the Scott Bader Corporation and the *Mellemfolkeligt Samvirke* movement. Suggestions that either Albert Bigelow or Guy Clutton-Brook might work with the centre in Dar es Salaam in cooperation with TANU's developing ideas of 'Ujamaa' – defined in the report as 'the "familyhood" African socialism' of Nyerere. Sutherland was unable to set out any concrete plans, but the apparent success of the relationship between the WPB and the Zambians in UNIP seemed – for the moment at least – to overcome any potential concerns that might have arisen from the lack of material developments on the ground in Dar es Salaam.

In September 1962, following the discussions led by Scott and Sutherland with representatives of Namibian independence movements as well as the ANC, the Africa Freedom Action organizers drafted proposals for a coordinated internal and external campaign, codenamed 'Operation Goya'.

The final plan was agreed following a meeting between the African Freedom Action executive and representatives of SWAPO, including Sam Nujoma and the South-West African National Union (SWANU), led by its external representative Nathanael Mbaeva. The plan envisaged sending two small teams into the country in November 1962 to launch a joint anti-pass campaign. This would be combined with a campaign for UN sanctions against South Africa, international protests against companies with operations in South-West Africa and an attempt by a WPB protest team to enter the country with SWANU and SWAPO activists.[147] In New York, Muste broadly welcomed the plans and began to coordinate efforts to mobilize US support for a campaign focused on South-West Africa. Scott, meanwhile, planned to secure a meeting with the

---

[146] 'Annual Council Meeting of WPB in London', 1 September 1962, SPC Muste 89/22 Africa Freedom Project Correspondence.
[147] Sutherland to Muste, et al., 16 September 1962, SPC Muste 89/22 WPB Correspondence.

UN Secretary General, U Thant to set out the WPB's position on South-West Africa. In addition, Muste hoped, Scott would be able to promote the plans for the training centre, which might provide a contrast with the kind of 'forceful action' the UN had deployed with tragic consequences in Congo. Together with Rustin, Muste was also beginning to make plans for protests at the South African consulate in New York.[148] Originally planned to coincide with debates on South-West Africa at the UN in mid-October, the focus of the protest expanded to include the constitutional crisis in Southern Rhodesia, prompted by the arrival of Zimbabwean nationalists in New York seeking to lobby for the release of Joshua Nkomo from detention. With Alvin Wolfe's work clearly still in mind, the protest would also aim to raise public awareness of 'the complex of political, economic and racial commitments extending from Katanga to the Union of South Africa all supported from the Western industrial nations'.[149] A demonstration was scheduled for 22 October, called jointly by a variety of organizations including CORE, ACOA and NAACP, and led by a delegation comprising A. J. Muste, A. Philip Randolph, Michael Scott and James Farmer.

Before the protest took place, however, Scott began to express doubts regarding the 'maturity' of Namibian activists, who were compared unfavourably to Kaunda and Nyerere.[150] In particular, Scott raised concerns about the lack of direct contact between external protest and the internal anti-pass campaign envisaged in 'Operation Goya', although Sutherland noted that this was somewhat surprising given that he already knew the Namibian activists when he proposed the project earlier in the year.[151] This seems to mark the point at which Scott, in many respects the founder of Namibian international solidarity campaigns, began to lose some of the credibility he had built up with SWAPO and SWANU leaders.[152]

While it was not unreasonable to raise concerns about the extent to which a civil disobedience campaign in South-West Africa would remain non-violent, Scott's position seems hard to reconcile with the arguments made by Muste and Sutherland in response to South African activists, namely that popular non-violent protest had not been given the chance to work. The efforts of the WPB thus turned towards diplomatic methods. Scott and Muste secured a meeting with U Thant, in which they planned to propose a deputation of figures from the WPB, Fellowship of Reconciliation and American Friends Service Committee to meet with leaders in southern Africa including Verwoerd and Welensky.[153] In many respects, this represented a retreat from the radical activism envisaged in the debates that led to the formation of the peace brigade and a return to the politics of delegation. Perhaps, most significantly, the proposal hinted that the relations between pacifists and national liberation movements were beginning to destabilize. Newspaper reports of the Trusteeship Committee hearings on Southern Rhodesia suggest that Scott's standing had declined considerably. 'Many African

---

[148] Muste to Sutherland, 24 September 1962, SPC Muste 89/22 WPB Correspondence.
[149] 'Minutes, WPB North American Regional Council', 8 October 1962, SPC Muste 89/39 Africa Freedom Action.
[150] Muste to Sutherland, 28 September 1962, SPC Muste 89/22 WPB Correspondence.
[151] Sutherland to A. J. Muste, 6 October 1962, SPC Muste 89/39 Africa Freedom Action.
[152] Yates and Chester, *The Troublemaker*, 255–62.
[153] Muste to Sutherland, 28 September 1962, SPC Muste 89/22 WPB Correspondence.

delegates . . . were shaking their heads with impatience', the *Guardian* newspaper reported, as Scott presented a petition claiming that a demonstration by African children had been broken up with tear gas.[154] In contrast, African movements in Dar es Salaam warmly welcomed the resignation of the UK representative on the Trusteeship Committee, Hugh Foot, widely regarded as an advocate of progressive constitutional changes in Southern Rhodesia.[155] This was perhaps a moment of minor significance in the campaign for independence in Zimbabwe, but it was a notable moment in the history of Western solidarity with African liberation movements, as the patience of both diplomats and African liberation movements seemed to be reaching their limits.

The plans for a large-scale protest in South-West Africa also faced increasing difficulties with funding and resources. In early October, Sutherland reported that Tanganyikan officials had declared that they had no funds to support the South-West African movements, SWAPO and SWANU. Sutherland concluded that it would be 'irresponsible' to launch a campaign without sufficient resources.[156] Fraught discussions around funding had been a consistent feature of attempts to coordinate international peace protests in support of nationalist movements in Africa in the early 1960s, but the correspondence between Muste and Sutherland revealed a constant preoccupation with resources, as Sutherland relied increasingly on support from the United States in order to cover the everyday costs of living as well as efforts to develop more expansive and expensive projects. At the same time, as the Tanganyikan capital became a hub for political exiles across southern and central Africa, the demands on pacifist philanthropy expanded. As Sutherland noted in desperation in September 1962, Africa Freedom Action had been providing small 'hardship' grants to a variety of individuals including Hastings Banda and Sam Nujoma. As the plans for Operation Goya were drafted, the movement's responsibilities towards UNIP were supplemented by requests from Namibian activists. 'Where is the money?' Sutherland cried, as his own credit had been exhausted.[157]

But, as Sutherland struggled to keep Africa Freedom Action in operation in Dar es Salaam, the political processes that had been the primary cause of its formation were moving towards a conclusion. The elections in Northern Rhodesia were held without any major incident on 30 October 1962. On one level, Kaunda's gamble, in agreeing to participate despite the deep misgivings about the hyper-complex electoral system, was misplaced, as UNIP could neither secure a majority of seats nor was it the largest party in the new legislature. The United Federal Party secured one more seat, but the seven seats secured by the Northern Rhodesian African National Congress under Nkumbula meant that neither the UFP or UNIP could form a government without its support. And with just under 80 per cent of the votes in the lower roll and 15 per cent in the upper, UNIP clearly carried the popular vote across the country. Suresh Ram followed Kaunda throughout the last week of the campaign and reported on his success in heroic terms, for his endurance on the campaign trail to his charismatic leadership of

[154] 'Rev. Michael Scott's Plea Before UN Misfires', *Guardian*, 5 October 1962, 17.
[155] 'Africans Applaud Briton for Quitting Post at U.N.', *New York Times*, 14 October 1962, 3; 'Sir Hugh Foot, Trusteeship Aide, Quits British Delegation at U.N.', *New York Times*, 12 October 1962, 6.
[156] Sutherland to A. J. Muste, 6 October 1962, SPC Muste 89/39 Africa Freedom Action.
[157] Sutherland to Muste, Scott and Rustin, 16 September 1962, SPC Muste 89/22 WPB Correspondence.

both a popular nationalist movement and as an 'asset to . . . the cause of nonviolence and world peace'.[158] The political strength of UNIP was less secure than it seemed, nor, was Kaunda firmly established as its leading authority. But, what power he held seemed to rest on his image as a 'principled, non-violent Christian leader, able to bridge the gap between diverse sections of Zambian society, white settlers keen to protect their privileges and Western powers seeking to protect the position of multinational mining corporations and resist the encroachment of communism'.[159] Insofar as that image was at least in part bolstered by the work of the World Peace Brigade and other pacifist activists in Britain and the United States, this was a success, albeit transitory and partial.

The end of the dream in Africa

By September 1962, Sutherland was beginning to complain openly of 'discouraging' signs in the relationship between Africa Freedom Action, TANU and PAFMECSA. Officials such as Oscar Kambona now proved elusive and that promises of resources failed to be honoured.[160] The situation continued to deteriorate in October, although some signs of partnership continued:

> People seem to be too busy to nail transport, housing, African personnel, and various other problems down. I'm writing a very serious letter to TAN with copies to Nyerere and Kambona. Koinange has disappeared completely! Supposed to be in Nairobi. On the positive side, Maswanya has been coming by and cooperating, Makasa continues being warm and confidential, and we are doing some solid work with the South West Africans on non-violence using April Carter's 'Direct Action' as a base.[161]

At the North American WPB Council meeting in early October 1962, council members discussed the issue of relations between South Asian communities and the new governing authorities in East Africa. Muste was tasked with setting up consultations between Suresh Ram and other South Asian leaders.[162] Ram had suggested that he begin a two-week-long fast to bring about a process of reconciliation, including specific proposals for Indian traders to replace English signage in their shops with Swahili, and establishing collective initiatives including cooperative stores. Muste wrote immediately to Narayan, asking him to travel to Tanganyika, and then made further enquiries into the history of communal tensions in the country.[163] In late

---

[158] Suresh Ram to Muste, 10 November, 1962, SPC Muste 89/22 WPB Correspondence.
[159] Larmer, *Rethinking African Politics*, 51.
[160] Sutherland to A. J. Muste, 18 September1962, SPC Muste 89/22 Africa Freedom Project Correspondence.
[161] Sutherland to A. J. Muste 6 October 1962, SPC Muste 89/39 Africa Freedom Action.
[162] 'Minutes, WPB North American Regional Council', 8 October 1962, SPC Muste 89/39 Africa Freedom Action.
[163] Muste to J. P. Narayan, 9 October 1962, SPC Muste 89/22 WPB Correspondence; Muste to Suresh Ram, 9 October 1962, SPC Muste 89/22 WPB Correspondence.

November, Sutherland travelled to Kampala in an attempt to raise funds for the training centre from those in the Asian community that had pledged their support to J. P. Narayan when he visited following the Mbeya conference in May. Sutherland encountered difficulties, not least with the Sino-Indian border war consuming a great deal of attention within pacifist networks.[164]

Faced with continuing financial woes, Sutherland began to seek work in Dar es Salaam, although he worried that the only available employment seemed to be in government which would, he felt, lead to a conflict of interest. Alongside Sutherland, Africa Freedom Action was also sustained by the efforts of Suresh Ram, as well as John Papworth, who had returned to East Africa in an effort to travel to Northern Rhodesia for the elections.[165] And they continued to seek a permanent base in Dar es Salaam. In November, Sutherland had found a potential building for the training centre in the vicinity of Kivukoni College. Locating a permanent site for the centre was increasingly urgent, he reported to the WPB in New York, as government officials had begun to enquire when Africa Freedom Action would vacate the building loaned to them by Nyerere. Their unstable circumstances were such that they were being asked to return their borrowed refrigerator.[166] Sutherland nevertheless took the decision to rent the Kivukoni house.[167] As the Northern Rhodesian elections concluded and the formation of the Tanganyikan republic loomed, Sutherland began to fear that African officials would lose patience with Africa Freedom Action unless a clear plan of action could be offered. He sought to identify a range of ideas, including a major conference on non-violence bringing together international pacifist leaders and African politicians.[168] From New York, though, Muste believed that progress with the training centre was driven by events in central Africa, and an understanding of the contribution that it might make depended on liaison with Kaunda, who no longer seemed in close contact with any in the WPB.[169] The close relationship between Africa Freedom Action and Kaunda thus seemed to limit the capacity of the peace activists to develop long-term plans for action. Moreover, in November, Michael Scott had returned to London to attend the annual conference of the Africa Bureau before returning to Africa, but instead had received messages from J. P. Narayan requesting his presence in India. Scott clearly felt unable to refuse, although Muste felt his decisions were made 'a little too emotionally'.[170]

Sutherland did, in fact, manage to meet both Kaunda and Nyerere in the last week of November and was able to provide an outline of the UNIP strategy following the elections. With Zambian independence and the dissolution of the Central African Federation being twin priorities, the primary aim of UNIP – as well as PAFMECSA – was to secure a coalition agreement with Nkumbula and the ANC. The hope was that talks in London might mean that a coalition would be in place by the final by-elections

---

[164] Sutherland to A. J. Muste, 20 November 1962, SPC Muste 89/22 WPB Correspondence.
[165] Sutherland to A. J. Muste, 30 October 1962, SPC, Muste 89/22 WPB Correspondence.
[166] Sutherland to Lazar, 7 November 1962, SPC Muste 89/39 Africa Freedom Action.
[167] Sutherland to A. J. Muste, 16 November 1962, SPC Muste 89/39 Africa Freedom Action.
[168] Sutherland to A. J. Muste, 20 November 1962, SPC Muste 89/22 WPB Correspondence.
[169] Muste to Sutherland, 26 November 1962, SPC Muste 89/22 WPB Correspondence.
[170] Ibid.

being held in Northern Rhodesia in the second week of December. With much of his efforts focused on assuaging the anger of UNIP supporters, Kaunda would (Sutherland reported) only be able to turn attention to the possibility of a seminar on non-violence.[171] Although the stalled development of the training centre might be regarded as an indication that African leaders took an instrumentalist view of non-violent action movements, interactions with the WPB organizers also suggest the existence of genuine ideological affinities. In December 1962, Suresh Ram interviewed Nyerere on his vision for Ujaama. The African socialist model of self-help, Nyerere suggested, was close to the ideas of Narayan, although the advantage in Tanganyika was that Nyerere had 'the chance to put those views into practice'.[172] The World Peace Brigade, Nyerere claimed, would 'provoke thought' and thus play a role in social reconstruction and 'creating the new society'.[173]

And yet, by early 1963, it was clear that the WPB had slipped from the elevated status it had once enjoyed in Tanganyika. In January, Sutherland continued to push his plans for a seminar on non-violence but struggled to elicit any interest – or face-to-face meetings with government officials. He began to talk openly of personal distress, which seems to have intensified after the celebrations to mark Republic day, to which neither Sutherland nor Ram was invited. He noted that he was finding it increasingly difficult to focus on the work setting up the centre when he felt he 'was not working in a situation where I feel I "belong"'. Moreover, although he admired the work that Ram was undertaking, they did not engage in 'real conclusion'. 'Anyhow' he concluded his letter to Muste, 'when is Michael coming back?'[174] Suresh Ram gave an update on developments with the training centre to the WPB Council in January 1963, who noted that the morale of the staff in Dar es Salaam was 'low with no prospect of action'. Michael Scott again raised Sutherland's proposal for an international seminar on non-violence, but Robert Gilmore argued that the costs of such an enterprise were beyond the means of the WPB. Gilmore then continued with a stark assessment of the prospects for the centre, which he regarded as an 'irrelevant relic sentimentally maintained long after its time of effectiveness'. The World Peace Brigade, he argued, was an organization that needed to employ its limited resources effectively by engaging opportunistically in specific circumstances. This had been the case in Northern Rhodesia in March 1962, but the political situation had since been transformed and it was no longer clear that the WPB was relevant. Rustin suggested, however, that the centre could be successful, given additional funds and a 'forceful director'. He wondered whether the threat of closure might reveal the position of African leaders, who should, he argued, take responsibility for the centre. Rustin also noted that, if the decision were taken to close the centre, Sutherland would need support, as his future and that of the centre were connected.[175]

---

[171] Sutherland to A. J. Muste, 30 November 1962, SPC – WPB – North American Council.
[172] Interview with Nyerere, 'Towards Ujamaa in Tanganyika', 10 December 1962 (Presented to WPB North American Council, March 1963), SPC – WPB – North American Council 1963–68.
[173] Ibid.
[174] Sutherland to A. J. Muste, 3 January 1963, SPC Muste 89/39 Africa Freedom Action.
[175] WPB Executive Committee Minutes, 9 January 1963, SPC Muste 89/22 WPB Executive Committee.

During January 1963, Scott began to develop his own set of proposals for a seminar on the political and economic situation in Africa, which Muste shared with the ACOA chair George Houser and the writer and social commentator Lewis Mumford. Scott's plan, which quoted extensively from Suresh Ram's interview with Julius Nyerere, aimed to address fundamental questions relating to economic development in post-colonial Africa, including the nature of the 'sovereignty and ownership of natural resources', and the role of international organizations in securing and regulating 'capital and technical aid'.[176] The North American Regional Council of the WPB, meanwhile, resolved to send a representative to Dar es Salaam to investigate the possibilities for future work in southern Africa. Specifically, the WPB representative would assess the degree to which the Tanganyikan government would support the centre, or whether it might amalgamate with Kivukoni College or the TANU training centre. A further option was discussed for a lecturer in non-violence to be appointed at Kivukoni.[177] But Rustin, who had initially seemed optimistic about the future of the centre, had already visited in February 1963 and concluded that Sutherland had lost control of the enterprise and had alienated his hosts; he therefore took the decision to close the centre.[178] However, it was Rustin, Sutherland recalled, who approached Nyerere to enquire about work in the civil service, and a role was found working with political refugees.[179] Sutherland continued to write voicing frustrations about relations with government officials. In March, he reflected that it was 'difficult to know which procedure is best because the establishment always counts on people running out of patience'.[180] But, he also continued to report back to Muste on the activities of southern African exiles in Dar es Salaam. Joshua Nkomo spoke at a public meeting in March, 'more on fire and alive' since his banning and arrest in Southern Rhodesia; alongside him on the platform was the Mozambiquan Eduardo Mondlane, who felt that advocates of non-violence were 'nice people to be protected from getting . . . hurt by the wicked Portuguese'.[181]

'Ignoring the temper of the people'

Recent work examining the historical narrative of the 'turn to armed struggle' in southern Africa has suggested that the responses of both state authorities and militant nationalists were contingent and that there were many, often contested, interpretations of 'violence' and the ends it was intended to achieve.[182] Similarly, 'non-violence' was ideologically and methodologically complex – as Scott himself acknowledged. On closer examination, the entangled relationship between violence and non-violence –

---

[176] Scott, 'Industry and Politics in Southern Africa', 20 January 1963, SPC Muste 89/22/ WPB Africa – Seminar on industry and politics in South Africa.
[177] Minutes, WPB North American Regional Council, 23 January 1963, SPC – WPB – North American Council 1963–68.
[178] D'Emilio, Lost Prophet, 329.
[179] Sutherland and Meyer, Guns and Gandhi, 64.
[180] Sutherland to A. J. Muste, 20 March 1963, SPC Muste 89/22 Africa Freedom Project Tanganyika.
[181] Ibid.
[182] Stevens, 'The Turn to Sabotage'.

as ideas, within movements, and in the actions of individual campaigners – suggests that they were mutually constitutive. We should therefore reconsider the value of historical analysis that relies purely on the notion of distinctive and dramatic 'turns'. Of course, the intransigence of settler regimes in southern Africa, engaged in what they understood as a struggle for survival, resulted in the narrowing of options for liberation movements. The emergence of armed force as the primary mode of opposition to colonialism and apartheid in southern Africa was a highly significant development. But the politics of violence was a multifaceted phenomenon that reflected both localized circumstances, the emergent political culture of nationalist movements and the nature of the connections between national movements, international organizations and transnational social movements.

The African Freedom Action march demonstrated the limited extent to which peace campaigners could support nationalist movements. Despite their attempts to identify the underlying structures of corporate interest that supported minority regimes in southern and central Africa, peace campaigners had insufficient material resources or political capital to directly challenge the institutions of state, finance and industry. Nor were there attempts to design alternative forms of political, social or economic power synonymous with the Bhoodan or Shanti Sena movements in India. Instead, local experiments such as Africa Freedom Action were wrapped into a generalized conception of a 'World' movement, whose ambition obscured its relative political weakness. In southern Africa, talk of passive resistance was being superseded by the notion of liberation struggle. In their initial call for volunteers, Scott, Rustin and Sutherland asserted that Africa Freedom Action was vital for 'the future of non-violent resistance in southern Africa', but, by the end of 1962, it was becoming clear that the principles of its African sponsors were diverging from those of the WPB. At a meeting of the Brigade's North American Committee in November, it was noted that 'the trend was away from a reliance upon non-violence and toward, on the one hand an increasing involvement in constitutional problems and political affairs . . . and on the other a passive resignation to the rise of violent action within their organisations'.[183]

In discussion with Bill Sutherland in Dar es Salaam in August 1962, South African nationalists Robert Resha and Tennison Makiwane argued that non-violence 'had been tried to exhaustion and that any leader who advocated it . . . would be ignoring the temper of the people'.[184] Such conversations with South African exiles prompted Sutherland to conclude that there had been a definitive change of direction since the conference in Addis Ababa in February 1962. He concluded that there was a 'programme of violence in South Africa' and covert cooperation between the ANC and China meant that a 'campaign of guerrilla tactics' would soon be launched.[185] From mid-1962, Sutherland and Ram also began to engage in discussions with ZAPU activists, fearing that, as in South Africa, the nationalist movement in Southern Rhodesia was turning to armed tactics, although they felt the 'temperament of the

---

[183] 'Minutes, WPB North American Regional Council', 14 November 1962, SPC, Muste 89/39 Africa Freedom Action.
[184] Sutherland to Muste, 31 August 1962, SPC Muste 89/22 WPB Correspondence.
[185] Sutherland to A. J. Muste, 18 September1962, SPC Muste 89/22 Africa Freedom Project Correspondence.

people' involved in the movements precluded 'another Mau Mau'.[186] The focus of pacifists on developing personal relationships with key organizers seemed predicated on the mutual sense that movements were built on the personalities of talented elites. Leadership seemed vital, and Kaunda remained a beacon of hope for the WPB. He had assured his pacifist contacts that non-violence was 'not only for today but for tomorrow and the day after', but he felt obliged to carefully re-examine his views on non-violence as Zambian independence approached. As Kaunda was transformed from the leader of a movement to the leader of a governing party, he began to grapple with the need to reconcile principles of non-violence with the necessary machinery of power. 'The business of statecraft', he mused, was 'enough to sober the keenest idealist'.[187] Shortly after the Mbeya meeting, in the aftermath of the march that never happened, Kaunda challenged his pacifist friends to find a solution to the dilemma he would face as a supporter of non-violence who would also bear the responsibility for defending his country against the settler forces to the south, and the Western-backed secessionists in the Katanga province of the Congo to the north. They had no clear answer.[188]

---

[186] Sutherland to A. J. Muste, 6 October 1962, SPC Muste 89/39 Africa Freedom Action.
[187] Kaunda, *Kaunda on Violence*, 37.
[188] Sutherland and Meyer, *Guns and Gandhi*, 96.

7

Aftermaths

Peace and decolonization

In late October 1964, just weeks after Muste circulated his mimeographed reflections on the challenges for a radical peace movement, Zambia celebrated its independence. Despite his challenge to pacifist supporters two years earlier, some had stayed in the country and were invited to attend official events marking the end of colonial control in the country. These included the Quaker representatives of the American Friends' International Service, Lyle Tatum and George Loft, the latter of whom had arrived in Africa in the late 1950s determined to play the role of 'neutral facilitator' in the political conflicts within the Federation.[1] Despite the failure of his efforts, Loft attended Zambian independence celebrations, which seemed an apparent victory for the work of pacifist networks in shaping the dynamics of decolonization. When Kaunda arrived at the event dressed in the uniform of a general in the newly formed Zambian Defence Force, the Quaker activist was devastated. In Sutherland's recollection, 'Loft had tears in his eyes, saying "Ah, we have lost him . . . we have lost him"'.[2] It was, Sutherland suggested, a moment that revealed the failure of pacifist purists to recognize the limits of a politics of persuasion.

For his part, Kaunda recognized his predicament but, perhaps more pertinently, acknowledged that tactics of passive resistance relied to a degree on social privilege. In his reflections on violence published two decades later, Kaunda turned to the example of South Africa to illustrate the role of class in determining the effectiveness of non-violent protest. A white South African protestor, beaten and jailed for their actions, would, Kaunda argued, be recognized as making a sacrifice in ways Black protestors – who faced arbitrary violence and legal restrictions as everyday hazards – would not. For the Black protestor, their action would be 'a distinction without a difference'.[3] To a degree, Kaunda's assertion provides an apt illustration of the fundamental dividing line between a politics of resistance centred on peace and one focused on bringing an end to a colonial system of government.

---

[1] Brooks Marmon, 'Neutrality of a Special Type: George Loft's Abortive Racial Reconciliation in the Federation of Rhodesia and Nyasaland, 1957–1960', *Safundi* 22, no. 4 (2021): 417–34.
[2] Sutherland and Mayer, *Guns and Gandhi*, 96.
[3] Kaunda, *Kaunda on Violence*, 57.

During 1963, Africa Freedom Action faded from the discussions among the organizers of the World Peace Brigade. In January, the North American Regional Council held a series of joint meetings with the American Friends Service Committee, which concluded that the future of non-violent protest in Africa would be determined by the degree of interest and need expressed by African political leaders. Without any specific calls for support from individuals such as Kaunda and Nyerere, the centre in Dar es Salaam was 'in a time of diminished effectiveness'.[4] It was agreed that a WPB representative should assess Nyerere's interest in the training centre, but the council had already begun to discuss how they could support Sutherland and make 'arrangements for any necessary transition period', and plans were made to despatch Bayard Rustin to Dar es Salaam to oversee the process.

The vision of a Dar es Salaam training centre for peace was thus abandoned, although there were hints that they might be revived in Zambia under Kaunda. But there is no clear finality in the story of Africa Freedom Action. Before exploring the conclusions that could be drawn from the history of the engagement between peace movements and the processes of decolonization up to 1962, it is useful to consider the afterlives of the campaigns that have been explored above. This final chapter thus begins by addressing three episodes in the aftermath of Africa Freedom Action that illustrate a kind of parting of the ways, or at least a retreat from efforts by peace campaigners to shape the dynamics of the politics of decolonization.

As the World Peace Brigade began to discuss options for the Dar es Salaam project, the focus of their attention had turned to a new campaign centred not in Africa, but in India, which would mark a new departure for central figures such as Michael Scott. The Asian Regional Council of the World Peace Brigade called on supporters in Europe and the United States to join a march from Dehli to Beijing, in response to the military conflict that had broken out over the border dispute between India and China. While it travels some distance from the book's primary focus on peace campaigners and anti-colonial activism in Africa, it is included as it represented the final attempt by the WPB to launch a meaningful pacifist intervention in conflict. But, in returning the narrative of international pacifist efforts to India, the site of the conference with which the story began, it illustrates the ways in which the visions of international solidarity that had offered a sense of hope in 1950 had, just over a decade later, begun to fracture and transform.

Peace activists also continued to advocate interventions in the politics of decolonization in southern Africa, as settler minority regimes in South Africa and Rhodesia sought to entrench white supremacy. The second section of the chapter thus explores the ways in which peace campaigners refocused their efforts to engage with colonialism in southern Africa onto the central issue of apartheid and sought to engage with the emerging transnational anti-apartheid movement. By the end of the 1960s, anti-apartheid, alongside peace, disarmament and opposition to US 'imperialism' in Vietnam, had become a nexus of global political issues that concerned a new generation of activists inspired in part by the activities of pioneers such as Scott in

---

[4] 'Minutes, WPB North American Regional Council', 23 November 1963, SPC – WPB – North American Council 1963–68.

the previous decade. But Scott and the Africa Bureau were no longer central figures and despite efforts by pacifist campaigners such as John Papworth – and the ubiquity of "peace" in countercultural discourse – the radical peace movement struggled to maintain relevance in an era shaped by a language of national liberation struggle and the development of armed anti-colonial resistance movements.

But first, this concluding chapter will examine African engagement in international debates around nuclear disarmament had continued after the Accra conference in 1960, with Nkrumah again taking the lead. As the organizers of Africa Freedom Action waited in Tanganyika, Ghana hosted the Accra Assembly for the World Without the Bomb, bringing together anti-nuclear weapons campaigners from around the world. A coming together of the representatives of Western, Soviet-aligned and Non-Aligned States, and both 'aligned' and 'non-aligned' disarmament campaigners, the Assembly represented a divergence between international disarmament diplomacy and the peace movement that had launched the Sahara protest in 1959. The conference in Accra is seen largely from the perspective of Homer Jack who attended the meeting as a representative of the US National Committee for a Sane Nuclear Policy (SANE), whose campaigning, in contrast to Muste and the CNVA, focused on conventional diplomacy and political lobbying. While the conference did not make a critical contribution to the progress of disarmament talks, it illustrates the distance between campaigners for non-violence and international nuclear disarmament efforts by the mid-1960s.

Non-aligned nuclear diplomacy: The Accra Assembly

As the Africa Freedom Action activists gathered and waited in Tanganyika in 1962, another legacy of the Sahara protest and Positive Action conference of 1960 was playing out in Africa. This parallel development represented a somewhat different engagement between African nationalism and transnational peace movements. For when the plans for a non-violent training centre withered, the exigencies of the Congo crisis diverted the attention of Ghanaian officials, and European anti-nuclear protestors returned north to continue their campaigns, the question of nuclear disarmament was not forgotten. Instead, anti-nuclear weapons policies were drawn into the international politics of non-alignment. After 1960, Nkrumah retained a commitment to world disarmament and began to weave the rhetoric of opposition to 'nuclear imperialism' into a discourse of development, in which the vast sums spent on arms could be directed instead towards social and economic programmes.[5] Disarmament was also consistent with Nkrumah's engagement with the development of the Non-Aligned Movement.[6] Plans for a proposed Accra Assembly were first mooted by Nkrumah in 1961 and discussed at the London conference on 'Disarmament and Reduction of World Tensions' organized by Canon Collins of the British CND.[7] Collins was keen

---

[5] Kwame Nkrumah, *Africa must unite* (London: Heinemann, 1964), 199.
[6] On Nkrumah and non-alignment, see Peter Willetts, *The Non-aligned Movement: The Origins of a Third World Alliance* (New York: Frances Pinter, 1978), 11–13.
[7] Collins, *Faith Under Fire*, 342 see also Duff, *Left, Left, Left*.

to promote dialogue between the non-aligned disarmament movements (essentially the non-governmental campaigns based in the West) and those aligned closely with the Soviet Union, notably the World Peace Council. Collins was a prominent member of a large delegation of Western campaigners who travelled to the World Congress for General Disarmament and Peace, held in Moscow in July 1962, which arguably represented the 'high water mark of cooperation between' these rival movements.[8] It was in this atmosphere of conciliation that the Accra was planned, and then held, just two months before the Moscow conference, in May 1962.

There was some scepticism about the location of an international conference in Ghana, given its political uncertainties and the tensions that had led to the imposition of the authoritarian detention laws that Randle and Sutherland had decried in 1960. It seemed to some observers, such as the American nuclear disarmament campaigner Homer Jack, that Nkrumah planned to exploit the conference as an attempt to bolster domestic support within Ghana. Jack, who we have seen had engaged with African issues since the early 1950s, met Nkrumah on a number of occasions, including the inaugural conference of the Non-Aligned Movement in Belgrade in September 1961, held just weeks after the Berlin Crisis. In common with many of the leaders who addressed the conference, Nkrumah's speech dwelt on the threat of nuclear war, declaring that 'aside from colonialism... no problem today is more urgent nor pressing than the problem of disarmament'.[9] He described the vast resources being dedicated to nuclear arms by the Soviet and Western Blocs and noted how, for the peoples of Africa, Asia and Latin America, debates around disarmament focused attention on the 'vast possibilities now denied... for increased standards of living, the development of housing, agriculture and industry, the planning of cities, and the eradication of illiteracy, ignorance, disease and want'. In this vision, disarmament was development. Non-aligned countries, Nkrumah argued, could play a critical role in brokering the system of inspection and arms control that would be central to a disarmament treaty. According to Jack, Nkrumah also mentioned plans for an international conference on disarmament in Accra, but further discussions did not take place until early in the following year.

In January 1962, Jack became involved in preparatory discussions for the conference, coordinating efforts to identify US representatives with colleagues in Europe, including Collins and CND. The list proposed by Jack – which included Linus Pauling, Lewis Mumford and Martin Luther King (or alternatively James Baldwin) – perhaps underlined the fissures between the government-focused efforts of groups such as SANE and the direct-action orientation of the Committee for Non-Violent Action. The acrimony that existed between the Committee of 100 and CND, and between Collins and Scott, did not appear to extend across the Atlantic, but there was nonetheless a distinct lack of overlap between the individuals involved with plans for the Accra Assembly and those who had been linked with the Positive Action conference and the World Peace Brigade. Collins' meeting in September 1961 did address this to a certain

---

[8] Wittner, *Resisting the Bomb*, 317.
[9] Nkrumah address at Belgrade, 4 September 1961, Kennedy Library, Non-Aligned Nations Summit Meeting, Belgrade, 1 September 1961, JFKPOF-104-004-p0086.

extent, as its participants included A. J. Muste, who afterwards wrote to Collins about ways of expanding US involvement. He felt that a new conference ought to draw 'certain elements' in order to give them a 'real feeling of participation' in the development of an international body. These would include Quaker groups such as the American Friends Service Committee, as well as CNVA and trades union groups. With long-standing experience of navigating between the socialist and Communist left, Muste was highly sensitive to the difficulties that ensued, especially in the United States, when ideas of a 'united front' rose to the surface. Ultimately, the aim was, as Muste saw it, the 'development of peace movements which are independent and, therefore, can be critical of the foreign policies of both blocks'.[10] However, Muste's optimism was not to manifest in any form of united disarmament conference. Instead, the Accra Assembly embodied Nkrumah's agenda for a disarmament conference that paralleled the aims of the non-aligned movement.

A preparatory conference was held in Zagreb in February 1962, during which separate committees discussed and drafted reports on five areas, from the reduction of international tensions to arms control regimes and the peaceful use of nuclear material. The final two committees examined economic aspects of disarmament, including an examination of the ways in which resources could be redirected towards issues of 'hunger, disease, ignorance, poverty and servitude'.[11] The reports from the first four committees provided concise overviews of the practical and technical challenges allied to the disarmament process; the fifth committee, however, was forced to reconcile disarmament with a much broader array of social and economic concerns. As such, its chair, the Ghanaian academic and Vice Chancellor of the Kwame Nkrumah University of Science and Technology, Robert Baffour, provided a broad overview rather than a detailed report. Perhaps more significantly, it was only in Baffour's statement that the question of colonialism was explicitly addressed. He argued that 'the problems of colonialism . . . are a danger to Peace and a proper subject therefore for discussion', and that more generally, disarmament was an issue that affected governments that did not have nuclear weapons programmes as much as those that did. Moreover, non-nuclear powers that sought 'to maintain colonialism through military strength' – which presumably included Portugal and South Africa – were another form of danger to world peace that ought to be considered by the Assembly.[12]

Despite these echoes of the language of the Positive Action conference of April 1960, the Accra Assembly framed the intersection of disarmament and colonialism in a significantly different manner than the rhetoric of 'nuclear imperialism' that had dominated two years previously. Nkrumah remained haunted by fears of neo-colonialism and determined to promote African political unity, but the Accra Assembly saw a series of debates that differed dramatically from the earlier conference. In contrast to the focus on anti-colonial struggles (and debates around the relative

---

[10] Muste to Collins, 25 September 1961, SPC, SANE B5 Misc Corre Collins.
[11] A sixth committee on the psychological dimensions of disarmament was also added during the preparatory conference. 'Press Release on the Pre-Assembly Meeting at Zagreb (February 24–28)', SPC Homer Jack Papers, JACK VII-3 Accra Assembly, 1962, Official Documents.
[12] 'Statement by the Chairman of the Fifth Committee', SPC Homer Jack Papers, JACK VII-3 Accra Assembly, 1962, Official Documents.

merits of violent and non-violent protest) in 1960, the Accra Assembly emphasized disarmament. It was an international rather than a pan-African meeting, and the debate was framed by a discourse of 'non-alignment' rather than 'African unity'. The emphasis on non-alignment was embodied in draft rules which reminded delegates that they were not 'attending in a representative capacity' or 'bound to any vote', although these measures might equally reflect Collins' agenda of creating an environment that could bring together groups from across the Cold War divide and insulate discussions from Communist versus anti-Communist tensions.[13]

The Accra Assembly also highlighted the complicated relationship between non-alignment and the evolving Cold War disarmament policies of the United States and the Soviet Union. As he made plans to travel to Accra, Homer Jack maintained close contact with US government officials about his plans to attend the Accra Assembly and the World Congress for General Disarmament and Peace in Moscow. William Chapman Foster, the Director of the US Arms Control and Disarmament Agency, inaugurated in September 1961, seemed to welcome Jack's involvement with the Accra conference, acknowledging that he would not represent the views of the US government, but that 'it will have a salutary effect if you state your views as your conscience prompts you'.[14] Thus, while the Accra Assembly was envisaged as an offshoot of the Non-Aligned Movement, its largest delegations represented the United States and the Soviet Union. These included figures with official connections, such as the former US Ambassador to the UN, James Wadsworth, as well as two physicists: Amrom Katz, an expert in aerial reconnaissance at the RAND Corporation, and William Higinbotham, who had worked on the US atomic weapons programme at Los Alamos during the 1940s and co-founder of the nuclear nonproliferation organization, the Federation of American Scientists. The ten-person Soviet delegation also contained figures of political substance including a former judge of the International Court of Justice and the Deputy Chair of the Presidium of the Supreme Soviet. Homer Jack contrasted the 'diverse' array of US delegates, who were free to speak independently of government policy (Wadsworth reportedly declared his opposition to US nuclear test policy), with the Soviet group, who adhered closely to the official line on disarmament policy, calling for 'general and complete disarmament', which Jack dismissed as mere 'incantation'.[15]

Other delegates included the Irish politician and prominent human rights activist Seán MacBride, the former Secretary of State for Commonwealth Relations Philip Noel-Baker, and British Labour MPs Anthony Greenwood and Judith Hart. Alongside Nkrumah, the only key individual from the 1960 conference who attended the Accra Assembly was E. C. Quaye. Nkrumah opened the conference with a dramatic declaration: 'Humanity is perched on the edge of a dangerous precipice from which one fatal miscalculation may bring mankind to the brink of annihilation'.[16] The Assembly would be, he hoped, a 'bold and courageous voice' in favour of disarmament.

[13] Ibid.; 'Accra Assembly Draft Rules', n.d. [c. May 1962], SPC SANE B5/Accra Assembly 1962.
[14] W. Foster to H. Jack, 31 May 1962, SPC SANE B 5/Accra Assembly, 1962.
[15] Jack, 'A Report to the National Committee for a Sane Nuclear Policy', 29 June 1962, SPC, SANE B5 Accra Assembly Reports 1962.
[16] 'Address of Osagyefo Dr Kwame Nkrumah', Accra Assembly – The World Without the Bomb, 21–28 June 1962, SPC, JACK VII-3 Accra Assembly 1962 Official Documents (3).

Anti-nuclear campaigners, he argued, had a moral authority, while disarmament was a practical necessity based on a realistic assessment of world tensions. He categorized four key sources of international tension: the legacies of the Second World War, the struggle between colonialism and freedom, ideological conflict and nuclear weapons. He spoke of Africa in terms of the dangers of Balkanization, with a particular emphasis on the possibility that small and weakened African states would become the kind of 'tinderbox' that the Balkans itself had in 1914. He also took the opportunity to rehearse key themes of his ideological vision of African Unity and the threat of neocolonialism, but he also sketched the outline of a plan for the demilitarization of Africa that would include not only the establishment of a nuclear-free zone across the continent but also the removal of all foreign military bases. This would be ensured by an 'ideological truce' that would avoid the continent becoming a site of proxy-Cold War conflict. And, just as importantly, an end to the nuclear arms race would release resources for development, which would do much to assuage the tensions 'which arise out of the disparity in wealth and opportunity for economic advancement'.[17]

The Assembly addressed an ambitious array of themes, but its primary focus remained that of nuclear disarmament. Its primary committee examined the 'reduction of international tensions' and recommended there should be a halt to further nuclear proliferation, the removal of nuclear weapons from central Europe, tougher with a reduction in armed forces 'so that . . . either side should become equal in number'.[18] Third World engagement with the disarmament debate was most strongly reflected in the fifth committee of the preparatory conference, which had focused on the relationship between disarmament and development. During the Assembly itself, the Ghanaian official Joseph Henry Mensah presented a discussion of 'Disarmament and Africa's Economic Development'. A former member of staff at the United Nations, Mensah had returned to Ghana to take up a post as a senior economist at for the government's Planning Commission. Mensah argued that, in contrast to the standard view, rather than reading the economic impact of disarmament purely in terms of its impact on nuclear powers, the economic drain of conventional armaments on developing countries was far greater. 'The world in which the great powers renounce their big bombs', Mensah asserted, 'must also be a world in which the smaller powers renounce their small bombs'.[19] Defence spending in Africa was not significant in global terms, but often represented a significant part of the government budget; armed forces were both a sign of prestige and a bulwark against 'naked imperialist oppression'. He therefore proposed a UN-sponsored disarmament conference, which would draft security guarantees and a non-aggression agreement in collaboration with NATO and Warsaw Pact countries. African disarmament would be a difficult task, Mensah suggested, as while 'governments are concerned about the threat to world and to themselves that is posed by great power conflict, but quite oblivious to the dangers of small power conflict'.

[17] K. Nkrumah, 'Address to Accra Assembly', 21 June 1962, SPC JACK VII-3 Accra Assembly, Official Documents.
[18] 'Report of the First Committee', 28 February 1962, SPC, SANE B5 Accra Assembly Reports 1962.
[19] Mensah, 'Disarmament and Africa's Economic Development', Accra Assembly – The World Without the Bomb, 21–28 June 1962, SPC SANE B5 Accra Assembly Documents 1962.

A more direct reference to colonialism came from the paper by Sierra Leone MP and trades unionist Isaac Wallace-Johnson, on 'Problems of Hunger and Disease'. Wallace-Johnson, who had worked with Nkrumah in the formation of the West African National Secretariat in London in the 1940s, had returned to Sierra Leone and became a founder of the United National People's Party in the mid-1950s. At the Accra Assembly, he argued that a 'world without the Bomb' would need to be a world free from colonialism. But, his speech made no reference to disarmament as such and offered a familiar line on the relationships between colonialism, capitalism and African poverty.[20] The Moroccan nationalist Alla al-Fassi offered a more detailed critique of foreign military bases, which he described as a 'relic of colonialism' that were 'capable of sheltering formidable atomic bombs'. While these bases were justified on the 'pretext' of protection, they revealed the weakness of newly independent states to guarantee their safety, al-Fassi argued. Moreover, Cold War strategic imperatives underpinned the aid and development policies of the major powers; these efforts were guided not by a 'struggle against poverty' but by 'ideological interests and a struggle for power'.[21] It was the United Nations, therefore, that should take the central role in the distribution of aid. Al-Fassi's vision of a world without atomic weapons thus relied on a strong and centralized international body, even as the events in the Congo were calling into question the capacity of the UN to ensure even basic levels of peace and political stability. These presentations revealed a divide that emerged from the work of the Assembly, between an agenda of Third World solidarity and Cold War non-alignment. Both were framed by strategic and ideological tensions between the post-war superpowers, but the former foregrounded anti-colonialism and post-colonial legacies. Thus, notwithstanding the differences between the Accra Assembly and the conference of two years earlier, the 1962 meeting again heard calls for efforts towards global disarmament to be aligned with agendas for development, the eradication of poverty and freedom from colonialism.

The Ghanaian government set out to create a permanent body to oversee the continuing work of the Assembly and created an office in Accra supervised by Ghanaian diplomat Frank Boaten as General Director. In the assessment of April Carter, this reflected the constraint imposed on peace activism by government-sponsored disarmament; the formation of a secretariat overseen by Boaten meant, she concluded, that 'autonomous peace activity was likely to be almost as difficult in new African states as in the Soviet bloc'.[22] But Boaten certainly worked hard to maintain the momentum of the conference and in the years that followed, he travelled widely within the circuits of international peace and disarmament movements. In early 1963, he addressed the Oxford Conference of Non-Aligned Peace Organisations, calling on delegates to avoid sharpening divisions along Cold War lines by focusing their opposition on the World Peace Council.[23] A few months later, he attended the founding conference of the OAU,

---

[20] Wallace-Johnson, 'Problems of Hunger and Disease', 21 June 1962, SPC, JACK VII-3 Accra Assembly 1962 Official Documents (2).
[21] 'Address by Prof Allal El Fassi', Accra Assembly – The World Without the Bomb, 21–28 June 1962, SPC, JACK VII-3 Accra Assembly 1962 Official Documents (2).
[22] Carter, *Peace Movements*, 74.
[23] Wernicke, 'The Communist-Led World Peace Council and the Western Peace Movements', 288.

where he admitted he struggled 'to get the conference to give serious consideration' to his proposals.[24] His efforts to promote the awareness of the debates around disarmament took him from Africa to the Congress for International Co-operation and Disarmament held in Australia in November 1964 and brought him indirectly into contact with prominent Third World nuclear scientists such as the Pakistani theoretical physicist Abdus Salam (who would play a key role in the development of his country's nuclear weapons programme in the 1970s).[25]

Other delegates at the Accra Assembly were able to engage directly with international disarmament processes. The chair of its committee on arms control and inspection, Seán MacBride, for example, delivered a well-received report on the debates in Ghana to the participants at the Geneva disarmament talks.[26] There were, nevertheless, some clear reservations, including regrets that the non-aligned delegates were unable to make 'bolder proposals', with the result that committee discussions became dominated by American and Soviet experts and thus a 'replica of the Geneva Disarmament conference'.[27] Homer Jack noted that there were many 'inevitable disappointments', not least in the small number of African participants, but also the 'failure of the Assembly as a whole to take many positive stands on outstanding cold war problems'.[28] While Western pacifists such as Jack were motivated in part by anti-Communist convictions, Cold War tensions – already a factor in the internal politics of movements such as SANE – were an evident constraint on international cooperation.[29] The form of non-alignment employed by the participants, described by Jack as 'a mathematical exercise in finding ideological equidistance between two poles', was perceived to be a far from effective route to disarmament.[30]

The Accra Assembly represented the ambition of non-aligned disarmament movements to mobilize Third World support during the early 1960s, when opposition to nuclear weapons among the African public seems to have been particularly strong.[31] As Allman suggests, the early 1960s saw growing evidence of Cold War power struggles playing out across Africa, leading activists such as Sutherland to pessimistic assessments of the declining opportunities for 'experimentation, and the space to imagine new worlds'.[32] International events later in 1962 would seem to underline this view. Five months after the Assembly, the revelations that the Soviet Union had begun to install strategic missile bases in Cuba catapulted the world into a crisis of nuclear

---

[24] F. Boaten to H. Jack, 14 May 1963, SPC, SANE B 5/Gen Corres, 'Atom Free Africa'.
[25] *Education – Journal of the New South Wales Teachers' Association*, 11 November 1964, 4. Shobana Shankar, *An Uneasy Embrace: Africa, India and the Spectre of Race* (Oxford: Oxford University Press, 2021), 121.
[26] S. MacBride to P. Noel-Baker, 5 September 1962, SPC, SANE B 5/Accra Assembly, 1962.
[27] H. Jack, 'The Accra Assembly – Report to SANE', 29 June 1962, SPC, SANE B5/Accra Assembly Reports 1962.
[28] Ibid.
[29] On anti-Communism in US peace movements, see R. Lieberman, *The Strangest Dream: Communism, Anticommunism and the US Peace Movement, 1945–63* (New York: Syracuse University Press, 2000).
[30] H. Jack, 'Accra Bans the Bomb', *Africa Today* 9, no. 7 (1 September 1962): 10–16. See also Wittner, *Resisting the Bomb*, 301–2.
[31] Ibid., 271.
[32] Allman, 'Nuclear Imperialism', 97; Sutherland and Meyer, *Guns and Gandhi*, 41–2.

diplomacy that has, in popular imagination, become cemented as a defining moment in the twentieth century. In this account, the Cuban Missile Crisis became the 'purest existential moment in the history of mankind', which both starkly illuminated the reality of nuclear Armageddon and gave impetus to political and diplomatic initiatives that would make its occurrence less likely.[33] More recent historical analyses of the crisis have begun to shed light on hitherto neglected aspects of the moment, including the significant mediating role played by the UN Secretary General U Thant as well as the need to re-centre Cuban initiatives, agendas and agency.[34] In similar ways, the Accra Assembly should not be considered merely a marginal moment in the history of non-governmental nuclear diplomacy. Non-aligned African states may well, as Allman suggests, have been subject to the influence of Cold War power struggles, but the Accra Assembly nonetheless represented a moment at which the Cold War superpowers, the non-aligned movement, disarmament movements and African governments could engage in a creative discussion of the possibilities for progress towards the limitation of nuclear threats.

For transnational peace activists, the nuclear threat was immanent in their conception of an interconnected world. And yet, Third World support for an anti-nuclear stance, which seemed widespread in early 1960, had become muted, even before the Cuban crisis. Attending an anti-nuclear weapons convention in New Delhi in June 1962, Muste noted that Nehru firmly opposed the proposal by former president Rajendra Prasad for India to declare its support for unilateral disarmament. It would, Nehru argued, stand in opposition to the democratic views of the majority of Indians.[35] Similarly, while the United Nations General Assembly had supported a resolution in 1961 calling for an African 'denuclearised zone', three years later Nkrumah dismissed calls for a delegation to protest against China's first atomic weapons test.[36] By the mid-1960s, it was increasingly difficult for leaders of post-colonial states to balance their earlier opposition to nuclear imperialism with the geopolitics of the Cold War. Despite the efforts of Boaten, the momentum from the Accra Assembly soon dissipated. When, in 1966, Nkrumah was deposed in a coup d'état, Boaten was redeployed to the Ministry of External Affairs, and plans for a second meeting in Accra were abandoned.[37]

From anti-colonialism to anti-apartheid

The cooperation between Nkrumah and Canon John Collins in the early development of plans for the Accra Assembly hints of another dynamic at play in the relations

---

[33] Don DeLillo, *Libra* (London: Penguin Books, 2011), 313; Alice George, *The Cuban Missile Crisis: The Threshold of Nuclear War* (London: Taylor & Francis Group, 2013), 114–15.
[34] A. Walter Dorn and Robert Pauk, 'Unsung Mediator: U Thant and the Cuban Missile Crisis', *Diplomatic History* 33, no. 2 (2009): 261–92; Mark Laffey and Jutta Weldes, 'Decolonizing the Cuban Missile Crisis', *International Studies Quarterly* 52, no. 3 (2008): 555–77.
[35] Danielson, *American Gandhi*, 293.
[36] Wittner, *Resisting the Bomb*, 390, 440.
[37] Boaten to Accra Assembly Council, 30 March 1966, SPC, JACK, VII-3 Accra Assembly 1962, Correspondence.

between Western and African anti-colonial movements: the personal rivalries that seemed to inflect international solidarity networks. As noted in Chapter 3, Scott wanted the Africa Bureau to transcend the 'stage army of the good' in British anti-colonial circles, dominated by powerful individuals whose motives and ideological alignments he viewed with some suspicion. With similar groups and individuals taking on leading roles in the disarmament movements that had emerged in the latter part of the 1950s, the early 1960s, saw the nexus of anti-nuclear weapons and anti-colonial protest movements begin to show signs of fracture. Long-standing conflicts and rivalries threatened to undermine the loose coalitions of anti-colonial and disarmament movements that had begun to capture public attention and support. The relationship between Scott and Canon John Collins, which had shown strains since the mid-1950s, became fraught by the start of the following decade. The pair differed in numerous ways, as Denis Herbstein has discussed in his account of Collins' decades-long efforts to maintain channels providing financial support for South African activists and their families.[38] In the late 1950s, Collins had overseen fundraising efforts in support of the defendants in the lengthy Treason Trial that followed mass arrests of leaders of opposition movements in 1956. Collins' endeavours with this Defence and Aid Fund came to be regarded with suspicion by Scott and others connected with the Africa Bureau, and in 1960 these had become increasingly hostile. Scott shared accusations made by Nana Mahomo, a PAC representative in London, that South African activists were unhappy with Collins, and that his fundraising efforts favoured the ANC. He also seemed anxious that the remit might expand beyond South Africa to include African protests against Central African Federation and beyond – areas in which the Africa Bureau had taken a close and active interest and felt a kind of proprietorial responsibility.[39]

A parallel dispute with Collins developed after Scott backed the formation of the Committee of 100 and Bertrand Russell's split from CND; Scott's radical action in the Sahara and stint in jail following the Swaffham protests contrasted with Collins' adherence to more 'respectable' forms of protest.[40] Civil disobedience might, he argued, be viewed as a 'sacrificial act', but could at the same time be a 'response to a deeply masochistic urge . . . a deliberately chosen and spectacular sacrifice is not the only form of self-sacrifice nor even always the most self-denying'.[41] Collins' sceptical view might, perhaps, seem less convincing when set alongside his efforts to channel funds to South Africans who had sought jail in the service of a political cause; his animus towards what he considered performative self-sacrifice reflected the depths of animosity that had developed between himself and Scott by the mid-1960s. During 1961, David Astor led discussions around the formation of a centralized committee to oversee the allocation of funds raised in Britain for South Africa. Collins eventually agreed to the establishment of a 'Board of Management' for Defence and Aid, but it soon became clear that the arrangement was unworkable.[42] Between 1959 and 1962,

---

[38] Herbstein, *White Lies*, 56–8.
[39] Collins, *Faith Under Fire*.
[40] Herbstein, *White Lies*, 59.
[41] Collins, *Faith Under Fire*, 336.
[42] Herbstein, *White Lies*, 66.

Collins and Scott had taken divergent paths in terms of their efforts to promote international solidarity with South African liberation movements. Scott, as we have seen, had focused on action and attempts to harness the energies of a new generation of radical activists and combine the causes of peace and anti-colonialism. Collins, in contrast, was the organizer and fixer. When the British campaign to boycott South African goods, launched by the Committee of African Organisations in the summer of 1959, began to founder later in the year (as the plans for the Sahara protest were being finalized), Collins gave his backing to a revived boycott campaign which would gain momentum into the following year and become one of the main foundations of the British Anti-Apartheid Movement.[43] And in December 1961, as Scott was preparing for the Brummana conference, Collins accompanied the ANC president Albert Lutuli as he travelled to Oslo to receive the Nobel Peace Prize.[44]

But Scott continued to develop plans for campaigns against apartheid in South Africa, via the Africa Bureau and WPB. In 1962, he set out a prospectus to reinvigorate the Africa Bureau's engagement with the 'New Struggle for Africa'.[45] His assessment of the prospects for peaceful democratic change in southern Africa was not optimistic:

> The fact remains that in the period that lies ahead, as the struggle against Apartheid becomes more bitter and violent, there will be an increasing need of interpretation of the nature of that struggle, the assertion of the claims of reason, justice and the art of the possible against white fanaticism and the black resentment it provokes.

Despite his long-standing and genuine alignment with African nationalist leaders, Scott's analysis suggested that agency lay in the hands of white governments and that Black groups were more reactive than proactive in their actions. Moreover, his emphasis on the 'art of the possible' gestures towards forms of political compromise that sit uneasily with his apparently uncompromising faith in non-violent action. The response to 'anti-colour emotion' (in both Africa and the United States) ought, he asserted, to be an internationally backed 'down to earth programme of practical economic possibilities . . . and venturesome application of science in the fields of agriculture, industry and economic and social planning'.[46] Much of this 1962 prospectus would be familiar to anyone who had known Scott since the 1940s, including its focus on migrant labour and large-scale development schemes. As in *Attitude to Africa* and on numerous occasions since its publication, Scott's proposals centred on notions of regional development influenced by Lewis Mumford, and drew again on Wolffe's account of the role of multinational mining corporations. There are hints of new influences in the memorandum, too. Along with the proposals for structural change, Scott also proclaimed the value of experiments in the 'utilisation of sun power for water boring etc'. Although there is no evidence of direct influence, Scott's interest in small-scale development technology seems to resonate with ideas that would become associated

---

[43] Skinner, *The Foundations of Anti-Apartheid*.
[44] Collins, *Faith Under Fire*, 227.
[45] Scott, 'The New Struggle for Africa: The Role of the Africa Bureau', BOD, Astor Papers MSS 15363/204 1962–67.
[46] Ibid.

with the economist E. F. Schumacher, who undergone a spiritual and intellectual crisis during the 1950s that had led him to reassess his conventional views on economics. After travelling to Burma in the mid-1950s, he met J. P. Narayan in London in 1958, who became interested in what Schumacher described as 'Buddhist Economics'.[47] In the mid-1960s, Schumacher would launch the Intermediate Technology Group (ITG), whose staff would include Julia Porter, manager of the Africa Bureau's Africa Development Trust, which would be merged with the ITG.[48] The connection between Schumacher and Scott's 1962 memorandum is tenuous, but persuasive; at the very least they illuminate the ways in which Scott continued to be attracted to radical proposals for social and economic development which could be incorporated into his model for systemic transformation. And yet, these remained a fundamentally diffuse and unfocused set of ideas when set in the context of a discussion of southern Africa politics and society.

In his memorandum to the Africa Bureau, Scott also urged the organization to 'take the initiative in building an international movement against apartheid'. Again, Scott's proposal betrayed the tension between his prophetic vision and distrust in the other organizations involved with promoting global solidarity against the policies of the South African government. His call might be read as an implicit critique of the work of organizations such as the American Committee on Africa, who in 1962 had drafted a call for an international 'Appeal for Action' against apartheid based on their earlier 'Declaration of Conscience' campaign of 1957.[49] The 1962 ACOA plan proposed an event in New York on Human Rights Day, with speakers including the South African political leader Oliver Tambo, the Zimbabwean activist Joshua Nkomo, as well as figures linked to Africa Freedom Action, including Koinange, Kaunda and Scott himself. But Scott's thinking may also have been focused on groups in Britain who had taken the lead in coordinating material assistance for South African resistance movements, lobbying for a programme of international sanctions against apartheid and promoting popular campaigns such as the consumer boycott movement in Britain.[50] But Scott's 1962 proposals suggest that he was motivated by more than inter-organizational rivalry and suspicion. His repeated references to 'international action' seemed also to reflect a determination to maintain the momentum of the activist zeal that he had experienced within the transnational networks that had launched the Sahara protest and World Peace Brigade.

As the focus of the political struggle in Northern Rhodesia turned to coalition-building, negotiation and the building of electoral support following the elections of October 1962, the former Africa Freedom Action volunteers began to look elsewhere for opportunities to display the vitality of non-violent action. In particular, pacifist activists steadfastly refused to give up plans to directly address the issue of apartheid in

[47] Robert Leonard, 'E. F. Schumacher and Intermediate Technology', *History of Political Economy* 50 (December 2018): 249–65.
[48] Ibid., 258, fn 19. See also Yates and Chester, *The Troublemaker*, 143.
[49] American Committee on Africa, 'Memorandum on Appeal for Action Against Apartheid', 11 June 1962; 'African Activist Archive', https://africanactivist.msu.edu/record/210-849-24626/, Accessed 10 October 2022.
[50] Gurney, '"A Great Cause"'.

South Africa. In October 1962, the former Africa Freedom Action volunteer marcher, John Papworth, drafted a proposal for a highly ambitious new Africa Freedom Action campaign. In his preamble, Papworth asserted that the original focus on Northern Rhodesia reflected the belief that a UNIP victory in elections would precipitate a collapse in colonial rule throughout southern Africa, including the independence of Angola and Mozambique as well as the British High Commission territories of Basutoland, Bechuanaland and Swaziland. But this somewhat bullish account of the situation in southern Africa was intended as a contrast with the greater challenge faced by opponents of colonialism in South-West Africa, Southern Rhodesia and South Africa, where the 'armed might' of the colonial authorities was 'commeasurate [sic] with the implacable hostility with which they regard African interests'. The struggle for power which would ensue, Papworth continued, would entail

> a loss of human life and a degree of human suffering more monstrous than anything the blood-boltered struggles of the African continent have so far yielded. What is more, the prospects of governments emerging which will be able to base their work on principles of justice, tolerance and charity, already dim, will become remote indeed. The conditions, the values, the attitudes of mind necessary for ordinary democratic forms of government may well. have been destroyed for a generation or more.[51]

The tone and style of Papworth's assessment of the prospects for liberation was not likely to enthuse observers, such as Lyle Tatum, whose sympathies for independence movements were tempered by a more cautious and pragmatic account of the political culture of colonialism in southern Africa. But the kernel of Papworth's vision was that 'only a minute fraction' of the international sympathy for African movements had been drawn into concrete action. He thus proposed the drafting of an 'appeal to conscience' signed by leading public figures. But the main aim of the declaration would be to form an international coordinating body, whose structures would enable a more ambitious programme of action to be launched. The second stage of this campaign would therefore be a global petition, supporting the original appeal and calling on the South African government. The scope of Papworth's grandiose plan is perhaps best illustrated by his confident assertion that the petition would aim to collect 100 million signatures around the world. Alongside the petition campaign would be a fundraising exercise to secure the resources to launch the third phase of the protest: a global boycott of South Africa.

Papworth argued that the rising strength of independent African and Asian countries and the more sympathetic view of the Kennedy administration towards anti-colonial movements would give his plan a greater chance of success. For contemporaries, the rising influence of the emerging bloc of independent African states at the United Nations did seem palpable; in August 1962, the US Assistant Secretary of State for African Affairs, Gerhard Mennon-Williams, had called – unsuccessfully – for the State Department to block export guarantees to US mining companies with interests in

---

[51] Proposal for Africa Freedom Action, 16 October 1962, SPC Muste 89/39 Africa Freedom Action.

South Africa. More significantly, the US government would impose an arms embargo on South Africa the following year, shortly before the UN Security Council voted in favour of a worldwide voluntary ban on weapons sales to the apartheid state.[52] But, these were largely symbolic gestures that failed to build a momentum for an internationally coordinated programme of sanctions.[53] Ultimately, Papworth's plan suffered from a failure to appreciate or account for the realities of South African trade relations around the world, in which African and Asian territories were far less significant than Britain, North America and Europe.[54]

As such, in its third phase, Papworth's plan began to diverge into political fantasy. Without any sense of an enforcement regime, Papworth declared that no South African ships or aircraft would be able to dock or land around the world. 'Not a gram of gold or a speck of diamond dust would be purchased', he added, nor any other industrial or agricultural product from South Africa. During the following year, a British Cabinet Office Working Committee suggested that South Africa had the capacity for a high level of self-sufficiency in the face of a boycott; more importantly, most advocates of economic sanctions recognized that the chief challenge would be in policing a boycott – which for some would require the deployment of naval forces to blockade the country.[55] Given the evidence of contemporary events around Cuba, it seems incredible that a pacifist would be recommending a course of action that would likely lead to the mobilization of a significant military force. But Papworth moved quickly on, 'assuming the success of such a boycott', which would, he assessed, be severe. He acknowledged that 'economic distress on a mass scale' would likely result in civil unrest and violence. In order to minimize this, Papworth also assumed that Africa Freedom Action would have worked with the United Nations in advance to have a force ready to undertake the necessary police action in the country and to 'provide an orderly basis for the transfer to majority rule'.[56] In this regard, Papworth's proposal seemed to reflect a fundamental misunderstanding of the global political economy; it seems more a pastiche of political pragmatism than a genuine programme for action. As a narrative account of the end of minority rule in southern Africa, it closely resembled Arthur Keppel-Jones' 1947 dystopian novel *When Smuts Goes*.[57]

But, in some respects, Papworth's plan prefigured the aspects of the global anti-apartheid movement that would develop over the following three decades. It imagined

[52] William Minter and Sylvia Hill, 'Anti-Apartheid Solidarity in United States-South African Relations: From the Margins to the Mainstream', in *The Road to Democracy in South Africa, 3 Part 1, International Solidarity*, edited by South African Democracy Education Trust (Pretoria: Unisa Press, 2008), 761.
[53] Ronald Segal, ed., *Sanctions against South Africa* (Harmondsworth: Penguin Books, 1964); see also Simon Stevens, 'Boycotts and Sanctions against South Africa: An International History, 1946–1970', (Ph.D. thesis, New York: Columbia University, 2016); Rob Skinner, '"Every Bite Buys a Bullet": Sanctions, Boycotts and Solidarity in Transnational Anti-Apartheid Activism', *Moving the Social* 57 (2017): 97–114.
[54] Ryan M. Irwin, *Gordian Knot: Apartheid and the Unmaking of the Liberal World Order* (Oxford: Oxford University Press, 2012).
[55] Skinner, *The Foundations of Anti-Apartheid*.
[56] John Papworth, 'A Proposal for Africa Freedom Action', 16 October 1962, BOD, Scott Papers. (5770) 48/2.
[57] Arthur Keppel-Jones, *When Smuts Goes: A History of South Africa from 1952 to 2010* (Pietermaritzburg: Shuter & Shooter, 1949).

a coalition of local campaigns into a wider, more diffuse movement; by the 1980s a global anti-apartheid coalesce around a loose grouping of national campaigns that, despite significant local differences, would be bound together by an emotional politics of 'solidarity' and moral principles of anti-racism.[58] At its strongest, this movement would be most effective in its consciousness-raising efforts that, as Papworth suggested, built on a general 'appeal to conscience'. Papworth was also correct in assuming that the United Nations and other inter- and supra-national organizations, such as the Commonwealth, European Community and Organisation of African Unity, would play a key role in mobilizing political action and declarations of solidarity. In contrast to Papworth's estimation of the power of UN agencies as such, these international efforts would, however, have their greatest impact in fostering a multiplier effect for external pressures on the apartheid state enacted by individual states and multinational corporations.

But Papworth's plan did receive some serious consideration and was, it seems, discussed at length by Scott, Muste, Rustin and others in New York. This group appeared to recognize some of its key flaws and, without dismissing it outright, Muste noted that they doubted the 'wisdom of spending...slender resources' on an appeal to public opinion, when the effectiveness of economic sanctions would depend on the attitudes and actions of a 'few great powers'. Muste noted that, although a public consumer boycott might have some impact in Britain, effective international action against apartheid would need to be rooted in diplomatic efforts and coordinated joint action led by a small group of powerful states including the United States and USSR.[59] But for Scott, the concept of 'international action' represented more than a scale of political engagement beyond the nation, or an attempt to combine localized campaigns in an effort to heighten their effectiveness. In 'The New Struggle for Africa' he presented international mobilization as something other than strategy; the practice of coordinating action between different national groups would be an end in itself. International action, he argued, would require the Africa Bureau to 'be the servant of an inter-dependence which is inevitable, but can be as exciting and adventurous as a voyage of discovery into space'.[60] He concluded his memorandum with an appeal to a new generation of activists:

> A call must go out to the younger generation of the world to resist the terror of old bigotries and false values that have no meaning today whether it be the legalised violence of western countries such as South Africa or the military violence of the Communist world against the growing liberal and humanist spirit which is trying to break through the hard crust of authoritarianism and state imposed uniformity.... The young of today in many countries are in ever increasing revolt against bigotry and authoritarianism... all who are discriminated against,

---

[58] Anna Konieczna and Rob Skinner, 'Introduction: Anti-Apartheid in Global History', in *A Global History of Anti-Apartheid 'Forward to Freedom' in South Africa*, edited by Anna Konieczna and Rob Skinner (Basingstoke: Palgrave, 2019), 1–30.
[59] Muste to Sutherland, 9 November 1962, SPC Muste 89/22 WPB Correspondence.
[60] Scott, 'The New Struggle for Africa: The Role of the Africa Bureau', BOD, Astor Papers MSS 15363/204 1962–67, 10.

must rise up and fight again for freedom in the world, but particularly the young, whatever their colour or race or nation or religion – because the old who have got control of the world are perpetuating the false values and divisions of humanity by establishment religions and outdated political creeds. And they have brought the civilised world to the brink of a crisis of its very existence.[61]

Scott had found inspiration in the younger activists of the DAC during his involvement with the Sahara protest and direct-action campaigns in Britain. He appears to have recognized the vitality of younger protestors, whose values and campaigns focused on issues, including peace, anti-racism, gender and sexuality, that constituted a rejection of the norms and principles of their parents' generation.[62] But this did not mean that Scott's activities remained relevant. By late 1962, although he remained a respected figure honoured for his pioneering role in promoting worldwide opposition to colonialism in southern Africa, the Anti-Apartheid Movement and Collins' Defence and Aid Fund had become the primary centres of both British and international campaigns on the issue that now dominated debate at the United Nations.[63] During the mid-1960s, his involvement with the Africa Bureau would diminish significantly. The catalyst for this was a lengthy absence from Britain in the cause of a campaign with which he first began to engage in the aftermath of the Africa Freedom Action project: the civil conflict in Nagaland on the north-eastern border of India and Burma.

Changing landscapes: The Dehli–Peking march

While Sutherland and Ram engaged in their unsuccessful efforts to establish the Dar es Salaam training centre, Scott, Rustin, Muste and other WPB activists had turned their attention further east. On 20 October 1962, just as tensions around Cuba between the United States and Soviet Union were reaching their peak, Chinese military forces launched a surprise offensive across the disputed north-eastern border between India and Tibet. While China withdraw its forces a month later, the brief conflict served to heighten the sense of a global Cold War crisis, undermined India's claim of leadership in the non-aligned world and underlined the changing nature of political power in a point-colonial world.[64] Soon after the initial offensive, Jayaprakash Narayan called for Shanti Sena volunteers to travel to the region, but other Gandhian activists, including Vinoba Bhave, seemed to support a more partisan view of the conflict.[65] As Devi Prasad noted in an assessment of the Border War produced in December 1962, the response by the Sarva Seva Sangh, the alliance of Gandhian organizations formed in 1948 led by Bhave, was to declare their sympathy for the Indian government and

---

[61] Ibid.
[62] Lent, *British Social Movements Since 1945*.
[63] Yates and Chester, *The Troublemaker*, 238–40.
[64] David R. Devereux, 'The Sino-Indian War of 1962 in Anglo-American Relations', *Journal of Contemporary History* 44, no. 1 (2009): 71–87; see also David M. Malone and Rohan Mukherjee, 'India and China: Conflict and Cooperation', *Survival* 52, no. 1 (2010): 137–58.
[65] Weber, *Gandhi's Peace Army*, 1st ed., 22.

pledge to work for 'economic and social revolution' rather than oppose the war with non-violent methods.[66]

Members of the World Peace Brigade, however, began to make plans for a 'friendship' march from Dehli to Beijing. The idea of a march was first proposed by the WPB and WRI activist Ed Lazar, a veteran of both the earlier CNVA peace marches in the United States and Europe. In this case, however, rather than raising public consciousness of the long-term problem of the nuclear Cold War, the aim was to express 'the friendship and unity of peoples irrespective of the policies pursued by their governments'.[67] In a working paper drafted in November 1962, before the Chinese withdrawal, Lazar set out an assessment of the border conflict that defined it as a consequence of the refusal to recognize the Communist Chinese government in Beijing within international institutions, but also as evidence of an emergent militancy in Indian foreign policy.[68] For peace activists, the conflict with China was set in the same analytical frame as the Indian invasion of Goa in late 1961, which had taken place just as Portuguese forces had begun to suppress the popular uprising against colonialism in Angola, and mobilized military forces in other African territories under its control. Lazar, therefore, suggested that the worldwide non-violent movement ought to launch a campaign to 'establish human ties with the Chinese and Indian people; to challenge them to live up to their past insights, wisdom and tolerance'. He proposed that a walk – led by either Vinoba Bhave or an international team of volunteers – should set out across India, continue through Ladakh in Indian-controlled Kashmir and then across the Himalayan mountains into China.

In late 1962, Muste travelled to India, where he met with Ed Lazar and J. P. Narayan before contacting the WPB regional councils to request support. At an emergency meeting held on New Year's Eve, the North American Council of the WPB agreed to Muste's request that the Council sponsor the march and send US participants including Rustin.[69] The plans were then discussed at a joint meeting of the WPB Executive and European Councils in London in January 1963, after which the three regional directors of the WPB published a memorandum setting out the plans for a march.[70] These were largely along the lines of Lazar's proposal, with the primary aim of the protest being to foster communication, understanding and friendship between the peoples of India and China. The plan envisaged a march of around fifteen individuals, two-thirds of whom would be international volunteers organized by the Peace Brigade. A number of conditions were set for WPB participation, following discussions at the London conference which raised concerns around the possibility that the march would be seen as supporting the Indian government, and that, in the view of Bayard Rustin, it needed to offer 'concrete alternatives to the border hostilities' rather than 'vague ideas of peace and friendship'.[71] The conditions stated explicitly that the protest would engage, in both India and China with 'positive nonviolent alternatives to the war in which their

[66] 'Action on China-India Border Conflict', 25 December 1962, SPC, WPB Dehli-Peking March.
[67] WPB Executive Committee Minutes, 9 January1963, SPC Muste 89/22 WPB Executive Committee.
[68] Lazar, 'Working Paper: China-India Conflict and the World Peace Brigade', 18 November 1962, SPC, WPB Dehli-Peking March.
[69] Minutes, WPB North American Regional Council, 31 December 1962, SPC – WPB – North American Council.
[70] 'Memorandum on Aims and Objectives', 14 January 1963, SPC, WPB Dehli-Peking March.
[71] WPB Executive Committee Minutes, 9 January1963, SPC, Muste 89/22 WPB Executive Committee.

countries are involved'. In reality these ambitions were somewhat compromised from the outset, as the Chinese activists with whom the organizers had initiated contact seemed to have at least indirect ties with the state, including Li Chuwen, a pastor at the Shanghai Community Church (and covert member of the Chinese Communist Party), and members of the Chinese People's Committee for World Peace (an affiliate of the World Peace Council).[72]

The marchers set out in early March 1963 and were immediately denounced by the official Chinese news agency as 'Indian reactionaries in collusion with US imperialism'.[73] The marchers' claim that their action was aimed at developing 'friendly relations' was dismissed as a 'false flag', while the reports also included a purported quote from Narayan stating that the march was designed to counter Chinese aggression. A week after it began, the demonstrators had reached the town of Gabhana in Alighar, around 100 kilometres from the capital. Divisions had already emerged within the Indian organizers, with Bhave having proposed that Gandhians should deploy non-violent action in service of the Indian state, while Narayan asserted that campaigners should oppose all militarism.[74] In Gabhana, Lazar reported that tensions had also developed between the Shanti Sena/WPB contingent and the Congress leader Pandit Sunderlal of the All-India Indian Peace Council, who had repeated some of the assertions of the Chinese press about Narayan's political position and anti-China stance. Caught up in local political disputes suffering from internal divisions, and thwarted by the refusal of the Chinese authorities to grant the marchers permission to enter the country, the project would ultimately be no more successful than Africa Freedom Action. A small group of marchers nevertheless continued across the country, and by September the group had reached the north-eastern province of Assam. The following month, they were finally halted at the border with Burma, and even Muste, returning from the United States to lead negotiations, failed to persuade Chinese officials to allow the march to continue.[75] Although some participants claimed success in bringing 'a message of disarmament, non-violence and friendship to millions of people in India',[76] the World Peace Brigade seemed again to have achieved little aside from revealing the contradictions and tensions within their movement.

For Michael Scott, the march brought a number of underlying tensions in his relationship to the WPB and to pacifism more generally into sharp focus. Since his first engagement with the United Nations in the 1940s, he had accepted moral and material support from the Indian government and had worked closely with Gandhian activists including Narayan. But he had also begun to take a close interest in an issue that would complicate these relationships. In 1960, he had come into contact with Angami Zapu Phizo, a leader of the separatist Naga nationalist movement on the border with Burma in the north-east of India.[77] Phizo worked for a time at the Africa Bureau, and the

[72] WPB Executive Committee Minutes, 9 January1963, SPC, Muste 89/22 WPB Executive Committee.
[73] 'Indian Reactionaries Begin Peace March', 2 March 1963, SPC, WPB Dehli-Peking March.
[74] Danielson, *American Gandhi*, 294.
[75] Ibid.
[76] George Willoughby, 'We Have Been Walking Six Months', [n.d. September 1963], SPC, WPB Dehli-Peking March.
[77] Yates and Chester, *The Troublemaker*, 243–4; Walker, 'Decolonization in the 1960s'.

Naga claims inspired the formation of the Minority Rights Group by Scott and Astor in 1962. The *Observer* would later receive widespread criticism in India for publishing reports on events in Nagaland.[78] In his campaign on behalf of the Naga and work with the Minority Rights Group, Scott would enter into a form of international advocacy that exposed the ambiguities of the post-war international system in ways that further undermined his reputation at the United Nations. As Astor later argued, the Naga claims revealed the UN to be a 'particularly inhospitable forum for the rights of minorities'.[79] And, as the recent analysis by Lydia Walker has shown, the difficulties Scott faced when attempting to present the Naga case in New York reflected the fault lines that defined acceptable and illegitimate political demands in the post-war world order.[80] Of course, as Director of the European Regional Council of the WPB, Scott was one of the first to be contacted by J. P. Narayan in October 1962 seeking advice on possible intervention in the conflict.[81] But when the march got underway in the following March, Scott's allegiances seemed to pull in different directions. Just four days after the marchers left the Indian capital, Scott returned to New Delhi, ostensibly to discuss organizational issues with Nehru. Instead, as Charles Walker later reported to Muste, the march suffered its 'first jolt' when Scott instead questioned Nehru at length on the conflict in Nagaland.[82] Together with signs of emerging 'internal ideological dissension', correspondence from the marchers seems to reveal more division than friendship.[83]

In May 1963, Scott tendered his resignation from the World Peace Brigade, feeling that his deep involvement with the Naga dispute, and the refusal of the WPB Council to consider becoming involved, made his position untenable. He added that the WPB had become 'a launching pad for projects involving small teams of people in conflict areas' rather than the large-scale 'international peace force' he had envisaged at the time of the Brummana conference.[84] Muste, in response, concurred with Scott's conclusion that his involvement (although Muste described it as a 'preoccupation') with the Naga dispute had a detrimental impact on the peace march. He also agreed that Scott's vision for the Brigade differed significantly from those of others involved in its formation. But he also suggested that Scott continue to act as Regional Director until he, Scott and Narayan were able to attend a meeting of the WPB Council together.[85] A month later, when J. P. Narayan had also suggested that he ought to step down from the WPB, Muste again insisted that such decisions ought to be made at the full meeting of the WPB Council.[86] In July, however, Scott confirmed his decision to resign from the World Peace Brigade. It was, he explained, a consequence of a dilemma with which he had long struggled concerning the distinctions between non-violence and pacifism. He was certain of his commitment to the former, but its distinctions from pacifism had been 'brought to head for me personally over my association with liberation

[78] Cockett, *David Astor*, 205–6.
[79] Jeremy Lewis, *David Astor* (London: Vintage Digital, 2016).
[80] Walker, 'Decolonization in the 1960s'.
[81] Telegram, Narayan to Scott, 24 October 1962, BOD Scott Papers 5770 Box 48 (2).
[82] Walker to Muste, 15 May 1963, SPC WPB Dehli-Peking March.
[83] Ibid.
[84] Scott to Muste, 17 May 1963, SPC, WPB Dehli-Peking March.
[85] Muste to Scott, 22 May, 1963, SPC, WPB Dehli-Peking March.
[86] Muste to Narayan, 4 June 1963, SPC, WPB Dehli-Peking March.

movements in Africa and with the Naga'.[87] His action on behalf of the Naga had, he claimed, resulted in Lazar requesting that he withdraw from the Dehli–Peking march. In his resignation letter, he also cited the tensions that had arisen between himself and Narayan around Nagaland but also Narayan's view of China. He thus reiterated his intention to resign, but also suggested that the WPB ought to consider 'the problem of relationships with other organisations and movements not committed to pacifism or necessarily to non-violence as an absolute article in itself'.[88] In 1963, Scott thus found himself in a similar position to Houser when he visited Angola in 1961; aligned with an organization engaged in an active violent conflict, he began to voice concerns over the viability of the WPB.

But, it is not clear whether he did sever his links with the WPB in July 1963. In conversation with Devi Prasad of War Resisters' International in early 1964, he spoke of his concerns about the WPB and that he was considering 'giving up his chairmanship'. He restated his belief that the Brigade had been formed without deciding on clear aims and made the extraordinary suggestion that it 'should be prepared to go and take control of the situation . . . even, if necessary, with arms'.[89] Prior to this, he had written in the *Observer* of the 'pacifist's dilemma' that had emerged, in which, unlike the 'old pacifism, pre-occupied with conscientious objection', contemporary campaigners for peace and justice 'are not necessarily committed to non-violence as a first principle'.[90] In the piece, ostensibly a review of a collection of essays on non-violence, Scott suggested that Naga efforts to appeal using non-violent means had been met with 'the armed might of the Indian army' had left them little choice other than turn to armed resistance. This was, of course, essentially the same argument that Fanon had made in Accra in 1960 and Mandela in Addis Ababa in 1962. Scott's comments in 1964 seem remarkable given that for much of the previous two decades, the means of peaceful resistance had been at least as important as the ends of democracy, self-determination and racial equality. It is also possible, as his biographers suggest, that Scott's engagement with the Nagaland conflict simply represented an activist career in decline.[91] But all peace campaigners found themselves facing a similar dilemma in the early 1960s. Muste noted that the majority were 'in agreement with the position of support for the freedom struggle . . . despite the violence perpetrated'. As editor of *Liberation*, he acknowledged that he had faced a significant degree of criticism for its support for the Cuban revolution.[92]

And yet, plans for non-violent intervention in worldwide conflicts continued to circulate in the mid-1960s. As the World Peace Brigade began preparations for its march across India in 1963, direct-action campaigners in Britain began to sketch out ideas for a new form of peace force known as the 'Crisis Contingent', which would train volunteers in preparation for interventions during critical events such as the Cuban Missile Crisis.[93]

[87] Scott to Muste and Narayan, 9 July 1963, BOD Scott Papers 5770 Box 48 (2).
[88] Ibid.
[89] Devi Prasad, 'Notes on a Conversation with Michael Scott', 25 February 1964, BOD, Scott Papers. (5770) 59.
[90] Scott, 'The Pacifist's Dilemma', *Observer*, 19 January 1964.
[91] Yates and Chester, *The Troublemaker*, 255–62.
[92] Muste to Narayan, 4 June 1963, SPC, WPB Dehli-Peking March.
[93] 'Report on the Project to Form a Crisis Contingent', 7 February 1963, London School of Economics, Special Collections (LSE), Papers of Pat Arrowsmith, ARROWSMITH 6 Folder 7 (1).

Two years later, members of the group set out proposals for a non-violent 'invasion' of Southern Rhodesia, supported by the British government. The feasibility of the plan would be tested via a 'socio-drama' in four scenes that would enact potential encounters, including meetings with the British prime minister Harold Wilson and African leaders, as well as the ultimate confrontation with armed Rhodesian security forces.[94] The plan concluded with the suggestion that it might be used to launch a revival of the World Peace Brigade. But, despite the belief of the Brigade's founders in 1962 that the engagement between peace activism and movements for national liberation was an opportunity to expand the influence of 'militant non-violence', three years later the movement seemed gripped by inertia and unable to undertake anything more than role-play. The Brigade was never formally dissolved, but instead 'fell into disuse'.[95] The legacies of campaigns such as Africa Freedom Action were ambiguous, although the participants would continue in their efforts to promote peace and freedom.

Endings, legacies and aftermaths

In 1963, as Michael Scott turned his attention to the Nagaland dispute, Rustin focused his efforts on a new project with one of his oldest political comrades, A. Philip Randolph: a major civil rights march in Washington to mark the centenary of the emancipation proclamation. Rustin had travelled to India for the start of the Dehli–Peking march, but quickly returned to the United States to resume work on what had been re-framed as a march for 'Jobs and Freedom' and, together with Randolph, managed to secure, through persuasion and compromise, a broad alliance of all civil rights groups, from the militant pacifists at CORE to the staunch opponents of civil disobedience in the NAACP.[96] The march was shaped by the political culture of social and civil rights protest in America, but, as Wittner has suggested, it also drew some inspiration from Rustin's experience at the Aldermaston march in 1958.[97] And, of course, the March on Washington followed in the wake of the ambitious projects Rustin had helped to coordinate in Africa. Rustin, appointed as a deputy director for the march, took command of the logistical challenge of coordinating the arrival, accommodation and care for over 100,000 demonstrators. In the event, it was estimated that up to four times that number participated in the March on Washington on 28 August 1963, which has become a centrepiece of the historical narrative of the civil rights movement and a touchstone for post-war American history. The pre-eminent image of the day was the majestic speech given by Martin Luther King, but the argument that the moment was made 'both possible and meaningful' by Rustin's planning is

---

[94] 'Proposals for a Non-violent Invasion of Rhodesia', 23 November 1965, LSE ARROWSMITH 6 Folder 7 (1).
[95] Charles C. Walker, 'Nonviolence in Eastern Africa, 1962–4', in *Liberation without Violence: A Third-Party Approach,* edited by A Paul Hare and Herbert H. Blumberg (London: Collings, 1977), 157–77, p. 175.
[96] Anderson, *Bayard Rustin,* 241–2.
[97] Wittner, *Resisting the Bomb,* 58.

persuasive.[98] Africa Freedom Action, meanwhile, has generally been little more than a footnote in the history of decolonization. In stark contrast to his work in Africa, Rustin helped to reshape the repertoire of US political activism, as the set-piece march on the capital, ending at the Lincoln Memorial became a 'culturally embedded' element of US politics.[99]

The story of the Africa Freedom Action march challenges historians to consider the meaning of 'significance' in our analysis of past events. In contrast to the March on Washington it was a 'non-event' that does not easily fit into a standard historical narrative concerned with cause and consequence, origin and effect. The march did not happen. Militant liberation struggles, not non-violent civil disobedience, marked the experience of decolonization in southern Africa in the 1970s and 1980s.[100] The campaigns examined in this book might seem marginal and insignificant, but the efforts of the World Peace Brigade and others nevertheless provide a compelling case study in the history of decolonization and the process through which Africa and the 'Third World' became a mooring point in the imagination and identities of western social movements. In the context of France, Christoph Kalter has argued that anti-colonialism was a defining characteristic of the radical 'New Left' that emerged during the 1960s and that the 'discovery' of the Third World (*tiers monde*) by French radicals emphasizes the interconnections between localities, organizations and actors in contemporary perceptions of global integration.[101] The interweaving of peace and anti-colonial movements in the late 1950s and early 1960s suggests that these interconnections extended beyond the field of radical left politics and included those who embraced conventional social democratic ideologies, such as Rustin and Muste, as well as those such as Scott whose political values were difficult to align with standard ideological polarities. If we must seek significance in the frustrated projects and unfulfilled ambitions of the Sahara team and the phantom march from Tanganyika to Northern Rhodesia, it is found perhaps in the ways in which these schemes illustrate the compelling influence of decolonization (both as process and vision) within radical activist networks.

The Sahara protest and the World Peace Brigade thus represented emergent forms of transnational social movements that were forged in the context of Cold War anxieties and drew inspiration from the process of decolonization. The protest against the French nuclear tests in 1960 originated in attempts to construct a pan-European anti-nuclear weapons movement, despite the fragility of the links between national movements. As Nehring suggests, moreover, these Western European movements were fundamentally shaped by national political cultures, rather than forms of global consciousness.[102] Instead, the activists that connected the Sahara protest and the World Peace Brigade, combined networks of pacifists and advocates

---

[98] Charles Bloomstein, quoted in Anderson, *Bayard Rustin*, 264.
[99] Tarrow, *Power in Movement*, 114.
[100] See for example, Alexander, McGregor, and Ranger, *Violence & Memory*; Simpson, *Umkhonto We Sizwe*.
[101] Christoph Kalter, *The Discovery of the Third World: Decolonization and the Rise of the New Left in France, c.1950–1976* (Cambridge: Cambridge University Press, 2016), 1; 5–6.
[102] Nehring, *Politics of Security*.

of Gandhian non-violence linking British and US anti-nuclear movements. These transatlantic networks had, moreover, close connections with African nationalist movements and pan-African networks, and it was these connections that facilitated the launch of transnational protests in Africa in 1960 and 1962. However, despite the intersection between African nationalist anti-colonial and transnational disarmament and peace movements, the resulting coalitions were often fraught and brittle. The Sahara protest and Africa Freedom Action revealed the fault lines between peace movements and nationalism, and while the wider ambitions of the World Peace Brigade sought to bring into being a transnational community with 'open, porous, revisable and interactive' boundaries, it ultimately reflected the limits of such an ambition.[103]

From the evaluation of the post-war crisis of colonialism in *Attitude to Africa* to the Sahara team's embrace of the campaign against 'nuclear imperialism' and the alignment of the WPB with UNIP, Western activists found common cause with African nationalism. But this alliance did not result in the formation of effective and long-standing transnational movements. Campaigns that aimed to cut across national borders seemed most fragile where they directly engaged with anti-colonial nationalist agendas. Moreover, the process of decolonization routinized the nation state; transnational campaigns established in the cause of national liberation carried within themselves the seed of their own contradiction. But transnational narratives are perhaps best understood not as an attempt to move beyond the framework of the nation as an analytical category, but instead reveal the ways in which processes of modernity, including decolonization 'occur in varied and often unpredictable ways'.[104] The campaigns against the French nuclear tests and the attempts to adopt Gandhian non-violence in the cause of national liberation movements in central Africa did not in themselves foster the development of powerful and long-lasting transnational movements. But they contributed to the development of a language of protest that centred on notions of solidarity and global liberation that would be adopted, adapted and reinterpreted in particular national and local contexts.[105]

The transnational dimension of Cold War peace movements emerged in the interactions of global networks of activists, rather than the development of movements across national boundaries. The Sahara protest and Africa Freedom Action helped to shape a radical political space that fostered the transmissions of values of social justice, human rights and environmental concern across the boundaries of the nation state. Transnational peace activists felt increasingly anxious about the nexus of Cold War nuclear rivalries and decolonization at the start of the 1960s. Responses to the French tests in the Sahara reveal those anxieties in sharp relief, insofar as they interwove universalist fears over the emergence of a new nuclear power with more particular national concerns. European activists felt such concerns in relation to their own

---

[103] On transnational movements and open communities, see Patricia Clavin, 'Defining Transnationalism', *Contemporary European History* 14, no. 4 (2005): 439.

[104] Bayly, et al., 'AHR Conversation', 1459.

[105] Håkan Thörn, *Anti-Apartheid and the Emergence of a Global Civil Society* (Basingstoke: Palgrave Macmillan, 2006); Konieczna and Skinner, *A Global History of Anti-Apartheid 'Forward to Freedom' in South Africa*.

particular experiences of decolonization. In the British case, these were embodied in the popular view that disarmament was a path back to world influence, while French campaigns against the tests were muted by anxieties over a more violent disengagement from the empire. African views, meanwhile, were shaped by the fear that independence would be tempered by the emergence of neocolonialism. The events in the Congo, South Africa and Algeria that shaped the debates around 'nuclear imperialism' were, moreover, viewed through a filter of Cold War anxieties.

Was non-violent resistance therefore a lost cause in the context of African decolonization? Advocates often defined solidarity in anachronistic terms, employing a universalist discourse that, despite espousing the interests of African people, retained much of the language of colonial liberalism. While Scott revealed the ambiguities of 'trusteeship' his prospectus for a new politics failed to provide an alternative discourse of freedom. As Lydia Walker discusses in her recent analysis of his engagement with South-West Africa and Nagaland, however, these campaigns confronted the fundamental dilemma of advocacy. Scott aimed to speak for African initiatives and ambitions but struggled to achieve this ambition without simultaneously undermining the capacity for African organizations and individuals to voice political claims on their own terms.[106] Kalter makes a similar argument in suggesting that post-colonial Third World solidarity liberated Western radicalism from the structures of the colonial period, but its knowledge and critical understanding of Western power 'owed its very existence to the globalisation of older, western categories' including notions of class, race, the nation, and development.[107] The radical non-violent action of the World Peace Brigade sought to build on the anti-colonial legacies of Gandhian resistance, but these were refracted through a lens shaped by interactions with the politics of nationalism.

Equally significant were the tensions between the ideals of Gandhian non-violence and the sometimes-brutal realities of state politics. Kaunda encountered these realities and challenged his Gandhian supporters to provide a solution. The Dehli-Peking peace march and Scott's engagement with the Naga dispute similarly provided evidence of the frictions between post-colonial states, supra-national idealism from 'above' and minority nationalist claims from 'below'. In this context, the organizers of such projects were forced to confront the relationship between their non-violent ethics and the resort to violence, either by the state in response to invasion or nationalist groups in response to state oppression. That is not to suggest that schemes for violent resistance had a practical advantage – not all revolutionary cadres would have the success (or luck) of Castro's rebels in Cuba, for example – but strict adherence to non-violent action seemed less persuasive in the face of the coercive power of the nation state. But campaigns such as Africa Freedom Action nonetheless provide a lens with which to examine the language of international solidarity with the Third World and more specifically with liberation movements in southern Africa that took shape in the 1960s and 1970s. Solidarity took a number of forms but underlying them all was

---

[106] Walker, 'Decolonization in the 1960s'.
[107] Kalter, *The Discovery of the Third World*, 434.

a sense of imminent crisis, an intensification of the struggle between white and Black nationalists, and a seemingly inexorable journey towards armed struggle.

Similarly, peace activists' proposals for practical forms of engagement through projects of social and economic development, despite parallels with projects of colonial knowledge and power, reflected the ambiguities of the post-colonial experience. As the Dar es Salaam training centre wound down its activities in early 1963, the representative of the Asian Regional Council of the WPB, Suresh Ram, interviewed Julius Nyerere. The Tanganyikan leader spoke with enthusiasm about his government's plans for development and the emotional excitement that had been generated by Ujamaa, its programme for African socialism. Nyerere addressed the similarities between his plan and those of the WPB leader Jayaprakash Narayan. Tanganyikans had an advantage over Narayan and his supporters, he argued, because they 'have the chance to put those views into practice . . . we can build up rural life, give it a modern look and make the people participate in the revolutionary process. They can see to accomplishing a revolution by their own endeavour'.[108] The future of the WPB, he suggested, would be in providing advice and support as Africans began to confront post-colonial social and economic challenges. In the ten years since the publication of *Attitude to Africa* the continent had been transformed, in ways that had not been predicted by its authors. But the similarities between Nyerere's vision for development and their earlier enthusiasm for the social transformations that could be initiated in Africa are striking. Moreover, the programmes of non-violent education envisaged by Randle and Sutherland in their ill-fated plans for training centres in Africa find echoes in more recent programmes for the development of 'peace by peaceful means'.[109] The failure to establish schools for non-violence in the early 1960s reflected circumstances in which state-sponsored assistance for African anti-colonial movements had already begun to focus on preparations for revolutionary violence; political contingencies were not congenial to transnational programmes for non-violence, but this did not mean that the programmes advocated by Randle and the WPB were inherently flawed.

In the conclusion of his 1964 essay on the problems of the peace movement, A. J. Muste quoted the British writer and journalist Mervyn Jones who, during the peak of the first wave of the nuclear disarmament campaign, had written that the central issue was not specific weapons, but the question of acquiescence to violence. 'If we consent to violence', Jones argued, 'then we have gone hopelessly astray'.[110] This, then, was the credo of those who sought to harness non-violence to the struggle against colonialism. The primary danger was the tendency for violence to be rationalized as the only realistic response to powerful forces of injustice. The struggle against colonialism seemingly overwhelmed the persuasive power of non-violence, and the evidence of the Sahara protest and Africa Freedom Action suggests that, by the mid-1960s, transnational advocates of non-violence were, as Charles Walker predicted,

[108] 'Towards Ujamaa in Tanganyika' an Interview with Julius Nyerere', 10 December 1962, SPC – WPB – North American Council 1963–68.
[109] Johan Galtung, *Peace by Peaceful Means: Peace and Conflict, Development and Civilization* (London: SAGE Publications, Limited, 1996), 270.
[110] Mervyn Jones, 'The Time Is Short', in *Conviction: Essays*, edited by Norman MacKenzie (London: MacGibbon & Kee, 1958).

unable to muster anything more 'sporadic protest', even as nationalist resistance against colonialism in Africa and elsewhere increasingly centred on militant armed struggle.[111]

The challenges encountered by the pacifists who sought to harness non-violence to the cause of decolonization highlight one of the central contradictions of the counter-cultural radicalism that developed in the West in the 1960s. Even as anti-colonial and civil rights protestors turned to militancy, the concept of 'peace' began to take hold as a central precept of a radical generation of politics and protest, symbolized by the widespread adoption of Gerald Holtom's nuclear disarmament emblem, first unveiled at the DAC-organized Aldermaston march of 1958.[112] From civil rights to student protests, 'new' social movements in the West drew on the language of peace in formulating protest identities that stood opposed to the imperialist and establishment values of previous generations. In his analysis of the prospects for peace campaigners in 1964, A. J. Muste remained convinced that the radicalism of non-violence had to be maintained. He urged pacifists to identify more 'creative forms of nonviolent action', rather than seek alliance with the political mainstream. In their struggle against violence and Communism, Muste argued that pacifists should seek not an alignment, but a 'rupture' with liberalism.[113] Instead, as he reached the final years of his life, he implored activists to look beyond nuclear weapons and civil rights and focus on US 'imperialism in the Congo, Vietnam and elsewhere'.[114] The struggle continued, but the means also remained paramount.

---

[111] Walker, 'The Idea of Non-violence'
[112] Andrew Rigby, 'A Peace Symbol's Origins', *Peace Review* 10, no. 3 (1998): 475–9.
[113] Danielson, *American Gandhi*, 302.
[114] Ibid., 303.

Bibliography

Archive material

Amistad Research Center, Tulane University
American Committee on Africa records
Bodleian Library, University of Oxford
Archive of David Astor (MSS 15363)
Records of the Africa Bureau and related organizations (MSS. Afr. s. 1681)
Papers of Guthrie Michael Scott (Mss 5770)
Lambeth Palace Library, London
Papers of Canon John Collins (MS 3294)
London School of Economics, Special Collections
Papers of the Campaign for Nuclear Disarmament (CND)
Special Collections on Peace, Politics and Social Change, University of Bradford
Archive of the Direct Action Committee Against Nuclear War (Cwl DAC)
Papers of Michael Randle (Cwl MR)
Special Collections, School of Oriental and African Studies, London
Papers of the Movement for Colonial Freedom
Swarthmore College Peace Collection
A.J. Muste Papers
Homer A. Jack Papers
Fellowship of Reconciliation Papers (DG 013)
Committee for Nonviolent Activism Records (DG 017)
UK National Archives
The Security Service: Personal Files (KV 2)
Colonial Office: Central Africa and Aden: Original Correspondence (CO 1015)
Dominions Office and Commonwealth Relations Office: Original Correspondence (DO 35)

Publications

Abraham, Itty. *The Making of the Indian Atomic Bomb: Science, Secrecy and the Postcolonial State*. London: Zed Books, 1998.
Adams, Anne V. and Esi Sutherland-Addy. *The Legacy of Efua Sutherland: Pan-African Cultural Activism*. Banbury: Ayebia Clarke, 2007.
Adi, Hakim. 'African Political Thinkers, Pan-Africanism and the Politics of Exile, c.1850–1970'. *Immigrants & Minorities* 30, no. 2–3 (2012): 263–91.
Ahlman, Jeffrey S. 'The Algerian Question in Nkrumah's Ghana, 1958–1960: Debating "Violence" and "Nonviolence" in African Decolonization'. *Africa Today* 57, no. 2 (2010): 66–84.

Ahlman, Jeffrey S. 'Managing the Pan-African Workplace: Discipline, Ideology, and the Cultural Politics of the Ghanaian Bureau of African Affairs, 1959-1966'. *Ghana Studies* 15 (January 2013): 337-71.
Alexander, Jocelyn and JoAnn McGregor. 'War Stories: Guerrilla Narratives of Zimbabwe's Liberation War'. *History Workshop Journal* 57 (2004): 79-100.
Allman, Jean. 'Nuclear Imperialism and the Pan-African Struggle for Peace and Freedom: Ghana, 1959-1962'. *Souls* 10, no. 2 (2008): 83-102.
Allman, Jean. 'Between the Present and History: African Nationalism and Decolonization'. In *The Oxford Handbook of Modern African History*, edited by John Parker and Richard Reid, pp. 224-40. Oxford: Oxford University Press, 2013.
Allman, Jean Marie. *The Quills of the Porcupine: Asante Nationalism in an Emergent Ghana*. Madison: University of Wisconsin Press, 1993.
Alter, Joseph S. *Gandhi's Body: Sex, Diet, and the Politics of Nationalism*. Philadelphia: University of Pennsylvania Press, 2000.
Anderson, Carol. *Eyes off the Prize : The United Nations and the African American Struggle for Human Rights, 1944-1955*. Cambridge and New York: Cambridge University Press, 2003.
Anderson, Carol. 'International Conscience, the Cold War, and Apartheid: The NAACP's Alliance with the Reverend Michael Scott for South West Africa's Liberation, 1946-1951'. *Journal of World History* 19, no. 3 (2008): 297-325.
Anderson, Jervis. *Bayard Rustin : Troubles I've Seen : A Biography*. New York: Harper Collins Publishers, 1997.
Anthony, David Henry. *Max Yergan: Race Man, Internationalist, Cold Warrior*. New York: New York University Press, 2006.
Auden, W. H. *New Year Letter*. London: Faber and Faber, 1941.
Bayly, C. A, Sven Beckert, Matthew Connelly, Isabel Hofmeyr, Wendy Kozol, and Patricia Seed. 'AHR Conversation: On Transnational History'. *The American Historical Review* 111, no. 5 (2006): 1441-64.
Bendjebbar, André. *Histoire secrète de la bombe atomique française*. Paris: Le Cherche Midi Editeur, 2000.
Bennett, Scott H. *Radical Pacifism: The War Resisters League and Gandhian Nonviolence in America, 1915-1963*. Syracuse Studies on Peace and Conflict Resolution. Syracuse, NY: Syracuse University Press, 2003.
Benson, Mary. *A Far Cry: The Making of a South African*, New ed. Randburg: Ravan, 1996.
Betts, Paul. *Ruin and Renewal: Civilizing Europe After World War II*. New York: Basic Books, 2020.
Betts, Raymond F. *Decolonization*. London: Routledge, 2004.
Bhebe, Ngwabi and Terence Ranger, eds. *Soldiers in Zimbabwe's Liberation War*. London: James Currey, 1995.
Biess, Frank. 'Feelings in the Aftermath: Toward a History of Postwar Emotions'. In *Histories of the Aftermath: The Legacies of the Second World War in Europe*, edited by Frank Biess and Robert G. Moeller, 30-48. New York: Berghahn Books, Incorporated, 2010.
Biess, Frank and Robert G. Moeller. *Histories of the Aftermath: The Legacies of the Second World War in Europe*. New York: Berghahn Books, Incorporated, 2010.
Birmingham, David. *Empire in Africa : Angola and Its Neighbors*. Athens: Ohio University Press, 2006.
Boggende, Bert den. 'Richard Roberts' Vision and the Founding of the Fellowship of Reconciliation'. *Albion: A Quarterly Journal Concerned with British Studies* 36, no. 4 (2004): 608-35.

Borstelmann, Thomas. *The Cold War and the Color Line : American Race Relations in the Global Arena*. Cambridge, MA: Harvard University Press, 2001.
Bourke, Joanna. *Fear: A Cultural History*, Paperback ed. London: Virago, 2006.
Brougher, Kerry. 'Art and Nuclear Culture'. *Bulletin of the Atomic Scientists* 69, no. 6 (November 2013): 11–18.
Buettner, Elizabeth. *Europe After Empire: Decolonization, Society, and Culture*. New Approaches to European History. Cambridge: Cambridge University Press, 2016.
Burke, Roland. *Decolonization and the Evolution of International Human Rights*. Philadelphia: University of Pennsylvania Press, 2010.
Burke, Roland. 'Emotional Diplomacy and Human Rights at the United Nations'. *Human Rights Quarterly* 39, no. 2 (2017): 273–95.
Burkett, Jodi. 'Re-Defining British Morality: "Britishness" and the Campaign for Nuclear Disarmament 1958–68'. *Twentieth Century British History* 21, no. 2 (2010): 184–205.
Burkett, Jodi. *Constructing Post-Imperial Britain: Britishness, "Race" and the Radical Left in the 1960s*. Houndmills, Basingstoke, and Hampshire: Palgrave Macmillan, 2013.
Butler, L. J. 'Britain, the United States, and the Demise of the Central African Federation, 1959–63'. *The Journal of Imperial and Commonwealth History* 28, no. 3 (2000): 131–51.
Campbell, J. T. *Songs of Zion: The African Methodist Episcopal Church in the United States and South Africa*. Chapel Hill: University of North Carolina Press, 1998.
Carter, April. 'The Sahara Protest Team'. In *Liberation Without Violence: A Third-Party Approach*, edited by A Paul Hare and Herbert H. Blumberg, 126–56. London: Collings, 1977.
Carter, April. *Peace Movements: International Protest and World Politics Since 1945*. London: Longman, 1992.
Catsam, Derek. *Freedom's Main Line : The Journey of Reconciliation and the Freedom Rides*. Lexington: University Press of Kentucky, 2009.
Catsam, Derek Charles. '"When We Are Tired We Shall Rest": Bus Boycotts in the United States of America and South Africa and Prospects for Comparative History'. *The Journal for Transdisciplinary Research in Southern Africa* 3, no. 1 (2007): 16.
Ceadel, Martin. *Pacifism in Britain, 1914–1945: The Defining of a Faith*. Oxford Historical Monographs. Oxford: Clarendon Press, 1980.
Ceadel, Martin. *Semi-Detached Idealists: The British Peace Movement and International Relations, 1854–1945*. 1 Online Resource (477 pages) vols. Oxford: Oxford University Press, 2000.
Chabal, Patrick and Nuno Vidal, eds. *Angola: The Weight of History*. London: Hurst & Company, 2007.
Christiaens, Kim. '"To Go Further Than Words Alone": The World Peace Council and the Global Orchestration of Vietnam War Campaigns During the 1960s'. In *Protest in the Vietnam War Era*, edited by Alexander Sedlmaier, 13–49. Palgrave Studies in the History of Social Movements. Basingstoke: Palgrave MacMillan, 2022.
Clavin, Patricia. 'Defining Transnationalism'. *Contemporary European History* 14, no. 4 (2005): 421–39.
Cockett, Richard. *David Astor and the Observer*. London: Deutsch, 1991.
Coffey, Rosalind. *The British Press, Public Opinion and the End of Empire in Africa: The 'Wind of Change', 1957–60*. 1 Online Resource vols. Britain and the World. Cham: Palgrave Macmillan, 2022.
Coll, Steve. *The Bin Ladens: An Arabian Family in the American Century*. New York: Penguin Press, 2008.
Collins, Lewis John. *Faith Under Fire*. London: Frewin, 1966.

Collins, Michael. 'Decolonisation and the "Federal Moment"'. *Diplomacy & Statecraft* 24, no. 1 (2013): 21–40.
Conrad, Sebastian and Sorcha O'Hagan. *German Colonialism: A Short History*. Cambridge: Cambridge University Press, 2012.
Cooper, Frederick. 'Possibility and Constraint: African Independence in Historical Perspective'. *The Journal of African History* 49, no. 2 (2008): 167–96.
Cooper, Frederick. 'Writing the History of Development'. *Journal of Modern European History* 8, no. 1 (2010): 5–23.
Cooper, Frederick. *Citizenship Between Empire and Nation: Remaking France and French Africa, 1945–1960*. Princeton, NJ: Princeton University Press, 2014.
Cooper, Frederick. 'Decolonizations, Colonizations, and More Decolonizations: The End of Empire in Time and Space'. *Journal of World History* 33, no. 3 (2022): 491–526.
Cotkin, George. *William James, Public Philosopher*, Reprint ed. Urbana: University of Illinois Press, 1994.
Cowen, M. and R. Shenton. 'The Origin and Course of Fabian Colonialism in Africa'. *Journal of Historical Sociology* 4, no. 2 (1991): 143–74.
Cowen, Michael and Robert W. Shenton. 'The Invention of Development'. In *Power of Development*, edited by Jonathan Crush, 27–43. London: Routledge, 1995.
Cowen, Michael and Robert W. Shenton. *Doctrines of Development*. London: Routledge, 1996.
Croft, Stuart. 'The Labour Party and the Nuclear Issue'. In *The Changing Labour Party*, edited by Martin J. Smith and Joanna Spear, 201–13. London: Routledge, 1992.
Crowder, Michael. 'Tshekedi Khama and Opposition to the British Administration of the Bechuanaland Protectorate, 1926–1936'. *The Journal of African History* 26, no. 2–3 (1985): 193–214.
Crowder, Michael. 'Tshekedi Khama, Smuts, and South West Africa'. *The Journal of Modern African Studies* 25, no. 1 (1987): 25–42.
Culverson, Donald R. *Contesting Apartheid : U.S. Activism, 1960–1987*. Boulder, CO: Westview, 1999.
Danielson, Leilah. 'Christianity, Dissent, and the Cold War: A. J. Muste's Challenge to Realism and U.S. Empire'. *Diplomatic History* 30, no. 4 (2006): 645–69.
Danielson, Leilah. '"It Is a Day of Judgment": The Peacemakers, Religion, and Radicalism in Cold War America'. *Religion and American Culture* 18, no. 2 (2008): 215–48.
Danielson, Leilah. *American Gandhi: A. J. Muste and the History of Radicalism in the Twentieth Century*. 1 Online Resource (x, 459 pages): Illustrations vols. Politics and Culture in Modern America. Philadelphia: University of Pennsylvania Press, 2014.
Darwin, J. *Britain and Decolonisation: The Retreat from Empire in the Postwar World*. Basingstoke: Macmillan Education, 1988.
Darwin, John. 'Decolonization and the End of Empire'. In *The Oxford History of the British Empire*, edited by Robin Winks, V: Historiography: 541–57. Oxford: Oxford University Press, 1999.
D'Emilio, John. 'Reading the Silences in a Gay Life: The Case of Bayard Rustin'. In *The Seductions of Biography*, edited by Mary Rhiel and David Bruce Suchoff. Culture Work, 59–68. New York ; Routledge, 1996.
D'Emilio, John. *Lost Prophet : The Life and Times of Bayard Rustin*. New York and London: Free Press, 2003.
Deutsch, Morton. 'William James: The First Peace Psychologist'. *Peace and Conflict: Journal of Peace Psychology* 1, no. 1 (1995): 27–35.

Devereux, David R. 'The Sino-Indian War of 1962 in Anglo-American Relations'. *Journal of Contemporary History* 44, no. 1 (2009): 71–87.
Dongen, Luc van, Stéphanie Roulin, and Giles Scott-Smith. *Transnational Anti-Communism and the Cold War: Agents, Activities, and Networks*. London: Palgrave Macmillan UK, 2014.
Dorn, A. Walter and Robert Pauk. 'Unsung Mediator: U Thant and the Cuban Missile Crisis'. *Diplomatic History* 33, no. 2 (2009): 261–92.
Duara, Prasenjit. *Decolonization: Perspectives from Now and Then*. 1 Online Resource (xvi, 312 pages): Map vols. Rewriting Histories. London ; Routledge, 2004.
Dubow, Saul. 'Macmillan, Verwoerd, And The 1960 "Wind of Change" Speech'. *The Historical Journal* 54, no. 4 (2011): 1087–114.
Dubow, Saul. 'Were There Political Alternatives in the Wake of the Sharpeville-Langa Violence in South Africa, 1960?'. *The Journal of African History* 56, no. 1 (2015): 119–42.
Elkins, Caroline. *Britain's Gulag : The Brutal End of Empire in Kenya*. London: Jonathan Cape, 2005.
Ellis, Stephen. 'The Genesis of the ANC's Armed Struggle in South Africa 1948–1961'. *Journal of Southern African Studies* 37, no. 4 (2011): 657–76.
Ellis, Stephen. *External Mission : The ANC in Exile, 1960–1990*. London: Hurst, 2012.
Emig, Rainer. 'Auden and Ecology'. In *The Cambridge Companion to W. H. Auden*, edited by Stan Smith, 212–25. Cambridge Companions to Literature. Cambridge: Cambridge University Press, 2005.
Escobar, Arturo. *Encountering Development: The Making and Unmaking of the Third World*. Princeton Studies in Culture/Power/History. Princeton, NJ: Princeton University Press, 1995.
Evans, Martin. *Algeria : France's Undeclared War*. Oxford: Oxford University Press, 2011.
Evans, Martin. 'Towards an Emotional History of Settler Decolonisation: De Gaulle, Political Masculinity and the End of French Algeria 1958–1962'. *Settler Colonial Studies* 8, no. 2 (2018): 213–43.
Fanon, Frantz. *The Wretched of the Earth*. Translated by Constance Farrington. New York: Grove Press, 1963.
Fanon, Frantz. *Alienation and Freedom*. Edited by Jean Khalfa and Robert J. C. Young. Translated by Steven Corcoran. London: Bloomsbury Publishing Plc, 2018.
Featherstone, David. *Solidarity: Hidden Histories and Geographies of Internationalism*. London: Zed Books, 2012.
Feichtinger, Moritz and Stephan Malinowski. '"Eine Million Algerier Lernen Im 20. Jahrhundert Zu Leben" Umsiedlungslager Und Zwangsmodernisierung Im Algerienkrieg 1954–1962'. *Journal of Modern European History* 8, no. 1 (2010): 107–35.
Ferguson, James. *The Anti-Politics Machine : 'development,' Depoliticization, and Bureaucratic Power in Lesotho*. Cambridge: Cambridge University Press, 1990.
First, Ruth, Jonathan Steele, and Christabel Gurney. *The South African Connection: Western Investment in Apartheid*. London: Temple Smith, 1972.
Freund, Bill. *Twentieth-Century South Africa: A Developmental History*. 1 Online Resource (x, 259 pages): PDF file(s) vols. Cambridge: Cambridge University Press, 2019.
Fryer, Peter. *Staying Power: The History of Black People in Britain*. London: Pluto Press, 1984.
Furnivall, J. S. *Netherlands India: A Study of Plural Economy*. Cambridge Library Collection - East and South-East Asian History. Cambridge: Cambridge University Press, 2010.

Galtung, Johan. *Peace by Peaceful Means: Peace and Conflict, Development and Civilization*. London: SAGE Publications, Limited, 1996.
Gandhi, Leela. *Affective Communities: Anticolonial Thought, Fin-De-Siècle Radicalism, and the Politics of Friendship*. Durham, NC: Duke University Press, 2006.
Gandhi, Mohandas Karamchand. *Hind Swaraj: Or, Indian Home Rule. With the Latest Foreword by the Author*. Madras: G.A. Natesan, 1921.
Gibbs, James. *Nkyin-Kyin: Essays on the Ghanaian Theatre*. Leiden: Brill, 2009.
Gill, Rebecca. '"Now I Have Seen Evil, and I Cannot Be Silent About It": Arnold J. Toynbee and His Encounters with Atrocity, 1915-1923'. In *Evil, Barbarism and Empire: Britain and Abroad, C. 1830-2000*, edited by T. Crook, R. Gill, and B. Taithe, 172-200. London: Palgrave Macmillan UK, 2011.
Gleijeses, Piero. *Conflicting Missions : Havana, Washington, and Africa, 1959-1976*. Chapel Hill: University of North Carolina Press, 2002.
Gleijeses, Piero. *Visions of Freedom : Havana, Washington, Pretoria and the Struggle for Southern Africa, 1976-1991*. Chapel Hill : The University of North Carolina Press, 2013.
Goedde, Petra. *The Politics of Peace: A Global Cold War History*. Oxford: Oxford University Press, 2019.
Goldsworthy, D. *Colonial Issues in British Politics 1945-1961*. Oxford: Clarendon Press, 1971.
Gordon, David M. *Invisible Agents: Spirits in a Central African History*. Athens: Ohio University Press, 2012.
Gordon, Rob. 'Not Quite Cricket: 'Civilization on Trial in South Africa': A Note on the First 'Protest Film' Made in Southern Africa'. *History in Africa* 32 (January) (2005): 457-66.
Grant, M. *After the Bomb: Civil Defence and Nuclear War in Britain, 1945-68*. London: Palgrave Macmillan UK, 2009.
Gregg, Richard Bartlett. *The Power of Non-Violence*. Philadelphia and London: J. B. Lippincott Co, 1934.
Grilli, Matteo. 'Nkrumah's Ghana and the Armed Struggle in Southern Africa (1961-1966)'. *South African Historical Journal* 70, no. 1 (2018): 56-81.
Gurney, Christabel. '"A Great Cause": The Origins of the Anti-Apartheid Movement, June 1959-March 1960'. *Journal of Southern African Studies* 26, no. 1 (2000): 123-44.
Hall, I. *The International Thought of Martin Wight*. New York: Palgrave Macmillan US, 2006.
Hare, A. Paul, and Herbert H. Blumberg, eds. *A Search for Peace and Justice : Reflections of Michael Scott*. London: R. Collings, 1980.
Häussler, Matthias. *The Herero Genocide War, Emotion, and Extreme Violence in Colonial Namibia*. 1 Online Resource (306 pages). vols. War and Genocide Ser., v. 31. New York: Berghahn Books, Incorporated, 2021.
Heinlein, Frank. *British Government Policy and Decolonisation, 1945-63: The Empire Commonwealth*. 1 Online Resource vols. British Politics and Society. London: Routledge, 2013.
Herbstein, Denis. *White Lies: Canon John Collins and the Secret War Against Apartheid*. Oxford: James Currey, 2004.
Hill, Christopher R. *Peace and Power in Cold War Britain: Media, Movements and Democracy, C. 1945-68*. London: Bloomsbury Publishing, 2018.
Hill, Christopher R. 'The Activist as Geographer: Nonviolent Direct Action in Cold War Germany and Postcolonial Ghana, 1959-1960'. *Journal of Historical Geography* 64 (April 2019): 36-46.

Hill, Christopher Robert. 'Britain, West Africa and 'The New Nuclear Imperialism': Decolonisation and Development During French Tests'. *Contemporary British History* 33, no. 2 (2019): 274–89.

Hill, Robert A. and Gregory A. Pirio. '"Africa for the Africans": The Garvey Movement in South Africa, 1920–1940'. In *The Politics of Race, Class and Nationalism in Twentieth-Century South Africa*, edited by Shula Marks and Stanley Trapido, 209–53. Harlow: Longman, 1987.

Hinton, James. *Protests and Visions : Peace Politics in Twentieth-Century Britain*. London: Hutchinson Radius, 1989.

Hodder, Jake. 'Conferencing the International at the World Pacifist Meeting, 1949'. *Political Geography*, Special Issue: Historical Geographies of Internationalism 49 (November 2015): 40–50.

Hodder, Jake. 'Waging Peace: Militarising Pacifism in Central Africa and the Problem of Geography, 1962'. *Transactions of the Institute of British Geographers* 42, no. 1 (2017): 29–43.

Hogg, Jonathan. *British Nuclear Culture: Official and Unofficial Narratives in the Long 20th Century*. London: Bloomsbury Publishing Plc, 2016.

Hogg, Jonathan and Kate Brown. 'Introduction: Social and Cultural Histories of British Nuclear Mobilisation Since 1945'. *Contemporary British History* 33, no. 1 (2019): 161–9.

Holloway, David. 'Nuclear Weapons and the Escalation of the Cold War, 1945–1962'. In *The Cambridge History of the Cold War: Volume 1: Origins*, edited by Melvyn P. Leffler and Odd Arne Westad, 1:376–97. The Cambridge History of the Cold War. Cambridge: Cambridge University Press, 2010.

Houser, George M. *No One Can Stop the Rain : Glimpses of Africa's Liberation Struggle*. New York: Pilgrim Press, 1989.

Howe, Stephen. *Anticolonialism in British Politics : The Left and the End of Empire, 1918–1964*. New York: Oxford University Press, 1993.

Hunt, Andrew E. *David Dellinger: The Life and Times of a Nonviolent Revolutionary*. New York: New York University Press, 2006.

Hunter, Emma. '"The History and Affairs of TANU": Intellectual History, Nationalism, and the Postcolonial State in Tanzania'. *The International Journal of African Historical Studies* 45, no. 3 (2012): 365–83.

Hunter, Emma. *Political Thought and the Public Sphere in Tanzania: Freedom, Democracy and Citizenship in the Era of Decolonization*. African Studies. Cambridge: Cambridge University Press, 2015.

Hunter, Emma. 'Languages of Freedom in Decolonising Africa'. *Transactions of the Royal Historical Society* 27 (December 2017): 253–69.

Hyam, Ronald. 'The Political Consequences of Seretse Khama: Britain, the Bangwato and South Africa, 1948–1952'. *The Historical Journal* 29, no. 4 (1986): 921–47.

Hyslop, Jonathan. 'Mandela on War'. In *The Cambridge Companion to Nelson Mandela*, edited by Rita Barnard, 162–81. New York: Cambridge University Press, 2014.

Jachec, Nancy. *Europe's Intellectuals and the Cold War: The European Society of Culture, Post-War Politics and International Relations*, Reprint ed. London: Bloomsbury Academic, 2020.

James, L. *George Padmore and Decolonization from Below: Pan-Africanism, the Cold War, and the End of Empire*. London: Palgrave, 2014.

James, Leslie and Elisabeth Leake. *Decolonization and the Cold War: Negotiating Independence*. London: Bloomsbury Publishing Plc, 2015.

James, William. 'The Moral Equivalent of War'. *Peace and Conflict: Journal of Peace Psychology* 1, no. 1 (1995): 17–26.

Jansen, Jan C., Jurgen Osterhammel, and Jeremiah Riemer. *Decolonization: A Short History*. 1 Online Resource vols. Princeton, NJ: Princeton University Press, 2019.

Jasper, James M. *The Art of Moral Protest : Culture, Biography, and Creativity in Social Movements*. Chicago and London: University of Chicago Press, 1997.

Jasper, James M.. 'The Emotions of Protest: Affective and Reactive Emotions In and Around Social Movements'. *Sociological Forum* 13, no. 3 (1998): 397–424.

Jocelyn, Alexander, JoAnn McGregor, and T. O. Ranger, eds. *Violence & Memory: One Hundred Years in the 'Dark Forests' of Matabeleland*. Social History of Africa. Oxford: James Currey, 2000.

Johnson, Charles Denton. 'Re-Thinking the Emergence of the Struggle for South African Liberation in the United States: Max Yergan and the Council on African Affairs, 1922–1946'. *Journal of Southern African Studies* 39, no. 1 (2013): 171–92.

Jones, Mervyn. 'The Time Is Short'. In *Conviction: Essays*, edited by Norman MacKenzie, 183–201. London: MacGibbon & Kee, 1958.

Jordan, Z. Pallo and Mac Maharaj. 'South Africa and the Turn to Armed Resistance'. *South African Historical Journal* 70, no. 1 (2018): 11–26.

Kalter, Christoph. *The Discovery of the Third World: Decolonization and the Rise of the New Left in France, c.1950–1976*. Cambridge: Cambridge University Press, 2016.

Kalusa, Walima T. 'The Killing of Lilian Margaret Burton and Black and White Nationalisms in Northern Rhodesia (Zambia) in the 1960s'. *Journal of Southern African Studies* 37, no. 1 (2011): 63–77.

Katz, Elaine. 'The Role of American Mining Technology and American Mining Engineers in the Witwatersrand Gold Mining Industry 1890–1910'. *South African Journal of Economic History* 20, no. 2 (2005): 48–82.

Katz, Hagai and Helmut K. Anheier. 'Global Connectedness: The Structure of Transnational NGO Networks'. In *Global Civil Society 2005/6*, edited by Helmut K. Anheier, Mary Kaldor, and Marlies Glasius, 240–65. London: SAGE Publications, Limited, 2005.

Kaunda, Kenneth. *Kaunda on Violence*. London: Sphere, 1982.

Kelly, John Dunham and Martha Kaplan. *Represented Communities : Fiji and World Decolonization*. Chicago: University of Chicago Press, 2001.

Kepe, Thembela and Lungisile Ntsebeza, eds. *Rural Resistance in South Africa : The Mpondo Revolts After Fifty Years*. Cape Town: UCT Press, 2012.

Keppel-Jones, Arthur. *When Smuts Goes : A History of South Africa from 1952 to 2010, First Published in 2015*. Pietermaritzburg: Shuter & Shooter, 1949.

King-Hall, Sir Stephen. *Defence in the Nuclear Age*. London: Victor Gollancz, 1958.

Klose, Fabian. *Human Rights in the Shadow of Colonial Violence: The Wars of Independence in Kenya and Algeria*, 1st ed. 1 Online Resource (369 xvii, pages) vols. Pennsylvania Studies in Human Rights. Philadelphia: University of Pennsylvania Press, 2013.

Konieczna, Anna and Rob Skinner, eds. *A Global History of Anti-Apartheid 'Forward to Freedom' in South Africa*. St. Antony's Series. Basingstoke: Palgrave, 2019a.

Konieczna, Anna and Rob Skinner. 'Introduction: Anti-Apartheid in Global History'. In *A Global History of Anti-Apartheid 'Forward to Freedom' in South Africa*, edited by Anna Konieczna and Rob Skinner, 1–30. St. Antony's Series. Basingstoke: Palgrave, 2019b.

Kosek, Joseph Kip. *Acts of Conscience: Christian Nonviolence and Modern American Democracy*. New York: Columbia University Press, 2011.

Kossler, Reinhart. *Namibia and Germany: Negotiating the Past*. 1 Online Resource (xiii, 377 pages) vols. Windhoek: UNAM Press, 2015.

Kraft, Alison and Carola Sachse. 'Introduction: The Pugwash Conferences on Science and World Affairs: Vision, Rhetoric, Realities'. In *Science, (Anti-)Communism and Diplomacy: The Pugwash Conferences on Science and World Affairs in the Early Cold War*, edited by Alison Kraft and Carola Sachse, 1–39. Boston: Brill, 2019.

Kraft, Alison, Carola Sachse, Alison Kraft, Carola Sachse, Alison Kraft, Carola Sachse, Alison Kraft, et al., eds. *Science, (Anti-)Communism and Diplomacy: The Pugwash Conferences on Science and World Affairs in the Early Cold War*. Boston: Brill, 2019.

Kuper, Leo. *Race, Class and Power: Ideology and Revolutionary Change in Plural Societies*. London: Duckworth, 1974.

Laffey, Mark and Jutta Weldes. 'Decolonizing the Cuban Missile Crisis'. *International Studies Quarterly* 52, no. 3 (2008): 555–77.

Lake, Marilyn and Henry Reynolds. *Drawing the Global Colour Line: White Men's Countries and the International Challenge of Racial Equality*. Critical Perspectives on Empire. Cambridge: Cambridge University Press, 2011.

Lal, Vinay. 'Nakedness, Nonviolence, and Brahmacharya: Gandhi's Experiments in Celibate Sexuality'. *Journal of the History of Sexuality* 9, no. 1/2 (2000): 105–36.

Lang, Michael. 'Globalization and Global History in Toynbee'. *Journal of World History* 22, no. 4 (2011): 747–83.

Lannoy, Richard. *The Speaking Tree, a Study of Indian Culture and Society*. London: New York University Press, 1971.

Larmer, Miles. '"A Little Bit Like A Volcano"-The United Progressive Party and Resistance to One-Party Rule in Zambia, 1964–1980'. *The International Journal of African Historical Studies* 39, no. 1 (2006): 49–83.

Larmer, Miles. *Rethinking African Politics : A History of Opposition in Zambia*. London: Routledge, 2016.

Larmer, Miles and Baz Lecocq. 'Historicising Nationalism in Africa'. *Nations and Nationalism* 24, no. 4 (2018): 893–917.

Lee, Christopher J., ed. *Making a World After Empire: The Bandung Moment and Its Political Afterlives*. Research in International Studies. Global and Comparative Studies Series ; No. 11. Athens: Ohio University Press, 2010.

Legg, Stephen, Mike Heffernan, Jake Hodder, and Benjamin Thorpe, eds. *Placing Internationalism: International Conferences and the Making of the Modern World*. London: Bloomsbury Academic, 2022.

Legum, Colin and Margaret Legum. *South Africa: Crisis for the West*. London: Pall Mall Press, 1964.

Lent, Adam. *British Social Movements Since 1945 : Sex, Colour, Peace and Power*. Basingstoke: Palgrave, 2001.

Leonard, Robert. 'E. F. Schumacher and Intermediate Technology'. *History of Political Economy* 50 (December 2018): 249–65.

Leonard, Robert. 'Between the 'Hand-Loom' and the 'Samson Stripper': Fritz Schumacher's Struggle for Intermediate Technology'. *Contemporary European History* 31, no. 4 (2022): 525–52.

Leow, Rachel. 'A Missing Peace: The Asia-Pacific Peace Conference in Beijing, 1952 and the Emotional Making of Third World Internationalism *'. *Journal of World History* 30, no. 1/2 (2019): 21–53.

Levey, Zach. 'Israel's Strategy in Africa, 1961–67'. *International Journal of Middle East Studies* 36, no. 1 (2004): 71–87.

Levy, Michael. *Ban the Bomb!* Stuttgart: Ibidem Press, 2021.
Lewis, Jeremy. *Penguin Special : The Life and Times of Allen Lane*. London: Viking, 2005.
Lewis, Jeremy. *David Astor*, Reprint ed. London: Vintage Digital, 2016.
Lewis, Su Lin and Carolien Stolte. 'Other Bandungs: Afro-Asian Internationalisms in the Early Cold War *'. *Journal of World History* 30, no. 1/2 (2019): 1-19.
Lewis, W. Arthur. 'Economic Development with Unlimited Supplies of Labour'. *The Manchester School* 22, no. 2 (1954): 139-91.
Lewis, W. Arthur, Michael Scott, Martin Wight, and Colin Legum. *Attitude to Africa*. Penguin Special, S159 ^A753690 ^A753690. Harmondsworth, Middlesex: Penguin Books, 1951.
Lieberman, Robbie. *The Strangest Dream : Communism, Anticommunism and the U.S. Peace Movement 1945-1963*, 1st ed. New York: Syracuse University Press, 2000.
Little, Lawrence S. *Disciples of Liberty: The African Methodist Episcopal Church in the Age of Imperialism, 1884-1916*. Knoxville: University of Tennessee Press, 2000.
Liu, Lydia H. 'The Question of Meaning-Value in the Political Economy of the Sign'. In *Tokens of Exchange: The Problem of Translation in Global Circulations*, edited by Lydia H. Liu, 13-41. Post-Contemporary Interventions. Durham, NC: Duke University Press, 2000a.
Liu, Lydia H., ed. *Tokens of Exchange: The Problem of Translation in Global Circulations*. 1 Online Resource (464 pages): 22 Black and White Photographs vols. Post-Contemporary Interventions. Durham, NC: Duke University Press, 2000b.
Liu, Zifeng. 'Decolonization Is Not a Dinner Party: Claudia Jones, China's Nuclear Weapons, and Anti-Imperialist Solidarity'. *Journal of Intersectionality* 3 (July 2019): 21-45.
Lodge, Tom. *Mandela : A Critical Life*. Oxford: Oxford University Press, 2006.
Lodge, Tom. *Sharpeville: An Apartheid Massacre and Its Consequences*. Oxford: Oxford University Press, 2011.
Macey, David. *Frantz Fanon : A Life*. London: Granta, 2000.
MacLellan, Nic and Australian National University Press. *Grappling with the Bomb: Britain's Pacific H-Bomb Tests*. 1 Online Resource (xxiv, 383 pages): Illustrations vols. Pacific Series. Acton, ACT: ANU Press, 2017.
Macola, G. *Liberal Nationalism in Central Africa: A Biography of Harry Mwaanga Nkumbula*. London: Palgrave, 2010.
Macola, Giacomo. 'Harry Mwaanga Nkumbula, UNIP and the Roots of Authoritarianism in Nationalist Zambia'. In *One Zambia, Many Histories: Towards a History of Post-Colonial Zambia*, edited by Giacomo Macola, Jan-Bart Gewald, and Marja Hinfelaar, 17-44. Leiden: Brill, 2008.
Macola, Giacomo, Jan-Bart Gewald, and Marja Hinfelaar, eds. *One Zambia, Many Histories: Towards a History of Post-Colonial Zambia*. Leiden: Brill, 2008.
Makalani, Minkah. *In the Cause of Freedom: Radical Black Internationalism from Harlem to London, 1917-1939*. Chapel Hill: University of North Carolina Press, 2011.
Malone, David M. and Rohan Mukherjee. 'India and China: Conflict and Cooperation'. *Survival* 52, no. 1 (2010): 137-58.
Mamdani, Mahmood. *Citizen and Subject : Contemporary Africa and the Legacy of Late Colonialism*. Princeton, NJ: Princeton University Press, 1996.
Mandela, Nelson. *Long Walk to Freedom : The Autobiography of Nelson Mandela*. London: Abacus, 1995.
Marable, Manning. *W. E. B. Du Bois: Black Radical Democrat*. London: Taylor & Francis Group, 1987.

Marcum, John A. *The Angolan Revolution. Vol.1, The Anatomy of an Explosion, 1950-1962*. Studies in Communism, Revisionism and Revolution; 1. Cambridge, MA: MIT Press, 1969.

Marmon, Brooks. 'Neutrality of a Special Type: George Loft's Abortive Racial Reconciliation in the Federation of Rhodesia and Nyasaland, 1957–1960'. *Safundi* 22, no. 4 (2021): 417–34.

Mason, David. 'The "Civitas" of Sound: Auden's "Paul Bunyan" and "New Year Letter"'. *Journal of Modern Literature* 19, no. 1 (1994): 115–28.

Massumi, Brian. *Politics of Affect*. Cambridge: Polity, 2015.

Mazower, Mark. *No Enchanted Palace : The End of Empire and the Ideological Origins of the United Nations*. Woodstock: Princeton University Press, 2009.

McKay, George. 'Subcultural Innovations in the Campaign for Nuclear Disarmament'. *Peace Review* 16, no. 4 (2004): 429–38.

McKinley, Dale T. 'Umkhonto We Sizwe: A Critical Analysis of the Armed Struggle of the African National Congress'. *South African Historical Journal* 70, no. 1 (2018): 27–41.

Milford, Ismay. 'Harnessing the Wind : East and Central African Activists and Anticolonial Cultures in a Decolonising World, 1952–64'. Thesis, European University Institute, 2019.

Milford, Ismay. 'Federation, Partnership, and the Chronologies of Space in 1950s East and Central Africa'. *The Historical Journal* 63, no. 5 (2020): 1325–48.

Milford, Ismay and Gerard McCann. 'African Internationalisms and the Erstwhile Trajectories of Kenyan Community Development: Joseph Murumbi's 1950s'. *Journal of Contemporary History* 57, no. 1 (2021): 3–23.

Minter, William and Sylvia Hill. 'Anti-Apartheid Solidarity in United States-South African Relations: From the Margins to the Mainstream'. In *The Road to Democracy in South Africa*, edited by South African Democracy Education Trust. [Main author], 3 Part 1, International Solidarity, 745–824. Pretoria: Unisa Press, 2008.

Minter, William, Gail Hovey, and Charles E. Cobb, eds. *No Easy Victories: African Liberation and American Activists over a Half Century, 1950-2000*. Trenton, NJ: Africa World Press, 2008.

Mollin, Marian. 'The Limits of Egalitarianism: Radical Pacifism, Civil Rights, and the Journey of Reconciliation'. *Radical History Review* 88, no. 1 (2004): 112–38.

Mollin, Marian. *Radical Pacifism in Modern America: Egalitarianism and Protest*. Politics and Culture in Modern America. Philadelphia: University of Pennsylvania Press, 2006.

Morier-Genoud, Éric., ed. *Sure Road? : Nationalisms in Angola, Guinea-Bissau and Mozambique*. Leiden : Brill, 2012.

Moyn, Samuel. *The Last Utopia: Human Rights in History*. London: Belknap Press of Harvard University Press, 2010.

Mukherjee, Mithi. 'Transcending Identity: Gandhi, Nonviolence, and the Pursuit of a 'Different' Freedom in Modern India'. *The American Historical Review* 115, no. 2 (2010): 453–73.

Mumford, Lewis. *The Culture of Cities*. London: Secker & Warburg, 1944.

Musso, Marta. '"Oil Will Set Us Free": The Hydrocarbon Industry and the Algerian Decolonization Process'. In *Britain, France and the Decolonization of Africa: Future Imperfect?*, edited by Andrew W. M. Smith and Chris Jeppesen, 62–84. London: UCL Press, 2017.

Naranch, Bradley, Geoff Eley, Geoff Eley, and Bradley Naranch. *German Colonialism in a Global Age*. Politics, History, and Culture. Durham, NC: Duke University Press, 2014.

Ndhlovu, Finex. 'Pan-African Identities and Literacies: The Orthographic Harmonisation Debate Revisited'. *South African Journal of African Languages* 42, no. 2 (2022): 207–15.
Nehring, Holger. 'The British and West German Protests Against Nuclear Weapons and the Cultures of the Cold War, 1957–64'. *Contemporary British History* 19, no. 2 (2005): 223–41.
Nehring, Holger. *Politics of Security: British and West German Protest Movements and the Early Cold War, 1945-1970*, 1st ed. Oxford Historical Monographs. Oxford: Oxford University Press, 2013.
Nesbitt, Francis Njubi. *Race for Sanctions: African Americans Against Apartheid, 1946–1994*. Bloomington: Indiana University Press, 2004.
Nevinson, Henry. *Fire of Life*. London: Harcourt & Brace, 1935.
Newitt, Malyn. 'Angola in Historical Context'. In *Angola: The Weight of History*, edited by Patrick Chabal and Nuno Vidal, 19–92. London: Hurst & Company, 2007.
Nkosi, M. Z. 'American Mining Engineers and the Labor Structure in the South African Gold Mines'. *African Journal of Political Economy / Revue Africaine d'Economie Politique* 1, no. 2 (1987): 63–80.
Nkrumah, Kwame. *Africa Must Unite*. London: Heinemann, 1964.
Pagedas, Constantine A. *Anglo-American Strategic Relations and the French Problem, 1960-1963: A Troubled Partnership*. London and New York: Routledge, 2013.
Palmer, Bryan D. 'The French Turn in the United States: James P. Cannon and the Trotskyist Entry into the Socialist Party, 1934–1937'. *Labor History* 59, no. 5 (2018): 610–38.
Pedersen, Susan. *The Guardians: The League of Nations and the Crisis of Empire*, 1st ed. Oxford: Oxford University Press, 2015.
Perham, Margery. 'The British Problem in Africa'. *Foreign Affairs* 29, no. 4 (1951): 637–50.
Plaatjie, Stephen. 'Conflict of Ideologies: The Anc Youth League and Communism, 1949–1955'. M.A., South Africa: University of Johannesburg (South Africa), 1994.
Plummer, Brenda Gayle. *Rising Wind: Black Americans and U.S. Foreign Affairs, 1935–1960*. Chapel Hill: University of North Carolina Press, 1996.
Plummer, Brenda Gayle, ed. *Window on Freedom : Race, Civil Rights, and Foreign Affairs, 1945-1988*. Chapel Hill: University of North Carolina Press, 2003.
Podair, Jerald, Jacqueline M. Moore, and Nina Mjagkij. *Bayard Rustin: American Dreamer*. Lanham, MD: Rowman & Littlefield Publishers, 2008.
Porter, Andrew. 'Missions and Empire: An Overview, 1700–1914'. In *Missions and Empire*, edited by Norman Etherington, 40–63. Oxford: Oxford University Press, 2005.
Posel, Deborah. 'The ANC Youth League and the Politicization of Race'. *Thesis Eleven* 115, no. 1 (2013): 58–76.
Power, Joey. *Political Culture and Nationalism in Malawi: Building Kwacha*. Rochester: University Rochester Press, 2010.
Power, Rob. 'The African Dimension to the Anti-Federation Struggle, ca. 1950–53: 'It Has United Us Far More Closely than Any Other Question Would Have Accomplished''. *Itinerario* 45, no. 2 (2021): 304–24.
Prasad, Devi. *War Is a Crime Against Humanity: The Story of War Resisters' International*. London: War Resisters' International, 2005.
Pringle, Yolana. 'Humanitarianism, Race and Denial: The International Committee of the Red Cross and Kenya's Mau Mau Rebellion, 1952–60'. *History Workshop Journal* 84 (October 2017): 89–107.
Pugh, Michael. 'Pacifism and Politics in Britain, 1931–1935'. *The Historical Journal* 23, no. 3 (1980): 641–56.

Ranger, Terence. 'The Invention of Tradition in Colonial Africa'. In *The Invention of Tradition*, edited by E. Hobsbawm and Terence Ranger, 211–62. Cambridge: Cambridge University Press, 1983.
Reginald, Maudling. *Memoirs*. London: Sidgwick and Jackson, 1978.
Rex, John. 'The Plural Society in Sociological Theory'. *The British Journal of Sociology* 10, no. 2 (1959): 114–24.
Rich, Paul B. *Hope and Despair : English-Speaking Intellectuals and South African Politics, 1896–1976*. London: British Academic Press, 1993.
Rigby, Andrew. 'A Peace Symbol's Origins'. *Peace Review* 10, no. 3 (1998): 475–9.
Riley, Charlotte Lydia. '"The Winds of Change Are Blowing Economically": The Labour Party and British Overseas Development, 1940s–1960s'. In *Britain, France and the Decolonization of Africa: Future Imperfect?*, edited by Andrew W. M Smith and Chris Jeppesen, 43–61. London: UCL Press, 2017.
Rizzo, Matteo. 'What Was Left of the Groundnut Scheme? Development Disaster and Labour Market in Southern Tanganyika 1946–1952'. *Journal of Agrarian Change* 6, no. 2 (2006): 205–38.
Roberts, George. *Revolutionary State-Making in Dar Es Salaam: African Liberation and the Global Cold War, 1961–1974*. African Studies. Cambridge: Cambridge University Press, 2021.
Robinson, Jo Ann. 'A. J. Muste and Ways to Peace'. *American Studies* 13, no. 1 (1972): 95–108.
Rotberg, Robert I. *The Rise of Nationalism in Central Africa : The Making of Malawi and Zambia, 1873–1964*. Cambridge, MA: Harvard University Press, 1965.
Sampson, Anthony. *Mandela : The Authorised Biography*. London: HarperCollins, 1999.
Saunders, Frances Stonor. *Who Paid the Piper?: The CIA and the Cultural Cold War*. London: Granta, 1999.
Scalmer, Sean. *Gandhi in the West : The Mahatma and the Rise of Radical Protest*. Cambridge and New York: Cambridge University Press, 2011.
Scalmer, Sean. 'Mediated Nonviolence as a Global Force: An Historical Perspective'. In *Mediation and Protest Movements*, edited by Bart Cammaerts, Alice Mattoni, and Patrick McCurdy, 115–32. Bristol: Intellect, 2012.
Scott, James C. *Seeing Like a State: How Certain Schemes to Improve the Human Condition Have Failed*. 1 Online Resource (xiv, 445 pages): Illustrations, Maps vols. Yale ISPS Series. New Haven, CT: Yale University Press, 1998.
Scott, Michael. *A Time to Speak*, 1st ed. Garden City, NY: Doubleday, 1958.
Segal, Ronald, ed. *Sanctions Against South Africa*. Harmondsworth: Penguin Books, 1964.
Shepard, Todd. *The Invention of Decolonization : The Algerian War and the Remaking of France*. Ithaca, NY: Cornell University Press, 2006.
Sherman, Taylor C. 'A Gandhian Answer to the Threat of Communism? Sarvodaya and Postcolonial Nationalism in India'. *The Indian Economic & Social History Review* 53, no. 2 (2016): 249–70.
Sherwood, Marika and Hakim Adi. *Pan-African History: Political Figures from Africa and the Diaspora Since 1787*. 1 Online Resource (216 pages) vols. London: Routledge, 2003.
Simpson, Thula. *Umkhonto We Sizwe: The ANC's Armed Struggle*. Cape Town: Penguin Books, 2016.
Simpson, Thula. 'Nelson Mandela and the Genesis of the ANC's Armed Struggle: Notes on Method'. *Journal of Southern African Studies* 44, no. 1 (2018): 133–48.
Simpson, Thula. 'Mandela's Army: Urban Revolt in South Africa, 1960–1964'. *Journal of Southern African Studies* 45, no. 6 (2019): 1093–110.

Skinner, Rob. 'Christian Reconstruction, Secular Politics: Michael Scott and the Campaign for Right and Justice, 1943–1945'. In *South Africa's 1940s : Worlds of Possibilities*, edited by Saul Dubow and Alan Jeeves, 246–66. Cape Town: Double Storey, 2005.

Skinner, Rob. 'The Anti-Apartheid Movement: Pressure Group Politics, International Solidarity and Transnational Activism'. In *NGOs in Contemporary Britain: Non-State Actors in Society and Politics Since 1945*, edited by N. J. Crowson, Matthew Hilton, and James McKay, 129–46. Basingstoke: Palgrave Macmillan, 2009.

Skinner, Rob. *The Foundations of Anti-Apartheid: Liberal Humanitarianism and Transnational Activism in Britain and the United States, c. 1919–64*. Basingstoke: Palgrave Macmillan, 2010.

Skinner, Rob. 'Bombs and Border Crossings: Peace Activist Networks and the Post-Colonial State in Africa, 1959–62'. *Journal of Contemporary History*, November 2014.

Skinner, Rob. "Every Bite Buys a Bullet': Sanctions, Boycotts and Solidarity in Transnational Anti-Apartheid Activism'. *Moving the Social* 57 (2017): 97–114.

Smith, Andrew W. M. and Chris Jeppesen, eds. *Britain, France and the Decolonization of Africa: Future Imperfect?* London: UCL Press, 2017.

Smith, Evan, Gavin Brown, Matthew Worley, Jacquelyn Arnold, Daniel Finn, Michael Fitzpatrick, Diarmaid Kelliher, Jack Saunders, J. Daniel Taylor, and Jodi Burkett. *Waiting for the Revolution: The British Far Left From 1956*. Manchester: Manchester University Press, 2017.

Smuts, Jan Christiaan. *Holism and Evolution*, 2nd ed. London: Macmillan, 1927.

Solomon, Mark. *The Cry Was Unity: Communists and African Americans, 1917–1936*. Jackson: University Press of Mississippi, 1998.

Spear, Thomas. 'Neo-Traditionalism and the Limits of Invention in British Colonial Africa'. *The Journal of African History* 44, no. 1 (2003): 3–27.

Steiner, Tina. 'Ports as Portals: D. D. T. Jabavu's Voyage to the World Pacifist Meeting in India'. *English Studies in Africa* 62, no. 1 (2019): 8–20.

Stevens, Simon. 'Boycotts and Sanctions Against South Africa: An International History, 1946–1970'. PhD, New York: Columbia University, 2016.

Stevens, Simon. 'The Turn to Sabotage by The Congress Movement in South Africa'. *Past & Present* 245, no. 1 (2019): 221–55.

Stolte, Carolien. "The People's Bandung': Local Anti-Imperialists on an Afro-Asian Stage'. *Journal of World History* 30, no.1/2 (2019): 125–56.

Stultz, Newell Maynard. 'Evolution of the United Nations Anti-Apartheid Regime'. *Human Rights Quarterly* 13, no. 1 (1991): 1–23.

Sutherland, Bill and Matt Meyer. *Guns and Gandhi in Africa: Pan African Insights on Nonviolence, Armed Struggle and Liberation in Africa*. Trenton, NJ: Africa World Press, 2000.

Suttner, Raymond. 'The African National Congress (ANC) Underground: From the M-Plan to Rivonia'. *South African Historical Journal* 49, no. 1 (2003): 123–46.

Suttner, Raymond. '"The Road to Freedom Is via the Cross" "Just Means" in Chief Albert Luthuli's Life'. *South African Historical Journal* 62, no. 4 (2010): 693–715.

Tarrow, Sidney. 'Modular Collective Action and the Rise of the Social Movement: Why the French Revolution Was Not Enough'. *Politics & Society* 21, no. 1 (1993): 69–90.

Tarrow, Sidney G. *Power in Movement: Social Movements and Contentious Politics*. Cambridge: Cambridge University Press, 1998.

Telepneva, Natalia. *Cold War Liberation The Soviet Union and the Collapse of the Portuguese Empire in Africa, 1961–1975*. Chapel Hill: University of North Carolina Press, 2021.

Thomas, Martin and Gareth Curless. *Decolonization and Conflict: Colonial Comparisons and Legacies*. London: Bloomsbury Academic, 2017.
Thomas, Martin and Andrew Thompson. 'Empire and Globalisation: From 'High Imperialism' to Decolonisation'. *The International History Review* 36, no. 1 (2014): 142–70.
Thörn, Håkan. *Anti-Apartheid and the Emergence of a Global Civil Society*. Basingstoke: Palgrave Macmillan, 2006.
Thörn, Håkan. 'The Meaning(s) of Solidarity: Narratives of Anti-Apartheid Activism'. *Journal of Southern African Studies* 35, no. 2 (2009): 417–36.
Tignor, Robert L. *W. Arthur Lewis and the Birth of Development Economics*. Princeton, NJ: Princeton University Press, 2020.
Tilly, Charles. *The Politics of Collective Violence*. Cambridge Studies in Contentious Politics. Cambridge: Cambridge University Press, 2003.
Tilly, Charles. *Contentious Performances*. New York: Cambridge University Press, 2008.
Toynbee, Arnold Joseph. *Civilization on Trial*. London: Geoffrey Cumberlege, Oxford University Press, 1948.
Troup, Freda. *In Face of Fear. Michael Scott's Challenge to South Africa. [With Plates, Including a Portrait]*. London: Faber & Faber, 1950.
Tuffnell, Stephen. 'Engineering Inter-Imperialism: American Miners and the Transformation of Global Mining, 1871–1910'. *Journal of Global History* 10, no. 1 (2015): 53–76.
Turner, Oliver. '"Finishing the Job": The UN Special Committee on Decolonization and the Politics of Self-Governance'. *Third World Quarterly* 34, no. 7 (2013): 1193–208.
Van Donge, Jan Kees. 'An Episode from the Independence Struggle in Zambia: A Case Study from Mwase Lundazi'. *African Affairs* 84, no. 335 (1985): 265–77.
Van Wyk, Anna-Mart. 'Apartheid's Atomic Bomb: Cold War Perspectives'. *South African Historical Journal* 62, no. 1 (2010): 100–20.
Veldman, Meredith. *Fantasy, the Bomb and the Greening of Britain: Romantic Protest, 1945–1980*. Cambridge: Cambridge University Press, 1994.
Vinson, Robert Trent. *The Americans Are Coming!: Dreams of African American Liberation in Segregationist South Africa*. Athens: Ohio University Press, 2012.
Von Eschen, Penny M. *Race Against Empire : Black Americans and Anticolonialism, 1937–1957*. Ithaca, NY: Cornell University Press, 1997.
Walker, Lydia. 'Decolonization in the 1960s: On Legitimate and Illegitimate Nationalist Claims-Making'. *Past & Present* 242, no. 1 (2019a): 227–64.
Walker, Lydia. 'Jayaprakash Narayan and the Politics of Reconciliation for the Postcolonial State and Its Imperial Fragments'. *The Indian Economic & Social History Review* 56, no. 2 (2019b): 147–69.
Waters, Chris. '"Dark Strangers" in Our Midst: Discourses of Race and Nation in Britain, 1947–1963'. *Journal of British Studies* 36, no. 2 (1997): 207–38.
Weber, Thomas. *Gandhi's Peace Army : The Shanti Sena and Unarmed Peacekeeping*, 1st ed. Syracuse, NY: Syracuse University Press, 1996.
Wellington, John H. 'A New Development Scheme for the Okovango Delta, Northern Kalahari'. *The Geographical Journal* 113 (1949a): 62–9.
Wellington, John H. 'Zambezi-Okovango Development Projects'. *Geographical Review* 39, no. 4 (1949b): 552–67.
Wells, H. G. (Herbert George). *The Work, Wealth and Happiness of Mankind*, New and rev. ed. London: William Heinemann, 1934.
Wells, H. G., Julian Huxley, and G. P. Wells. *The Science of Life*. London: Cassell, 1931.

Wernicke, Günter. 'The Communist-Led World Peace Council and the Western Peace Movements: The Fetters of Bipolarity and Some Attempts to Break Them in the Fifties and Early Sixties1'. *Peace & Change* 23, no. 3 (1998): 265–311.

Wernicke, Günter and Lawrence S. Wittner. 'Lifting the Iron Curtain: The Peace March to Moscow of 1960–1961'. *The International History Review* 21, no. 4 (1999): 900–17.

Westad, Odd Arne. *The Global Cold War : Third World Interventions and the Making of Our Times*. Cambridge: Cambridge University Press, 2016.

Westad, Odd Arne. *The Cold War: A World History*, 1st ed. New York: Basic Books, 2017.

White, Luise and Miles Larmer. 'Introduction: Mobile Soldiers and the Un-National Liberation of Southern Africa'. *Journal of Southern African Studies* 40, no. 6 (2014): 1271–4.

Wight, Martin. *British Colonial Constitutions, 1947*. Oxford: Clarendon Press, 1952.

Wilder, Gary. *Freedom Time: Negritude, Decolonization, and the Future of the World*. Durham, NC and London: Duke University Press, 2015.

Willetts, Peter. *The Non-Aligned Movement : The Origins of a Third World Alliance*. New York: Nichols Pub. Co, 1978.

Williams, Elizabeth. *The Politics of Race in Britain and South Africa : Black British Solidarity and the Anti-Apartheid Struggle*. London: I.B. Tauris, 2012.

Williams, Susan. *Colour Bar: The Triumph of Seretse Khama and His Nation*. London: Penguin UK, 2007.

Wittner, Lawrence S. *Rebels Against War the American Peace Movement, 1941–1960*. New York: Columbia University Press, 1969.

Wittner, Lawrence S.. *Resisting the Bomb: A History of the World Nuclear Disarmament Movement 1954–1970*. Stanford, CA: Stanford University Press, 1997.

Wittner, Lawrence S.. *Confronting the Bomb : A Short History of the World Nuclear Disarmament Movement*. Stanford, CA: Stanford University Press, 2009.

Yates, Anne and Lewis Chester. *The Troublemaker : Michael Scott and His Lonely Struggle Against Injustice*. London: Aurum, 2006.

Young, Robert J. C. 'Fanon and the Turn to Armed Struggle in Africa'. *Wasafiri* 20, no. 44 (2005): 33–41.

Index

Accra Assembly-'The World Without the Bomb' (1962)   191–8
activism   17–18, 50, 74
   non-violent   1–5, 14–17, 24, 39, 50, 60–1, 73–5, 78, 106–8, 115, 117, 119, 121–7, 141–6, 156, 159, 164, 167, 179, 188, 201, 206, 208, 211–14 (*see also* non-violent civil disobedience)
   and personal life   22–3, 59–64, 86, 184–5
Africa Bureau   12, 21, 39, 54, 59, 61, 63–4, 71–2, 77–8, 80, 85–7, 155, 156, 184, 191, 199–201, 204–5, 207
   formation of   28–9, 65–70
Africa Freedom Action   7, 151, 157–8, 160–4, 166, 168–84
African National Congress (South Africa)   2, 8–9, 56, 82, 136–7, 139, 152, 159, 173, 178–80, 187, 199–200
Afro-Asian Solidarity Conference   114, 121
Aldermaston, Nuclear Weapons Research Establishment (UK)   87–8, 98, 104, 116, 134, 165, 210, 215
Algeria   2, 7, 8, 41, 89–93, 97–8, 100, 103, 112, 114, 116, 119–24, 126, 129, 130, 136, 138–40, 152, 170–1, 175, 179, 213
All-Africa Peoples' Conference, Accra (1958)   85, 153, 154
All-Africa Peoples' Conference, Tunis (1960)   119, 122
American Committee on Africa   25, 78–9, 87, 135, 138–9, 151, 155, 156, 181, 186, 201
American Friends Service Committee   24, 58, 140, 165, 176, 180, 181, 190, 193
Americans for South African Resistance   56, 79

Angola   7, 8, 44, 131, 140, 157, 159, 202, 206, 209
   Baixa de Cassanje uprising (1961)   135–6, 138–9
anti-apartheid movement   6, 7, 57, 58, 67, 79–81, 94, 134–8, 178, 190, 198–205
anti-Communism   68, 87, 197 n.29
anti-Vietnam War protest   6, 16, 56, 190, 215
apartheid   2, 3, 8, 9, 27, 38, 45, 53, 54, 56, 66, 71, 73, 82, 121, 137, 140, 148, 159, 175, 179, 187
armed resistance   2–3, 54, 73, 76, 77, 119, 122, 124–7, 134–40, 152, 156, 158–9, 170, 187, 209, 211, 213
Arrowsmith, Pat   85, 90, 209 n.93
Astor, David   28, 34, 43, 61–5, 67, 68, 86, 199, 208
Attitude to Africa   21, 28, 33–8, 40–2, 44, 45, 48–9, 51, 54, 56, 62, 65, 67, 129, 200, 212, 214
Azikiwe, Nnamdi   58, 78

Balewa, Abubaker   97, 100
Banda, Hastings   72, 182
Bandung Conference (1955)   13, 28
Barden, A. K.   130, 133 n.76, 158
Benson, Mary   23, 33, 61–5, 67
Bhave, Vinoba   133, 140–2, 149, 180, 205–7
Bigelow, Albert   88
Birmingham, Walter   101, 126–7
Boaten, Frank   196, 197 n.24, 198
Bourdet, Claude   91
Bourguiba, Habib   112
boycott campaigns   15, 18, 73, 88, 94, 113, 125, 133, 138, 154, 169, 175, 200–4
Britain. *See* United Kingdom
Brock, Hugh   27, 50, 78, 84–6, 90, 93, 160

Brockway, Fenner   66–7, 71, 76–7, 81, 84–6, 93, 122
Brooke, Anthony   64, 143
Brummana conference (1961–2)   145–7, 149–51, 158, 160, 164, 177, 200, 208
Bureau of African Affairs (Ghana)   82, 105–6, 121, 158
Burkina Faso. *See* Upper Volta
Butler, R. A.   170–2

Campaign for Nuclear Disarmament (UK)   1, 12, 87–9, 95, 102, 103, 113, 134, 191, 192, 199
Canada   99–100
Carter, April   85, 87, 92, 95–6, 100, 103–4, 126–8, 183, 196
Castro, Fidel   85, 138, 213
Central African Federation   53–4, 69–78, 80, 94, 125, 151, 154–5, 161–2, 164, 166, 167, 170–2, 174, 184, 199
China   8, 29, 146, 187, 190, 198, 205–7, 209
Chona, Mainza   124–5, 156 n.25
Christian pacifism   3, 16, 24–6, 33, 59, 74–5, 102, 127, 135
civilization   32, 37–8, 45–6, 48–9, 87
Cold War   3, 6–9, 11–12, 34, 45, 55, 57, 68–9, 80, 82, 83, 86, 89, 91, 114, 116, 120, 122, 133, 134, 143, 147, 148, 157, 159, 173, 175, 194–8, 205, 206, 211–13
Collins, Canon John   33, 43, 80, 86, 87, 102–3, 134, 191–2, 194, 198–9, 205
colonial development   32, 34, 40–8, 50–1, 70–1, 76, 79
Committee for Non-Violent Action   7, 88, 96, 101–5, 165, 191, 193, 206
Committee of 100   103, 133, 167, 192, 199
Committee of African Organisations   94–6, 100, 102, 103, 107, 200
communism   2, 5, 12, 35, 41, 67, 68, 82, 166, 183, 215
Congo   2, 106, 119, 131–3, 135–6, 139, 147, 148, 153, 159, 174, 175, 181, 188, 191, 196, 213, 215
Congress of Racial Equality (CORE)   17, 25, 26, 54–6, 60, 79, 80, 181

Convention Peoples' Party (Ghana)   35, 54, 79, 107, 113
Council of African Affairs (USA)   55, 79–80
Creech Jones, Arthur   37, 67
Cuba   85, 138, 152, 197–8, 203, 205, 209, 213

Dar es Salaam training centre for non-violence   159, 170, 172, 177–86, 190
Davidson, Basil   65–6
Defence and Aid Fund (UK)   134, 199, 205
Defiance Campaign (South Africa 1952)   54, 57, 68, 73, 79, 135
de Gaulle, Charles   89–90, 92, 94, 113–14, 120
Delhi-Peking Friendship March (1963)   205–10
Dellinger, David   16
Desai, Narayan   146, 149, 160
Dhadda, Siddhartha   144, 158, 160
Diallo, Abdoulaye   106, 112
Direct Action Committee Against Nuclear War (DAC)   7, 85, 87, 88, 90–6, 99–105, 107, 112, 113, 115, 205, 215
disarmament, nuclear   1, 3, 5–7, 9–12, 27, 50–1, 56, 80, 83–4, 86–93, 100–1, 103–4, 113–21, 134, 157, 165, 191–9, 211–12
Drake, John St. Clair   132, 153
du Bois, W. E. B.   51, 79, 80, 132
du Puigaudeau, Odette   97, 99

ecology   47–8
Einstein, Albert   88
European Congress for Nuclear Disarmament (1959)   90–1
European Defence Community   89

Fabian Colonial Bureau   32, 37, 39, 66, 69, 71
Fairfield Foundation   68
Fanon, Frantz   119, 124, 126, 135, 138–40, 209
Farmer, James   25, 26, 54, 181
Fellowship of Reconciliation (FOR)   1, 3, 24–7, 33, 38, 54, 58, 59, 63, 76, 78, 91, 128, 140, 181

Index

France   7–8, 89–93, 96–7, 99, 100, 104, 111, 113–14, 119–23, 127, 131, 132, 211

Gandhi, Manilal   28, 56–7
Gandhi, Mohandas   2, 15–16, 21, 24, 26–7, 31, 46, 60, 69, 123, 124, 126, 128–9, 142, 148, 154
Gbedemah, Komla   79, 96–7, 100, 105–7, 109, 120, 133
Germany   12, 27–31, 89, 91, 149
Ghana   2, 7, 23, 58, 71, 78, 82, 85, 90, 93–113
Ghana Council for Nuclear Disarmament   96
Goa, annexation of (1961)   142–3, 206
Gomani, Phillip   75–6
Gregg, Richard   27, 128, 132, 141

Hammarskjöld, Dag   141, 175
Hemingford, Lord   63, 65, 67, 86
Herero people   21–3, 27–32, 65, 72
Houser, George   25, 26, 50, 56, 59, 79, 85 n.7, 135, 138–40, 153, 186, 209
Hoyland, Francis   101, 102, 104, 106
Hydrogen Bomb   83, 86–7, 91, 134

India   2, 4, 5, 12, 14–15, 21–8, 33, 46, 54, 69, 93, 114, 119, 128, 129, 133, 142–3, 149, 160, 171, 172, 187, 190, 198, 205–10
Indo-China Border War (1962)   205–10

Jabavu, Davidson   28
Jack, Homer   56–8, 69–70, 191–4, 197
Japan   83, 113, 142

Kapwepwe, Simon   154, 159, 180
Kaunda, Kenneth   7, 135, 149, 151, 153–60, 164–78, 181–5, 188–90, 201, 213
Kawawa, Rashidi   160, 161, 163
Kenya   2, 41, 54, 73, 76–7, 85, 94, 102, 111, 171, 173
Khama, Seretse   66, 69, 80
Khama, Tshekedi   30–2, 44, 66
King, Dr Martin Luther   88, 143, 192
Koinange, Mbiyu   76, 167, 169, 178, 183, 201

Labour Party (UK)   66, 67, 69, 71, 76, 88–9, 101, 154, 156, 166, 170
Lazar, Ed   206, 207, 209
League of Nations   29–30, 39, 142
Legum, Colin   2, 34–8, 40–1, 45, 48, 67
Lewis, W. Arthur   34, 38, 41–3
Lierde, Jan van   147
Loft, George   189
Lucky Dragon, The   83, 104
Lumumba, Patrice   2, 106, 147
Lutuli, Albert   2, 135, 137, 139, 177, 179, 200

Macbride, Seán   194, 197
Macmillan, Harold   98, 110–11, 114, 116, 162
Mahereru, Frederick   31–2
Makiwane, Tennison   158, 187
Makonnen, Ras   106
Malawi. *See* Nyasaland
Mandela, Nelson   2, 5, 137, 140, 159, 178–9, 209
March on Washington (1963)   210–11
Marquand, David   116
Martin, Pierre   92, 93, 106, 109, 113, 126, 144–7
Maswanya, Saidi   163, 178, 183
Maudling, Reginald   162–3, 167
Mbeki, Govan   2, 138 n.100
Mendès-France, Pierre   89, 113
Minority Rights Group   208
Mokhehle, Ntsu   106
Morgue, Efua   78
Morocco   90, 91, 93, 100, 113, 120–1
Movement for Colonial Freedom (MCF)   59, 77, 81, 94, 116
Mpondoland uprising (1960)   137
Mumford, Lewis   48–9, 86, 175, 186, 192, 200
Murumbi, Joseph   76, 77, 102–3
Muste, A. J.   1–5, 26, 56, 58–60, 64, 88, 101, 105–8, 121, 128, 132, 143, 148–9, 153, 158, 160, 164, 171, 174, 178–86, 189, 191, 193, 198, 204–9, 211–15

Nagaland   205, 208–10, 213
Namibia   21, 173, 180–2. *See also* South-West Africa

Narayan, Jayaprakash 26, 129, 141–3, 146, 148–9, 160, 171–3, 183–5, 201, 205–9, 214
National Association for the Advancement of Colored People (NAACP) 32, 80, 181, 210
National Committee for a Sane Nuclear Policy (SANE) 88, 191–2, 197
nationalism 5, 10–13, 18, 26–8, 35–8, 46, 49, 50, 68, 70, 76–82, 88, 89, 115–16, 121, 124–6, 131, 140, 151, 152, 154–6, 158, 165–6, 175–7, 187, 191, 212–14
National Liberation Front (FLN, Algeria) 100, 103, 122–4
National Peace Council (UK) 54, 66
Nehru, Jawaharlal 60, 133, 143, 198, 208
Nhlapo, Jacob 56
Nigeria 58, 78, 85, 93, 97–100, 106, 111–13, 124
Nkrumah, Kwame 35, 58, 71, 82, 85, 95, 96, 98–9, 100 n.92, 110, 113, 114, 120–5, 127, 128, 130, 132, 133, 136, 148, 158, 191–4, 198
Nkumbula, Harry 71, 151, 154, 155, 178, 180, 182, 184
non-alignment 89, 116, 123, 191–8, 205
'non-aligned' disarmament 6, 191–2, 196, 197
non-violence, training 58, 64, 108, 119, 121, 125–30, 132–3, 144–6, 148–9, 169, 177, 184–6, 214
non-violent civil disobedience 14–17, 25, 27, 39, 50, 54, 73–5, 77, 88, 119, 154, 155, 177, 199, 211
Northern Rhodesia 54, 69–71, 137, 148, 149, 151, 153–7, 160–6, 168–71, 175–8, 180, 182, 184–5, 201–2, 211. See also Zambia
Northern Rhodesian African National Congress 71, 151, 153–4, 176, 182
nuclear weapons 7–9, 83–4, 86–94, 97, 100, 111, 116–17, 130, 144, 192–5, 197–8, 211–15
Nujoma, Sam 178, 180, 182
Nyasaland 54, 69, 70, 72–7, 94, 111, 154, 155, 161, 172
Nyasaland African Congress 73–4, 76, 154

Nyerere, Julius 95, 148, 149, 158–62, 164, 168–9, 171, 173, 180, 181, 183, 185–6, 190, 214

Okavango delta irrigation scheme 44, 145, 175
'Operation Gandhi' 27, 50, 86
'Operation Goya' 180–2

pacifism 1–5, 15–17, 21–8, 51, 54–6, 64–5, 92–3, 114–15, 127–9, 139–44, 148, 157, 172, 207–9, 215
Padmore, George 78, 82, 93, 96, 106, 112
Pan-African Freedom Movement of East and Central Africa (PAFMECA) 125, 151, 158–9, 167, 169, 171, 180, 183, 184
Pan-African Freedom Movement of East, Central and Southern Africa (PAFMECSA). See Pan-African Movement of East and Central Africa (PAFMECA)
pan-Africanism 10, 17, 71–2, 78, 82, 94–5, 106, 112, 115–16, 122, 125, 134, 136, 158
Pan-Africanist Congress (PAC, South Africa) 81, 130, 137, 158–9, 173, 179, 199
Papworth, John 166, 169, 184, 191, 202–4
Peace News 85–6, 93, 138, 156
Peace Pledge Union (UK) 50, 95, 142
Perham, Margery 33, 35–8, 64
Peter, Esther 103–4, 106, 126
Phizo, Angami 207
Phombeah, Dennis 95–6
'Positive Action' 18, 82, 122–8, 132, 133, 157, 172
Postive Action' conference (Accra 1960) 120–7, 146, 191–3
Prasad, Devi 205, 209
Priestley, J. B. 87

Quakers 14, 22, 24, 33, 56, 58, 66, 85, 87, 102, 115, 126, 143, 145, 149, 167, 189, 193
Quaye, E. C. 104, 106, 107, 109, 111, 149, 194

Ram, Suresh   172, 177, 180, 182–7, 205, 214
Randle, Michael   85, 87, 95–6, 100–4, 106, 109, 111–12, 115–16, 120, 122, 126–33, 143, 146, 148, 149, 157, 192, 214
Randolph, A. Phillip   88, 105, 128, 181, 210
Reggane, atomic test site   91, 99, 110, 112, 115, 125
Royden, Maude   142
Russell, Bertrand   86, 103, 133, 166, 199
Rustin, Bayard   17, 25–6, 50, 56, 58–60, 63, 64, 78–9, 87–8, 101–7, 109, 120, 128–9, 143, 149, 153, 158–64, 167–70, 172, 181, 185–7, 190, 204–6, 210–11

Sahara Protest   7–8, 90, 92–7, 100–10, 113–17
Schweitzer, Albert   57, 69, 86–7
Scott, Michael   4–6, 12–13, 144, 145, 149, 190–1, 207–10, 213
  activism and personal life   61–4
  Africa Freedom Action   169–78, 187–8
  anti-colonialism   28–32, 34–40, 54, 57–8, 65–8, 72–8, 85, 119–22, 134, 157, 158, 161, 167, 180–1, 186, 199–201, 204–5
  Communism   5, 12, 35, 67–9
  development and ecology   42–9, 51, 174–5
  nuclear disarmament   85–7, 90, 101–3, 105–6, 109, 112, 120–2, 133, 157, 192
  pacifism and non-violence   21–8, 50–1, 74–5, 128–30, 134, 159, 164, 185
  Sahara protest   101–12
Scott Bader Corporation   180
Service Civil International   93, 106–7
Shanti Sena movement   133, 140, 142–3, 146, 187, 205, 207
Sharpeville Shootings (South Africa, 1960)   119, 123, 130, 136–8, 158
South Africa   2, 5, 8, 9, 12, 22, 24, 27–33, 36, 42, 45, 46, 48–50, 53, 54, 56–7, 68, 81–2, 87, 110, 114, 119, 121, 123, 130–1, 134–40, 148, 158–9, 175, 178–81, 187, 189, 199–205, 213
South Africa, Communism   2, 5, 136–7, 152, 159
Southern Rhodesia   54, 70–3, 129, 165, 171, 176, 181, 182, 186, 190, 202, 210. *See also* Zimbabwe
South-West Africa   21–2, 27, 29–31, 69–70, 148, 178, 180–2, 202, 213
Soviet Union   8, 11, 55, 96, 100 n.92, 148, 165, 192, 194, 196, 197, 205
Sutherland, Bill   56, 59, 78–9, 82, 96, 100–2, 104, 106, 107, 109, 115, 120–2, 124–5, 128, 130–3, 144, 146, 148, 153, 157–60, 163, 164, 169, 172, 173, 178–87, 189, 190, 192, 197, 205, 214
Swaffham, anti-nuclear protest (1958)   85, 88, 90, 199

Tanganyika   2, 95, 125, 148, 151, 154, 156, 158–64, 166–78, 182–6, 191, 211, 214
Tanganyikan African National Union (TANU)   95, 151, 159, 160, 163–4, 169, 173, 180, 183, 186
Tanzania. *See* Tanganyika
Tatum, Arlo   85, 143, 145, 149, 160, 176
Tatum, Lyle   165, 176, 189, 202
Toynbee, Arnold   35, 45–6
Trocmé, André   91–2, 101, 104

uMkhonto wi Sizwe (MK)   136
Union of Democratic Control   65
United Kingdom   6–7, 12, 24, 34–40, 50–6, 66–8, 78–82, 84–9, 94–9, 111, 113, 115–16, 134, 153–4, 156–7, 164–7, 201, 204, 205, 209
United National Independence Party (Zambia)   7, 124, 151, 154, 157, 159, 160, 162–3, 165–74, 176–8, 180, 182–5, 202, 212
United Nations   21–2, 26–35, 39, 45, 54, 59, 61, 62, 65, 73, 74, 85, 98, 131, 138, 141, 148, 173–7, 179, 198, 202–5, 207–8
United Nations Special Committee on Decolonization   173–7

United Nations Trusteeship Committee 22, 30–3, 69, 101, 145, 181–2
United States of America 1–5, 7–8, 11, 16, 17, 24, 26, 33, 51, 54–9, 69, 82, 86–7, 90, 96, 101, 107, 133, 135, 139, 145, 149, 155, 157, 178–9, 182, 194, 206, 210
Upper Volta 7, 108, 109, 112, 120

Walker, Charles 14–15, 140, 208, 214
War Resisters International 88, 102, 106, 141, 143, 209
Welbeck, Nathaniel 106, 135
Welensky, Roy 71–2, 155, 161–2, 164, 171, 176, 178, 180, 181
Wight, Martin 34–8, 40–1, 45, 48
Willoughby, George 96, 101–4
Winneba Training Centre 130–4, 146

Wolfe, Alvin 174–5, 181
World Movement for World Federal Government 96–7
World Pacifist Conference (1949) 21–8
World Peace Brigade 7–8, 14, 140–52, 156–7, 159–61, 165–88, 190, 200, 206–13
World Peace Council 6, 91, 123, 165, 192, 207

Xuma, Alfred 57

Zambia (nationalism) 7–8, 17, 124, 135, 151–62, 165–8, 171–2, 175–6, 180, 184, 188–90
Zambia (*see* Northern Rhodesia)
Zimbabwe. *See* Southern Rhodesiaa